THE POLITICAL PHILOSOPHY OF
MICHAEL OAKESHOTT

The
POLITICAL PHILOSOPHY
of
MICHAEL OAKESHOTT

Paul Franco

YALE UNIVERSITY PRESS
NEW HAVEN AND LONDON 1990

TO MY PARENTS, FRANK AND PATRICIA FRANCO

Set by Best-set Typesetters Ltd, Hong Kong
Printed and bound in Great Britain by
Biddles Ltd, Guildford and King's Lynn

Library of Congress Cataloging-in-Publication Data

Franco, Paul, 1956–
    The political philosophy of Michael Oakeshott/Paul Franco.
       p.   cm.
    Includes bibliographical references.
    ISBN 0-300-04686-3
    1. Oakeshott, Michael Joseph, 1901–   —Contributions in political
science.   I. Title.
JC257.0244F73   1990
320'.01—dc20   89-29189
                                                      CIP

CONTENTS

CONTENTS

ACKNOWLEDGEMENTS

I would like to thank Professors Nathan Tarcov, Joseph Cropsey, and Russell Hardin of the University of Chicago for their care in reading and commenting on an earlier version of this work. I would especially like to thank Professor Tarcov, who commented extensively on this earlier version, and who also provided crucial encouragement at the outset of the project. Professor Timothy Fuller of Colorado College first introduced me to political philosophy and to the thought of Michael Oakeshott. This study owes a great deal to his original and continued inspiration. Finally, I would like to thank my wife Jill for her assistance, both editorial and otherwise, during the completion of the book.

I

INTRODUCTION

Of the major contemporary political theorists, Michael Oakeshott has in some ways been the most difficult to get hold of. The reason for this may lie in the fact that he does not fit comfortably into any of the conventional categories we use to make sense of the world of political theory. Labels such as "conservative," "liberal," "idealist," "historicist," "traditionalist," and "individualist" all fail to specify adequately his complex and distinctive position. As one writer has put it,

> [Oakeshott] is a traditionalist with few traditional beliefs, an "idealist" who is more sceptical than many positivists, a lover of liberty who repudiates liberalism, an individualist who prefers Hegel to Locke, a philosopher who disapproves of *philosophisme*, a romantic perhaps (if Hume could also be called one), and a marvelous stylist. Oakeshott's voice is unique.[1]

The price of such "uniqueness," however, is often exclusion from current debate. And since such exclusion in Oakeshott's case would be a mistake, let me state at the outset just what I think he has to contribute to contemporary political philosophy.

There are three aspects of Oakeshott's work which merit serious consideration, and which will receive continuous attention in this study. The first concerns his theory of philosophy and of political philosophy. It is well known that philosophy (and especially political philosophy) has suffered serious challenges in the twentieth century from various forms of positivism and historicism, science and social science. Anyone who engages in political philosophy today must be prepared to answer these challenges and provide an initial justification for his activity. This Oakeshott has done, and with a depth and tenacity that few of his contemporaries have matched. As we shall see, he never loses sight of the "meta-political" question of the nature and possibility of philosophy, and much of this study will be given over to elucidating his answer to it.

The second aspect of Oakeshott's philosophy I shall stress is his critique of rationalism, along with the positive account of practical rationality he develops in the course of it. This, of course, is the best-known part of Oakeshott's philosophy, and it is perhaps less in need of explanation than the other parts. Indeed, so large does this aspect loom in the reception of Oakeshott's thought that I have been led at times to diminish its importance – or at least to prevent it from over-shadowing the other aspects which I believe are necessary to under-standing Oakeshott's whole position. Nevertheless, it cannot be doubted that this critique of rationalism and the elaboration of a more practical and contextual conception of rationality in opposition to it constitute one of the most interesting and important aspects of Oakeshott's philosophy. What he has to say in this regard not only has enormous political implications but is of the utmost relevance to the whole issue of human rationality which has moved to the center of current philosophical debate.

Oakeshott's third and most important contribution to contempor-ary political philosophy comes in the area of liberal theory. In his theory of civil association he provides us with what is perhaps the most sophisticated and satisfying contemporary statement of liberal-ism to date. It is a statement which owes much to Hegel, rejecting the natural rights and atomism of traditional liberal theory. Here, too, Oakeshott shows himself difficult to peg according to conventional categories. The highly procedural character of his theory of civil asso-ciation in some ways aligns him with so-called "deontological" liberals such as Rawls, Nozick, Hayek, and Dworkin. But the Hegelian and historical aspects of his theory allow him to answer the criticisms "communitarians" such as Sandel and Taylor have levelled at the deontological project. Besides this advantage, Oakeshott's theory also gives due consideration to the idea of authority – a topic almost always stinted in contemporary liberal theory (e.g., by Rawls). Finally, I will show that Oakeshott has done more than any other contemporary thinker to purge liberalism of the economism and materialism which have often appeared to constitute its moral ideal and rendered it vul-nerable to attacks from both the Right and the Left.

Oakeshott's defense of the idea of political philosophy, his critique of rationalism, and his restatement of liberalism are the broad themes which frame this study. It is time now to see how they are more particularly developed in the course of it. A word, first, about my method. I have proceeded mainly by way of careful exposition of Oakeshott's texts. There is, alas, no other way to understand a philos-opher, especially when he is as careful a writer as Oakeshott. Further-more, I have taken these texts in roughly chronological order. There is in Oakeshott's career a certain exemplary movement from the elaboration of a general philosophical point of view in the early *Ex-perience and its Modes* (1933) to the treatment of the more specific problems of political philosophy in the later *On Human Conduct* (1975). I have done nothing more than avail myself of it.

I begin, then, in chapter 2 with a thorough analysis of *Experience and its Modes*, the early work in which Oakeshott analyzes the major forms of experience or knowledge – philosophy, history, science, practice – and determines the relationships which obtain between them. Careful study of this work serves as a necessary corrective to the view of Oakeshott – based largely on an exclusive reading of the essays in *Rationalism in Politics* – as a "Burkean conservative" or a right-wing ideologue. It reveals Oakeshott for what he truly is – a philosopher with a view as comprehensive as it could be, neither parochial nor narrowly ideological. Most commentators have recognized the importance of *Experience and it Modes* for understanding Oakeshott's later political philosophy,[2] but there exists as yet no full-scale analysis of this crucial early work. Such an analysis I have undertaken in chapter 2, bringing out not only the work's significance for the later writings but also its roots in nineteenth- and twentieth-century idealist thought.

In my analysis of *Experience and its Modes*, I focus on what I take to be the book's central concern: namely, the idea of philosophy. Since the middle of the nineteenth century the nature and role of philosophy have come increasingly into question due to the growth of the separate sciences, both natural and historical. What, in this era of science and social science, is the real task of philosophy? is a question to which many twentieth-century philosophers have addressed themselves, among them Husserl, Heidegger, Croce, and Collingwood. And it is to this fundamental question that I think Oakeshott's own reflection in *Experience and its Modes* must be seen as a response. Defining philosophy as radically self-critical thought – experience without reservation or presupposition – he demonstrates how it abolishes and supersedes the limited standpoints of both science and history. Positivism and historicism, two dogmas which have posed serious challenges to philosophy in the twentieth century, are both repudiated in *Experience and its Modes*. Oakeshott's rejection of historicism deserves special emphasis here, since it is to some form of historicism that he is commonly seen as subscribing. But Oakeshott is no historicist in the sense of believing philosophy to be somehow "liquidated" by history or in any way reducible to history. Philosophy for him is both independent of and superior to historical understanding. And he holds to this position throughout his career.

Besides positivism and historicism, there is one other dogma about philosophy that is rejected in *Experience and its Modes*: what might be called "pragmatism,"[3] or the view that philosophy is somehow subordinate to, bounded by, or in the service of, practical life. The world of practice, according to Oakeshott, like the worlds of science and history, is abstract; it is built upon certain abstract presuppositions which philosophy as the quest for a perfectly concrete and coherent world of experience necessarily seeks to overcome. Philosophy has nothing to gain from, much less contribute to, such an abstract world of experience. It is only by throwing off the insistent abstractions of practical life that philosophy can achieve its concrete end.

It cannot be doubted that Oakeshott's emphasis on the despotism of practice constitutes one of the most distinctive aspects of his analysis in *Experience and its Modes*. What he says about the despotism of science of course finds an echo in many modern, anti-positivist writers; but not so his critique of the despotism of practice (both in philosophy and in history). Unlike many other anti-positivist writers – Nietzsche and Heidegger, for example, or even Rorty – Oakeshott does not proceed to reduce all thought to the horizon of "life" or "praxis." He preserves the categorial distinction between theory and practice and thus avoids the politicization of philosophy and history which has been one of the great catastrophes of our time.

Having mentioned Oakeshott's distinction between theory and practice, let me say something more about this most controversial aspect of his philosophy. The distinction rests ultimately on Oakeshott's belief that practice, like any other form of non-philosophical experience, is modal or conditional; that it rests upon, and presupposes throughout, certain uncriticized assumptions. Practical life consists in the continual exploration and integration of experience in terms of these unquestioned and unproblematic assumptions. Philosophy, on the other hand, begins by questioning these assumptions that are taken for granted in practical life and without which practical life would collapse. The philosopher is concerned not with integrating experience *in terms of* these assumptions but with relating these assumptions to a larger context and with establishing a coherence of an altogether different kind. He cannot *apply* his conclusions to the world of practice because they derive from a rejection of the very principle upon which that world is organized. Practical life, Oakeshott tells us in *Experience and its Modes*, takes place in a kind of "mental fog" – we might say an unquestioned horizon. And philosophy as self-conscious, self-critical thought can only serve to disperse this mental fog upon which practical success and satisfaction depend. "What is farthest from our needs is that kings should be philosophers."[4] Though Oakeshott utters this sentence in *Experience and its Modes*, the understanding of the relationship between theory and practice on which it rests remains essentially the same all the way through to *On Human Conduct*.[5] It is, without doubt, one of the central tenets of his political philosophy.

What the implications of the view of philosophy set forth in *Experience and its Modes* are for political philosophy Oakeshott does not explicitly say in that work. For these we must turn to a less well-known essay published five years later, "The Concept of a Philosophical Jurisprudence," in which Oakeshott explicitly takes up the question of "the meaning and possibility of a philosophy of law and civil society." I consider this essay at some length in chapter 3 because it reveals so clearly the link between the idea of philosophy set forth in *Experience and its Modes* and the idea of political philosophy embodied in Oakeshott's later works, especially *On Human Conduct*. Here again philosophy is defined as absolutely critical thought – thought without reservation or presupposition – and Oakeshott spends some time drawing out what this implies for the relationship between a philosophical jurisprudence and other types (analytical, historical, sociological, etc.) of jurisprudence: a philosophical jurisprudence cannot be conceived as simply one explanation of the nature of law among others; it is the criterion by which all other explanations must be judged. More positively, he shows how philosophical reflection on law begins with our ordinary understanding of law and proceeds by critically exploring what is implied in this pre-philosophical experience. Philosophy is here understood in Socratic fashion as getting to know more fully and clearly what in some sense we know already, a formula Oakeshott repeats in *On Human Conduct*.[6] Of course, where we end in philosophical inquiry is far from where we begin, and this means that our philosophical conclusions can neither be *checked* by appeal to common sense (as some "analytic" philosophers have suggested)[7] nor *applied* to practical reality. Philosophy for Oakeshott, in addition to being radically critical, is a radically transformative activity.

Toward the end of "The Concept of a Philosophical Jurisprudence," Oakeshott suggests something like an agenda for legal and political philosophy today, and at the top of this agenda he puts the study of the history of legal and political philosophy. We cannot hope to carry the philosophical inquiry into law and politics any further, he maintains, without a profound understanding of what has gone before. In chapter 3 I consider some of Oakeshott's early writings on the history of political philosophy, largely with a view to what they reveal about his notion of political philosophy. The suggestion in these writings that, in interpreting a past philosopher, we look to his philosophical reasons rather than his moral and political conclusions or opinions supports Oakeshott's general view of philosophy as a fundamentally explanatory and not an ideological activity. Theory is once again sharply distinguished from practice.

In these writings is also disclosed a certain reading of the tradition of modern political philosophy, which I try to reconstruct toward the end of chapter 3. Here I take up Oakeshott's famous interpretation of Hobbes and try to determine more exactly wherein the importance of this thinker lies for him. The main significance of Hobbes for Oakeshott lies in his radical break with the rationalism of the natural-law tradition and his revolutionary movement of will to the center of political philosophy. Despite this achievement, however, Oakeshott still thinks Hobbes lacks something vital to modern political philosophy: namely, an adequate theory of volition. And he looks to Rousseau's notion of the "general will," Hegel's notion of the "rational will," and Bosanquet's notion of the "real will" for inspiration in overcoming this defect. I spend some time considering this idealist tradition of the general or rational will in chapter 3 because it forms the essential background for Oakeshott's philosophical project in *On Human Conduct*. It is as a further stage in this idealist reflection on will and the state that I interpret his political philosophy in chapter 5.

A considerable stretch of time (almost forty years) separates the largely methodological reflections of "The Concept of a Philosophical Jurisprudence" from the full-blown statement of Oakeshott's political philosophy in *On Human Conduct*. In between come the essays eventually collected in *Rationalism in Politics* (also some important essays not included in that volume). These essays, which I take up in chapter 4, form an important background to the later work of political philosophy. They also relate back to *Experience and its Modes* in important ways. It is to this latter connection that I would like to address myself first. But before doing so, I must first mention another aspect of *Experience and its Modes* (besides the idea of philosophy defended there) which is crucial to understanding this connection.

Underlying the whole of *Experience and its Modes* is a certain theory of knowledge or logic of human experience. This logic, which has its roots in Hegel and was later elaborated in England by F. H. Bradley and Bernard Bosanquet, rests on a rejection of the strict separation of universal and particular which characterizes traditional logic. Its watchword is the "concrete universal," which is said to unite universality and particularity. And it postulates coherence instead of correspondence as the criterion of truth and reality. In chapter 2 I argue that the formulation of this "concrete" logic in Oakeshott's case (as in Collingwood's) owes much to his attempt to account for historical knowledge, a task for which traditional logic had proved inadequate. Be that as it may, this concrete logic also proved fruitful when applied to the realm of practical activity. Here it allowed Oakeshott to steer a course between the extremes of empiricism, on the one hand, and rationalism, on the other (as well as between "objectivism and relativism"). And it enabled him to grasp the organization of practical life in more complex terms than conformity to fixed principles or purposes.

Now, it is my contention that the essays in *Rationalism in Politics* should be read in the light of this concrete logic elaborated in *Experience and its Modes*. By doing so we get a better idea of the exact character of Oakeshott's critique of rationalism in these essays – its distinctiveness vis-à-vis other critiques of rationalism, scientism, and positivism – and a better view of the positive view of human activity which lies behind this critique. Reading *Rationalism in Politics* in the light of *Experience and its Modes* also results in a revision of the conventional portrait of Oakeshott as a "Burkean conservative." As I try to show in chapter 4, Oakeshott's so-called "traditionalism" has a completely different ground than the traditionalism of Burke. Oakeshott's notion of tradition arises out of a genuinely philosophical analysis of human activity and in no way presupposes (as I think Burke's appeal to tradition does) a belief in the wisdom or rationality of history. The "method of nature" or its modern equivalent – "evolution" – has no place in Oakeshott's assessment of the significance of tradition.

By emphasizing the philosophical character of Oakeshott's critique of rationalism and his idea of tradition, I try to answer those critics who discern a more ideological intention behind these concepts, or who think that Oakeshott contradicts himself by confusing theory and practice, description and prescription. I also address the common criticism that "tradition" is inadequate as a normative principle or as a guide to practical conduct. My argument (briefly) is that "tradition" for Oakeshott is not primarily a norm but (as I have already indicated) a philosophical concept arising out of a philosophical analysis of human activity. With it he is concerned not so much to tell us what we ought to do as to describe what in fact we do do whenever we act. Human activity is unavoidably "traditional," and from this follows the limited practical advice that we should not try to do that which is inherently impossible: "to try to do something which is inherently impossible is always a corrupting activity."[8] In short, "tradition" is an inadequate guide to conduct only because it does not purport to be a guide at all.

The implications of Oakeshott's critique of rationalism for our understanding of politics and concrete governmental activity I pursue in the final section of chapter 4. Drawing on some of the more explicitly political essays from the time of *Rationalism in Politics* (roughly the forties and fifties), I try to uncover the meaning of Oakeshott's "politics of scepticism," with their emphasis on liberty, individuality, the diffusion of power, and the rule of law. At the same time I examine his critique of the diametrically opposed "politics of passion," with their emphasis on central planning and the pursuit of a common purpose. Here again Oakeshott's divergence from Burkean conservatism comes into view. Oakeshott's conservatism does not appeal to any sort of metaphysical or religious beliefs for sanction or support; nor does it hark back to a more integrated and traditional form of society. Oakeshott's conservatism (as he himself tells us) ultimately has more in common with the skeptical conservatism of Montaigne, Hobbes, and Hume than with the religious or cosmic conservatism of Burke.

It must be admitted that the decidedly "libertarian" character of these latter writings does not immediately or obviously harmonize with the more "traditionalist" or historicist insights of *Rationalism in Politics*; and some commentators have suggested that there is a tension between these two aspects of Oakeshott's thought.[9] While I do not think this is the case, I also do not think the connection between the "libertarian" and "traditionalist" aspects of Oakeshott's thought – sometimes styled in terms of his Hobbesianism and his Hegelianism – has yet been adequately explained. My own attempt to relate them rests on emphasizing the procedural and non-purposive character of Oakeshott's understanding of "tradition." The considerations which compose a tradition do not command specific actions, nor are they instrumental to a substantive purpose. Like the considerations of a language – an analogy to which Oakeshott recurs more than once in *Rationalism in Politics* – they are the terms in which any substantive action or utterance must take place. It is in this sense that the organization of society in terms of the rule of law may be said to be "traditional." Such an organization provides a matrix or language in terms of which a multitude of individual purposes – and not just a single purpose – may be pursued. Here politics is understood to be a secondary (though necessary) activity: not the pursuit of substantive satisfaction but the custody of the matrix in terms of which substantive satisfactions are pursued.

The connection I am drawing between the "libertarian" and "traditionalist" (or Hobbesian and Hegelian) aspects of Oakeshott's thought becomes much clearer in his magnum opus, *On Human Conduct*, which I treat in chapter 5. In this work, Oakeshott substitutes the term "practice" for "tradition" and thus avoids the misleading substantive and communitarian connotations contained in the latter. He also brings out more explicitly than before the procedural and non-instrumental character which lay behind the notion of tradition in *Rationalism in Politics*. A "practice" – more specifically, a moral practice – is a set of procedural or adverbial considerations which qualify but do not determine conduct, and which are not instrumental to any extrinsic substantive purpose. It is a vernacular language of intercourse and understanding which is instrumental (if at all) only to the exercise of agency itself. There is no agency which is not the acknowledgement of some such moral practice, just as there is no individual utterance or speech which is not in any language in particular.

Now it is as a moral, non-instrumental practice – a vernacular language of intercourse and understanding – that Oakeshott theorizes civil association, or association in terms of the rule of law, in *On Human Conduct*. This, I argue in chapter 5, is one of the significant achievements of this consummate work of political philosophy. It is

an achievement by which Oakeshott's "libertarianism" is reconciled
with his "traditionalism," his Hobbesianism successfully synthesized
with his Hegelianism. This understanding of *On Human Conduct* of
course differs from that which sees it as a betrayal of Oakeshott's
earlier Hegelianism or historicism, which sees a "tension" between
the legalistic ideal of civil association in *On Human Conduct* and the
critique of universalistic rationalism in *Rationalism in Politics*.[10] Such a
view fails to grasp the profoundly Hegelian character of *On Human
Conduct*; the fact that it is an attempt to understand civil association as
a *Sittlichkeit*. For me, Oakeshott's Hobbesianism or individualism is
not in tension with his Hegelianism. What makes his theory of civil
association in *On Human Conduct* interesting and important is precisely
that it successfully synthesizes these two strands of thought, combining
liberal individualism with a more sophisticated historical outlook.

This brings us back to one of the major themes mentioned at the
outset of this introduction, namely, liberalism. Oakeshott's theory of
civil association can, I think, plausibly be seen as a restatement or
reformulation of liberalism. It is true that Oakeshott himself does not
use this term to style his political philosophy, finding it too ambiguous
and loaded down with meanings that do not convey his own. Nevertheless, his theory, in its concern for liberty, its appreciation for
individuality, and its defense of the rule of law, cannot but be characterized as liberal. That Oakeshott can be seen as a liberal theorist
does not mean, however, that he finds nothing wrong with liberal
theory as it has been traditionally formulated. He does. That is why
I speak of his political philosophy as a restatement or reformulation
of liberalism. It is an attempt to purge liberalism of some of the
more questionable metaphysical and ethical assumptions which have
marked it since its inception. Two such defective assumptions are
highlighted in my account of Oakeshott's restatement of liberalism:
first, the negative and abstract individualism which has marked liberal theory from Hobbes to Mill (or even Nozick); second, the
materialism or economism which has sometimes appeared to constitute liberalism's moral ideal.[11] Let me say a little more about
Oakeshott's attempt to overcome each of these two perceived weaknesses in traditional liberal doctrine.

With respect to the first – the abstract and negative individualism
of traditional liberal theory – Oakeshott's connection to the idealist or
Hegelian tradition of political thought once again comes to sight. The
idealists, of course, rejected this particular liberal assumption – not
individualism per se, but the negative and atomistic understanding of
it. And there is considerable evidence (especially in his earlier writings)
that Oakeshott endorsed their attempts to overcome it. In chapter 3
I look at some of these idealist attempts to reformulate the relationship between individual and government, will and law, freedom

and authority – attempts such as are represented by Rousseau's notion of the "general will," Hegel's notion of the "rational will," and Bosanquet's notion of the "real will" – with a view to gaining a firmer grasp of Oakeshott's own philosophical project. In chapter 5 I try to show how his theorization of civil association as a moral practice in *On Human Conduct* fits into this general idealist framework. It is my contention that by conceiving civil association as a moral, non-instrumental practice, Oakeshott overcomes the opposition between individual and government, will and law, freedom and authority, which has dogged liberal thought ever since Hobbes; and that he does so in a manner more consistent than some of his idealist predecessors.

In this connection, it is worth pointing out Oakeshott's divergence from other libertarian conservatives. It is clear that Oakeshott's Hegelianism will not allow him to defend liberty and the individual by invoking the libertarian opposition between "government" and "individual." And, indeed, he is frequently to be found criticizing libertarian conservatives for calling upon such abstract notions as "natural rights," the "private individual," and "laissez-faire" when defending the liberal state against such anti-liberal alternatives as socialism and totalitarianism. Against them he insists that the "individual" is not natural but an historic achievement, and that "government" has played a decisive role in this achievement. In his emphasis on the historicity of individuality and on the interdependence of individual and government, then, Oakeshott diverges sharply from more conventional libertarian conservatives. He is no believer in a mythical laissez-faire or even in a Nozickean "minimal state." For him the crucial consideration is not the quantity of government but its mode.

The second weakness in traditional liberal doctrine to which Oakeshott's restatement may be seen as a response is liberalism's materialism, its emphasis on economic productivity and prosperity. Once again Oakeshott's idea of civil association as a moral (i.e., non-instrumental) practice provides the key to dissolving this traditional link between liberalism and economic prosperity. To be related in terms of the satisfaction of wants, an "economy," or even "capitalism," is to be related in terms of an *instrumental* practice and ultimately in terms of a substantive purpose. And this is not civil association. In sharply distinguishing civil association from the idea of economic welfare or prosperity, I argue in chapter 5, Oakeshott distances himself from such libertarian writers as Friedman and Hayek, who do tend to recommend liberalism in utilitarian and economic terms. He also proves himself more consistent than liberal theorists such as Rawls and Nozick, who, despite their protests to the contrary, end up buttressing their deontological theories with substantial appeals to economic efficiency and well-being. In short, Oakeshott succeeds – as perhaps no other contemporary thinker has – in freeing liberalism from the utilitarianism, materialism, and economism which have haunted it since the seventeenth century. This I take to be one of his most significant achievements.

Earlier I characterized Oakeshott's theory of civil association as the most sophisticated and satisfying contemporary statement of liberalism to date. I do not want to give the impression, however, that there are no problems with the theory. In the final section of chapter 5, I consider the most common charge that is levelled against the theory, namely, that it is too formalistic. Though I find this criticism for the most part misconceived, it nevertheless points to a certain unsatisfactory sketchiness in Oakeshott's theory of civil association. We are frequently left wondering what the theory really means for politics as we know it. In this regard, it might be said for Oakeshott that at least he remains true to his distinction between theory and practice. In his theory of civil association he offers us nothing resembling a blueprint for society.

In the conclusion of this study, I try to situate Oakeshott in the contemporary debate over liberalism. This debate has largely been framed in terms of the antinomy of "deontological" liberalism and "communitarianism"; and I have already remarked that Oakeshott doesn't fit comfortably into either of these camps. This is perhaps his virtue. No doubt his idea of civil association as a non-instrumental, non-purposive practice has more in common with the procedural or juridical ideal of deontological liberals such as Rawls, Nozick, Dworkin, and Hayek. Nevertheless, in its rejection of atomism and its incorporation of a more historical and hermeneutic conception of the self, it seems less vulnerable to the criticisms communitarians such as Sandel and Taylor have levelled at the deontological project. Beyond this, civil association's resolute opposition to the materialism and economism which have always been entwined with liberalism makes it less vulnerable to the more radical communitarian critiques of thinkers such as MacIntyre.

Let me conclude this introduction where I began, namely, with the difficulty of classifying Oakeshott. As is evident to anyone who has read his books, Oakeshott's position is quite complex and not easy to characterize. Therefore I have primarily devoted myself in this study to the task of interpreting and integrating his thought; of showing how all the parts fit together and amount to more than an eclectic composition. I have tried to make Oakeshott's "uniqueness" a little more intelligible, both within its own terms and within the terms of the larger traditions to which it belongs. In so doing, though, I have left aside for the most part the equally important task of criticism (though I have addressed the criticisms that have been made by others). In this regard, my study remains incomplete. I fortify myself, however, with the words Collingwood once wrote in reviewing *Experience and its Modes*: "I have tried to expound Mr. Oakeshott's thesis rather than criticize it, because it is so original, so important, and so profound that criticism must be silent until his meaning has long been pondered."[12] I think there is still some justification for this procedure today. Without deprecating the need for criticism, I think the complexity of Oakeshott's position and its susceptibility to misunderstanding make this first step of interpretation important and indispensable.

II

EXPERIENCE AND ITS MODES *AND*
THE IDEA OF PHILOSOPHY

Although we are ultimately interested in Oakeshott's substantive political philosophy in this study, there are a number of preliminary, one might say "meta-political," considerations which must be addressed before we can begin to approach the substantive political doctrine. Most important among these is Oakeshott's idea of philosophy. Time and again in the course of this study we will see that at the heart of Oakeshott's political philosophy lies a doctrine about the nature of philosophy. This doctrine he elaborated most fully in his first book, *Experience and its Modes*. It is to this rather precocious book, therefore, that we must turn our attention first.

1. Aim and Background of the Work

In the introduction to *Experience and its Modes* Oakeshott states clearly that the purpose of the book is to discover the implications of a certain conception of philosophy: namely, the idea of philosophy as "experience without presupposition, reservation, arrest or modification." "It is an attempt, not to formulate a system, but to see clearly and to grasp firmly a single idea – the notion of philosophy as experience without reservation or arrest, experience which is critical throughout, unhindered and undistracted by what is subsidiary, partial or abstract."[1] This conception of philosophy – what it means and what it implies – will be the focus of this chapter. I intend simply to follow the argument of *Experience and its Modes*, but to do so with a view almost exclusively to the announced main theme of philosophy.

This is not quite as easy as it may sound. For in the course of expounding his idea of philosophy in *Experience and its Modes*, Oakeshott is led to consider a number of non-philosophical forms of experience – specifically history, science, and practice – at some length. Why he finds it necessary to do so will occupy us in a moment. For now it is enough to point out that this procedure inevitably distracts from the main theme of the book, that is, philosophy. What Oakeshott has to say about history, for example, is interesting in itself apart from the role it plays in the argument about philosophy; and the same can be said of his discussions of science and practice. Nevertheless, I will be concerned with his analyses of these forms of experience, at least initially, only insofar as they shed light on his idea of philosophy.

But the larger question is, of course, why Oakeshott, in elaborating a theory of philosophy, finds it necessary to devote the bulk of his discussion to analyzing various forms of non-philosophical experience. It seems to me that the answer to this question should not only explain why Oakeshott's theory of philosophy takes the particular form that it does, but also the significance of the theory for our time. And I would like to suggest that the answer is to be sought in the special situation of philosophy in our time, the situation philosophy has confronted ever since the so-called "collapse" of idealism in the middle of the nineteenth century. That this situation has largely been determined by the growth of the separate sciences, especially the humanistic or historical sciences, is indisputable. And with this growth the role or task of philosophy has come increasingly into question. "What, in the era of such sciences, is the real task of philosophy?" This, according to Werner Brock, an historian of philosophy writing in 1935, is the central problem that has been posed to "German philosophy in the last century and especially in the last decades"; and as evidence he cites the works of such thinkers as Nietzsche, Dilthey, Husserl, Jaspers, and Heidegger.[2] In a review of Brock's book, Oakeshott writes that this question of the task of philosophy in an age of science is a question that has been posed not only to the recent German tradition but to the tradition of English philosophy as well.[3] And it is to this fundamental question that I think Oakeshott's own reflection in *Experience and its Modes* must be seen as a response.

But in order to grasp the significance of Oakeshott's argument more firmly, we must consider a few of the more common answers that were being given to the question of the task of philosophy in this age of science just prior to and at the same time as the writing of *Experience and its Modes*. Brock mentions two fundamental positions with respect to this question. In the first, which belongs for the most part to the nineteenth century, the task of philosophy was thought to consist in the synthesis or systematization of the results of the various sciences. The names of Comte, Wundt, Fechner, Lotze, and Eduard von Hartman are associated with this positivistic attempt to construct a philosophical synthesis of the separate sciences. And not surprisingly —or even unjustifiably – their philosophico-scientific efforts usually met with the derision of those actually engaged in real scientific or historical work at the time. A more respectable, though no less positivistic, answer to the question of the task of philosophy came from the neo-Kantians (Hermann Cohen foremost among them), who conceived the task of philosophy to be, not the synthesis of scientific results, but the inquiry into the presuppositions, principles, and methods of the special sciences. The neo-Kantians reduced philosophy to the *scientia scientarum*.[4]

It is interesting to note that, in the introduction to *Experience and its Modes*, Oakeshott picks out both of these conceptions of the nature and task of philosophy for special consideration. "[I]t is scarcely to be expected, in these days, that we should not be tempted to take up with the idea of philosophy as, in some sense, 'the fusion of the sciences', 'the synthesis of the sciences' or the *scientia scientarum*." But such conceptions of philosophy, he argues, remain hopelessly wedded to the point of view of science. Each takes the methods and results of science to be absolute and beyond criticism. It is given to philosophy only to reflect on these methods and results without in any way criticizing or transforming them. And yet, he asks, "what are the sciences that they must be accepted as the datum, and as a datum not to be changed, of valid knowledge? And if we begin with the sciences, can our conclusions be other or more than merely scientific? These and other questions like them are what anyone must consider who, in search of a complete and satisfactory world of experience, is tempted by science."[5]

Oakeshott seeks to answer the fundamental question of the task of philosophy in this age of science in a different way from that implied in the notions of philosophy as the "synthesis of the sciences" or the *scientia scientarum*. He wants to get away from the notion of philosophy as a kind of second-order reflection on experience, a kind of reflection which simply accepts the methods, aims, and results of other forms of experience as absolute, unquestionable, uncriticizable. Philosophy for him has its own aims, methods and results – ones that transcend those of science or history. Philosophy is not second-order reflection on experience but first-order reflection which transforms, supersedes, and destroys whatever it reflects upon. "Philosophical experience," he writes toward the end of *Experience and its Modes*, "by no means stands above the battle of experience; it is experience itself. It is at once the field and the battle, the strength and what remains undefeated in every combatant, the promise and the criterion of victory."[6]

But such a view of philosophy cannot simply be asserted, it must be established. And it can only be established by showing exactly in what way philosophy surpasses other forms of experience and provides what they themselves seek but cannot provide. This, finally, is the reason why Oakeshott spends the better part of *Experience and its Modes*, a book ostensibly devoted to the idea of philosophy, analyzing various forms of non-philosophical experience. His intention is critical. His aim is to liberate philosophy from the methods, results, and authority of the separate sciences; to define a role for philosophy beyond that of a mere appendage of science, a part of history, or an adjunct to practice. Of course, this liberation is not simply negative; it is a liberation *to* or *for* distinctive new tasks. Nevertheless, *Experience and its Modes* remains largely negative in character, emancipatory, leaving the applications of its idea of philosophy to the problems of morals, politics, and art for future discussion. In this sense *Experience and its Modes* is a propaedeutic to a complete philosophy; as Oakeshott himself puts it in the introduction, "if not a philosophy, at least a foundation upon which to build one."[7]

It is perhaps worth pausing here to notice an implication of the foregoing analysis, an implication which will emerge more sharply in the discussion to follow. Of late it has become not uncommon to find Oakeshott mentioned along with Richard Rorty as an exponent of a "non-foundationalist" conception of philosophy. This association undoubtedly first suggested itself when Rorty himself, in *Philosophy and the Mirror of Nature*, invoked Oakeshott's notion of "conversation" to evoke his own understanding of philosophy and its relationship to other modes of knowing.[8] But if what I have said so far about Oakeshott's conception of philosophy in *Experience and its Modes* is true, it cannot be identified with Rorty's anti-foundationalist conception.[9] This is not to deny there are any links between these two thinkers. Oakeshott certainly rejects the notion of philosophy (which Rorty ascribes to Kant) as a kind of master-discipline which legitimates and ultimately dictates to other disciplines; the view of philosophy (or "Philosophy," as Rorty likes to denote it) as a kind of ur-inquiry which helps us to pursue all other inquiries, asking questions about certain normative notions (e.g., truth, rationality, goodness) in the hope that we might better realize them.[10] With such a "foundational" and intrusive notion of "Philosophy" Oakeshott will have nothing to do, as will become apparent shortly. Nevertheless, he does not (like Rorty) so loosen his conception of philosophy that it loses all distinctiveness. He would certainly reject the blurring of the line between philosophy and other disciplines implied in Rorty's characterization of the philosopher as an "all-purpose intellectual" and a "culture-critic."[11] He is, as I have already suggested, very concerned to distinguish philosophical inquiry from all other types of inquiry. And this is one of the things that links him to the Kantian tradition Rorty is frequently to be found criticizing.[12] In short, though Oakeshott agrees with Rorty that philosophy is not "foundational" in the sense of pre-empting the other modes of knowledge, he nevertheless differs from Rorty (at least so far as *Experience and its Modes* is concerned) in holding philosophy to be a categorially distinct discipline, and indeed a discipline which in some sense supersedes and judges other modes of knowing.

I have stated that my focus in this chapter is Oakeshott's idea of philosophy. But I do not want to give the impression that *Experience and its Modes* is simply or solely concerned with philosophy and its relationship to the various forms of non-philosophical experience. It is also concerned with the relationship of these forms of non-philosophical experience to one another – of science to history, of history to practice, of science to practice, and so forth. Oakeshott is of the opinion that the most serious form of intellectual error – to which he gives the name *ignoratio elenchi*, or the fallacy of irrelevance – arises from the failure to keep the various modes of experience separate and distinct. And therefore he devotes considerable space in *Experience and its Modes* to separating and distinguishing them. He is particularly concerned – as not only *Experience and its Modes* but also many of his early articles and reviews attest – to protect history from the irrelevant intrusions of science and the practical attitude, and practical life from the irrelevant intrusions of science and history (especially as these latter have been used to criticize the claims of religion).

This logical differentiation of the various modes of experience from one another (and the consequent exposure of the fallacy of *ignoratio elenchi*) clearly constitutes one of the major themes of *Experience and its Modes*. But since my focus in this chapter is on Oakeshott's idea of philosophy, I have been forced to give it a subordinate place. Nevertheless, I do treat at some length below Oakeshott's distinction between history and science, since the problem of the relationship between these two forms of knowledge has occupied a central place in philosophical reflection for the last one hundred years or so, and since what Oakeshott has to say about this problem is not uninteresting.

There is yet another aspect of *Experience and its Modes* which will receive continuous, if subordinate, attention in the pages which follow. It concerns the theory of knowledge or logic of human experience upon which Oakeshott's understanding of philosophy and the various modes of experience ultimately depends. This logic can be characterized as being both non-empiricist and non-rationalist. It rests on a rejection of the strict separation of universal and particular, thought and perception, theory and fact, which characterizes traditional logic. More positively, it rests on the notion of the "concrete universal," which is said to unite particularity and universality. I will have more to say about this "concrete" logic in a moment, when I consider the philosophical background of *Experience and its Modes*. For now I only want to point out that this logic enables Oakeshott (as we shall see) to grasp both history and practice as genuine worlds of knowledge instead of as welters of mere facts. It also provides the foundation (as we shall see in subsequent chapters) for the analyses of practical activity which are found in *Rationalism in Politics* and *On Human Conduct*.

I would like to conclude these introductory remarks on *Experience and its Modes* now by briefly considering the philosophical background of the work. Oakeshott frankly acknowledges in the introduction that his view "derives all that is valuable in it from its affinity to what is known by the somewhat ambiguous name of Idealism." And he goes on to say that the works from which he is "conscious of having learnt most are Hegel's *Phänomenologie des Geistes* and Bradley's *Appearance and Reality*."[13] It remains to flesh out a little this idealist tradition (about which Oakeshott himself says nothing more), which forms such an essential context for the doctrine of *Experience and its Modes*. And I will concern myself for the most part with British idealism, since it is this tradition which stands most immediately in the background of Oakeshott's thought.

Let me begin with what British idealism was originally directed against: namely, British empiricism. It was against the empiricist theory of knowledge, especially as it had been formulated by Mill, that Bradley's philosophy (for example) first took shape. Specifically, he rejected the empiricist notion that knowledge somehow begins with psychical particulars (i.e., "ideas" or "impressions") and then proceeds (by way of "association") to universals. In knowledge or experience, Bradley argued (and here he was simply following Hegel), we do not begin with separate and independent particulars, but with meanings, universals; and it is only on the basis of such universals that inference can take place. The brute and atomistic datum from which the empiricist supposes thought and induction take their start simply does not exist.[14] This critique of the empiricist belief that knowledge begins from or is founded upon the immediate facts of perception was later taken up and extended by such followers of Bradley as Bernard Bosanquet and Harold Joachim. Like Bradley, these thinkers rejected the rigid distinction between mediate and immediate experience upon which the whole empiricist doctrine was founded. There is no such thing as immediate experience, they argued, experience of isolated particulars without meaning or relation. All experience is in some way intellectual or infected with thought.[15]

The idealist critique of the empiricist notion of the "given" was not, of course, a merely negative doctrine. It ultimately involved a completely different positive conception of the nature of knowledge, of truth, and even of reality. No longer could knowledge, for example, be pictured as a building resting on indubitable and incorrigible "foundations."[16] Nor could truth be conceived in terms of correspondence to a fixed and solid "datum." In place of "correspondence" the idealists put systematic coherence as the criterion of truth (and of reality as well).[17] Individual facts and judgments are true (or real), according to this coherence view, only insofar as they belong to a larger system or whole. And as knowledge grows, these facts and judgments are susceptible to correction in light of the changing whole.

It is only with the achievement of an absolutely coherent world of experience that these individual constituents can take on final stability. Of course, the idea of an absolutely coherent world of experience, of a single system of non-contradictory knowledge, is implied in the coherence-notion of truth from the start. And to this perfectly coherent, non-contradictory world of experience the idealists gave the name of "the absolute."

Before going on to speak of the absolute in connection with Bradley and Hegel, I would like to dwell for a moment on an implication of the foregoing analysis of truth. From that analysis it should be clear that coherence is not to be confused with mere formal consistency. Formal consistency involves the arrangement of already accepted truths, the imposition of a universal form on the fixed materials of knowledge. But such distinctions – between the whole and its parts, between form and materials, between the universal and the particular – are alien to the idealist logic I am outlining. Indeed, they belong to the traditional formal logic against which – along with empiricist logic – the idealists were rebelling. The coherence the idealists have in mind is not something outside the elements that comprise it; it is not a coherence of static units or fixed constituents. And if we have to speak of a "form" or a "universal," it must be understood that this form or universal interpenetrates the material parts, giving them their particular character. In short, we have to do here with the idealist notion of the "concrete universal" – the type of universal which (in contradistinction to the abstract universal of traditional logic) characterizes a complex whole or system.[18] This notion of the concrete universal is absolutely central to idealist logic, and it plays an important role (as I have already suggested) in Oakeshott's own understanding of knowledge and experience.

Let us return to the absolute – which we may now also characterize in terms of the concrete universal. It is, of course, the idea (or ideal) which stands at the center of the two books Oakeshott mentions as having learned most from, namely, Hegel's *Phenomenology* and Bradley's *Appearance and Reality*. In both these books we find an exposition of the absolute as the one self-subsistent, non-self-contradictory reality which is implied by our cognitive experiences but which those cognitive experiences themselves fail to achieve. In the *Phenomenology* Hegel traces the dialectical process by which the absolute emerges and finally comes to be revealed to the philosopher. In *Appearance and Reality* Bradley pursues a somewhat more modest line of inquiry, showing how reflection on our self-contradictory experiences (or "appearances") forces us to the conception of a single, non-self-contradictory, totally self-subsistent experience or reality, that is, the absolute. I characterize this effort as more modest because Bradley, unlike Hegel, does not attempt to arrange the various forms of experience in a hierarchy of increasing coherence and concreteness leading up to the absolute – although he does acknowledge that such a task is what would be involved in a complete philosophy, which he himself does not claim to provide.[19]

A more substantial difference between Hegel and Bradley arises, however, in their respective understandings of the relationship between thought and reality. For Hegel, as we know, ultimate reality is finally revealed to the philosopher, grasped in philosophical thought – this is one of the meanings of the famous sentence that the real is rational. But Bradley never accepted this doctrine of the rationality of the real, this identification of thought and ultimate reality. For him, discursive thought always remains to some extent relational and therefore self-contradictory; it never attains the immediacy or undivided unity which he associated with "Feeling" and attributed to reality in its fullest sense. Thus, though philosophical reflection may lead us to see the necessity of the absolute, it is not itself to be identified with the absolute.[20] This doctrine of the rift between thought and reality, it should be pointed out, was not taken over by Bradley's followers. Bosanquet and Joachim, for example, maintained the identity of philosophical thought and ultimate reality; and insofar as they did they remained truer to the Hegelian source.[21] Oakeshott, too, as we shall see, is more Hegelian than Bradleian in this regard. Philosophy as experience without reservation or presupposition is ultimately identified with the absolute.

Having referred to Hegel's *Phenomenology* and Bradley's *Appearance and Reality*, it is perhaps worth mentioning a third book which undoubtedly exercised some influence on Oakeshott in the writing of *Experience and its Modes*: namely, Collingwood's *Speculum Mentis*. Published some nine years before *Experience and its Modes*, *Speculum Mentis* bears a number of striking resemblances to Oakeshott's book. It too is cast in the form of a philosophy of the forms of experience. And it too draws heavily on the tradition of idealist thought I have sketched above. Reflecting on the major forms of experience – art, religion, science, and history – Collingwood shows that none is completely autonomous or self-contained, all are merely phases or stages in the development of absolute knowledge. It is only in philosophy that this absolute knowledge implied in all our experiences is finally and explicitly achieved. Collingwood's exposition of the absolute, it should be noted, is modelled on the Hegelian dialectic. The various forms of experience are arranged in a hierarchy of increasing coherence and concreteness, and each successive form is shown to emerge out of and resolve the self-contradictions of the previous form. In this latter aspect Oakeshott, as we shall see, does not follow Collingwood (or Hegel, or even Bradley, for that matter). Nevertheless, there remain a great many similarities between *Speculum Mentis* and *Experience and its Modes*, and where I could I have noted them below.

So much, then, by way of introduction to *Experience and its Modes*. With this preliminary understanding of the aim and background of the book, we may now proceed to the argument itself.

2. The Concepts of Experience and a Mode of Experience

Oakeshott's idea of philosophy is ultimately connected with a certain view of the nature of human experience. And lest there be any confusion, Oakeshott states at the outset that "experience" here does not refer simply to a part of the whole, namely that part which pertains to the subject and stands over against the object or reality. All such dualisms between subject and object, experience and reality, he rejects. "Experience" stands for the whole which comprehends both subject and object, and which is inseparable from reality.

> "Experience" stands for the concrete whole which analysis divides into "experiencing" and "what is experienced". Experiencing and what is experienced are, taken separately, meaningless abstractions; they cannot, in fact, be separated. Perceiving, for example, involves a something perceived, willing a something willed. The one side does not determine the other; the relationship is certainly not that of cause and consequent. The character of what is experienced is, in the strictest sense, correlative to the manner in which it is experienced. These two abstractions stand to one another in the most complete interdependence; they compose a single whole.[22]

Oakeshott here merely restates what may be considered one of the central tenets of philosophical idealism: namely, that the objects of experience are not independent of our experiencing of them; that they are, in fact, in some sense constituted by mind or thought. But it should also be observed that he does not set up the "subject" or "experiencing" as the sole reality and make it the cause of "what is experienced." To such subjective idealism Oakeshott – and his idealist predecessors as well – stands unalterably opposed. It was only in the minds of "realist" critics that idealism was identified with subjective idealism, and it was on this confusion that their "refutations" of idealism ultimately depended.[23]

What is this view of experience to which Oakeshott's idea of philosophy is ultimately connected? Essentially it is the monistic view which I ascribed above to previous idealist thought. It is the view that experience (which, again, is inseparable from reality) forms "a single whole, within which modifications may be distinguished, but which admits of no final or absolute division."[24] Neither experience nor reality is composed of separate parts or departments. There is, in the end, only one experience and one reality; only a single system of experience to which all our experiences belong. And this single system of experience is not to be thought of as the "sum-total" of our experiences. It is just this notion of experience as an aggregate or a collection that Oakeshott wants to avoid by speaking of it as a system or a whole. Individual experiences, he insists, "are not fixed and finished units, merely to be added to, or subtracted from one another. Experiences can destroy one another, amplify one another, coalesce, suffer change, transformation and supersession."[25]

This notion of experience as a single, undivided whole entails, as we shall see, a change in the way we usually conceive such forms of experience as history, science, and practice. For, on such a view of experience, these forms of experience can no longer be conceived as separate *kinds* of experience corresponding to separable *parts* of reality. Instead, they will be conceived as modifications of the single whole of experience. But there is an even more fundamental distinction than that between the various forms of experience which Oakeshott's view of experience may be taken to deny: namely, the empiricist distinction between mediate and immediate experience; the distinction – as it has traditionally been formulated – between thought and perception or thought and sensation. It is to this ancient distinction that Oakeshott turns first in the course of expounding his view of experience.

The view Oakeshott wishes to recommend is that there is no absolute or final distinction between thought and more elementary or "immediate" forms of experience such as sensation, perception, volition, intuition, or feeling. Thought is not simply a particular form of experience; it is ultimately inseparable from experience. Experience, as we have already heard, admits of no final or absolute division; and experience everywhere, according to Oakeshott, involves thought or judgment.[26]

In order to explain this point, he takes the case of sensation – sensation being the form of experience with perhaps the strongest claim to being immediate and independent of thought or judgment. Implied in this claim is the idea that what is given in sensation is something "isolated, simple, exclusive, and wholly unrelated; transient, inexpressible, unsharable and impossible of repetition." But reflection reveals that no sensation is of this simple sort. The sensation of yellow, for example, "is never isolated and unrelated, unmodified by previous experience"; it "is characterized by connection with previous experiences recognized as different or similar either in kind or degree." It is, in a word, "recognized"; and this recognition "involves us at once in judgment, in inference, in reflection, in thought." The element of thought or judgment here remains implicit to be sure. But that does not make it any less operative. For Oakeshott, "judgment and explicit, conscious inference and proposition are not identical." Nothing in experience escapes the minimal condition of recognition. "Experience is always and everywhere significant." And this is what

Oakeshott means when he says that experience always and everywhere involves thought or judgment.[27]

Why it has been considered important to discover a form of immediate experience outside thought (in sensation or perception, for example) Oakeshott does not find difficult to understand. The whole attempt belongs to a more general conception of knowledge which, as one writer puts it, "has long commanded the allegiance of philosophers . . . : that of a construction whose solidity is entirely determined by the solidity of the foundations so that if the foundations are not totally secure, the whole will topple."[28] Oakeshott himself characterizes this naive picture of knowledge in the following way: "Experience, it is said, must begin somewhere, and if thought involves mediation, it cannot begin with thought. 'It is as if one should say that in building a wall every brick must be laid on the top of another brick and none directly on the ground.'" He can see in all this, though, "nothing but the distorting influence of a false analogy." We must, he argues, rid ourselves of the notion "that thought requires raw material, a datum which is not judgment." "In thought there is nothing analogous to the painter's colours or the builder's bricks – raw material existing apart from the use made of it." Thinking, he insists in one of the key passages of *Experience and its Modes*

> begins neither from sense-data, nor from given feelings or perceptions; it begins neither from what is immediate, nor with the manifold, the contradictory and the nonsensical. What is at first given in experience is single and significant, a One and not a Many. The given in thought is the complex situation in which we find ourselves in the first moments of consciousness. There is nothing immediate or "natural" in contrast to what is mediate or sophisticated; there are only degrees of sophistication.[29]

What is it that Oakeshott really wants to draw our attention to in this account of the given in experience? Not simply to the fact that the given is mediate or consists of ideas. The passage just quoted emphasizes another aspect of the given. The given is said to be not only mediate but also "single and significant, a One and not a Many." What receives expression here is Oakeshott's crucial notion of a "world." We begin in experience, Oakeshott tells us, not simply with ideas but with a *world* of ideas. And by a world he means a "complex, integral whole or system; wherever there is a world there is unity." Unity is what characterizes the world given in experience, the situation in which we find ourselves in the first moments of consciousness. Nothing in experience is simply separate, unique, isolated, or without relations. Even in the case of sensation, as we have just seen, what is given is at the very least a something recognized. And recognition implies relations, a world, a complex, differentiated, and significant whole. It is perhaps this "worldliness" of experience, even more than its "ideality" (of course, for Oakeshott, the two are inseparable), which distinguishes Oakeshott's view of experience.

It is important at this point to distinguish the unity which belongs to a world from that which belongs to a class. The unity of a class, Oakeshott tells us, has its seat in an "essence" or a "principle." This essence or principle is arrived at by abstracting from a collection of particulars a common element or factor. It is, in short, an abstract universal, and the unity it supports is also said to be abstract. The unity of a world, on the other hand, is not arrived at by abstracting from the particulars which comprise it. Indeed, it is nothing other than these particulars in their mutual coherence. The unity which belongs to a world or system is one

> in which every element is indispensable, in which no one is more important than any other and none is immune from change and rearrangement. The unity of a world of ideas lies in its coherence not in its conformity to or agreement with any one fixed idea. It is neither "in" nor "outside" its constituents, but is the character of its constituents in so far as they are satisfactory in experience.[30]

In a world or system, universal and particular are inseparable. The universal is, in short, a "concrete universal." Though Oakeshott himself does not use the term here, it is quite clear that what he theorizes under the rubric of the "unity of a world" is nothing other than this idealist notion of concrete universality.[31] It is a notion which, as we shall see, plays a crucial role in his understanding of the various forms of human knowledge and activity.

That we begin in unity does not of course mean there remains nothing left to do or achieve in experience. For the unity which characterizes the world of ideas with which we begin is only partial and imperfect. It is partial and imperfect because it is not yet explicit but only implicit. For Oakeshott, the process in experience is a process by which the partially integrated world of ideas given in experience is transformed into a world which is more of a world, which is a more coherent world. More specifically, it is a process of making explicit the unity which is already implicit in that given world of ideas. In "the development of a given world or system of ideas," he writes, "we proceed always by way of implication. We never look *away from* a given world to another world, but always *at* a given world to discover the unity it implies."[32]

The process in experience, then, for Oakeshott, consists in the continuous elucidation of the implications of a given world of ideas. And the criterion of this process is always coherence. Indeed, the pursuit of implications and the pursuit of coherence are really one and the same thing: the attempt to see our world of experience as a single, interrelated whole. To explore or elucidate the implications of a given world of ideas means to relate what may at first appear separate and independent to a context in which this appearance of separateness is dissolved. According to Oakeshott, separate and independent ideas or "facts" always "imply a wider relationship than that in which they are first or frequently conceived."[33] To elucidate that wider relationship or context is what he means by elucidating the implications of a given world of ideas. It is a process by which mere separateness and independence are broken down, and mere diversity gives way to unity. What is achieved is the coherence of a world of ideas.

What Oakeshott is driving at perhaps becomes a little clearer when we consider the criterion of experience from another standpoint, namely that of individuality. Individuality can also be conceived as the criterion of experience, according to Oakeshott. But individuality for him does not mean mere separateness or particularity. When individuality is sought in what is separate from and exclusive of its world or environment, we have to do with an abstract conception of individuality. An idea "separated and held apart from its world or environment," abstracted and divorced from its implications, enjoys only a precarious individuality. Such an idea is ultimately dependent and incomplete; it points beyond itself and hence is not self-contained. It is self-containedness, self-completeness, which Oakeshott ultimately identifies with individuality. Individuality must be sought not simply in what is separate but in what is separate *and* self-contained. The "concrete" individual is not exclusive but inclusive of its world or environment.

> And when this suggestion is pressed to the end, it becomes clear that individuality is the reverse of particularity, that it must be sought ahead and not behind, in what is self-complete and not in what is merely isolated, in what is whole in itself and not in mere solitariness. It must be sought in the world of ideas which an isolated idea implies. For, whenever an idea points beyond itself, however distinct it may appear, it has demonstrated its own lack of individuality, and is powerless to resist inclusion in what is more individual than itself.[34]

When individuality is conceived in this "concrete" way, it can be nothing else but the criterion of experience; it is but another expression for the coherence of a world of ideas. Of course, everything in experience partakes to some extent of individuality. But on Oakeshott's view, individuality is always a matter of degree. And only that which is absolutely independent and self-contained is unlimitedly individual (and unlimitedly real). The individuality of an idea which only appears to be independent and complete is a merely "designated" individuality. And for Oakeshott, the end in experience is always to replace what is merely "designated" with what is "defined."

Experience is not mere designation, which is satisfied with what is separate because it appears to be complete; it is definition, which is characterized by the unremitting pursuit of concrete individuality. And individuality is, in the world of experience, but another name for the point at which experience is obliged to stop; it is the world of experience as a coherent whole.[35]

The end or criterion of experience, then, according to Oakeshott, is the achievement of an absolutely coherent world of experience. It is what his idealist predecessors called the absolute or "the individual." And wherever this concrete end or purpose "is pursued without hindrance or distraction," he calls it "philosophy." Philosophy is simply experience itself, "experience without reservation or presupposition, experience which is self-conscious and self-critical throughout, in which the determination to remain unsatisfied with anything short of a completely coherent world of ideas is absolute and unqualified."[36]

This is, of course, the definition of philosophy with which we began. We are certainly in a better position now to understand what it means than we were then. But before we can fully grasp its meaning, there is one final aspect of Oakeshott's doctrine of experience which we must consider. It concerns the relationship of philosophical experience to the rest of our experience. For it cannot be supposed that we are always – or even very frequently – engaged in this philosophical pursuit of what is finally satisfactory in experience. What role, we want to know, does the rest of our experience have to play in the elaboration of an absolutely coherent and concrete world of experience? What contribution do other and more familiar forms of experience have to make to the concrete whole of experience? In asking these questions we reach what is perhaps the most difficult and distinctive aspect of Oakeshott's teaching concerning the nature of experience and the nature of philosophy: the notion of modality.

So far we have seen that in experience "there is a movement directed towards the achievement of a coherent world of experience." But at any given point this movement may, according to Oakeshott, be "arrested," and a separate world of ideas constructed at the point of the arrest. "In experience," he writes, "there is the alternative of pressing forward towards the perfectly coherent world of concrete ideas or of turning aside from the main current in order to construct and explore a restricted world of abstract ideas." In this latter case, he says, the full obligations of experience are avoided; "the attempt to define, the attempt to see clearly and as a whole, is surrendered for the abstract satisfaction of designation."[37]

The world of ideas that results from such an arrest in experience Oakeshott calls a "mode" of experience – recalling Spinoza's distinction between "substantial" (or self-dependent) and "modal" (or dependent) being. By calling it a "mode" he means to call attention to the fact that such a world of ideas is not a separate *kind* of experience but the whole of experience arrested – modified – at a certain point. Thus he asserts that a mode of experience "is not a separable part of reality, but the whole from a limited standpoint. It is not an island in the sea of experience, but a limited view of the totality of experience. It is not partial (in the literal sense), but abstract."[38] This follows, of course, from Oakeshott's view of experience as a single whole. Experience (or reality) is not cut up into parts; it can, however, be viewed from abstract standpoints. It is precisely the abstract (as opposed to the partial) character of these non-philosophical worlds of ideas that Oakeshott insists upon and that he wishes to call our attention to by referring to them as "modes." To conceive the various forms of non-philosophical experience in terms of modification is to conceive them in terms of abstraction.

We must wait to pass judgment on the ultimate validity of Oakeshott's theory of modality until we see how well it explains some of the more important forms of our experience. For the moment we are only concerned to see if these abstract modes of experience have any contribution to make to the concrete whole of experience, to the achievement of an absolutely coherent world of experience. And it is quite clear from what has been said so far that they do not. Oakeshott conceives these modes of experience as "arrests" in the concrete process of experience, as "divergencies" from the concrete purpose in experience. They lead away from and contribute nothing toward the elaboration of a concrete and absolutely coherent world of experience. The concrete whole, Oakeshott insists, is not a collection or combination of abstract modes of experience. He rejects the view that conceives each form or mode of experience as a body of absolutely valid results "which must be thrown into the total world and without which that world would fall short of totality" – a view which receives expression in the assertion that the coherence of the world of experience depends on its being "in harmony with the results of the special sciences." Such a view implies, according to Oakeshott, "that the more half-truths we entertain, the more certain we are of achieving in the end a fully coherent world of experience." Most importantly, it

loses sight of the fact that these modes of experience are abstract worlds of ideas; it misconceives the character of abstraction. An abstract world of ideas is an arrest in experience. It is not a part of reality; it is not an organization of a separate tract of experience; it is the organization of the whole of experience from a partial and defective point of view. And no collection or combination of such abstractions will ever constitute a concrete whole. The whole is not made of abstractions, it is implied in them; it is not dependent upon abstractions, because it is logically prior to them.[39]

Abstract modes of experience such as history, science, or practice, then, contribute nothing to the overall coherence of our world of experience. Indeed, they lead away from the achievement of an absolutely coherent world of experience; they hinder it, distract from it. A complete and satisfactory experience is to be had, therefore, only by avoiding all such modifications of experience. And such avoidance may take one of two forms. Either it may take the form of "mere failure to be diverted from the concrete purpose in experience." Or it may take the form of an active "rejection of any form of experience which falls short of the character of experience."[40]

It is clearly this latter, active form of avoidance which Oakeshott thinks is called for, given the confusing and distracting circumstances of actual existence. Thus he maintains that it is the "main business" of philosophy conceived as experience without reservation, arrest or modification to consider and reject various arrests or modifications which offer themselves as distractions to the pursuit of a concrete world of experience.

> For ordinarily our experience is not clear and unclouded by abstract categories and postulates, but confused and distracted by a thousand extraneous purposes. And unless we are exceptionally fortunate, a clear and unclouded experience is to be realized only by a process of criticism and rejection. In philosophy . . . it is not less necessary to be unwearied in rejection than in invention, and it is certainly more difficult.[41]

And in order to carry out this critical task, it is necessary that philosophy consider the exact character of every abstract world of ideas which offers itself as a distraction; for "it is difficult to avoid what is imperfectly recognized and impossible to overcome what is only vaguely conceived." This, finally, is the reason why the bulk of *Experience and its Modes* is taken up with lengthy analyses of what Oakeshott takes to be "the main arrests or modifications in experience," namely, history, science, and practice.[42]

At this point in the argument Oakeshott distinguishes his critical project in *Experience and its Modes* from the more specifically Hegelian attempt to determine the exact degree of defect in each of the modes "and thus to determine a logical order or hierarchy of modes." Here he undoubtedly has in mind Collingwood's *Speculum Mentis*. In that work (as I have already remarked) Collingwood too considers the major forms of experience – art, religion, science, history, and philosophy – but (unlike Oakeshott) he arranges them in a hierarchy of increasing coherence and concreteness; each successive form is shown to emerge out of and resolve the self-contradictions of the previous form. Such a project, however, Oakeshott thinks involves a "misconception of the business of philosophy." He does not deny that the modes represent different degrees of abstraction, but he argues that from the standpoint of philosophy these differences are "irrelevant"; "from that standpoint all that is visible is the fact of abstraction, of defect and shortcoming." In order to realize its character, "it is not necessary for philosophy to determine the exact degree of defect belonging to any presented abstract world of ideas, it is necessary only to recognize abstraction and overcome it."[43]

It is absolutely essential that we follow Oakeshott in his critical analyses of history, science, and practice; otherwise his view will remain hopelessly abstract for us and ultimately carry no conviction. But as we follow these analyses, we must always bear in mind the end toward which they are taken up: namely, criticism and rejection. Oakeshott considers history, science, and practice not simply for themselves but because each offers itself as a distraction in the search for a complete and satisfactory world of experience. He considers each of these worlds of ideas, therefore, "solely from the standpoint of its capacity to provide what is satisfactory in experience."[44] The fundamental question he addresses to each of these worlds is, does it constitute the concrete whole of experience or not? Once it is discovered that it doesn't, the mode is rejected, avoided, overcome, and the search for a genuinely coherent world of experience is resumed. It is in terms of this specific and fundamentally critical intention that Oakeshott's inquiries into history, science, and practice in *Experience and its Modes* are to be understood.

Before we take up Oakeshott's analyses of the chief modes of experience, however, we would do well to consider in a little more detail the method of criticism and rejection involved in them. We now know that philosophy according to Oakeshott must assume a critical posture with respect to the non-philosophical modes of experience. But philosophy, he insists, cannot *simply* dismiss or reject these forms of experience. Though in philosophy "it is not less necessary to be unwearied in rejection than in invention," he adds that "in philosophy nothing may be merely rejected."[45] And with respect to science he remarks that, whatever defect we may discover in it, "it is impossible to dismiss such a world of experience as merely invalid and look for a philosophy beyond it in some other, different world; that is too easy an escape. . . . [N]othing can be dismissed as mere error."[46]

What Oakeshott is driving at with these remarks is that philosophy cannot simply criticize the various modes of experience from the outside, as it were, applying a completely alien standard to them. Philosophy must somehow embody what the modes themselves seek but cannot satisfy in full. The standard it applies must be one which the criticized mode itself in some sense admits. That this is indeed the case is part and parcel of Oakeshott's conception of a mode of experience. For a mode of experience is not defined by its renunciation of the criterion of experience, namely coherence, but by its failure to take this criterion seriously. The critical authority of philosophy vis-à-vis the modes of experience thus rests on the fact that it satisfies (or pursues explicitly) the criterion of coherence which the modes themselves recognize (albeit implicitly) but fail to satisfy in full. Philosophical criticism here is not external but immanent. It involves not simply rejection but affirmation of the truth a mode of experience partially possesses. Such criticism discovers not only the error in the half-truth but also the half-truth in the error.[47]

This process by which an abstract mode is avoided or overcome may also be described in terms of supersession (again, in contrast to mere rejection). "Every experience whatever," Oakeshott argues, "submits to the criterion of coherence, and in so far as it is abstract, an arrest in experience, it calls out for its supersession by what is complete." According to this conception, a mode of experience can resolve its incoherence only by surrendering its explicit character as a mode and allowing its implicit character as experience to assert itself. Every mode of experience, according to Oakeshott, "constitutes a self-contradiction": its explicit character as a mode contradicts its implicit character as experience; the explicit aim it pursues contradicts the criterion of coherence it implicitly acknowledges. And the only way this self-contradiction which inheres in a mode can be resolved is "by the surrender of its modality, its character as a world of ideas." Supersession thus involves both completion and abolition. Philosophy, in completing a mode of experience, necessarily abolishes it as a world.[48]

One final implication of this relationship between the concrete whole of experience (or philosophy) and an abstract mode of experience remains to be noticed. Philosophy can do nothing to further the aims of any abstract world of experience. This means, in the cases Oakeshott has chosen, that philosophy must leave history to the historians, science to the scientists, and practice to the virtuosi of the practical realm. Philosophy supersedes an abstract mode of experience, but (Oakeshott insists) it cannot take its place. "No experience save that which belongs exclusively to its mode can help to elucidate the contents of an abstract world of ideas." Philosophy does not perfect a mode within the abstract terms of that mode. Philosophy *supersedes* every abstract world of ideas and consequently "is merely destructive of the abstract world as a world."[49]

To pass in argument from what is concrete to what is abstract, or vice versa, is an example of what Oakeshott calls *ignoratio elenchi*, or the fallacy of irrelevance. As I noted above, this fallacy can also refer to the confusion between one abstract world of ideas and another.[50] But since my concern in this chapter is with Oakeshott's idea of philosophy, I have focused on the fallacy primarily as it applies to the confusion between what is concrete and what is abstract. The notion of *ignoratio elenchi* in this latter sense is of particular importance to Oakeshott's whole understanding of the crucial relationship between theory and practice. The full significance of the notion, however, as well as of all that has been sketched so far, will emerge more clearly and concretely in the explications of Oakeshott's analyses of history, science, and practice which follow.

3. History

By taking up Oakeshott's analysis of historical knowledge first I am doing no more than following the order of *Experience and its Modes* itself. Nevertheless, it remains a question why Oakeshott himself begins with history. The prominent role reflection on historical knowledge plays throughout his philosophical career leads one to doubt that the position of the chapter on history is simply arbitrary.[51] In a review of *Experience and its Modes*, published in *The Cambridge Review*, Collingwood wrote that Oakeshott's theory of the modes of experience

> has been arrived at, I suspect, mainly from an intense effort to understand the nature of historical knowledge. Mr. Oakeshott writes of history like an accomplished historian, who, driven into philosophy by the problems of his own work, has found current philosophies impotent to cope with their philosophical implications; and in that sense the chapter on history seems to me the real nucleus of the book.[52]

Disregarding for the moment that this sounds more like a description of the genesis of Collingwood's own philosophy than of Oakeshott's, let us ask, What in particular about Oakeshott's theory of experience and its modes suggests that it was framed largely with the epistemological problems of history in mind?

I have already remarked on the non-empiricist character of Oakeshott's concept of experience. In experience, on Oakeshott's view, we do not begin with absolute data or fixed facts (frequently conceived in terms of the "immediate" facts of perception). Rather, we begin with a world of ideas, a world in which the so-called "facts" are only half-known, a world in which nothing is fixed, solid, or absolute. And the process in experience is not one in which an inferential superstructure is built on the absolutely solid foundation of immediate or perceptual fact. It is a process by which a given world of ideas is transformed into a more coherent world; a process by which we come to know better, more certainly, what we knew only imperfectly and inadequately at first.

There can be no doubt that the non-empiricist process Oakeshott sees operating in all experience seems immediately more plausible as a description of the historian's experience than, say, of the natural scientist's. For the natural scientist does seem to begin with the immediate facts of perception, and to proceed by building on top of that absolutely certain foundation. In natural science the analogy of the builder and his bricks (which, as we have seen, Oakeshott finds so misleading) does at least seem plausible. And it might be added, it is from reflection on natural science that the empiricist or inductive model of knowledge has traditionally derived its strongest support. Historical knowledge, on the other hand, cannot very easily be made to fit with this purely empiricist model of knowledge. For in history there are no "data" to speak of; nothing is simply "given." The facts which the historian tries to ascertain have, unlike the facts of science, disappeared; they need to be reconstructed. The ostensible object of history, the past course of events, is simply not "there" for the historian in the same way nature seems to be "there" for the scientist. The past, as Collingwood observes in *The Idea of History*, "consists of events that have finished happening and are no longer there to be observed."[53] This simple but significant fact, which comes to sight through reflection on historical knowledge, demands that we rethink history (and perhaps all knowledge) in terms other than those suggested by reflection on natural science. I do not think it entirely misleading to see Oakeshott's theory of experience as arising, at least in part, in response to this demand.[54] The affinities between his concept of experience in general and the idea of history in particular, however, will become clearer as we follow Oakeshott in his analysis of historical knowledge.

So much, then, for the paradigmatic position of history in Oakeshott's philosophy of experience as a whole. It is time now to turn to his analysis of history proper. As I have already indicated, Oakeshott's reflections on each of the main modes of experience are carried out with a view to the question of its capacity to provide what is completely satisfactory in experience. He is concerned to determine whether the form of experience in question be the concrete whole of experience or merely an abstract mode of experience. But in the case of history there is a prior point to be considered, a point implicit in the distinction I drew between history and science above. It concerns the experiential character of history. Before it can be determined whether history be the concrete whole of experience or merely an abstract mode of experience, it must first be shown that history is a form of experience at all. It must be shown that history is a world of thought or ideas and not simply a world of empirical or "objective" fact; that it is a world "constructed" and not simply "discovered" by the historian. A naive objectivism denies the experiential character of history. And in order to counter this objectivism, Oakeshott considers the denial in two of its most common forms: in the assertion that history is a mere series of successive events; and in the assertion that history is the objective course of events.

He first takes up the argument that history does not constitute a world of experience or ideas because it does not constitute a world but only a series. The distinguishing mark of a world, as we have already seen, is unity; the constituents of a world are coexistent and inter-dependent. But history, so this argument runs, does not consist in what is coexistent but only in what is successive. Schopenhauer made this point in his well-known attack on history. "History," he wrote,

> lacks the fundamental characteristic of science, namely the subordina-tion of the objects of consciousness; all it can do is present a simple co-ordination of the facts it has registered. Hence there is no system in history as there is in other sciences. . . . [N]owhere does it know the particular by means of the universal, but always comprehends the particular directly, creeping along the ground of experience, as it were. The real sciences, on the other hand, excel it, since they have attained to comprehensive con-cepts by means of which they command and control the particular. . . . The sciences being systems of concepts, speak always of kinds; history always of individuals.[55]

And Bosanquet made exactly the same point when he spoke of history as a "tissue of mere conjunctions" and the "doubtful story of suc-cessive events."[56] History, both Schopenhauer and Bosanquet are saying, is a mere series of isolated particulars; it is not a whole or a world, but a sum; "it enumerates, but cannot integrate."[57]

Oakeshott grants that history certainly appears to the unreflective historian – the historian as such – as a series of separate and suc-cessive events. But he goes on to argue that history is not logically constituted as such a series. In the first place, "history is concerned only with that which appears in or is constructed from record of some kind." An event which has left no trace in record is not part of the so-called "historical series." In short, the "historical series" is not the same as the "time series." But further, "history does not consist in a bare, uncritical account of whatever has survived in record." The historian does not simply accept whatever happens to have survived in record in whatever order it happens to appear. He is both selective and critical with respect to his "authorities." He translates them, he simplifies them, he adds to them, and frequently he contradicts them if he thinks they are not telling the truth. Ultimately everything the historian includes in his narrative must fit together to form a coherent, non-contradictory whole. All the pieces criticize one another. And once this element of criticism is admitted, the whole notion of history as a series of successive events breaks down. If the terms of the so-called "historical series" offer criticism of one another, then we no longer have to do with a mere series but with a world. No term stands "isolated and self-evident"; each is "guaranteed by the series as a whole." And "wherever the terms of a 'series' so far lose their isola-tion and come to depend upon the criticism and guarantee of other, perhaps subsequent terms, and of the 'series' as a whole, there is no longer a series of what is successive, but a world of what is co-existent."[58]

But denial of the view that history constitutes a world of ideas has taken a second form. It is commonly believed, Oakeshott points out, that history "is an 'objective' world, a world of past events to be discovered, unearthed, recaptured; it consists of what actually happened, and that (at least) is independent of what we think; it is a world, not of ideas, but of events. History, in short, is the course of events." This view, too, Oakeshott remarks, comes to us backed by "the prejudices and assumptions of the historian," whose scientific ideal is to narrate the past *wie es eigentlich gewesen ist*, and whose criterion of objectivity is an impossible freedom from experience.[59]

Though this is what the historian commonly believes, the division of the world of history which it implies – the separation of the "course of events" from "our interpretation of it," and "of history from historiography" – will not bear philosophical scrutiny, Oakeshott argues. "The distinction between history as it happened (the course of events) and history as it is thought, the distinction between history itself and merely experienced history, must go; it is not only false, it is meaningless." It is meaningless because the course of events as such is past and incapable of entering present experience. The course of events has finished happening and is no longer "there" to be observed; it is, in the strictest sense, unknowable, a nonentity. "There is no history independent of experience; the course of events, as such, is not history because it is nothing at all." The only history we have is that which the historian "makes." Oakeshott concludes, "History is experience, the historian's world of experience; it is a world of ideas, the historian's world of ideas."[60]

The notion that history is the historian's present world of experience and not the past course of events is of crucial importance to Oakeshott's entire theory of history. But we must not conclude from this that Oakeshott means to proclaim a radical historical relativism or skepticism. In asserting that history is the experience of the historian, he is not saying that history consists of the historian's experience "as such, merely as *his* experience." For Oakeshott, it must be remembered, experience is always a *world* of ideas; it is never simply immediate, merely mine. It is true, he concedes, that experience is always somebody's experience. But this fact never constitutes anything more than a single abstract aspect of experience. My experience is always mine, but it is never merely mine; never merely *my* psychical state. My experience is always also, for example, relatively true or false. "If my experience were my psychical states as such and nothing more, I should be obliged to take every experience at its face value; to question would be contradictory, to doubt impossible."[61] Experience everywhere, as we have already seen, involves judgment; it is, therefore, always more than merely mine, more than my psychical state as such.

Having established that history is a form of experience, a world of ideas, Oakeshott proceeds next to show that it pursues the process characteristic of all experience. "The datum in all experience is, we have seen, a world of ideas, and the process in all experience is to make a given world more of a world, to make it coherent." And this is the case in historical experience, though again the historian himself frequently does not recognize it. The unreflective historian commonly supposes that history "begins with the collection of data" or "with the collection of material"; only then can history proceed to the task of "criticism and synthesis" or "interpretation." But history, Oakeshott argues, does not begin with the collection of raw data or material. No knowledge begins with "mere particles of data" or with "isolated facts." Whatever comes before the historian as data or material has a meaning, belongs to a world. And what in the first place gives it its significance is the "homogeneous system of ideas or postulates" in terms of which the historian "is conscious of whatever comes before him." It is this initial system of postulates, and not the "facts," which is first from the standpoint of logic. In addition to a system of postulates or presuppositions, the historian, according to Oakeshott, comes to whatever he happens to be studying with a general view of the course of events, a hypothesis to guide him in his inquiry. It must be kept in mind, though, that this hypothesis or "preconception" about the general course of events does not derive from what is merely incidental to the historian's situation; it is itself governed by his initial system of postulates.[62]

But it is not only the conception of the initial datum that Oakeshott finds inadequate in the naive view (which he generally ascribes to the historian himself) of the process in historical knowledge. He also rejects the conception implied in this view of what the initial datum undergoes as thought proceeds. On the naive view, as we have seen, history is said to begin with the collection of data or material, which are always conceived as "isolated facts." After these "isolated facts" have been collected, the historian then proceeds to the task of "criticism and synthesis." The important thing to be noticed here is that the "facts" with which the historian is said to begin, the so-called "data," are conceived as fixed and absolute. The historian may add new facts to the old facts; he may connect them, synthesize them, or construct a theory out of them. But whatever he does, his activity is never understood in any way to change or transform them. The "facts," according to this naive empiricist view, always retain their original character; they are given only "to be incorporated, not to be transformed."[63]

This view of the relationship between what is given and what is achieved cannot, however, be maintained once the given is conceived as a world of ideas. For Oakeshott, as we have seen, the process in all experience is a process by which a given world of ideas is transformed into a more coherent world. But we must not think of this transformation of the initial datum of knowledge in terms of mere incorporation. As our knowledge advances, Oakeshott argues, the initial datum itself changes. The given facts are not fixed and inviolable; they are completely dependent on the whole world to which they belong. Any change in this world necessarily involves a transformation of the "facts" themselves. For Oakeshott, fact and world – fact and interpretation, fact and theory – are inseparable. He draws out this implication of the "worldly" or systematic character of fact in general thus:

> In a system each constituent rests upon the whole. . . . And at whatever point we take it up, we take up the whole, for the so-called constituents of a system are no more than the accidental creations of the circumstances in which we came to apprehend it. And again, these constituents have no individuality or character of their own in isolation from the whole which they constitute; their character is their place in the system. To modify the system as a whole is to cause every constituent to take on a new character; to modify any of the constituents is to alter the system as a whole.[64]

And it is on account of this "worldly" or systematic character of fact that the process of knowledge is not, for Oakeshott, "a process of mere accretion." Every addition to our knowledge, he argues, involves the transformation of an entire world of ideas; the creation of an entirely new world of ideas. Since knowledge always forms a system, "each advance affects retrospectively the entire whole, and is the creation of a new world."[65]

In historical knowledge this systematic or "concrete" character of fact is particularly well exemplified. Indeed, here is one of those places where Oakeshott's general theory of experience seems to have learned from history. At any rate, the concreteness of historical fact prevents us from conceiving the process of historical knowledge in terms of a process of incorporation or accretion. The task which confronts the historian, Oakeshott argues, "is to detect what modification a new discovery, a new experience produces in the world of history as a whole." Each new discovery in history is "not the discovery of a fresh detail, but of a new world."[66] The process in historical thought is not one in which new facts are simply "added" to old facts, or old facts are simply "incorporated" unchanged into a new world of fact. The facts of history are not fixed, absolute, inert. Every advance in historical knowledge involves a revision of all that has up to that point counted as fact.

By considering the process of historical knowledge, the process by which historical facts are established, we gain a better understanding of what Oakeshott means when he designates coherence as the criterion of historical truth. Coherence is, of course, the criterion of all truth, according to Oakeshott. Nevertheless, it is not difficult to see how reflection on historical knowledge in particular might have suggested coherence as a general criterion of truth. In history, as we have seen, there is no "objective" course of events, nothing outside the historian's present world of experience by which the truth of that world might be established. The truth of the historian's world of experience cannot lie in its correspondence with "what was"; it cannot even be shown to consist (as Oakeshott goes on to show) in its agreement with the "original authorities."[67] The truth of the historian's world of experience can only lie in its internal coherence. And the most important implication of this view of historical truth is – once again – that the so-called "facts" of history have no independence vis-à-vis the interpretation or world of ideas to which they belong. "[I]t is impossible to establish the truth of historical facts piecemeal." Oakeshott elaborates on this most important implication of the coherence-notion of historical truth thus:

> The truth of each fact depends upon the truth of the world of facts to which it belongs, and the truth of the world of facts lies in the coherence of the facts which compose it. In historical experience, as in all other experience, there are no absolute data, nothing given which is immune from change; each element rests upon and supports every other element. Each separate "fact" remains an hypothesis until the whole world of facts is established in which it is involved. And no single fact may be taken as historically true, and beyond the possibility of transformation, until the whole world of facts has achieved a condition of stable coherence.[68]

So far Oakeshott has been concerned to show, against a naive objectivism, that history is experience, the historian's present world of experience, and not the past course of events or "what actually happened." But his whole thesis is not simply that history is experience, but that it is a *modification* of experience; it is the whole of experience viewed from a limited standpoint. The specific character of this modification is what we must now consider. What, we want to know, are the particular postulates in terms of which the historian organizes the whole of experience or reality?

The master-postulate or category of historical experience, according to Oakeshott, is the idea of the past. History is experience *sub specie praeteritorum*. It is the attempt to organize the whole of experience in the form of the past; to see all that is present as evidence of a past that has not survived. But the past in terms of which the historian organizes his present experience is not just any past; it is a special past. According to Oakeshott, there is not in experience a single past. The notion of a single past still participates in the objectivist error that the past is something "there" lying "behind" the present. The past in experience is always postulated; and consequently there are several different pasts corresponding to the several different modes of experience. The historical past – the past postulated in history – is but one of these; it is a special past which must be distinguished from other pasts, most importantly (in Oakeshott's view) from the practical past.[69]

The practical past, according to Oakeshott, is the past when it is viewed in relation to the present.

> Wherever the past is merely that which preceded the present, that from which the present has grown, wherever the significance of the past lies in the fact that it has been influential in deciding the present and the future fortunes of man, wherever the present is sought in the past, and wherever the past is regarded merely as a refuge from the present – the past involved is a practical, and not an historical past.

This practical attitude toward the past is perhaps best exemplified in religion. In both Judaism and Christianity, for example, the past plays an important role. But it is, for Oakeshott, always a practical past. For the Hebrew people, "the past had meaning . . . only in so far as it was seen to be their past; their concern was with its life, not with its deadness; for them it was saga, it was (in fact) a mythology, an effort to make actual and impressive their beliefs about the present world and about the character of God." In Christianity the so-called "historical element" partakes of this same practical character: "the past is designed to justify, to make valid practical beliefs about the present and the future, about the world in general"; to give those beliefs "force" and "liveliness."[70]

The practical past, then, is the past for the sake of the present. The historical past, on the other hand, is "the past for its own sake." The past that the historian is interested in, Oakeshott argues, "is a dead past; a past unlike the present." This, indeed, is the *differentia* of the historical past: its deadness, its dissimilarity from and irrelevance to the present.[71] By distinguishing the historical past from the practical past in this way, Oakeshott means to avoid that variety of historical skepticism in which the past is simply assimilated to the present. Though emphasizing the presentness of historical fact, he rejects the view that (in Croce's phrase) all history is contemporary history. The historical past is certainly present insofar as it is not the past course of events; insofar, that is, as it is experience. But this is by no means all that can be said of the historical past. And it certainly does not imply that the past in history is the mere reflection of the contemporary world as such.[72]

Related to this deadness is another feature of the historical past, according to Oakeshott. In addition to thinking it dead and unlike the present, "the historian is accustomed to think of the past as a complete and virgin world stretching out behind the present, fixed, finished and independent, awaiting only discovery.... In short, the past *for* history is 'what really happened'." Oakeshott stresses that this is the past only as it is *for* history. "It is what the historian is accustomed to believe"; it "encourages" him; "it is difficult to see how he could go on did he not believe his task to be the resurrection of what once had been alive." Nevertheless, it is obvious that, given what Oakeshott has already argued, this view of the past which belongs *explicitly* to history cannot "be maintained unmodified." For "it implies that history is not experience"; that history is the past course of events, "what really happened." And this naive view of history we have already seen to be erroneous. The historical past, because it is experience, must be present; but (Oakeshott insists) it is not simply present, present through and through. "[T]he pastness of the world of historical experience involves a modification of its presentness, involves a modification of its character as experience." And this modification of the presentness of experience is precisely what constitutes the abstractness of historical experience. Put another way, historical experience is self-contradictory: its *explicit* form as past contradicts its *implicit* character as experience. Oakeshott sums up the contradiction that is history in this way:

> The historical past is always present; and yet historical experience is always in the form of the past. And this contradiction must remain unresolved so long as we remain within the world of historical ideas. History, because it is experience, is present, its facts are present facts, its world a present world of ideas; but because it is history, the formulation of experience as a whole *sub specie praeteritorum*, it is the continuous assertion of a past which is not past and of a present which is not present.[73]

The historian, according to Oakeshott, is guilty of a certain kind of philosophical error. And this error or naïveté is indispensable to his carrying on his activity. The historian supposes the past to be a "complete and virgin world stretching out behind the present, fixed, finished and independent, awaiting only discovery." In short, he supposes the past to be "what actually happened." And if he only thought through the implications of his experience, as the philosopher does, he would realize that the past cannot be of such a character. He would realize that the historical past is really present and not past; that it is the organization of his own present consciousness and not a separate tract of reality lying behind the present which he simply "discovers." But Oakeshott maintains – and this is the difficult point – that the historian cannot transcend this presupposition of *was eigentlich geschehen ist* without at the same time ceasing to be an historian. This belief in the pastness of the past is essential to the historian; it "encourages" him; "it is difficult to see how he could go on did he not believe his task to be the resurrection of what once had been alive." Or again, "the notion of the past cannot be dismissed from history without dismissing history itself."[74] In short, philosophical sophistication can only lead away from the abstractions of historical experience. To recognize the self-contradiction that lies at the heart of history is to transcend it.

This, as I have said, is a difficult point, and Oakeshott himself concedes as much. It may seem to some, he writes, "that history can be freed from its attachment to the past without at the same moment being freed from itself."[75] But even supposing the historian's awareness of the illusoriness of *was eigentlich geschehen ist* need not lead to historical skepticism, there still remains "a second characteristic of history which establishes its abstract character on an even firmer foundation." This second characteristic is the conception of individuality which belongs to historical experience. The individual of history is, according to Oakeshott, ultimately "designated" and not "defined."[76] This requires some explanation.

For Oakeshott, it will be remembered, individuality is not the same thing as particularity or singularity. He rejects the positivistic conception of individuality, which is based on separateness from environment and exclusivity. He conceives individuality instead in terms of inclusiveness and completeness. Individuality "is the reverse of particularity"; it must be sought ahead in what is self-complete and not behind in what is merely isolated. Individuality, on this view, is always a matter of degree, and absolute individuality is the concrete end or criterion of experience. "Experience is not mere designation, which is satisfied with what is separate because it appears to be complete; it is definition, which is characterized by the unremitting pursuit of concrete individuality." And since the end in all experience is definition, "wherever in experience satisfaction is achieved in a world of merely designated individuals . . . experience has fallen short of its own character."[77]

Now, the individual of history, Oakeshott argues, of which historical events, institutions and persons are examples, is characterized by a certain amount of continuity with its environment; but ultimately its identity is established through discontinuity and separateness from environment. Certainly history is not concerned, as is sometimes asserted, with what is absolutely particular or singular; with what is "unique." History does not consist of a series of unique moments or events. History of this sort, Oakeshott contends, "has never been written" and "never could be written"; "what is absolutely singular is absolutely unknowable." Nevertheless, though not absolutely singular, the individual of history is not absolutely complete either; it must at some point distinguish itself from its environment; it is conceived finally in terms of separateness rather than self-completeness.

Oakeshott thus describes the individuality that belongs to historical experience in terms of "the double conception of continuity and discontinuity." The identity of an historical individual is "established by means of the principle of discontinuity" and "maintained by means of the principle of continuity." An historical event, for example, "is never a mere point-instant.... Its capacity for establishing its individuality lies in the discontinuity, the relative break which seems to precede it; and its capacity for maintaining its individuality lies in the continuity, or relative absence of break, which it can show."[78]

The individuality of the historical individual is, then, only relative and, for Oakeshott, ultimately arbitrary. "Anyone who has considered the matter," he writes, "knows well enough how arbitrary the individuality of an historical event is. One historical event is distinguished from another by the flimsiest partition; there is nothing solid or absolute in their character." And it is just this arbitrariness, this merely designated character of the historical individual, which finally convicts historical experience of abstraction and incoherence. Nor can history ever completely overcome this defect. It is difficult, Oakeshott observes, for the historian to remain unaware of the arbitrariness of the historical individual; he is constantly tempted "to abandon the terms of the presupposition." But the process by which the merely presupposed and designated individual is absorbed into its environment can only go so far. "[A]llow the designated individual of history to disappear altogether into its environment," he maintains, "and history is destroyed." "Historical experience, like all abstract experience, is always on the verge of passing beyond itself. Its movement tends to supersede the conception of individuality upon which it is based, while at the same time it insists, as it must insist, upon retaining it."[79]

The notions of the past and of the individual which belong to history[80] reveal it to be an abstract and defective mode of experience, not the concrete whole of experience. And this means, from the standpoint of philosophy, that it must be avoided, rejected, overcome. History can only serve to hinder and distract from the pursuit of an absolutely coherent world of experience. "History is a world of abstractions. It is a backwater, and, from the standpoint of experience, a mistake. It leads nowhere; and in experience, if we have been unable to avoid it, we can regain the path to what will afford satisfaction only by superseding and destroying it."[81]

This implies, among other things, that there is nothing in history of which philosophy can ever make use. Everything in history is vitiated by abstraction, and what is abstract can make no contribution to the coherence of the whole. Nor, by the same token, may philosophy ever take upon itself the task of making the world of historical experience more coherent – for example, by drawing connections between historical facts, or discovering a plan or plot in them. The "philosophy of history" is, for Oakeshott, an example of *ignoratio elenchi.* The philosopher can have nothing to do with the abstractions of history. And the philosophico-historical speculations of the philosopher of history can only be irrelevant to the historian (or possibly the object of legitimate derision). Because history is a world of abstractions, "those who have made it their business to press experience to its conclusion can choose only between avoiding it or superseding it."[82]

Perhaps the main significance of Oakeshott's analysis of history as an abstract mode of experience is that it repudiates any sort of radical or skeptical historicism. "Historicism" is, of course, a notoriously ambiguous term, but here I understand by it the reduction or assimilation of all knowledge (including philosophical knowledge) to historical knowledge.[83] It should be clear by now that historicism in this sense is no part of Oakeshott's theory of knowledge or of philosophy. Philosophy is in no way reducible to or liquidated by history. History is an abstract world of experience, and philosophy as concrete experience begins by avoiding or rejecting this world of abstractions. Nor can a philosophy be refuted by tracing it to its historical setting or situation. Place and time, Oakeshott tells us, are irrelevant to philosophy. Of course, every philosophy has a place and a time, an historical setting; but these are irrelevant to it *as a philosophy.* What we want to know about a philosophy is whether it is true or not, whether it is valid. And no amount of historical investigation will help us answer this philosophical question.[84]

With respect to this question of historicism, it is perhaps instructive to compare Oakeshott with Collingwood. There is, as I have already noted, much that links these two thinkers, not least their common preoccupation with the problem of historical knowledge. But in Collingwood there is a tendency to historicism that is absent from Oakeshott's thought. As the editor of *The Idea of History* points out in his preface to the work, Collingwood, like Croce, "came to think that 'philosophy as a separate discipline is liquidated by being converted into history'."[85] Oakeshott too, in a review of *The Idea of History,* draws attention critically to this historicistic tendency in Collingwood's thought. "[I]t must be observed that, almost imperceptibly, Collingwood's philosophy of history turned into a philosophy in which all knowledge is assimilated to historical knowledge, and consequently into a radically sceptical philosophy."[86] In this extreme historicistic direction Oakeshott did not follow Collingwood. Not only in *Experience and its Modes* but in his later writings as well, the categorial distinction between philosophy and history is strictly maintained.

It is perhaps worth noting (in conclusion) that Oakeshott diverges from Collingwood not only in his understanding of the relationship between history and philosophy, but also in his understanding of the nature of historical knowledge itself. Specifically, he rejects Collingwood's doctrine of historical "re-enactment."[87] In various reviews from the forties and the fifties, as well as in the essay "The Activity of Being an Historian," Oakeshott comes more and more to emphasize (in contradistinction to Collingwood) the difference between an historical understanding of actions or events and the self-understanding of an agent or participant. Of course, the distinction was there from the start in *Experience and its Modes*, where the "historical past" is differentiated from the "practical past"; but it becomes much more explicit in the later writings. In a long review of E. H. Carr's *The Bolshevik Revolution, 1917–23*, for example, Oakeshott criticizes Carr for failing to translate the actions and utterances of his subjects from the idiom of practice into the idiom of history. The task of the historian, he says, is not simply sympathetic re-enactment but to understand "men and events more profoundly than they were understood when they lived and happened."[88] He repeats this point in "The Activity of Being an Historian": "It would appear that the task of 'the historian' is . . . to understand past conduct and happening in a manner in which they were never understood at the time; to translate action and event from their practical idiom into an historical idiom."[89] It is clear from statements such as these that Oakeshott rejects Collingwood's doctrine of historical re-enactment.[90] For him the task of the historian is to understand the past, not as, but better than, it understood itself.

4. Science

The necessity of considering science from the standpoint of philosophy, from the standpoint, that is, of its capacity to provide what is satisfactory in experience, is not difficult to understand. For some time now science, of all the non-practical forms of experience, has most frequently been taken for the absolute in experience, the model of or gateway to all genuine knowledge. This identification of natural science with knowledge itself is what is known as "positivism." And it cannot be doubted that this false philosophy constitutes one of the main targets of *Experience and its Modes*.

Oakeshott's antagonism to positivism and the positivistic conception of philosophy is made clear in the introduction to *Experience and its Modes*. There he writes that "it is scarcely to be expected, in these days, that we should not be tempted to take up with the idea of philosophy as, in some sense, 'the fusion of the sciences', 'the synthesis of the sciences' or the *scientia scientarum*." Behind these notions of the nature and task of philosophy lies the positivistic belief in the absoluteness of scientific methods and results; the belief that philosophy must accept these methods and results unquestioningly. And yet, Oakeshott asks, "what are the sciences that they must be accepted as the datum, and as the datum not to be changed, of valid knowledge? And if we begin with the sciences, can our conclusions be other or more than merely scientific?"[91] In a similar vein, he writes: "The notion . . . that philosophy has anything to learn from the methods of scientific thought, or that the conclusions of philosophy 'must be in harmony with the results of the special sciences', is altogether false."[92]

In order to maintain his idea of philosophy, then, Oakeshott must show that science does not provide what is finally or completely satisfactory in experience; that it is not the concrete whole of experience but only an abstract mode. And of course this requires that he consider the exact character of scientific experience. The procedure he follows is essentially the same one we saw him apply to historical experience. One difference, however, is that he does not find it necessary (as he did in the case of history) to show that science is indeed a world of experience and not simply a world of "pure fact." That the world of science is a world of experience, a world of thought, is not really controversial.[93] The scientist, unlike the historian, does not conceive his knowledge to be knowledge of "pure fact." The scientist does not deny that his knowledge is to some extent constructed, the product of thought; that the laws he discovers are not simply a matter of empirical perception.

What is contentious, though, according to Oakeshott, is "the character and degree of the modification which scientific experience introduces into experience."[94] Though the scientist recognizes the experiential character of his knowledge, he fails to grasp its essential abstractness. He fails to see that science is not experience, absolute and self-critical, but a modification of experience. And what more than anything else prevents the scientist from seeing the abstractness of his activity is the belief that the methods of science are exactly fitted to a reality which lies outside scientific thought, that is, nature. It is true that the scientist is not prey to exactly the same objectivist delusion that the historian is. Nevertheless, he still believes that there is a reality outside his experience to which his experience corresponds. He believes that his knowledge rests on the absolutely solid foundation of the facts of nature, facts generally conceived to be immediately given in perception. The theory of science has long been based on some such empiricist or objectivist foundation. The matter of science, nature, has been conceived as independent of scientific thought; and the method of science has been thought to be specially "adapted" to this independent and objective nature.[95]

It is primarily against this empiricist or objectivist conception of scientific knowledge that Oakeshott reacts in his analysis of scientific experience. His view of the critical authority of philosophy vis-à-vis science depends on his refuting the view that scientific knowledge simply corresponds to reality; that it is founded on concrete fact. He must show that science is not empirical in the sense of being specially adapted to nature; that its method is not simply inductive. He must show that the facts, no less than the conclusions (i.e., laws, generalizations), of science are the product of scientific thought; that scientific experience is not a special kind of thought concerned with a special kind of object, but a special organization of the whole of experience. In short, he must show that the method of science and the matter of science are absolutely correlative.

Oakeshott sets out to undermine the empiricist theory of science by first observing that scientific experience does not begin, logically speaking, with the mere "observation" of the world around us. The "kind of semi-detached observation of uniformities in the world of perception" with which scientific experience is frequently said to begin he relegates to a pre-scientific stage of experience he calls "natural history." The desire which animates natural history, the desire "for an escape from the private, incommunicable world of personal experience as such, into a world of common and communicable experience, a world of experience upon which universal agreement is possible," certainly animates science proper as well; indeed, Oakeshott takes "absolute communicability" to be the "sole *explicit* criterion of scientific ideas." But natural history is unable to fulfill this end; it remains confined to the incompletely communicable world of perception.[96]

Science, then, in order to achieve its end of absolute communicability, must "leave behind the world of perception." "Science begins," Oakeshott argues, "only when the world of 'things' opened to us by our sensations and perceptions has been forgotten or left on one side." The world with which we begin in science is not the world of which we are aware when we first open our eyes; it is not the world of perception; nor is it the world of common sense or of ordinary practical consciousness (nothing, according to Oakeshott, "hinders the full development of scientific thought" more than the practical interest). The world given in scientific experience has been arrived at through abstraction from these nearer and more familiar worlds; it is a world of abstractions, a world not of hard "facts" but of ideas. "The world of scientific experience is, then, created by a transformation of our familiar world; in science there is no attempt to elucidate the character of this world of perception in which we live, what is attempted is the elucidation of the world of absolutely stable experience." This postulated end of scientific experience determines its character as purely quantitative experience. The world of scientific experience is, for Oakeshott, the world *sub specie quantitatis*, the world conceived under the category of quantity.[97]

Thus, in scientific experience, we do not move from an "external" world of sensible "things" to a world of abstract scientific ideas; we always move within a single homogeneous world of quantitative ideas. Scientific experience, Oakeshott argues, does not begin with the "collection of data" or with mere "observation"; it begins with a partially integrated world of quantitative ideas, "a world in outline, the sketch of a world." In the course of scientific thought this outline is gradually filled in and elaborated: first by means of hypothesis, which is always framed in terms of the quantitative structural concepts originally given in scientific experience; and only later by means of observation and experiment. At several points in the argument Oakeshott stresses the wholly subordinate role of experiment and observation in scientific thought. The observations and experiments of science are always carried out with some purpose in mind. In the first place, they are "limited and controlled by hypothesis. Science knows nothing of a collection of miscellaneous data, it knows nothing of a haphazard accumulation of materials." And in the second place, scientific observations and experiments are "limited also by the postulated character and end of scientific knowledge"; that is to say, they are always quantitative. Scientific observations are always measurements, never percepts. "The eye of the scientific observer is a measure; scientific perception is itself measurement. The data of scientific knowledge are never mere 'observations'."[98]

From the "data" of scientific thought Oakeshott goes on to consider the conclusions of scientific thought. The conclusions of science, he argues, are always generalizations; but more specifically, they are always *statistical* generalizations. The observations of science, we have seen, are measurements; and "the only way of generalizing measurements is statistical," according to Oakeshott. A statistical generalization – as opposed to a collective or enumerative generalization – does not refer categorically to individual observations or particular cases. "It is a generalization which refers to a series or a body of observations as a series or a body." With respect to science, "a statistical generalization is a résumé of scientific observations, but a résumé independent of the character of any single observation." Given their statistical nature, no scientific generalization can be disproved by a single observation or counterexample alone, according to Oakeshott; "a single observation," he comments, "is never of any significance in science."[99]

So far Oakeshott has considered science in terms of its "method," the process by which it creates and elucidates a world of quantitative ideas. He turns next to consider the "matter" of science, that is, nature. On one view, the method of science is thought to be "dictated" or specially "adapted" to the character of its matter, nature. But Oakeshott rejects this view of scientific knowledge; indeed, he calls it "the most vicious and crippling fallacy the theory of scientific knowledge has ever entertained." For him, the method and the matter of science, what is experienced in science and the manner in which it is experienced, are absolutely correlative.[100] This is implied in what he has already said about the process of scientific knowledge. The "nature" which is the subject-matter of science is not simply "the world of which we are aware when we open our eyes"[101]; it is a specialized world wholly determined by the postulated end of scientific experience. In scientific experience we do not move from an external and concrete world of nature to a world of abstract scientific ideas; we always move within a single homogeneous world of quantitative ideas. Nature for the scientist is nothing other than the world *sub specie quantitatis*, the world conceived entirely in terms of measurements.

One implication of this view of the subject-matter of science – an implication I will explore at greater length below – ought to be noticed here: namely, there is nothing to prevent the "human" from being assimilated to the scientist's "nature." For Oakeshott, there is nothing inherently contradictory in the notion of a science of man or a science of society, so long as these are conceived quantitatively. To exclude man or society from scientific treatment clearly involves, on his view, a misconception of the nature of science. Nature as the subject-matter of science is not a separable part of reality, to be distinguished from the realm of the "human"; it is the whole of reality conceived under the category of quantity. And for this reason man and society are no less susceptible to scientific study than anything else.

Up to this point Oakeshott has only specified the character of scientific experience without raising the all-important question of its validity. But it is quite clear that his analysis of scientific knowledge throws the question of its validity into an entirely new light. No longer can it be maintained that science is true, that is, absolutely true, even if only with respect to a certain part of reality. For what is asserted in science is asserted of the whole of reality. Science, as we have seen, is an attempt to give coherence to the whole of reality; and, according to Oakeshott, it must be judged in the light of this attempt. The question is whether science is an absolutely coherent world of ideas or not. Is it the concrete whole of experience, or is it merely the whole from a limited and abstract standpoint?

There can be little doubt as to what Oakeshott's answer to this question will be. His entire analysis of scientific experience is dominated by the view that science "is the attempt to find a common, uniform and impersonal world, rather than a world which is absolute and concrete; it is the attempt to abolish superstition rather than establish what is absolutely true."[102] But what, we want to know, is the specific error in virtue of which science remains an incompletely coherent and wholly abstract world of experience?

According to Oakeshott, the essential abstractness of scientific experience lies in its hypothetical or suppositional character. Science, he argues, is hypothetical through and through. And by this he means more than that in science hypothesis is used as a method of discovery. He means that even the conclusions of science, and not simply the means by which those conclusions are arrived at, are hypothetical. Of the hypothetical character of his knowledge in this sense the scientist is not necessarily aware. The element of supposal (as Oakeshott refers to it here) is implicit. It emerges into explicitness only in the course of philosophical reflection on scientific knowledge.

What Oakeshott says about the character of scientific generalizations reveals fully the hypothetical, the merely suppositional, nature of scientific knowledge. These generalizations, we have learned, are always statistical generalizations. Each is a "résumé of scientific observations, but a résumé independent of the character of any single observation." Scientific generalizations "do not refer categorically to particular cases" or to actual concrete observations. A scientific generalization only "asserts a relation or a consequence, and never the existence of what is related." Thus the world of science is a world of supposals about reality, not a world of categorical judgments about reality. Oakeshott dismisses scientific knowledge as "merely generalized knowledge"; "nowhere in the whole range of scientific experience is there to be found a generalization categorically asserted."[103]

But we must not think that because Oakeshott characterizes the world of science as a world of supposals he means to dismiss it as a world of "mere supposals," a purely conceptual world containing no assertion of reality. Oakeshott's theory of knowledge has nothing in common with that easy-going pluralism which sees the various forms of experience as independent and self-contained worlds that do not point beyond themselves to reality. For him, all worlds of experience contain some reference to reality, though in varying degrees of explicitness; no world of experience is a world of "mere ideas," a world coherent in itself but asserting nothing of reality. For this reason he argues that the world of scientific experience is not a world of "mere supposals"; "a mere supposal, a supposal that asserts nothing of reality, is contradictory and impossible in experience."[104]

By arguing that science is a world of supposals, then, Oakeshott is not arguing that there is no assertion of reality in science; only that the assertion of reality in scientific judgment remains implicit. Explicitly science is supposal; it remains satisfied in its explicit aim with a world of supposals about reality. But implicitly science refers to and depends upon concrete reality. It is precisely because its explicit character contradicts its implicit character that science falls short of complete coherence. Science is self-contradictory and to that extent incoherent. And until the assertion of reality that is implicit in science becomes explicit, scientific experience will remain incoherent. But this becoming explicit of the assertion of reality implicit in scientific experience involves the destruction of the world of science as a distinctive world; once accomplished, nothing remains of the explicit aim which distinguishes scientific experience from all other forms of experience.[105] One could say that, just as the historian ceases to be an historian once he frees himself from the illusion of *was eigentlich geschehen ist*, so the scientist, once he recognizes the merely hypothetical character of his knowledge, necessarily ceases to be a scientist. With the achievement of this self-consciousness, science loses its *raison d'être* and appears as a merely misguided attempt to achieve a completely coherent world of ideas.

Science, then, is not the concrete whole of experience; it is only an abstract mode of experience. And Oakeshott draws from this result the expected implication. Scientific knowledge as abstract knowledge "has no contribution whatever to make to our knowledge of reality." There is nothing in scientific experience of which philosophy can make use in its pursuit of an absolutely coherent world of experience. Philosophy is in no sense a synthesis of scientific results; nor need it be in harmony with scientific results. The results as well as the methods of science are, from the standpoint of philosophy, abstract and defective from end to end. "Philosophy," Oakeshott concludes, "must begin by rejecting alike the method and the results of the arrest in experience called science."[106]

5. History and Science

At the beginning of the previous section I mentioned the anti-positivistic character of Oakeshott's theory of science, and this, I hope, is now evident. By showing science to be an abstract world of experience, Oakeshott undermines the positivistic claim that scientific knowledge is the only true form of knowledge; that scientific experience is absolute and beyond criticism. This critique of the pretensions of science has the positive effect of vindicating the autonomy and critical authority of philosophy vis-à-vis science; of liberating philosophy from the methods and results of science. Philosophy, Oakeshott shows, need not accept the methods and results of science. And philosophy is not to be conceived as the synthesis of scientific results or as the *scientia scientarum*.

But Oakeshott's critique of positivism is not confined to the question of the relationship between philosophy and science. It also involves a complete reassessment of the relationship between history and science.[107] Though I have indicated that my main concern in this chapter is with Oakeshott's idea of philosophy in *Experience and its Modes*, I do not think the issue of the autonomy of historical knowledge vis-à-vis scientific knowledge can simply be passed over. It is, I think, one of the central problems to which the book – and Oakeshott's theory of modality as a whole – addresses itself. Therefore, I intend to devote a few pages to Oakeshott's understanding of the distinction between history and science.

Of course, by the time Oakeshott came to it, a good deal of reflection had already been devoted to this problem of distinguishing history from science.[108] To a large extent this reflective activity had been actuated by a humanistic desire to keep the realm of morals and individual action from being reduced to a mere object of scientific analysis. The attempt to vindicate history as a form of knowledge distinct from natural science was thus also an attempt to vindicate the autonomy of the human vis-à-vis the merely natural. And consequently the principle for distinguishing history from science was frequently sought in the distinction between their respective subject-matters; in the Kantian (or neo-Kantian) distinction between the human and the natural, spirit and nature.

From what has been said so far, it is clear that for Oakeshott the distinction between history and science cannot consist in the fact that history deals with man while science deals with nature. History and science are, for Oakeshott, *modes* of experience. This means that they are not to be understood as specific kinds of thought concerned with special types of object. A mode of experience is not a separate *kind* of experience which concerns itself with a separate *part* of reality; it is the whole of experience (or reality) viewed from a limited or abstract standpoint. The character of any mode of experience is determined not by its subject-matter but by the category in terms of which it organizes experience and reality.

Oakeshott's rejection of subject-matter as a principle for distinguishing history from science is perhaps best illustrated in his discussion of the so-called "human" sciences, the sciences of man and society. As I mentioned above, for Oakeshott there is nothing inherently contradictory about a science of man or a science of society, so long as these are conceived quantitatively. This is not an uncontroversial view. It is frequently argued, for example, that disciplines such as sociology, economics, and psychology cannot become sciences in the full sense because of their "human" subject-matter. Clearly the exclusion of these disciplines from the world of science – especially on such a basis – involves, on Oakeshott's view, a misconception of the nature of science. For him, man and society are no less susceptible to scientific study than "nature," since scientific thought is not concerned with a special subject-matter or a specific part of reality but with the whole of reality from a limited standpoint. To illustrate his point, he considers the particular cases of economics and psychology.

With respect to economics, Oakeshott repudiates the view that it cannot become a science in the full sense because it deals with complex human actions, motives, and desires; the view that the complexity of its data prevents economics from achieving the mathematically exact generalizations of, say, physics. The fact is, he argues, the generalizations or laws of economics do not refer to actual, historical or individual events or actions. Economics is concerned only with a limited aspect of all actions and events, an aspect which is non-historical, non-individual, and susceptible to mathematical or quantitative formulation. Insofar as economics approaches the condition of a science, it conceives "its material not in human terms of behaviour, action, desire, satisfaction, etc., but in such quantitative terms as those of cost, price, utility and disutility." Economics, like any other science, is not a science of individual or historical actions and events. "It is a science of measurements. Its generalizations do not refer to a 'human' world of desires, feelings, wants and satisfactions, but to a world of impersonal quantitative conceptions and their relations."[109]

Oakeshott also argues that there is nothing inherent in the character of psychology to prevent it from assuming scientific, that is, quantitative, form. He of course rejects the argument "that psychology cannot be a science in the full sense because it is concerned with 'mental' as distinct from 'physical' phenomena." Science is not an attempt to elucidate the "physical" world but the whole of reality under the category of quantity. If psychology can be shown to partake of this purpose, then its scientific character will be established. Oakeshott also rejects the notion that psychology cannot be fully scientific because it is concerned with concrete human behavior, with individuals or living personalities. Such research – under which he includes psychoanalysis – never amounts to anything more than natural history. Again, science is not concerned with individuals, nor with anything that comes untransformed from the world of percepts. Oakeshott emphatically asserts that "there can be no such thing as a 'science of individual behaviour'." A scientific psychology must be thoroughly quantitative; which means, in the first place, that it must achieve "a world in outline" with genuinely quantitative structural concepts. Psychology, Oakeshott believes, has not gone as far in this regard as economics (it has, of course, developed considerably since). Nevertheless, concepts such as sensation and attention, which have been quantitatively conceived, seem to him more promising for the development of a scientific psychology than concepts such as imagination, memory, or consciousness, which have yet to achieve quantitative form.[110]

What Oakeshott says here about the possibility of a scientific psychology and a scientific economics only serves to illustrate his larger point that the postulated end of a particular mode of thought – and not its special subject-matter – ultimately determines its character. There is nothing contradictory in the idea of a science of the psyche, a science of society, or a science of politics,[111] so long as these are conceived quantitatively and do not take themselves for more than they are. The distinction between history and science does not consist in the fact that the one is concerned with man while the other is concerned with nature. Rather, the distinction between these two modes of thought consists in the fact that they have entirely different purposes and rest on entirely different presuppositions. Science is the attempt to elucidate the world under the category of quantity; history is the attempt to interpret the whole of experience as evidence of a past that is independent of and utterly unlike the present.

But that Oakeshott does not see the idea of a science of man and of society as necessarily contradictory does not mean that he denies the possibility of confusion and contradiction in the world of knowledge. Indeed, one of the main purposes of *Experience and its Modes* is to determine the character of such confusion and contradiction.[112] Confusion, Oakeshott argues however, does not arise from the attempt to apply a particular mode of thought to a putatively inappropriate subject-matter. Rather, it arises from the attempt to meld together, from the failure to observe the categorial differences between, two different modes of thought. Thus, though a science of man or society is not a contradiction according to Oakeshott, a science of history or historical events certainly is. For it involves the mixing together of two utterly different worlds of ideas, two worlds of ideas with utterly different purposes and constructed on entirely different principles. He rejects the positivistic notion that history merely ascertains the facts, leaving it to the "science of history" to discover laws connecting those facts.[113] Indeed, the entire notion of "causes" or "laws" in history, upon which the positivistic view depends, he finds contradictory. But in order to understand why, we must consider one final and very important postulate of historical experience which I have delayed discussing until now: namely, the principle of historical explanation.

Oakeshott's understanding of historical explanation is intimately connected with his understanding of the historical individual. As we have seen, Oakeshott conceives the historical individual non-positivistically as insecurely distinguished from its environment. The historical individual is not constituted by being cut off from everything that surrounds it; by being made free of all its connections and relations. The individuality of an historical event, for example, does not consist in separateness from its environment but in a certain propensity to coalesce with its environment. Because this is the character of historical events, Oakeshott rejects the notion of cause as a category of historical explanation. Causality is not consonant with the character of historical events. And whatever else the categories of historical explanation may be, they must, according to Oakeshott, be consonant with the presuppositions of historical thought. In order to understand his thinking on this most important issue of the kind of explanation that is appropriate to history, let us examine Oakeshott's rejection of causal explanation in history more closely.

Of course, the notion of cause covers a variety of conceptions. And Oakeshott begins by dismissing as irrelevant to history causes such as God and the stars which, used to explain everything, end up by explaining nothing. He also rejects as alien to history the notion of causality belonging to science. According to this notion, a cause is conceived as "the minimum conditions required to account for any example of an observed result." Such a notion of causality, however, is applicable only to a world of abstract instances; it cannot be applied to a world of concrete events. History has no use for abstractions such as climate, geographical conditions, or economic conditions as the *sole* cause of events. These causes are excluded, though, not because of their subject-matter, but because they do not accord with the presuppositions of history.[114]

But there is another notion of cause which Oakeshott seems to take more seriously and discusses at greater length: "the notion that some events are causal in the sense of being decisive." But causality in this special sense of decisiveness, he argues, is also alien to historical thought; like the strict notion of causality mentioned above, it contradicts the character of historical events. "[T]he process by which an event is made a cause is a process which deprives it of its historical character." To make an historical event a cause in this sense involves abstracting it from the historical process, isolating it from its environment, making it free of all its relations and connections. Once this is done, it ceases to be an historical event at all. Nothing in history – neither events nor the individual will – "is isolable in this manner." The postulate of historical experience which causal explanation violates is (again) that of the historical individual, which is never securely distinguished from its environment (as the individual in scientific experience always is).[115]

Oakeshott's own conception of historical explanation is implied in his criticism of the concept of cause as a category of historical explanation. There are no causal historical events; no decisive or even essential historical events. These are contradictions in terms. "[E]very historical event is necessary. . . . No event is merely negative, none is non-contributory."[116] The principle of explanation implied in this fact Oakeshott calls the "unity or continuity of history." This, he argues, is "the only principle of explanation consonant with the other postulates of historical experience." According to this principle of explanation, the task of the historian is to fill in the details of the course of events to such an extent that no event seems sudden, strange, unexpected, or catastrophic. The historian must proceed like the novelist, who presents his characters "in such detail and with such coherence that additional explanation of their actions is superfluous." The historian never explains by referring to some principle outside the course of events, but only by adding more details, more events; to appeal to some external reason or universal cause signifies failure. On this point Oakeshott is emphatic: "the method of the historian is never to explain by means of generalization but always by means of greater and more complete detail."[117]

For Oakeshott, then, causal explanation, the kind of explanation appropriate for the abstract individuals of scientific experience, is absolutely inappropriate for the world of history and historical individuals. And this, in general, is the basis of his dismissal of any attempt to unite scientific and historical thought in the form of a "science of history." To recapitulate: these two worlds, according to Oakeshott, have utterly different purposes, and have been constructed on entirely different principles. The observations of history, which are always percepts and in terms of historical individuals, cannot serve as material for scientific generalizations, since such generalizations always only relate to quantitatively determined observations. Historical "facts" can never serve as data for scientific generalizations because they are never in the form of measurements.

Of course, few so-called "sciences of history" have sought to organize the facts of history under strictly scientific, that is, statistical, laws. In general, they have made the more modest claim of discovering laws, regularities, and recurrences of a more general nature. Nevertheless, such sciences of history still claim to unite historical and scientific thought. And on this ground Oakeshott finds them thoroughly confused and misconceived. He develops this criticism by considering the assumptions of one such science of history, anthropology.

Anthropology[118] claims to be both historical and scientific. Its claim to being scientific is not meant to deny that it deals with concrete historical actions, institutions, and events. Anthropology does not begin with purely quantitative conceptions of man, society, culture, or religion; its data are not measurements. The claim that anthropology is a science, therefore, has generally taken a modified form. Anthropology, it is argued, does not seek to frame "strictly scientific laws, but general laws of some kind." Some of these generalizations, Oakeshott maintains, are no more than enumerative or collective judgments of historical facts; they are in no sense statistical or scientific. Sometimes, however, "a more extended form of generalization is attempted." Such generalizations "go beyond what is actually observed," while still referring "to historically determined events or occurrences, and not to a series of quantitatively conceived observations as such." These generalizations are based on what is called "the Comparative Method," which Oakeshott (quoting Frazer) describes as "borrowing the links in one chain of evidence to supply the gaps in another." Though Oakeshott believes this to be "the only coherent suggestion yet made for a method of generalizing historical observations," he does not think it can avoid destroying – like the scientific method in the strict sense – the historical character of those observations. The comparative method must assume, he argues, that the world of anthropology possesses "the characteristics of atomism and limited variety." But these characteristics belong only to the world of science, "which secures for itself a world of limited variety, a world of repetitions and recurrences, by assuming a world of pure measurements." Since the observations of anthropology are historical and not quantitative, the presupposed character of those observations is violated by the comparative method no less than by the strictly scientific method. Oakeshott concludes, therefore, that anthropology is either "history or it is nothing."[119]

Behind all such attempts to establish a science of history there lies the positivistic belief that history, because it is concerned only with individual facts, somehow falls short of genuine knowledge. For the positivist – indeed, for the better part of the tradition of European philosophy for which Schopenhauer speaks in his anti-historical remarks quoted above[120] – the hallmark of genuine knowledge is its generality or universality, which he finds exemplified in natural science and absent in history. History, it is granted, perhaps forms the empirical basis for a genuine science, but it is not genuine knowledge itself. The merely empirical, isolated, and individual facts of history must be organized, connected, generalized, by a super-historical science of history before true knowledge of the human world is attained.

It should be clear from all that has been said so far that for Oakeshott any such positivistic attempt to convert history into science or to create a science of history is marked by confusion about the nature of both history and science. There is no such thing as "empirical" history and hence no science of such. The facts of history are never "there," ready-made for the historian, only to be perceived; they are the conclusions of a complicated process of historical inference. And not only are these historical facts not "empirical" facts, they are in no sense assimilable to the quantitative observations of science, which are the only conceivable data for scientific generalization. More broadly, science and history are, as we have seen, absolutely exclusive worlds of ideas; they are absolutely divergent attempts to organize the whole of experience in terms of certain mutually exclusive categories. Historical experience cannot be superseded by a super-historical science of history; it can only be destroyed.

6. Practice

The last mode of experience Oakeshott takes up is practice. Once again, he is concerned primarily with the question of whether practical experience is capable of providing what is finally satisfactory in experience; whether it is a completely coherent world of experience. More precisely, he is concerned to show that practice is an abstract mode of experience; that it does not provide what is finally satisfactory in experience; and that it must be avoided or superseded.

This critical examination of practical experience occupies a most important place in Oakeshott's view as a whole. For among the various modifications of experience, practice is the most alluring and distracting. Far more frequently than either science or history, practice has been taken to be the concrete whole of experience; what is absolute and satisfactory in experience. "The reduction of the whole of experience either to scientific experience or to historical experience," Oakeshott writes,

> has found general consent only upon rare occasions and in peculiar circumstances. But anyone who, at any time, comes forward with the suggestion that the world of practical experience is itself what is absolutely and finally satisfactory in experience; that it belongs to the character of thought to be for the sake of action, is assured in advance of the concurrence of the majority of mankind.[121]

This statement comes perhaps as something of a surprise, given what I have already said about Oakeshott's anti-positivism. Nevertheless, it is clear from *Experience and its Modes* that for Oakeshott the despotism of practice is to be feared at least as much as the despotism of science. In the introduction to *Experience and its Modes*, practice, even more than science, is invoked as the antagonist to his conception of philosophy. Philosophy, he argues, must be sought for its own sake, not for the sake of action. "It depends for its existence upon maintaining its independence from all extraneous interests, and in particular from the practical interest." Nor does philosophy alone suffer from this despotism of practice, according to Oakeshott. History, too, "has been, and still is, almost wholly obscured by the confusion which exists with regard to its relationship with practical experience." Even, "the emancipation of science from the despotism of practice," has been "slow and uncertain."[122] In short, the practical is our most constant and familiar mood; and it is escaped only with great difficulty. This insistence on the despotic and limiting character of practical life runs though almost all of Oakeshott's writings and is one of the things which distinguishes his anti-positivism from that of many of his contemporaries.[123]

Before Oakeshott can consider the question of whether practice is indeed the world of concrete experience, he must first address the question of whether it is a world of experience at all. The experiential character of practice is frequently denied, and in this regard it resembles history. The world of practice is said to be a world of "pure facts," not a world of ideas; a "tissue of mere conjunctions," and not a genuine world of knowledge. Oakeshott confronts this objection to his contention that practice is experience by considering, first, the view that practical activity is not a world of *ideas*, and secondly, the view that it is not a world.

"Practice, it will be said, is activity but not thought; and the world of practice is a world of actions, not of ideas." Oakeshott disposes of this objection somewhat perfunctorily by referring the reader to his general view of experience. There is nothing which is not experience, he argues; and all experience involves thought or judgment; therefore, practice is a world of thought.[124] But what is Oakeshott really arguing here? What view of practical activity is he arguing against?

We must not think that in arguing that practical activity is a world of ideas, a world of thought, Oakeshott is simply arguing that our actions are always preceded by thought. Indeed, this in some ways is the view he is reacting against. He is reacting against the dualistic view which sees practical activity as divided into two parts: a "subjective" idea or intention, and an "objective" action. The former, on this dualistic view, precedes the latter and is thought to be its "cause." Thought, in other words, does not reside *in* the action itself but lies somehow *behind* it. The meaning of the action is to be sought in the subjective intention which lies behind it.

All this is incompatible with the view of experience which Oakeshott has been maintaining. He argues instead that the meaning of an action lies in the action itself and not behind it. Understanding an action, whether it be our own or someone else's, does not presuppose knowledge of a conscious intention behind or antecedent to the action. The meaning is itself objective; the action has a place in a world of ideas. Thus Oakeshott argues that "'action' is not the product of thought, it is itself a form of thought. An 'external' or 'objective' world of doings and happenings which is not a world of ideas is a mere fiction." And this rejection of the dualism of thought and action extends to the dualism of thought and will as well. "Volition is itself thought and not the mere result of thought."[125]

A "more weighty contention," according to Oakeshott, is the view that practical activity "is not a *world* of experience but a tissue of mere conjunctions." Practical activity, on this view, is a mere collection of ideas – of instincts, intuitions, feelings, or opinions – and not a world of knowledge. We have already encountered a similar view with respect to history; we need only remember Schopenhauer's remark that "there is no system in history," only "a simple coordination of the facts it has registered." Oakeshott was able to overcome this empiricist view of history with a more profound understanding of the inter-relationship between the particular and the universal, fact and interpretation, in historical experience. His logic of the concrete universal enabled him to comprehend the systematic character of individual historical fact. And it is this same concrete logic which enables him to see practical experience as more than a tissue of mere conjunctions, a collection of desires, wants, and impulses without system or unity.

Our practical judgments, Oakeshott argues, are not simply intuitive or instinctual; nor are they a matter of mere opinion. But this is not to say that everything we do is reflective or self-conscious. Oakeshott does not deny that many of our practical judgments are non-reflective and take place, so to speak, beneath consciousness. Nevertheless, this does not mean that they are immediate intuitions or feelings. Again we must refer to Oakeshott's general view of experience. Nothing in experience is radically immediate, not even sensation or perception. All experience involves thought or judgment. And though this thought may take place below the level of consciousness, implicitly, nevertheless it is clear that nothing in experience is unrecognized, isolated, random, without a world. And this goes for even the most "intuitive" and "instinctual" of our value-judgments.[126]

The "yet more formidable contention" that "practical activity is not a world of knowledge because it is a mere collection of opinions" also collapses upon examination of its implications. "The view is that there is nothing in practical experience beyond a multiplicity of separate opinions. . . . Some people think one thing, and some another; some desire one thing, some another." But differences, Oakeshott argues, do not imply the absence of a common world or criterion; quite the contrary. "If anything were a matter of *mere* opinion there could be no difference of opinion. It belongs to the character of a mere opinion that it can never be contradicted: in the region of mere opinions, what one asserts the other never denies." Precisely because there are differences of opinions on questions of value, practical activity is more than a collection of mere opinions. It is a world of knowledge whose criterion must be – as it is for all worlds of knowledge – coherence. Which is not to say that practical experience is always rational. Oakeshott does not deny "that much of our practical experience borders upon the condition of mere opinion. Nowhere is the criterion of judgment more negligently applied than in practical experience." But he is not concerned here with what is explicitly achieved in practical experience but with what is implicitly asserted. And in practical opinion – as in supposal or imagination – "there is implicit assertion, reference to reality."[127]

For Oakeshott, then, practical life does not consist of isolated "actions, volitions, feelings, intuitions, instincts or opinions"; it is a world of experience. Nothing in it is simply given, immediate, brute, irrational, or unconditional. Every action, intuition, and opinion belongs to a world of meaning and is what it is by virtue of having a place in that world. None escapes the criterion of experience; each must be judged in terms of its contribution to the coherence of the world of practical ideas. Oakeshott's view of practical experience has nothing to do with any sort of simple-minded relativism.

Having established that the world of practice is indeed a world of experience, Oakeshott is concerned next to show that it is an abstract mode of experience and not the concrete totality of experience. But before we follow him in his argument, we must first be clear as to the nature of the defect he intends to bring out with respect to practical experience. The abstractness and incompleteness Oakeshott is interested in demonstrating has nothing to do with the incompleteness, imperfection, and lack of system of which we are all aware in our personal practical experience. Though he does not deny the fact that our practical experience seems to be "full of irrationality, prejudice and contingency," and that nowhere shall we find "a completely integrated world of practical experience, a life which is a perfect system" – still, Oakeshott argues that this is a fact or truth not "relevant to the determination of the character of practical experience from the standpoint of the totality of experience." "In deciding the character of practical experience from that standpoint," he explains in a remark which sheds enormous light on his philosophical procedure in *Experience and its Modes* and on the entire notion of abstraction,

> what we must consider is not the character of the practical experience of which we are conscious, but the character of practical experience which is implied in our actual experience. And our unawareness of the systematic and organized world implied in our random experiences is no argument whatever against the existence of such a world. It means merely that we are not ordinarily conscious of its existence.

He concludes, therefore, that we must "look elsewhere for a demonstration of the absolute inadequacy of the world of practical experience."[128]

The "essential abstractness" of practical experience arises, according to Oakeshott, not from its "present incompleteness" or "its apparent lack of organization"; rather, it arises from "the terms in which the attempt in practice to achieve what is ultimately satisfactory in experience is conceived and executed."[129] Thus he proceeds in his demonstration of the inadequacy and essential abstractness of practical experience by considering the categories in terms of which it organizes the whole of present experience and tries to achieve an absolutely coherent world of experience.

The *differentia* of practice Oakeshott locates in the idea of action or alteration of existence. What "distinguishes practical activity from all other worlds of experience," he writes, "is that in it the alteration of existence is undertaken." Practice is the alteration of "what is" to make it agree with an unrealized idea, a "to be" which is "not yet." Even when the maintenance of "what is" is desired, such alteration is undertaken. For maintenance always takes place in the face of threatened change and therefore also involves a discrepancy between "what is" and a "to be" which is "not yet." "To maintain," Oakeshott, argues, "is always to change." Practical activity thus always "implies change, and involves a world in which change is both possible and significant, a mortal world." Oakeshott puts this same point about the *differentia* of practice in a slightly different way. What is distinctive about practice, he says, is not the end it pursues, that is, coherence,

> but the means followed to achieve this end. In practice a coherent world of experience is achieved by means of action, by the introduction of actual change into existence. And the aspect of mind involved is the will; practical thought is volition; practical experience is the world *sub specie voluntatis*.[130]

Practice, then, presupposes two discrepant worlds: a world of "what is" and a world "to be" which is "not yet." Practical activity is simply the attempt to reconcile these two discrepant worlds, to alter "what is" so as to agree with an unrealized "to be." What Oakeshott is going to argue is that the discrepancy between these two worlds can never be finally resolved, and that therefore practice can never achieve a completely satisfactory or coherent world of experience. But in order to see why this is so, we must examine the character of these two worlds presupposed in practice more closely.

Practice implies or presupposes, to begin with, a world of "what is," a world of practical fact. And it is of the utmost importance, according to Oakeshott, that we recognize that this world of practical fact *is presupposed*; that it has an entirely presupposed character. Though what is undertaken in practice is the alteration of existence, nevertheless the general character of fact remains the same from the world given to the world achieved in practical activity. Practice "implies a world of ideas not itself directly qualified by action"; implies a conception of fact which remains unchanged in the transformative process of practical activity. And the fundamental characteristic of practical fact is that it is mutable, transient. This instability is what distinguishes practical fact from all other worlds of fact. Both science and history presuppose a world of unchanging fact; only practice "assumes a world of mutable, transient fact." This means that whatever "cannot change, cannot, for practice, be a fact." As we have already seen, action or volition presupposes "a world in which change is both possible and significant, a mortal world." Severed from this assumption of mortal, mutable fact, "there could be no practical activity."[131]

But practice not only presupposes a world of "what is," a world of practical fact; it also presupposes a world in some sense discrepant from this world of "what is," a world "to be" which is "not yet." But, Oakeshott argues, this "to be" which is implied in practice is never merely "not yet." Because practice, like any other mode of experience, pursues coherence and is never mere activity or alteration for the sake of alteration, the "to be" of practice is also what is more coherent than "what is." And coherence in practice is always conceived in terms of value; the "to be" of practice is always conceived as "what ought to be." Once again Oakeshott stresses that this world of value is only a *presupposition* of practice. "Valuation is involved in practical activity as a necessary implication." Just as there could be no practical activity severed from the assumption of a world of mutable, transient fact, so there could be no practical activity severed from the presupposition of a world of value; of a world both discrepant from and more coherent than the world of "what is."[132]

Oakeshott goes on to consider the world of value implied in practical activity in greater detail. He is concerned to show that it is a genuine world of experience, and that, as such, it is not simply "subjective," or "emotive," or "ideal." For Oakeshott, the world of value is a world of thought and contains an assertion of reality; it has a certain "objectivity" (if this is understood not to imply independence of experience), and this objectivity is conceived in terms of coherence.[133]

But what Oakeshott is particularly interested in showing with respect to the world of value is that it is not reducible to the world of practical fact. It has its own coherence which is not the coherence of the world of "what is here and now." It contains a unique assertion of reality. The relationship between the world of practical fact and the world of value is thus governed by the same principle which governs the relationship between any two worlds or modes of experience, according to Oakeshott: "to pass directly from one to the other, or to attempt an explanation of one in terms of the other, must always involve an *ignoratio elenchi*." This puts the famous distinction between "facts" and "values" on a slightly different basis. The distinction between the world of "what is here and now" and the world of value does not consist in the one being "real" and the other "ideal," or in the one being "objective" and the other "subjective." For Oakeshott, both are worlds of being. What differs is their "mode of being."[134]

Though independent in this respect, the world of value, according to Oakeshott, is nevertheless bound to practice as a presupposition and necessary implication of practical activity. Valuation exists for practice (it is not self-contained), and practice is the alteration of existence. Practice implies 'the attempt to break down the discrepancy between "what is" and "what ought to be" through action. Practical activity

> goes further than mere valuation which . . . distinguishes between "what is here and now" and "what ought to be", but implies no attempt to reconcile them. Practice is the world *sub specie voluntatis*, and the will is not satisfied with mere valuation. What it attempts is the reconciliation of "what is here and now" and "what ought to be". Its business is to realize in the world of practical fact what exists and is already real in the world of value.[135]

Practice, then, is never mere valuation, but always action, "the actual, point-by-point qualification of 'what is here and now' by 'what ought to be'." And therein for Oakeshott lies its radical defectiveness. It is the means by which practice seeks to establish a coherent world of experience which condemns it to ultimate failure and self-contradiction. For the resolution of the discrepancy between "what is here and now" and "what ought to be" which practice undertakes "can never finally be accomplished."

> No sooner is it realized at one point in the world of practical existence, than a new discord springs up elsewhere, demanding a new resolution, a fresh qualification of "what is here and now" by "what ought to be". A theoretical resolution would be, if it were successful, a final resolution. But, since practical activity undertakes not this general resolution, but the particular resolution of all instances of this discrepancy, it undertakes what, from its nature, can never be brought to a conclusion.

Every success in practical life is partial and contains the seeds of new imperfections, future tasks. "Nowhere in practice is there uninterrupted progress or final achievement."[136]

It is precisely this endlessness of practical experience which for Oakeshott (here following Bradley and Hegel) constitutes its essential abstractness. Nor is this endlessness simply incidental to practical experience but of its essence. To resolve the discrepancy between "is" and "ought" once and for all would involve the destruction of the world of practical experience itself. In short, practice, like all abstract modes of experience, is self-contradictory. On the one hand, it postulates a discrepancy between "what is here and now" and "what ought to be." This discrepancy, as Oakeshott never tires of telling us, is not simply inevitable in practical life, it is presupposed by it. Practice depends on there being a discrepancy between "what is" and "what ought to be." On the other hand, practice attempts to break down this discrepancy, to resolve it, through action. Thus what is attempted in practice is the abolition of the condition which makes it possible in the first place. Practice cannot achieve what it aims at without destroying itself. "Permanent dissatisfaction," Oakeshott concludes,

> is inherent in practical experience; the explicit assertion of reality in practical judgment is never complete and consequently the world of practical experience as a world, is, from the standpoint of the totality of experience, abstract and incoherent. It is an abstract mode of experience, an arrest in experience.[137]

It follows from this, as we well know by now, that practical experience "must be rejected *in toto*." The pursuit of coherence in such an abstract mode of experience can only lead away from concrete truth and reality. Practice, like any other mode, is a divergence from the concrete purpose in experience. To take it up is to abandon the pursuit of what is finally satisfactory in experience, an absolutely coherent world of ideas.

> Not until we have become wholly indifferent to the truths of this world of practice, not until we have shaken off the abstractions of practical experience, of morality and religion, good and evil, faith and freedom, body and mind, the practical self and its ambitions and desires, shall we find ourselves once more turned in the direction which leads to what can satisfy the character of experience.

Because it is an abstract mode of experience, practice contributes nothing to the overall coherence of the totality of experience. From the standpoint of the totality "it is no more than a *cul-de-sac*, a regrettable mistake, perhaps a youthful folly, which, if it cannot be avoided, must be superseded."[138]

An important implication of this view of the relationship between philosophy and practical experience is that the conclusions of philosophy cannot be established or disproved by appeal to practical experience. Practice as abstract and defective experience cannot "afford any contribution to, or offer any relevant criticism of, philosophical propositions." The attempt to establish or refute a philosophical proposition by appeal to practical experience constitutes an *ignoratio elenchi*.[139] Oakeshott clearly rejects the view underlying much "analytic" moral philosophy that philosophy is capable only of analyzing – showing the "meaning" of, revealing the "logical structure" of – knowledge we already possess in, say, common sense. The conclusions of common sense – or of morality or religion – are in no sense absolute for philosophy; nor are they simply to be accepted as valid or true by philosophy. The conclusions of philosophy are never simply "based" on pre-philosophical practical experience. And this means, *a fortiori*, that their truth cannot be checked by appeal to such experience. The "analytic" view of the relationship of philosophy to practical experience remains mired in the empiricism Oakeshott wishes to escape.[140]

Practical experience, then, is irrelevant to the world of philosophical ideas; and to subject the conclusions of philosophy to the criticism of practice or life is to commit an *ignoratio elenchi*. But this is only half the story, according to Oakeshott. He insists equally (and sometimes more than equally) on the irrelevance of philosophy to the world of practical experience, the world of practical ideas. To subject life to the criticism of philosophy is also to commit an *ignoratio elenchi*. The only relevant criticism of practical experience is that of life. "[P]ractice is the tireless pursuit of a more satisfying way of life"; it is the attempt to make coherent a world of practical ideas. And philosophy, which is engaged in the unconditional pursuit of what is absolutely satisfactory in experience, "can make no relevant contribution to the coherence" of this abstract world of practical ideas. "Practical truth is not ultimate truth"; it "is the truth that we can live by and act upon; it is the truth which can give freedom." And this pursuit of practical truth, this attempt to make coherent a world of practical experience, is carried furthest, according to Oakeshott, in morality and especially religion.[141] So far as practice is concerned, religious ideas such as God, salvation, and immortality are true, and philosophy can make no relevant criticism of them.[142]

Oakeshott does not diminish the inimicality of philosophy to practice. For him practice takes place – it must take place – in a kind of "mental fog." Philosophy as self-conscious and self-critical thought, when brought to bear on practical experience, can only disperse this "mental fog" on which practical success and satisfaction depend.

> It is not the clear-sighted, not those who are fashioned for thought and the ardors of thought, who can lead the world. Great achievements are accomplished in the mental fog of practical experience. What is farthest from our needs is that kings should be philosophers.

Oakeshott has no compunction about admitting what for Nietzsche was the most serious charge that could be brought against philosophy: that it is an escape from living, a refuge from life. "Philosophy," he states austerely, "is not the enhancement of life, it is the denial of life"; it is (with reference to Plato's *Phaedo*) the study of dying and death. And therefore the attempt "to replace life with philosophy by subjecting life to the criticism of philosophy, must be set on one side as misguided." "Philosophy can and must supersede practical experience; but it cannot take its place."[143]

What Oakeshott here concludes about the relationship of philosophy to practice echoes what he has already said about the relationship of philosophy to both history and science (and, for that matter, to any abstract mode of experience). That philosophy is a radical undertaking which involves the renunciation of any and every attempt to achieve anything less than an absolutely coherent, concrete world of experience constitutes, as I have tried to show, the main teaching of *Experience and its Modes*. Philosophy for Oakeshott is not the sum-total of experiences – such a view contradicts what he takes to be the character of experience – but the concrete whole which is implied in all experiences. The relationship of philosophy to other forms of knowledge is not to be conceived in terms of the aggregative relationship of a whole to its parts but in terms of the complex relationship which holds between what is concrete and what is abstract. The concrete whole, as has been pointed out several times already, is never made up of its abstractions, it is implied in them. To achieve an absolutely coherent, concrete world of experience, every abstract world must be avoided, or if that is not possible, superseded, overcome.

"We come back in the end, then," Oakeshott concludes, "to what was suggested at the beginning: the view of philosophical thought as the pursuit, for its own sake, of an unlimited, unmodified experience, and at the same time as a mood, a turn of mind." And he is not unaware of the extremely paradoxical and in many respects emotionally unsatisfying character of this idea of philosophy. Indeed, this is why he describes philosophy as a "mood." "A man cannot be a philosopher and nothing else; to be so were either more or less than human. Such a life would, indeed, be at once febrile and insipid and not to be endured." He expresses the questionability of the whole endeavor beautifully in the final paragraph of the book:

> There is perhaps something decadent, something even depraved, in an attempt to achieve a completely coherent world of experience; for such a pursuit requires us to renounce for the time being everything which can be called good or evil, everything which can be valued or rejected as valueless. And no matter how far we go with it, we shall not easily forget the sweet delight which lies in the empty kisses of abstraction. Indeed, the attempt to find what is completely satisfactory in experience is so difficult and dubious an undertaking, leading us so far aside from the ways of ordinary thought, that those may be pardoned who prefer the embraces of abstraction. For, if these give but little satisfaction, and give that little not for long, it is at least a tangible and certain satisfaction while it lasts and one not to be despised.[144]

It is an exalted – if somewhat austere – notion of philosophy which receives expression in *Experience and its Modes*. And I would like to conclude this chapter by once again contrasting this outlook on philosophy with the more skeptical outlook of Richard Rorty. As I indicated earlier, Oakeshott has of late come to be associated with Rorty, largely as a result of the latter's appropriation of the term "conversation" to evoke his own anti-foundationalist conception of philosophy. As I suggested there, and as has become clearer over the course of my exposition of *Experience and its Modes*, Oakeshott's conception of philosophy cannot be identified with Rorty's anti-foundationalist conception. While Oakeshott certainly agrees with Rorty that philosophy is not "foundational" in the sense of being substitutable for other modes of knowledge, he nevertheless differs from Rorty in holding philosophy to be a categorially distinct discipline, and indeed a discipline which supersedes and in some sense judges other modes of knowing. Oakeshott the skeptic is definitely not skeptical about the possibility of philosophy – at least so far as *Experience and its Modes* is concerned.

I add the latter proviso because we do not know yet whether Oakeshott's view of philosophy changes after *Experience and its Modes*. Indeed, when Rorty invokes the notion of "conversation," it is the Oakeshott of *Rationalism in Politics*, and not the Oakeshott of *Experience and its Modes*, that he is invoking. And one of the questions we will be asking ourselves in a later chapter is whether Oakeshott's conception of philosophy changes from *Experience and its Modes* to *Rationalism in Politics*, as some commentators have suggested.[145] Without disposing of the issue, let me express an initial doubt about this interpretation of Oakeshott's development, since it involves an inexplicable reversion on Oakeshott's part to his earlier views in the later *On Human Conduct*. Be that as it may, we must now turn our attention to the application of Oakeshott's idea of philosophy in *Experience and its Modes* to the problem of political philosophy.

III

FROM PHILOSOPHY TO POLITICAL PHILOSOPHY

There is little in *Experience and its Modes* to indicate that its author would eventually make his most lasting contribution to twentieth-century thought in the field of political philosophy. Save for in a single footnote, political philosophy is not even mentioned in the work. Nevertheless, the view of philosophy set forth there forms – as I hope to show in this chapter – the crucial starting-point from which Oakeshott's entire political philosophy begins. At the foundation of Oakeshott's political philosophy lies, more than anything else, a doctrine about the nature of philosophy. And this doctrine is substantially the one which he expounds and defends in *Experience and its Modes*.

The connection between Oakeshott's idea of philosophy in *Experience and its Modes* and his conception of political philosophy can best be seen, I think, in some of his earlier writings on political philosophy (roughly from the period of *Experience and its Modes*). And therefore in this chapter I intend to examine these writings – in particular the long article entitled "The Concept of a Philosophical Jurisprudence" – with a view to bringing out this connection. Some of these writings are quite occasional – reviews, and so forth. Also, to a large extent they are critical in nature, concerned more with rejecting erroneous notions of the nature of political philosophy than with the construction of a positive political teaching. Nevertheless, they do contain suggestions of a more constructive nature: intimations of the direction Oakeshott thinks philosophical inquiry into politics ought to take in the twentieth century. These intimations, which are largely conveyed through Oakeshott's reading of the history of political philosophy, I pursue in the third part of this chapter.

1. The Meaning of a Philosophical Theory of Law and Politics

Before turning to "The Concept of a Philosophical Jurisprudence," I would like to take one last look at *Experience and its Modes* to see if it contains any indication as to how the idea of philosophy it pursues might be applied to the field of political philosophy. We find that it does (albeit indirectly) in the brief discussion of the nature of ethical thought toward the end of the book. Passing over for the moment his characterization of ethical thought (along with political philosophy) as "pseudo-philosophical,"[1] we find Oakeshott there making two points which we will see recurring with some frequency in his discussions of the nature of political philosophy.

First, he denies the view, traditional since Aristotle, "that the moral philosopher is a man who delivers judgments of value"; that ethics is somehow practical or normative. Ethics, he argues, is the attempt to *define* our moral and practical concepts. And this attempt to define is something quite different from the attempt to construct or make coherent a world of values. Indeed, the two attempts positively exclude one another. Because they belong to two different and exclusive worlds of ideas, namely the philosophical and the practical, what is relevant to one is absolutely irrelevant to the other. Philosophical definition can do nothing to further the aims of practice. And our practical beliefs can contribute nothing to the coherence of a philosophical world of ideas. All this, of course, simply reiterates what Oakeshott has already said about the relationship between philosophy and practice. The judgments which belong to each of these worlds of ideas are, as we have seen, irrelevant to one another. And therefore a truly *philosophical* ethics will never be able to offer any sort of practical guidance.[2]

The second point Oakeshott makes with respect to ethical thought concerns the nature of philosophical definition; and again it is a point which follows directly from the view of experience which he has already explained in the preceding chapters of *Experience and its Modes*. He makes the point while trying to meet the objection that the concepts of the moral world are ultimately irreducible and not susceptible to philosophical definition. This objection asserts that the concepts of the moral world are indefinable; or that, if definable, they are so only in terms of the concepts and categories which belong to the moral world. But such a view contradicts what Oakeshott has already said about the nature of definition. No concept for him is in principle indefinable; for every "concept whatever contains a reference to the whole of reality, every judgment whatever is an explicit or implicit assertion of reality, and the definition of a concept, the ultimate meaning of a concept, is simply the indication of its reference to reality." And this implies that an adequate definition of a concept can never be achieved in terms of the abstract world or context in which it is first presented to us. Definition involves relating what is abstract to something else, to a world or context which is not abstract but concrete; it involves making explicit the reference to reality which remains only implicit in our abstract experience. And this process of making explicit what is inherently implicit is, as we have already seen, a transformative process; the abstract concepts with which we begin are utterly transformed in the process of being referred to reality or the totality of experience. Thus, since the moral world is an abstract world, and "the reference of a moral concept to reality is always merely implicit," "the definition of a moral concept must involve the transformation of its character, the making explicit what is inherently implicit." Definition involves transformation and supersession, according to Oakeshott. And for this reason he concludes that it is impossible to explain (or define) philosophically the abstract concepts of morality and practice "without explaining them, as such, away."[3]

In some ways this second point implicitly contains the first. At the same time, it expresses what is perhaps the most distinctive feature of Oakeshott's idea of philosophical explanation; the feature which has (as we shall see) the greatest consequences for his entire understanding of the nature of political philosophy. I mean the transformative character of thought, especially of philosophical thought. For Oakeshott, as we have seen, what we begin with in experience is never absolute or completely satisfactory; it is simply where we begin. And as we concretely reflect on this initial "datum," and try to see it in a context wider than the one in which it first presents itself to us, it soon begins to lose those abstract features which at first identified it for us. We leave behind one world and enter another. Of course this does not happen all at once. But at some point in the course of reflection we become aware that the old world and everything in it has changed and been transformed utterly. It is some such process that Oakeshott discerns as we pass from the abstract to the concrete in thought. And it is precisely because he sees such a total transformation taking place that he finds absurd the notion of "applying" the concrete knowledge we have gained in the process to the abstract world from which we began. Philosophy can offer no practical guidance because it has left behind the abstract concepts and categories upon which the practical world depends.

The importance of this point for Oakeshott's entire conception of political philosophy will, I think, become clearer as we consider some of his other writings from the period of *Experience and its Modes.* Therefore, let us pass immediately to the essay in which Oakeshott gives the fullest account (at least among his writings from the thirties) of his conception of the nature and task of political philosophy: namely, "The Concept of a Philosophical Jurisprudence."

The object of the essay, as he states at the outset, "is to consider the meaning and possibility of a philosophy of law and civil society."[4] He is especially concerned, as we soon find out, to determine the relationship of a *philosophical* explanation of the nature of law – that is, of a *philosophical* jurisprudence – to the various forms of explanation which currently constitute the world of jurisprudence. The link to *Experience and its Modes* is obvious. But whereas in *Experience and its Modes* Oakeshott is concerned with the relationship of philosophy to the various modes of experience, in "The Concept of a Philosophical Jurisprudence" he is concerned with the relationship of a philosophical explanation of a certain phenomenon, namely, law, to the various explanations of that phenomenon which flow from the modes. Still, the principal point remains the same. Philosophy is not one mode of experience among others, it is the concrete whole which the modes imply. And philosophical explanation is not simply one explanation among others, it is the criterion by which all other explanations must be judged.

It is just this fundamental characteristic of philosophy and of philosophical explanation which is missing in current conceptions of the philosophy of law, according to Oakeshott. The world of jurisprudence today, he writes, is an unresolved variety or chaos of explanations of the nature of law.

> The first, and I believe greatest, defect common to all the current conceptions of philosophical jurisprudence is that it is conceived as one kind of explanation of the nature of law among others in a variety which it is not even considered necessary to attempt to resolve. By a wide tolerance it is allowed to exist; but such tolerance is only an excuse for a failure to recognise that an unresolved variety is the same thing as confusion and that until a relationship, or series of relationships, have been established between these different kinds of interpretation the confusion will remain.[5]

The problem with current conceptions of philosophical jurisprudence, then, is that it is conceived as one kind of explanation of law among others, no more valid or comprehensive than any other explanation. And before looking more closely at these current conceptions – or misconceptions – we would do well to have a more definite idea of the variety of kinds of explanation in which philosophical jurisprudence is placed.

Oakeshott considers four of the more prominent kinds of explanation which currently make up the world of jurisprudence. In the first place he considers "analytical jurisprudence." This kind of explanation of the law is characterized by "two fundamental presuppositions": first, "that there are certain basic elements in law *qua* law"; and second, "that these are the essential principles of law, that in them lies the nature of law." Next, he considers "historical jurisprudence," which he argues is based on a rejection of the essentialism underlying analytical jurisprudence. Historical jurisprudence seeks not the essential nor the universal but the individual. For historical jurisprudence the nature of law lies not in certain abstract principles but in its history. Closely related to historical jurisprudence are the economic

and sociological interpretations of the nature of law. But what ultimately distinguishes them both from historical jurisprudence is the
"attempt to limit the historical context of law to what is believed
to be the essential character . . . of a civilisation and its history."
Whereas in historical jurisprudence "there is no point in the exploration of the historical context at which we can justifiably stop," in
economic and sociological jurisprudence this concrete movement of
historical thought is arrested and the historical context limited to
what are believed to be the essential determinants of legal rules and
ideas. In the case of economic jurisprudence it is the material means
of production which are taken to be essential, decisive. In sociological
jurisprudence the context is widened to include "the total physical
and social environment of the law."[6]

Here, then, are a number of different kinds of explanation of the
nature of law. And it is important to recognize that they are not
"complementary methods of inquiry" but "mutually exclusive types
of explanation." The differences between them, like the differences
between the modes of experience, are not differences of emphasis or of
subject-matter; "they are differences of principle."[7] To accept one
theory is to deny the others. It is because the world of jurisprudence is
constituted by an unresolved variety of mutually exclusive explanations of the nature of law that Oakeshott calls it a "chaos." It is a
situation philosophy might be expected to remedy. But on current
conceptions of philosophical jurisprudence, philosophy only contributes to the confusion; it adds one more dissonant voice to the
cacophony.

Oakeshott considers five of these current misconceptions of the
philosophy of law, each of which "assumes that a philosophical interpretation of law is merely one interpretation among others, to be
pursued if we feel inclined, to be tolerated or dismissed as ineffectual."
First, there is the view that the philosophy of law is the application of
some previously thought-out philosophical doctrine to law and legally
organized society. It is, according to Oakeshott, the "least adequate"
of all the current conceptions of a philosophical jurisprudence. But it
displays in an extreme form the view of the relationship of philosophy
to the philosophy of law which underlies them all. The philosophy of
law is conceived here as resting on a philosophy but not as being itself
philosophical. If it is philosophical, it is so only in "a derivative
sense."

> According to this view the only genuinely philosophical part of a philos-
> ophy of law is something prior to and independent of the consideration of
> legal concepts which the philosophy of law itself comprises. Philosophy is
> related to the philosophy of law merely as a presupposition, and the con-
> sideration of legal concepts . . . is never itself a philosophical consideration,
> it is merely a consideration which presupposes some philosophical doctrine
> or other.[8]

The second view Oakeshott considers also exhibits this tendency to think of the philosophy of law as a two-stage affair in which philosophical ideas are "applied" to legal facts. According to this view, what distinguishes philosophical jurisprudence from all other types "is its *a priori* method." That is, it proceeds by first examining "certain abstract ideas such as Right, Duty, Obligation 'in relation to Morality, Freedom and the human Will generally'," and then deduces from these "a coherent system of law and legal relations."[9] Oakeshott's difficulties with this view are twofold. First, he does not think that the quality of being a priori sufficiently or unambiguously differentiates philosophical explanation from any other type. If a priori means beginning from general principles instead of observed facts, then every inquiry is a priori; this we know from *Experience and its Modes*. And if a priori means "not from experience," then no inquiry is a priori; the "absolutely *a priori* is the nearest thing to the absolutely absurd." Second, Oakeshott does not think that the "attempt to devise a perfect system of law and legal relationships" falls within the scope of the philosophy of law. He elaborates why in his objections to "the third, and perhaps most common, conception of the nature of a philosophy of law," the "ethical" (more properly the "normative") conception of philosophical jurisprudence.[10]

According to this conception, the philosophy of law is the consideration of legal rules and arrangements in terms of their goodness and badness, and the determination of the end the law ought to pursue. The purpose of such a philosophy of law is, "not to define the nature of 'right', but to determine the rightness or wrongness of the legal arrangements of a society; not to define a criterion, but to deliver precepts, and to construct an ideal system of legal relationships." It will be clear from what Oakeshott has already said about the nature of ethical thought in *Experience and its Modes* why he rejects this view of the nature of philosophical jurisprudence. And, indeed, he hardly elaborates here on the reasons he gave there for rejecting a normative moral (or political) philosophy. Definition of our moral and legal concepts, he argues, is one thing, the practical evaluation of these concepts and the construction of a world of value another. And philosophy is properly concerned with the former. "To investigate the nature of a moral criterion is an ethical and a philosophical enquiry; but to determine the goodness and badness of a law involves a moral judgment which the philosopher as such is in no better position to give than any other member of society." This latter engagement really belongs to what Oakeshott calls a "theory of legislation" rather than to a genuinely philosophical theory of law.[11]

The fourth view of the philosophy of law which Oakeshott considers is the "sociological" view: the view that the purpose of philosophical jurisprudence "is to provide a view of the nature of law appropriate to the needs of society."[12] This view is distinguished from the sociological jurisprudence mentioned above in that it is a theory of philosophy rather than a theory of law per se. The defects of this view are those which belong to the sociology of knowledge in general: it claims to transcend the very conditions in terms of which it understands all other knowledge. The sociology of knowledge is self-contradictory. Besides this, Oakeshott does not think it can be shown that the different philosophies of law are each confined to a single time and place or to a single set of social circumstances. He mentions both the natural-law theory and the natural-rights theory as examples of theories, which, though born in the ancient world, continue to flourish in the modern world.[13]

The fifth and final view Oakeshott considers is the view that philosophical jurisprudence consists in relating the conclusions of the various non-philosophical forms of jurisprudence to "general principles."[14] In other words, philosophical jurisprudence is conceived here as the synthesis of the results of the special legal sciences. And we need hear no more to know that Oakeshott rejects this view out of hand. For it is just such a view of philosophy which we have seen him attack explicitly in *Experience and its Modes*. Philosophy is not the synthesis of the special sciences – "what are the sciences that they must be accepted as the datum, and as the datum not to be changed, of valid knowledge?" As Oakeshott puts it here in "The Concept of a Philosophical Jurisprudence":

> [T]he notion that it is the business of philosophy to accept the conclusions of special inquiries – history, jurisprudence, physics, etc. – and relate them, unchanged, to "general philosophical principles", though once popular, is now on all hands seen to be the nonsense that it always was. For philosophy these "conclusions" are never, and never could be, mere data to be accepted; to consider them as such involves a misconception of the nature of knowledge, of philosophical inquiry and of the character of the so-called "conclusions". Any genuine synthesis of "results" must be a reinterpretation; and in interpretation what is given is accepted, not categorically as something already established, but hypothetically as a useful starting-place for thought.[15]

Apart from his specific objections, there are, as we have seen, two general criticisms which Oakeshott raises against all of these conceptions of the philosophy of law. In the first place, all erroneously conceive philosophical jurisprudence as merely one among a multiplicity of mutually exclusive explanations of the nature of law, neither more comprehensive (though the fifth as "synthesis" aspires to be) nor more self-critical than any other kind of explanation. Secondly, in none of these conceptions is philosophy related to the philosophy of law in any but the most external way. Philosophy stands to the philosophy of law merely as a presupposition. The philosophy of law is philosophical only in the sense that it presupposes some philosophical doctrine or other; which is to say it is not really philosophical at all. The philosophy of law does not itself seem to be characterized by genuine philosophical, that is, critical, thinking.

Now, these two points are really very closely linked, the first defect following from the second. If the philosophy of law were conceived as being itself philosophical instead of as simply resting on a philosophy, then it would cease to be merely one explanation among others and become the criterion by which all other explanations are judged. This, of course, does not obviously or directly follow; it presupposes a certain conception of the nature of philosophy: the notion of philosophy as absolutely critical thought with which we are familiar from *Experience and its Modes*. In "The Concept of a Philosophical Jurisprudence" Oakeshott briefly recapitulates his idea of philosophy, at the same time making explicit how this idea of philosophy can be applied to the problems of political and legal philosophy.

He begins with a proposition very much in the vein of *Experience and its Modes*. Philosophical knowledge for him, he says, "is not a special kind of knowledge derived from some special source of information. . . . Philosophical thought and knowledge is simply thought and knowledge without reservation or presupposition."[16] Philosophy, he goes on to explain, is not esoteric, starting from "some remote region of experience known only to the philosopher." Rather, it "begins with the concepts of ordinary, everyday knowledge," and it seeks to extend our knowledge of these concepts by discovering what is *implied* in them. The task of philosophy is fundamentally one of definition. "And definition is the making clearer of something which is already to some extent apprehended and therefore to some extent clear . . . it is making more definite what is already to some extent defined." Oakeshott insists on the continuity between philosophical and pre-philosophical experience. The philosopher does not begin with universal doubt. Pre-philosophical experience is not simply nescience; it implicitly contains a reference to the whole or the totality of experience; and the task of the philosopher is to make this implicit reference explicit. In philosophy we never pass "from mere ignorance to complete knowledge"; we always pass from what is only half-known, what is known confusedly and indistinctly, to what is known more fully and systematically. The process in philosophy "is always one of coming to know more fully and clearly what is in some sense already known."[17]

Now, it might seem that the essentially Socratic view of philosophy Oakeshott here sets forth – namely, that philosophy consists in analyzing and drawing out the implications of knowledge we already possess – allies him with, besides Socrates (or Kant or Hegel), certain "analytic" philosophers. There are, of course, similarities. But we must be clear on the no less important differences. That philosophy begins with and analyzes the knowledge contained in our ordinary, everyday concepts – so far Oakeshott is in agreement with the analytic view. But for the analytic philosopher, this initial knowledge remains in some sense absolute; it is a datum which philosophy may analyze but can never criticize or go beyond. It is just such a view that Oakeshott denies when he asserts that the conclusions of philosophy must be "new," must differ from the commonsense notions with which philosophical inquiry begins. "There *must* be disagreement between a concept as it is for, say, common sense, and as it is for philosophy." In the course of philosophical inquiry the pre-philosophical or common-sensical concept with which we began undergoes a radical transformation; it is transformed and superseded. This means, obviously, that the conclusions of philosophy cannot be checked by appeal to ordinary experience or common sense. Such experience is defective from the standpoint of philosophy. "'Verification' in philosophical enquiry," Oakeshott writes, "lies always ahead in what the concept is to become, and never behind in what it was when we first began work upon it." Which does not mean, however, that the philosopher is relieved of the responsibility of showing in detail how his philosophical definition "is connected with and arises out of the less comprehensive definition with which we began.... [H]is definition must be presented as a conclusion from a continuous argument."[18]

Oakeshott sums up his view of the process of philosophical inquiry and of the relation of philosophical explanation to other forms of explanation by casting it in slightly different terms. All explanation or understanding, he suggests, may be seen as a matter of placing that which is to be explained, an only partially known "text," in some sort of "context." Of course, many such contexts suggest themselves, but each "is seen itself to require explanation," a context in which it too can be understood and made coherent. Philosophy, on this view, is simply "the search for a context which does not require a further setting in order to be understood, a universal, self-complete context." This self-complete context Oakeshott has denominated "the totality of experience" in *Experience and its Modes*. It is a context which cannot be gone beyond, "a context which criticism cannot turn into a text itself requiring a context." It is, in short, absolute.[19]

For Oakeshott, then, philosophical explanation is the relation of a text (such as law) to a universal, self-complete context. And the process may be seen as involving two main stages. "First, there is the identification, the mere designation of the subject of inquiry." If, for example, we are concerned to define the concept "law," "we must first know how to apply the word 'law'. And this is learnt only by a critical examination of the ways in which the word is ordinarily used." But this is only the beginning of inquiry; "such an examination leaves us with merely the definition of a word, leaves us with merely the identification of a thing. We have one thing clearly before us, but we have nothing else; we have the text, but its full meaning is still to seek. We must, then, proceed, secondly, to the definition of the context." Definition, for Oakeshott, is "not merely having the one thing (in this case of a philosophical jurisprudence the one thing is 'law') clearly before us"; it is "knowing it in a world of related things, knowing it in its context."[20] Collingwood puts a similar point in his *Principles of Art*. Definition, he remarks,

> necessarily means defining one thing in terms of something else; therefore, in order to define any given thing, one must have in one's head not only a clear idea of the thing to be defined, but an equally clear idea of all the other things by reference to which one defines it.[21]

Definition, both Oakeshott and Collingwood agree, involves understanding something – a text – in terms of its context. And the context in terms of which a philosophical definition is constructed is distinguished by being a self-complete, a thoroughly self-critical, context; a context which supersedes all other contexts.

Now, what precisely is the connection between these remarks of Oakeshott's on the nature of philosophical inquiry and the criticisms he made earlier of current conceptions of philosophical jurisprudence? The chief defect he discovered in current notions of philosophical jurisprudence was that they conceived philosophical jurisprudence as merely one among a number of mutually exclusive and equally valid explanations of the nature of law. It should be clear now that this defect is remedied in Oakeshott's conception of a *philosophical* jurisprudence. A jurisprudence that is philosophical in the sense Oakeshott has outlined ceases "to be merely one among a number of unrelated explanations of law." It stands at the end of the process of concrete and critical reflection on the nature of law, having superseded all other limited or partial views, at once the most complete explanation of the nature of law and the criterion by which all other explanations must be judged. This process of critical reflection might begin with the essentially abstract definition of law found in, say, analytical jurisprudence; and from there it might pass to wider, more concrete contexts from which to view law (e.g., politics, history, economic organization, social structure, etc.). But sooner or later we arrive at a context which itself does not require further explanation, a context which is immune from criticism and cannot be superseded. And this, for Oakeshott, is the standpoint of the philosophy of law.[22]

Here I would like to turn aside for a moment to consider one of Oakeshott's earliest articles, "The Authority of the State,"[23] because it well illustrates the philosophical procedure we have been discussing. In this article Oakeshott addresses himself to the question of the nature of the state. Remarking that we are initially confronted by a multiplicity of different conceptions of the state, he argues (much in the manner of "The Concept of a Philosophical Jurisprudence") that we must not simply acquiesce in this multiplicity.

> What is important . . . is that we should understand the relationship of these different conceptions. Some writers assume that they are bare alternatives and invite us to choose which we will, but pluralism run to seed is not an engaging spectacle. Others take them to be merely conflicting, but to set one against another is not the way to get the truth out of ideas. Others again imagine a complete conception of the state to be constructed from the contributions of lesser and different conceptions, but this also is a relationship foreign to the nature of ideas; a complete conception was never achieved by adding together conceptions in themselves imperfect. In place of these, however, the view I wish to suggest is that a complete conception of the state is one which supersedes all others and beside which they appear neither as possible alternatives, nor as contradictions nor as contributions, but as abstractions to be supplanted.

He goes on to consider some of the more common of these conceptions of the state – the state understood as a piece of territory, as a collection of legal or economic persons, as the secular whole, and finally as the political machinery of government – rejecting each as an abstraction from concrete social reality. With respect to the identification of the state with government, for example, he writes: "Governmental activity is not a self-explanatory activity; its end is always beyond the perfection of itself; it deals with an aspect of life, never with the whole of it." This political conception of the state may be less abstract than, say, the economic conception of the state; nevertheless, it falls far short of concreteness. Where, then, is a concrete conception of the state to be found?

> If it is to be a concrete fact, the state must be self-subsistent, something which carries with it the explanation of itself and requires to be linked on to no more comprehensive whole in order to be understood. And it appears to me that nothing fulfils these conditions save the social whole which is correlative to individuals who are complete and living persons; or, in other words, the totality in an actual community which satisfies the whole mind of the individuals who comprise it. All that falls short of this is an abstraction which requires this to explain it.[24]

Oakeshott here seems to end up with a full-blown Hegelian definition of the state, an impression that is confirmed when he goes on to reject the separation of the state from society.[25] We will be pursuing Oakeshott's relationship to Hegel and Hegelianism later on in this chapter. Here I am mainly interested in the connection between "The Authority of the State" and the reflections on philosophical method in "The Concept of a Philosophical Jurisprudence." Indeed, one of the things that is interesting about this early article is that in it Oakeshott's Hegelianism reveals itself more as a philosophy of explanation

– based on the complex relationship of the abstract to the concrete – than anything else. This applies to his rejections later on in the article of identifications of the *authority* of the state with either legislative authority or popular consent. These conceptions of the authority of the state are rejected once again on the basis of being abstract, neither self-complete nor self-explanatory.[26]

Returning now to "The Concept of a Philosophical Jurisprudence," we have seen that it is the criterial character of philosophical jurisprudence – its critical authority vis-à-vis other types of explanation of the nature of law – which Oakeshott lays the greatest emphasis on in his discussion. It is the absence of this critical or criterial character in current conceptions of philosophical jurisprudence which convicts them of error in his eyes. But what beyond this does Oakeshott have to offer in the way of setting the philosophy of law (and of civil society) on a proper course? He has certainly identified an important feature of a philosophical theory of the nature of law: namely, that it supersedes all other theories and serves as a criterion by which they are to be judged. But he has yet to indicate where as a matter of actual procedure we might begin today in constructing a genuinely philosophical theory of law and civil society.

It is to this more practical problem that Oakeshott turns in the last few pages of "The Concept of a Philosophical Jurisprudence." Briefly, he argues that at the top of the agenda for the philosophy of law should stand "a thorough reconsideration of the history of the philosophy of law." Such a reconsideration he believes will give us a firmer consciousness of the direction philosophical inquiry into the nature of law and civil society should take today and of what still remains to be done in that inquiry.[27] It is quite clear that Oakeshott's own philosophizing on law and civil society takes its start from reflection on the history of legal and political philosophy. And therefore in the second and third parts of this chapter I propose to examine a number of his writings which touch on this history (mainly from the thirties and forties) as a prelude to the consideration of his political philosophy proper.

2. Recovering the Tradition of Political Philosophy

Oakeshott states toward the end of "The Concept of a Philosophical Jurisprudence" that "the greatest hindrances which stand in the way of a fresh and profitable start with the philosophical enquiry into the nature of law are the prevailing ignorance about what has been accomplished in this enquiry, and the prejudice, that springs from this ignorance, that little or nothing has been accomplished." Therefore, he suggests that "the first item on our agenda" be:

a thorough reconsideration of the history of the philosophy of law, and in particular of the great texts which belong to that history.... The philosophical enquiry into the nature of law is not something we can begin today *de novo*, and spin out of our heads and out of our present experience, without reference to what has gone before.[28]

We must immerse ourselves in the history (or more precisely, the "tradition") of philosophical jurisprudence before we can begin to construct a philosophical theory of law of our own.

This is, of course, easier said than done. The philosopher of law has much to learn from the history of the philosophy of law; but he can learn from it only if he changes his attitude toward it, only if he begins to appropriate it in a more profound way. For too long, Oakeshott argues, the history of philosophical jurisprudence has concerned itself with the conclusions or opinions which are to be found in a philosophical doctrine. But these conclusions or opinions are mere abstractions. Every concrete philosophical doctrine consists not only of conclusions or opinions but also of reasons given for those conclusions or opinions; "it provides a *ratio decidendi* for every *obiter dictum*." And it is with these reasons or *rationes decidendi* that the philosopher-historian ought primarily to be concerned. They in a way *are* the conclusions of a philosophical doctrine. We need to know them "not merely in order to be able to judge whether the conclusions are well-founded, but in order to know what the conclusions themselves are. In a philosophical doctrine the *what* and the *why* are genuinely inseparable, and this is one of the peculiarities of philosophy."[29]

Oakeshott calls, then, for a new approach to the history of legal and political philosophy; or if not exactly a new approach, at least one which differs from the traditional historical (and historicizing) approach. The historical approach, by occupying itself solely with conclusions and "the supposed effects or influence of those conclusions," succeeds only in destroying the tradition of philosophical jurisprudence as a source of inspiration. In contradistinction to this merely historical approach, Oakeshott's approach might be called "philosophical." Indeed, in order to further distinguish what he has in mind from conventional history, he speaks of the "tradition" of philosophical jurisprudence rather than of its "history." By "the tradition of philosophical jurisprudence" he means "the history of philosophical jurisprudence philosophically conceived, seen as a living, extemporary whole in which past and present are comparatively insignificant."[30] This tradition, he maintains, is single and continuous, though our narrow focus on conclusions, opinions and effects has blinded us to its unity and continuity. It is a tradition not "of conclusions or even of questions" but of philosophical inquiry. Questions and answers may change over time, but something abides through these changes:

namely, philosophy itself (presumably as Oakeshott conceives it), the tradition of philosophical inquiry.[31]

Oakeshott's ideas on the history of legal and political philosophy are only briefly and very generally sketched in "The Concept of a Philosophical Jurisprudence." In order to grasp them more firmly, we must turn to some of his other writings on the history of political thought from this period. Two articles in particular, one on Bentham and one on Hobbes,[32] elaborate Oakeshott's views on what is involved in understanding and interpreting a past thinker. Written some years before "The Concept of a Philosophical Jurisprudence" (six and three years respectively), they anticipate most of the ideas which are briefly sketched in the last few pages of that essay. In them we find the same emphasis on reasons over conclusions or opinions in understanding a philosophical doctrine; also the emphasis on the peculiarity of philosophical inquiry, its peculiarly radical character.

The Bentham article is largely an attack – not only on Bentham but on the "new Bentham" of recent scholarship. In such scholarship we find an attempt to rehabilitate Bentham by elevating him to the status of a great critical thinker, a philosopher who transcended his time and anticipated a number of more recent developments in philosophical and political thought. This, however, is not Oakeshott's view of the man who tried to create an objective science of morals and legislation. For him Bentham is a creature of the eighteenth century, not a precursor to the nineteenth; and he is the exact opposite of a critical thinker and a philosopher: he is a *philosophe*. And what more than anything else distinguishes the *philosophe* from the philosopher, according to Oakeshott (besides his faith in indiscriminate knowledge), is his "general credulity," the uncritical quality of his mind. The *philosophe* "begins with a whole miscellany of presuppositions which he has neither the time, the inclination nor the ability to examine." In short, the mind of the *philosophe* is one that touches everything superficially but never searches anything profoundly. And in this regard Bentham is, Oakeshott insists, the *philosophe* par excellence.[33]

But it is not so much Bentham that interests Oakeshott in this article as the historical method which has led to such a false estimate of his importance and originality. This method is concerned more with discovering "anticipations" in a thinker's thought than with whether a particular matter is developed subtly or profoundly. It concerns itself exclusively with the conclusions of a man's thought and with the after-effects or consequences of those conclusions. Of one scholar whose approach to Bentham exhibits this abstract concern with "effects" and "anticipations" Oakeshott writes:

[T]he criterion of importance which Mr. Ogden suggests is this: wherever in a writer who died a hundred years ago any ideas (however random, disconnected and undeveloped) appear which "anticipate the modern view" of the matter, that writer is important. What makes a long-dead writer important are "the echoes of modernity which reverberate through the fabric of this system." And, whatever we may think of this criterion, since Bentham was a *philosophe*, a man with an inventive mind, a man of innumerable "ideas" none of which he worked out fully, it is not difficult, if we adopt it, to represent him as "a giant" in the history of English thought.[34]

In the same vein he continues:

"Bentham was an ingenious man, and if we look hard enough we shall certainly find in his works some "remarkable anticipations" of fairly modern views. But what of it? Does that make him a giant? A thinker like Bentham does not trouble to discriminate or confine himself; he skims the cream.[35]

Nor does the preoccupation with effects and influence simply lead us to misjudge the rank of a thinker, according to Oakeshott; it also prevents us from understanding what he actually thought, what his ideas actually are. When we concern ourselves with effects or consequences, we look only to a thinker's conclusions. But conclusions by themselves, we have already learned, are mere abstractions. In order to understand what the conclusions themselves are we must look at the reasons, the *rationes decidendi*, which lie behind them. In philosophy the *what* and the *why* are inseparable. By focusing exclusively on Bentham's conclusions and after-effects, scholars have not only misjudged the profundity (or superficiality) but also the *character* of his thought.

Bentham as a thinker belonged essentially to the eighteenth century, and this fact has been obscured by writers on Bentham because they are determined to direct their attention away from what Bentham actually thought and the eighteenth-century presuppositions of his thought, towards the so-called after-effects or consequences of his thought. What has practical consequence is, almost always, the idea itself severed from the grounds and reasons which lie in the mind of the thinker, the mere *obiter dictum*. Cremation, contraception, coeducation, this or that reform of the law, may be advocated for a hundred different reasons, and what is influential is, usually the bare advocacy of the view. But when we come to consider what a man actually thought, it is not these bare ideas which are important, but the grounds or reasons for them which he believed to be cogent, the *ratio decidendi*. And in the case of Bentham, these grounds and reasons were all typical of eighteenth-century thought, and nearly all fallacious. For Bentham, so far from having thought out his first principles, had never given them a moment's consideration.[36]

The point Oakeshott makes here is the same one we saw him make toward the end of "The Concept of a Philosophical Jurisprudence": namely, that in order to understand a past thinker we must look not

only at his conclusions but at the reasons he gives for those conclusions, his *rationes decidendi*. Though here he suggests we look at
Bentham's *rationes decidendi* in order to see how conventional he really
was, in other places he suggests we do this precisely to see how
original and radical a philosopher is. This is eminently so in his
writings on Hobbes, especially in the early article "Thomas Hobbes"
published in 1935. This article is important not only because it defines
Oakeshott's basic approach to Hobbes, but also because it underlines
his fundamental conviction of the peculiarity of philosophy and of the
peculiar difficulty in interpreting a great political philosopher.

The article is cast in the form of a review of some of the more recent
literature on Hobbes, and it is guided by two basic questions: What
have we learned so far about Hobbes? And what have we still to learn?
But before addressing these questions directly, Oakeshott first takes
note of certain elements in the contemporary interest in Hobbes which
he regards as "unhealthy." Specifically, he objects to attempts to see
Hobbes's significance in the fact that he anticipated certain developments in politics, or in the fact that he held political opinions which
seem to be validated by current political experience. This, of course,
reminds us of the criticisms made in the Bentham article of a similar
preoccupation with mere opinions and conclusions, anticipations and
effects. There the focus on mere political opinions was said to obscure
the conventionality and superficiality of Bentham's thought. Here it is
argued that such a focus blinds us to what Hobbes really has to offer
us: namely, "a comprehensive view of the nature of political life."
Every man, Oakeshott writes,

> has his political opinions, and sometimes they are opinions which will
> interest and inspire ages other than his own. But a political philosopher
> has something more, and more significant, than political opinions: he has
> an analysis of political activity, a comprehensive view of the nature of
> political life, and it is this, and not his political opinions, which it is
> profitable for a later and different age to study. And if it is contended that
> these political opinions belong themselves to that analysis, it must, never-
> theless, remain a mistake to lift a few of them out of the system of his
> thought and give them an independent existence just because when
> regarded in this way they seem to meet present needs.[37]

The true teaching of a philosopher like Hobbes, then, is not to be
found in mere political opinions. Nor is it to be found in mere conclusions severed from the reasons which lie behind them. Here Oakeshott makes the same point we encountered in "The Concept of a
Philosophical Jurisprudence" and "The New Bentham" about the
reasons or *rationes decidendi* being more important than the conclusions
in a philosophical doctrine.[38] He goes on to argue that disregard for
the reasons upon which Hobbes's views are based has led to mis-

interpretation of those views. In particular, he thinks the failure to appreciate the profoundly systematic character of Hobbes's thought – the tendency to see it as a mere collection of opinions – has prevented us from fathoming Hobbes's meaning. "We are content to take [his] doctrines separately and are reluctant to follow Hobbes back to the foundation of his thought: we find embedded in its superstructure ideas with which we think ourselves familiar and, ignorant of what lies underneath, we do not question that familiarity."[39]

Oakeshott gives three examples of misinterpretation arising from the failure to appreciate the systematic and philosophical character of Hobbes's thought. And in all three cases, it is the *moral* reading of an essentially *philosophical* doctrine which leads to error. In the first, we find it asserted that human nature according to Hobbes is essentially selfish or egoistic; and that this doctrine of the selfishness of man is the foundation upon which Hobbes builds his political philosophy. But Oakeshott responds that

> when we turn to what Hobbes actually wrote, and treat it as a systematic whole, we find that the essential selfishness of man is not, in Hobbes, a premise, but (if the doctrine is to be found anywhere) is a conclusion, the result of a long and complicated argument. His premise is a doctrine of solipsism, a belief in the essential isolation of men from one another, and expounded as a theory of knowledge.[40]

This consideration ultimately bears on Oakeshott's understanding of Hobbes's individualism, which (he argues) is not based on a "moral opinion" about human nature but "upon a theory of knowledge, upon a thoroughgoing nominalism and an almost extreme solipsism."[41] The second misunderstanding Oakeshott takes up concerns the alleged "realism" of Hobbes's doctrine of authority. He denies this allegation, however, arguing that Hobbes's doctrine of authority has its origins not in a kind of moral realism but in a philosophic doctrine of knowledge. Hobbes's doctrine of authority

> begins not from a view of the *moral* character of man as so many theories of authority begin, but from a view of the nature of man merely as an experiencing being. Hobbes's theory of law and government has, indeed, no ethical foundation, in the ordinary sense, but it is conceived throughout in purely naturalistic terms, and begins in the theory of knowledge.[42]

Finally, Oakeshott comments on Hobbes's "so-called Erastianism," which he claims "is different from the Erastianism of Erastus and different from the Erastianism of any other writer because it is based on different reasons." His is a philosophical view, based on philosophical reasons, while theirs is no more than a prudential opinion about what is expedient. "Hobbes's view is based upon, not moral principles, but the principles of his theory of knowledge, upon his doctrines of nominalism and solipsism; theirs is based upon expediency and an observation of the world. And consequently they have, at bottom, little or nothing in common." For Oakeshott, no two philosophical doctrines may be said to be the same unless their conclusions *and* the reasons given for those conclusions alike coincide.[43]

The antithesis between moral and political *philosophy*, on the one hand, and moral observation and *opinion*, on the other, is evident in all three of the examples above. It appears again, in a slightly more subtle way, in Oakeshott's long review of Leo Strauss's *The Political Philosophy of Hobbes: its Basis and its Genesis*.[44] This review is of particular interest, not only because it underlines the sharp distinction Oakeshott wants to draw between the moral point of view and the philosophical point of view, but also because it confronts a prominent historian of political philosophy with whom Oakeshott would seem to have a great deal in common. Very generally, Oakeshott and Strauss both see the history of political philosophy as somehow essential to the philosophical inquiry into politics today; both share a keen appreciation of the radical quality of philosophical thought; both attempt to recover the radical character of the political philosophy of the past; and both set themselves against various levelling interpretations of past political philosophies – interpretations which either minimize important differences between philosophers, overemphasize superficial similarities, ignore subtleties, or search for ahistorical "anticipations." Nevertheless, despite these affinities, and despite his tremendous admiration for Strauss's book,[45] Oakeshott does ultimately express some disagreement with Strauss's overall interpretation of Hobbes. I wish briefly to consider his criticisms because they further illuminate his conception of political philosophy. I do not, however, intend to adjudicate between the two interpretations, for that would involve a complete consideration of the relevant texts in Hobbes and take us far beyond the scope of the present discussion.

Oakeshott's main criticism focuses on what seems to be the central thesis (or at least one of the central theses) of Strauss's book: namely, "that the real basis of [Hobbes's] political philosophy is not modern science" but a "specific moral attitude" growing out of "pre-scientific" reflection on "men and manners."[46] Hobbes's political philosophy, Strauss argues, is not (like Spinoza's) a naturalistic philosophy; it is based on a "moral attitude" which is capable of distinguishing between permissible and impermissible appetite or passion. Fear of death is seen by Hobbes to be fundamentally just, and vanity or pride fundamentally unjust. "Thus not the naturalistic antithesis of morally indifferent animal appetite (or of morally indifferent striving after power) on the one hand, and morally indifferent striving after self-preservation on the other, but the moral and humanist antithesis of fundamentally unjust vanity and fundamentally just fear of death is the basis of Hobbes's political philosophy."[47]

This, according to Strauss, is Hobbes's "original view, not yet distorted by scientific 'explanations,' of human life"; it is the "original" foundation for his political philosophy.[48] But Strauss has more in view than the narrow question of the historical *genesis* of Hobbes's political philosophy. He goes on to argue that this moral doctrine "is not merely the 'original,' but that it is the 'real' basis of Hobbes's political philosophy"; it "is not merely the genesis, but it is also the *basis* of Hobbes's mature political philosophy."[49] It is at this point that Oakeshott finds himself no longer able to follow Strauss's argument. For in order to establish his thesis, Strauss needs to show, not only that there is a development in Hobbes's later writings toward a more "mechanical" theory, but that the "science" in these writings has been "merely superimposed upon a theory the real basis of which [is] independent of 'science'." And this Oakeshott thinks Strauss fails to do. For him the replacement of the "moral attitude" by a more "scientific" (really a more "philosophical") theory represents a genuine advance in and transformation of Hobbes's thought and not a mere superimposition. "It is, really, one thing to prove (as Dr. Strauss proves) that there is a marked change and development towards a more and more "scientific" theory in the *Elements of Law, De Cive* and *Leviathan*," but it is quite another

> to infer that this "original" theory was never really abandoned. It is indeed certain that, in his latest writings, Hobbes did abandon it – Dr. Strauss admits as much; and it is a lapse from the scrupulous attention that Dr. Strauss usually pays to the smallest movement of Hobbes's intellectual history, to suppose that this abandonment was unintentional and not the real Hobbes.... For example, the whole period of his life in which he "turned to history" for the material of his political philosophy Hobbes later considered to have been misguided; and the view expressed in all his later writings of the essential wrongness of all opinion as such, must lead us to conclude that, as far as Hobbes himself was concerned, a political philosophy based upon a moral opinion or "attitude" was insecurely based. Somehow this merely moral basis had to be transformed, and Hobbes accomplished the transformation.[50]

The point Oakeshott here urges against Strauss is essentially the one we found him making in the earlier article on Hobbes. The antithesis between moral and political philosophy, on the one hand, and moral observation and opinion, on the other, is once again asserted. For Oakeshott, too (as he says of Hobbes), a political philosophy based on a merely moral opinion or "attitude" falls short of being genuinely philosophical. It may be that Hobbes's political philosophy *was* originally based on a "moral attitude"; but because Hobbes was above all a philosopher and therefore devoted to the tireless exploration of the postulates and conditions of political life, he could not long remain satisfied with this merely moral basis.

In his earlier article on Hobbes, Oakeshott continually points to the epistemological (in contradistinction to the merely moral) foundations of Hobbes's political teaching.[51] And it is, no doubt, this epistemological tendency which he finds increasingly asserts itself in the course of Hobbes's philosophical development. In this sense Hobbes's philosophy becomes more "naturalistic," and perhaps even more "scientific." But for Oakeshott, "science" in Hobbes's case is not simply to be equated with "the method of Galileo" or with modern natural science. Indeed, he criticizes Strauss for too narrowly construing what "science" means for Hobbes. Hobbes, he argues,

> was never a scientist in any true sense, that is, his "science" is really conceived throughout as an epistemology. He is never concerned with the scientific observation of the natural world, but always with what the character of the world must be if we are to have any knowledge of it; he is not concerned with the natural world for its own sake, but with the causes of sensation.[52]

Hobbes's movement from a moral to a more "naturalistic" basis for his political philosophy thus represents, for Oakeshott, a movement toward a more coherent and philosophical interpretation of political life; and it marks a genuine advance in Hobbes's thought. It is in his more positive evaluation of Hobbes's development toward a more "scientific" (i.e., philosophical) theory of law and politics that Oakeshott fundamentally diverges from Strauss. In summary, he grants that Strauss "has proved his case that at some early period Hobbes did conceive his political philosophy in terms of moral fear of violent death and an immoral vanity or pride." But he thinks Strauss

> is wrong in supposing either that [Hobbes's] early theory was conceived entirely in moral terms, or that the replacement of "vanity" by "the striving for power" (that is, by a "neutral" term) was not a real advance in Hobbes's theory and conceived as such by him. Hobbes's theory may not be of the *simple* "naturalistic" character that it has been supposed to be, but neither is it of the *simple* moral character Dr. Strauss suggests. It is "naturalistic" not in contrast to "moral," but in an attempt to find a firmer basis than merely moral opinion.[53]

So far I have confined myself to Oakeshott's criticism of Strauss's claim that the "real" basis (and not simply the "original" basis) of Hobbes's political philosophy lies in a specific moral doctrine or "attitude." But there is another important aspect of Strauss's book about which Oakeshott has something to say: that aspect which has to do with the question of Hobbes's relation to the tradition of political philosophy. Strauss argues that Hobbes is the originator of a new tradition in political philosophy; and that his distinctive innovation consists in the substitution of natural "right" for natural "law" as the basis of political order and obligation. This substitution of a subjective claim or "right" for "law" constitutes for Strauss the fundamental difference between modern and classical political philosophy. And because it becomes explicit for the first time in Hobbes, he calls him "the founder of modern political philosophy."[54] Oakeshott makes two points with respect to Strauss's claim here. In the first place, though he accepts Strauss's thesis that Hobbes's political philosophy represents a break with the natural-law tradition, he still thinks Strauss "exaggerates slightly Hobbes's originality." Hobbes certainly broke away from the tradition of natural law which ultimately derives from the thought of Plato and Aristotle, but that does not mean that he belonged to no tradition in particular, or that he founded an entirely new one. His selection of will over law as the basis of the state puts him squarely in the Epicurean tradition, according to Oakeshott. And he criticizes Strauss in all three of his reviews for not recognizing Hobbes's obvious affinities with this tradition.[55]

The second point Oakeshott makes concerns the significance of Hobbes's political philosophy for all later moral and political thought. And it must be admitted that what he has to say on this score relates only tangentially to Strauss's book and seems to have more to do with his own interpretation of the history of modern political philosophy and with his conception of the task of political philosophy today. For this reason it is of particular interest to us. Taking off from Strauss's claim that Hobbes's substitution of will for law became the starting-point for all later political thought, Oakeshott adds that Hobbes still lacked something vital to modern political thought: namely, a satisfactory theory of volition. Granted that "Hobbes set an example followed in one way or another by almost every later political thinker by starting with will instead of law," still

> he never had a satisfactory theory of volition, and the whole Epicurean tradition to which he belonged did not bear fruit until this lack was remedied, and the remedy was, in fact, the union of a reconstituted natural law theory with Hobbes's Epicurean theory – a union indicated in such phrases as Rousseau's "General Will", Hegel's "Rational Will" and Bosanquet's "Real Will".

The programmatic intention of this passage becomes explicit in the next few lines.

> The most profound movement in modern political philosophy is, as I see it, a revivification of the Stoic natural law theory achieved by the grafting upon it an Epicurean theory; it springs from the union of the two great traditions of political philosophy inherited by Western Europe from the ancient world. Its greatness is that it is a genuine theory and not a merely eclectic composition; and that it has not yet succeeded in finding an entirely satisfactory expression is certainly not a sign of its moribund condition.[56]

Here Oakeshott indicates pretty clearly the direction he thinks philosophical inquiry into politics should take in the twentieth century. The task of contemporary political philosophy is to carry through the theoretical attempt begun by Rousseau and Hegel, the attempt to synthesize "the two great traditions of political philosophy inherited by Western Europe from the ancient world" – what Oakeshott names elsewhere the "Rational-Natural" tradition and the tradition of "Will and Artifice."[57] What exactly this means or involves is not yet clear. In some ways Oakeshott has done nothing more than restate in historical form the aims and claims of the idealist or Hegelian theory of the state. But this label does not carry us very far. In order to determine more precisely what direction Oakeshott thinks philosophical inquiry into politics should take in the twentieth century – what he conceives the task of political philosophy today to be – we must consider more closely his reading of the history of political philosophy. We must particularly concern ourselves with his understanding of the essential development of modern political thought from Hobbes through Hegel (or, bringing it into the twentieth century, Bosanquet). For, as we shall see, Oakeshott's own political philosophy is closely linked with his reading of this tradition of modern political philosophy.

3. A Reading of the Tradition of Modern Political Philosophy

He begins, of course, with Hobbes. No account of Oakeshott's understanding of the tradition of modern political philosophy can fail to come to terms with his interpretation of Hobbes. Hobbes is the political philosopher about whom Oakeshott has written most; and it is upon his interpretation of Hobbes that Oakeshott's reputation still to a large extent rests. Why is Hobbes so important for Oakeshott? What is it in Hobbes that he finds crucial to political philosophy ever since Hobbes? What is it that Oakeshott himself gets from Hobbes? And where does he find Hobbes's political philosophy ultimately inadequate? These are the questions we must ask ourselves in trying to determine Oakeshott's relationship to Hobbes.

First let us take up the question of why Hobbes is so important for Oakeshott. The answer to this question, though implied in his review of Strauss, is perhaps most clearly indicated in Oakeshott's 1946 introduction to *Leviathan*.[58] There the significance of Hobbes is seen to lie in his being the first thorough expositor of the alternative to the rational-natural tradition of political thought which Oakeshott associates with Plato and Aristotle and the natural-law theorists who followed them. Instead of resorting to reason and nature, this alternative explores political life in terms of the master-conceptions of will and artifice.[59] We have already seen Strauss defending much the same view of Hobbes's deviance from Plato and Aristotle and the whole classical natural-law tradition. Like Strauss, Oakeshott sees the distinctive innovation of this alternative to the rational-natural tradition in its substitution of "right" for "law," of will for the dominion of reason. Nevertheless, he adds some nuances of his own to this antithesis of Hobbes and antiquity; and we would do well to pay some attention to them, since they serve further to illuminate the fundamental difference he sees between ancient and modern political philosophy.

What, for Oakeshott, seems to separate Hobbes most from his rational-natural predecessors is his conception of the nature and role of reason. It is Hobbes's skepticism about the power of reason, his appreciation of the limitations of reasoning, which seems to impress Oakeshott most when writing on Hobbes. In his introduction to *Leviathan*, for example, he argues that the thread which unites Hobbes's philosophy is "not any doctrine about the world" (i.e., materialism) but a doctrine about the nature of philosophy and reasoning. Hobbesian "reasoning" is to be sharply distinguished from the "Reason" of the rational-natural tradition. Reasoning, according to Hobbes, is capable of yielding only hypothetical or conditional knowledge. It concerns itself solely with hypothetical causes and effects; and it can never pass beyond the names of things to the real nature of things. Oakeshott calls this "at once a nominalist and profoundly sceptical doctrine," and traces it to late scholasticism.

> The lineage of Hobbes's rationalism lies, not (like that of Spinoza or even Descartes) in the great Platonic-Christian tradition, but in the sceptical, late scholastic tradition. He does not normally speak of Reason, the divine illumination of the mind that unites man with God; he speaks of reasoning. And he is not less persuaded of its fallibility and limitations than Montaigne himself.

Concomitant with this narrowing of reason is the expansion of the role of passion in human life. Indeed, the whole relationship between reason and passion is transformed by Hobbes's replacement of the sovereign "Reason" of antiquity with hypothetical "reasoning." Reason no longer rules the passions, becoming instead their instrument. Once again Oakeshott points to the medieval roots of this new view of the relationship between reason and passion. Hobbes's skepticism and individualism are said to be "the gifts of later scholastic nominalism; the displacement of Reason in favour of will and imagination and the emancipation of passion were slowly mediated changes in European thought that had gone far before Hobbes wrote."[60]

What does Hobbes's skeptical doctrine about the nature and role of reason mean for his understanding of politics? Oakeshott shows that Hobbes's rejection of the rationalism of the "Platonic-Christian tradition" entails the replacement of reason by will as the foundation of political authority. Hypothetical reasoning is incapable of imposing duties or obligations. Legitimate authority can only derive from an act of will on the part of the person who is obligated, that is, from individual consent. For Hobbes (as Oakeshott is fond of pointing out), there can be "no obligation on any man, which ariseth not from some act of his own."[61]

It is thus Hobbes's voluntarism and individualism which receive the greatest emphasis in Oakeshott's introduction to *Leviathan*. And he is particularly concerned there to refute the view that Hobbes, though an individualist at the beginning of his theory, ends up as some kind of absolutist. He reminds us that the rule of Hobbes's sovereign is not arbitrary but the rule of law; and that the silences of the law contain substantial freedom. But perhaps more relevant to our current train of thought is his contention that "law as the command of the Sovereign holds within itself a freedom absent from law as Reason or custom: it is Reason, not Authority, that is destructive of individuality."[62] He explains what he means in another passage. Law as command, in contradistinction to law as reason or custom, implies freedom in the person commanded in two ways.

> First, it implies a liberty of mental activity, for it cannot be carried out by an automaton but only by one who is mentally aware of it and understands it. And secondly, it implies a liberty of initiative; for all commands are abstract and general, are indifferent to the details of their execution, and assume the ability in the subject to fill in the detail and translate the generality into an act in which this generality is fulfilled. In every act there lies a part which is not commanded; or rather, the object in a command is never a concrete act but always an abstract generality.... [H]owever large a proportion of the acts of the subject are under the control of command, there remains inside every act of obedience an area of unassailable liberty.[63]

This passage is worth noting for a couple of reasons. First, it anticipates remarkably Oakeshott's later reflections on the relationship between law and moral autonomy in *On Human Conduct*. And secondly, it discloses more precisely the link between freedom and authority which plays such an important role in Oakeshott's political thought and forms the basis of his affinity with Hobbes. The link between Hobbes's doctrine of authority and his individualism receives its most vivid expression, however, in the following passage from the introduction, a passage to which we will have occasion to refer more than once in the course of this study:

It may be said, then, that Hobbes is not an absolutist precisely because he is an authoritarian. His scepticism about the power of reasoning, which applied no less to the "artificial reason" of the Sovereign than to the reasoning of the natural man, together with the rest of his individualism, separate him from the rationalist dictators of his or any age. Indeed, Hobbes, without being himself a liberal, had in him more of the philosophy of liberalism than most of its professed defenders.[64]

So much can be gathered from Oakeshott's introduction to *Leviathan*. But it is in the later essay "The Moral Life in the Writings of Thomas Hobbes" that he treats Hobbes's view of the relationship between reason and passion, and of the role of reason in the moral life in general, at length and in masterful detail.[65] The question around which the essay revolves is whether the conduct which Hobbes held to be pre-eminently rational, namely, endeavoring peace, he also held to be morally obligatory; and if so, whether he was not in this contradicting his view of reason as merely instrumental, as a mere "servant, revealing the probable causes of events, the probable consequences of actions and the probable means by which desired ends might be attained"; put another way, whether he was not "being forgetful of his view that 'reason serves only to convince the truth (not of fact, but) of consequence' and . . . taking improper advantage of that older meaning of 'reason' in which it was recognized to have the qualities of a master or at least of an authoritative guide."[66]

Oakeshott argues (briefly) that Hobbes's authentic view was that, in the absence of a positive law (or genuine law-maker) commanding it, there is no *natural* obligation to endeavor peace. Though Hobbes unquestionably held the endeavor for peace to be most rational, he did not for that reason consider it to be morally obligatory.[67] Hobbes therefore does not, in his theory of moral obligation, contradict his general view of reason as merely hypothetical or instrumental, incapable of delivering categorical injunctions. He does not, in short, abandon "reasoning" for the sovereign "Reason" of the rational-natural tradition. Oakeshott acknowledges that there are places where Hobbes writes as though he did believe there were "natural laws" imposing a "natural obligation" on men to endeavor peace; but he ascribes to Hobbes in these places an exoteric intention to show his contemporaries where their duties lay and to conceal his more radical teaching.[68]

This, of course, is the mere gist of a highly nuanced discussion of Hobbes's theory of moral and civil obligation, but it provides further evidence of what the importance of Hobbes consists in for Oakeshott. Simply stated, his importance seems to lie in his radical break with the natural-law tradition and the idea of reason which forms its central presupposition. Instead of a law discernible by reason Hobbes put will, the individual will, as the basis of the state; and he did so with a logical consistency and clarity which had up to that time (and rarely since) been attained. Therein lies Hobbes's significance for Oakeshott. Hobbes was the first political philosopher to overcome in a consistent and self-conscious fashion the ancient rationalism which has its roots in Plato and Aristotle and ultimately issues in natural-law theory. To be sure, Hobbes is a rationalist in his own way; but his rationalism has its roots in the skeptical, late scholastic tradition and not in the tradition of pagan antiquity. Hypothetical and instrumental reasoning, not "Reason," sovereign and injunctive, lies at the heart of Hobbes's rationalism. And reason thus understood can never take the place of passion, will, and imagination in the creation of political order.[69]

Besides the argument about Hobbes's theory of moral and civil obligation, there is another aspect of "The Moral Life in the Writings of Thomas Hobbes" which should be mentioned here. It concerns the contention (of Strauss, among others) that Hobbes is to be seen as a "bourgeois" moralist – the author of a new, "bourgeois" morality, a "bourgeois hedonist."[70] Oakeshott emphatically rejects this understanding of Hobbes's moral outlook. Hobbesian man he sees as driven not simply by fear and the desire for security but also by pride, honor and magnanimity. And though he concedes that it may at first appear that Hobbes defends the morality of the tame man by making fear of death the primary motive for endeavoring peace, he argues that there is evidence in Hobbes's writings of an alternative derivation of the endeavor for peace out of the passion of pride. The existence of this aristocratic element in Hobbes's moral outlook belies the simple designation of it as "bourgeois." Beyond that, Oakeshott argues that the suggestion of "a single approved condition of human circumstances for all conditions of men" in "bourgeois morality" sets it off from Hobbes's "morality of individuality," which involves no such common substantive purpose.[71]

With respect to this issue of "bourgeois morality," it is interesting to contrast Oakeshott's view of Hobbes with his view of Locke. For the bourgeois tendencies he denies to the former he generously ascribes to the latter. Most of the evidence for Oakeshott's view of Locke comes from a short article he wrote in 1932 – the tercentenary of Locke's birth. This is a fascinating document insofar as it reveals Oakeshott's profound dissatisfaction with a certain very prominent strand of liberalism, as well as the anti-bourgeois, radically individualistic springs of this dissatisfaction. The liberalism he criticizes is of course Lockean liberalism, which he characterizes in terms of its "boundless but capricious moderation." "Locke," he writes,

> was the apostle of the liberalism which is more conservative than conservatism itself, the liberalism characterised not by insensitiveness, but

by a sinister and destructive sensitiveness to the influx of the new, the liberalism which is sure of its limits, which has a terror of extremes, which lays its paralysing hand of respectability upon whatever is dangerous or revolutionary.

He goes on to observe that this Lockean brand of liberalism is no longer able to secure adherents because it has become boring, and that its fate may be to die of neglect.

The moderate individualism of Locke has no attraction for those who have embraced a radical, an Epicurean individualism. Locke's "steady love of liberty" appears worse than slavery to anyone who, like Montaigne, is "besotted with liberty." Democracy, parliamentary government, progress, discussion, and the "plausible ethics of productivity" are notions – all of them inseparable from the Lockean liberalism – which fail now to arouse even opposition; they are not merely absurd and exploded, they are uninteresting.[72]

Apart from disclosing Oakeshott's dissatisfaction with Lockean liberalism, these remarks also point up once again the significance of Hobbes for Oakeshott. For it is Hobbes who (along with Montaigne) embodies the radical, Epicurean individualism which is opposed to the moderate Lockean variety in the passage quoted above. The implication of this passage when read in conjunction with some others on Hobbes is that, where a liberalism inspired by Locke no longer commands respect, one inspired by Hobbes may. In one place Oakeshott even says that Hobbes has more of the ground of liberalism (i.e., individualism) in him than Locke.[73] And, related to this, he sees Hobbes as much more consistent than Locke in his rejection of natural law and his putting of will or consent as the basis of the state. Finally, Oakeshott rejects Locke's doctrine of natural rights held against the state and the opposition of "individual" and "government" that this doctrine implies. Here again Hobbes's more "authoritarian" view of the state seems to score.[74] In all of this can be discerned, I think, a project to reformulate liberalism on a more Hobbesian basis. At least this is a claim I will pursue when I come to treat Oakeshott's political philosophy proper.

Hobbes is obviously an important thinker for Oakeshott, and we have been trying to determine more precisely wherein that importance lies. But we also know that Oakeshott does not simply swallow Hobbes without qualification. Although he credits Hobbes with having discovered one of the essential elements of modern political philosophy – namely, the individual will as the basis of the state – this remains *only one* of the essential elements of modern political thought. Despite his adoption of will instead of law as the starting-point for his political philosophy, Hobbes nevertheless lacks something which Oakeshott takes to be absolutely vital to modern political thought:

namely, an adequate theory of volition.[75] We must now try to determine what is meant by this criticism.

Oakeshott himself does not specify what he finds wrong with Hobbes's theory of volition. Nevertheless, he gives some indication of the direction from which his criticism would come when he remarks that this lack has to some extent been remedied in later, idealist theories of the will – in Rousseau's theory of the "general will," in Hegel's theory of the "rational will," and in Bosanquet's theory of the "real will."[76] What is it in Hobbes that these theories all end up rejecting or radically modifying?

One might say that they reject or modify precisely that individualism or solipsism which Oakeshott so emphasizes in his interpretation of Hobbes. But here a distinction must be drawn between the individualism Oakeshott generally celebrates in Hobbes – which is more of an ethical idea or (as he later puts it) an historic disposition – and that individualism which involves certain questionable assumptions about the nature of the self and its relations to others as well as to the state – for example, Hobbes's view that man is by nature a creature shut up in his own sensations and imagination, "the victim of solipsism," "an *individua substantia* distinguished by incommunicability."[77] It is this latter, "negative" individualism in Hobbes (and even more in Locke)[78] which comes increasingly under attack in the idealist theories mentioned above. Specifically, these theories reject the separation of will and thought – the assimilation of will to appetite – that is implied in Hobbes's definition of the will as "the last appetite in deliberating"; and they reject the opposition between individual freedom and government which is implied in Hobbes's image of the isolated individual in the state of nature who, upon entering civil society, surrenders part of his natural freedom in order to enjoy the remainder. Instead of regarding the state as a (necessary) restriction on our natural freedom and individuality, these idealist theories project the state as in some sense the realization of freedom and the condition of true individuality.

With this new understanding of the relationship of the individual to the state also comes a new explanation of the ground of political obligation – and here the connection with the problem of the will mentioned above becomes clearer.[79] Hobbes, we know, tried to found political obligation on the explicit consent of the governed through the social contract. But there were problems with this contractarian account of political obligation from the start, the principal one being that it failed to account for the actual obligations of the vast majority of persons who had never explicitly consented to the authority of their sovereigns. In response to this latter difficulty the doctrine of tacit consent was developed, but this was a doctrine that seemed to drain "consent" of all its real, voluntaristic meaning. The idealists proposed another solution. Retaining the essential Hobbesian thesis that will or consent is the basis of political obligation – the thesis that "will, not force, is the basis of the state" – they sought to reinterpret will and consent in such a way as to avoid the difficulties encountered by contract theory. The thrust of the idealist theory of the general will is that political obligation and authority rest on will or consent, not in the sense that they have been explicitly consented to in a formal act of will, but in the sense that they correspond to the "real" or "rational" will of the governed. The whole contractarian apparatus is here abandoned, and in its place is put a theory of will which distinguishes between the "real" and merely "apparent" interests of the individual. The difficulties of the contract theory are thus avoided, since political authority and obligation no longer rest on the explicit consent of the governed. We always consent to the authority of the state, even when we are not conscious of doing so, insofar as the state enforces our "real" or "rational" will.

The first step in the elaboration of this idealist theory of the general will was of course taken by Rousseau. That he took this step not without considerable vacillation, ambiguity and contradiction has often been remarked and is certainly true. In Rousseau the individualism is constantly struggling with a more positive conception of the state; and the vestiges of the old contract doctrine are never completely abandoned. Nevertheless, at least one part of Rousseau's political thought – that having to do with the "general will" – points away from the negative individualism of Hobbes and of the whole social contract tradition. In the *Social Contract* Rousseau sharply differentiates between the general will, which has the common interest in view, and the merely private will of individuals. And he suggests that it is the former which is to be identified with true freedom. The individual remains free even when he appears to be coerced by the state. As Rousseau puts it in a famous sentence: "[W]hoever refuses to obey the general will shall be constrained to do so by the entire body; which means only that he will be forced to be free."[80] Later on in the book he asserts that it is the general will which makes human beings citizens and free. And when an opinion contrary to one's own prevails in the assembly, "that proves nothing except that I was mistaken, and what I thought to be the general will was not. If my private will had prevailed, I would have done something other than what I wanted. It is then that I would not have been free."[81] It is the chapter "On the Civil State," though, that most clearly reveals Rousseau's departure from the contract tradition and its identification of freedom with the isolated individual in the state of nature. There he speaks of the "remarkable change" that comes over man when he passes from the state of nature to the civil state: justice replaces instinct, "the voice of duty replaces physical impulse," and "right replaces appetite." Through the social contract a man loses his "natural freedom" only to gain "civil freedom," which (Rousseau indicates) is the more genuine freedom. Civil freedom brings moral freedom, "which alone makes man truly master of himself." And in words which look forward to the moral doctrine of Kant he asserts that "the impulse of appetite alone is slavery, and obedience to the law one has prescribed for oneself is freedom."[82]

The notion that the general will represents an individual's "real" or "rational" will as opposed to his merely actual, appetitive and momentary will, that it aims at his "true" interest as opposed to his merely "apparent" interest, is only imperfectly and inconsistently developed by Rousseau. Too often he conceives the general will as in some sense compounded of conscious or expressed individual wills.[83] And it was for this reason that he was criticized by Hegel. In his *Lectures on the History of Philosophy*, Hegel praises Rousseau for being the first to make free will the basis of the state, but he goes on to criticize Rousseau for taking free will in the sense of "the casual free will of each individual."

> The notion of Freedom must not be taken in the sense of the arbitrary caprice of an individual, but in the sense of the rational will, of the will in and for itself. The universal will is not to be regarded as compounded of definitively individual wills, so that these remain absolute; otherwise the saying would be correct: "Where the minority must obey the majority, there is not freedom." The universal will must really be the rational will, even if we are not conscious of the fact; the state is therefore not an association which is directed by the arbitrary will of individuals.[84]

Hegel repeats this criticism in the *Philosophy of Right*. Once again he praises Rousseau for "adducing the will as the principle of the state." But once again he criticizes him for taking will in the sense of the arbitrary individual will instead of in the sense of the rational will.

> Unfortunately, . . . as Fichte did later, he takes the will only in a determinate form as the individual will, and he regards the universal will not as the absolutely rational element in the will, but only as a "general" will which proceeds out of this individual will as out of a conscious will. The result is that he reduces the union of individuals in the state to a contract and therefore to something based on their arbitrary will, their opinion, and their capriciously given consent.[85]

These criticisms of Rousseau perhaps overemphasize one aspect of his thought and miss the significant commonality between his view of will and freedom and Hegel's own. Nevertheless, in Hegel we find the idealist theory of the general or rational will much more consistently developed than in Rousseau. In the *Philosophy of Right* the fiction of the social contract is completely abandoned.[86] Hegel does not, however, abandon the essential Rousseauan (really Hobbesian) starting-point

of will and freedom as the basis of the state. But he does not, as
Rousseau sometimes did, identify will with the casual free will of the
individual. Rather, he speaks of the "rational will," which is in no
way to be understood as proceeding from or being generated by the
conscious wills of individuals. "Confronted with the claims made for
the individual will," he writes, "we must remember the fundamental
conception that the objective will is rationally implicit or in conception, whether it be recognized or not by individuals, whether their
whims be deliberately for it or not."[87] The state may be said to be
based on will or consent only insofar as it embodies this rational or
objective will. Nor does Hegel identify freedom with the arbitrary
caprice of the isolated or pre-political individual. This freedom he
pejoratively designates as "negative" in opposition to the "positive"
freedom that is attained in the state. The state, for Hegel, so far from
being a restriction on some sort of original or natural freedom, is itself
the realization of freedom properly understood.[88]

Though Hegel certainly offers a more positive account of the relationship of the individual to the state than is found in previous liberal
thought, it is not to be supposed that he fails to take the "individual"
seriously or that he advocates the subordination of the individual to
the state. In the *Philosophy of Right* the modern state is differentiated
from the ancient state precisely by its recognition (especially in the
economic sphere) of individuality or the right of subjectivity. Hegel
writes: "The right of the subject's particularity, his right to be satisfied, or in other words the right of subjective freedom, is the pivot and
centre of the difference between antiquity and modern times."[89]
Hegel does not reject the *value* of the individual which lies at the
heart of so much liberal thought, but he does reject the particular
interpretation of the nature and conditions of individuality which
generally characterizes such thought. The individuality that the liberal
values is not to be understood as something existing prior to the state,
but rather as itself the product or gift of the state. Hegel thus rejects
the "negative individualism" of previous liberal thought but not its
concern with individuality and individual liberty.

Further light can be shed on Hegel's concept of the rational will by
considering Bosanquet's notion of the "real will" as it is developed in
The Philosophical Theory of the State.[90] There are several reasons for
paying special attention to Bosanquet here. In the first place, Oakeshott mentions him along with Rousseau and Hegel (in the passage
quoted above) as belonging to the most profound movement in modern
political philosophy. In the second, the implications of Rousseau's
concept of the general will and Hegel's concept of the rational will are
more fully developed and to some extent clarified in Bosanquet's
political philosophy. Finally, it cannot be doubted that Bosanquet's
political philosophy stands more immediately in the background of

Oakeshott's thought than the political philosophies of either Rousseau or Hegel. It was Bosanquet who, along with Green and Bradley, was mainly responsible for mediating Hegelian ideas to English political thought at the beginning of the century. And Oakeshott was certainly not exempt from this influence early on in his career, though we may find that he later emancipated himself from it.

Bosanquet, like Hegel, distinguishes between the conscious, arbitrary, momentary will of the individual and the "true" or "real" or "rational" will which it implies. And he asks the very pertinent question as to what this distinction can possibly mean. What does it mean to speak of a "real will" which is distinct from my "actual will"? "How can there be a Will which is no one's Will? and how can anything be my Will which I am not fully aware of, or which I am even averse to?" He goes on to answer this question by first pointing to the familiar fact that we frequently desire things which would not satisfy us if we got them. What we casually desire from one moment to the next frequently does not correspond to what we would want and will if we took the future into account or if we considered our actions in terms of their overall contribution to the systematic whole which is our self. Our "actual" will, "which we exert from moment to moment as conscious individuals," rarely corresponds to our "real" will, which seeks to compose our complex wants and wishes into a harmonious whole. Our "actual" will is contradictory, and it is contradiction which our "real" will seeks to remove.

> A comparison of our acts of will through a month or a year is enough to show that no one object of action, as we conceive it when acting, exhausts all that our will demands. Even the life which we wish to live, and which on the average we do live, is never before us as a whole in the motive of any particular volition. In order to obtain a full statement of what we will, what we want at any moment must at least be corrected and amended by what we want at all other moments; and this cannot be done without also correcting and amending it so as to harmonise it with what others want, which involves an application of the same process to them. But when any considerable degree of such correction and amendment had been gone through, our own will would return to us in a shape in which we should not know it again, although every detail would be a necessary inference from the whole of wishes and resolutions which we actually cherish. . . . Such a process of harmonising and readjusting a mass of data to bring them into a rational shape is what is meant by criticism. And criticism, when applied to our actual will, shows that it is not our real will; or, in the plainest language, that what we really want is something more and other than at any given moment we are aware that we will, although the wants which we are aware of lead up to it at every point.[91]

It is in our "real" will, then, not in our arbitrary "actual" will, that true freedom is to be found, according to Bosanquet. He refers to the

Kantian formula, "The free will is the will that wills itself." A will wills itself when it wills an object that is adequate to its *whole* want and not simply to a momentary and partial desire. The desires of such a will are not "narrow and partial desires, in the fulfilment of which a man feels choked and oppressed as in a blind alley which grows narrower and narrower." Rather, they are desires adjusted to the whole compatible with the systematic aims of the self. For the will to will itself the objects which present themselves to casual volition must undergo a process of criticism by which they are adjusted to the whole; by which the narrow, selfish, and partial elements in them are purged away and purified. It is only by submitting its desires to such criticism that the will can find an object which truly and wholly satisfies it; which does not limit it but opens the way to further development of its capacities. This is what it means for the will to will itself. And such a will willing itself is what is meant by the "real" or "rational" will.[92]

Now Bosanquet, like Hegel, identifies this "real" or "rational" will with the state. Like Hegel, he sees the state – its laws and its institutions – as embodying the intelligence and rationality of a people. It is in the evolution of the customs, laws, and institutions which comprise society or the state that the process of criticism by which the "actual" will is slowly disciplined and transformed takes place. In the state "we find at once discipline and expansion, the transfiguration of partial impulses, and something to do and to care for, such as the nature of the human self demands." It is there that the individual finds "an outlet and a stable purpose capable of doing justice to his capacities – a satisfying object of life."[93] The state as the embodiment of our "real" will constantly carries us beyond our average everyday selves, correcting and amending our immediate wants so that they harmonize with what we want at other moments and also with what others want. In short, the state liberates the self by disciplining it; it creates the conditions for genuine self-realization.

It should be pointed out, though, lest Bosanquet be taken for laying the basis for some sort of political absolutism or *étatisme*, that "state" here does not mean simply coercive political machinery. It has a much broader connotation than that, comprising social as well as political forces, influences, institutions, and associations. At this point in the argument, where Bosanquet is more concerned with breaking down the abstract distinction between self and others, individuality and society, than with defining the distinctive role of the state, "state" and "society" are treated as practically convertible terms. Bosanquet does later, however, go on to distinguish the state from society as a whole, and to enunciate a doctrine of the limits of state action. The distinctive character of the state, he argues, lies in force; and since force is not *in pari materia* with the spiritual or moral end of society, the state can only indirectly promote that end. Bosanquet fundamentally agrees with both Kant and Green, who confined state action or law (on account of its compulsive character) to external actions. The state's role in the promotion of the end of society, namely, freedom or individuality, is thus largely a negative one; it hinders hindrances to self-realization. In the end, men cannot be *forced* to be free; the state as compulsive force cannot directly promote the good for man.[94]

I will have more to say about this doctrine of the limits of state action later on, for it is a doctrine which Oakeshott seems to reject. But for the moment I would like to conclude this brief survey of idealist political thought by underlining what seems to me to be its distinctive contribution to modern political philosophy: namely, its emphasis on the essential role of the state (or society) in the realization of freedom and individuality; its rejection of the isolated individual possessed of certain natural rights as the basis of the right order. Nowhere does this insight into the correlativity of the individual and the state, this idea "that assertion and maximization of the self and individuality first become possible and real in and through society," receive such sustained expression as in Bosanquet's *Philosophical Theory of the State*. The book is informed throughout by a rejection of the "individualism" of such thinkers as Bentham, Mill, and Spencer, who interpret government and law as essentially antagonistic to the self or true individuality of man. The "individualism" of these thinkers, Bosanquet argues, is based on a false understanding of the individual or self. For them, the individual is what it *prima facie* appears to be – something separate and cut-off from everything that surrounds it. The political problem becomes one of fencing this individuality off from outside (i.e., social) forces; of protecting the purely private individual from the intrusion of government. But a completely different conception of the self and of individuality breathes in Bosanquet's (and of course Hegel's) philosophy. No longer is this private, negative, and exclusive self taken to be the locus of individuality.

> It is not in the nooks and recesses of the sensitive self, when the man is most withdrawn from things and persons and wrapped up in the intimacies of his feeling, that he enjoys and asserts his individual self to the full. This idea is a caricature of the genuine experience of individuality. It is true that to feel your individuality is to feel something distinctive, which gives you a hold and substance in yourself and a definite position among others, and, it may be, against them. But on careful consideration, it will be found that this substance and position are always maintained by some kind of determinate achievement or expansion on the part of the self. It always comes from taking hold of the world in some definite way; which just because it is definite and affirmative, is at once a distinct assertion of the self, and a transition from the private self into the great community of reality.[95]

We have been considering the so-called idealist theory of the state and the doctrine of will and self that goes along with it. We were led to take this path by some remarks of Oakeshott's concerning the lack of a coherent theory of volition in Hobbes. This lack, he indicated, has to some extent been remedied in the reflections of Rousseau and Hegel and Bosanquet on the "general" or "rational" or "real" will. And it was in the direction suggested by such idealist reflection that he saw "the most profound movement in modern political philosophy." That this assessment is Oakeshott's considered opinion and not a stray overstatement may be verified by looking at some of his other writings at the time. In a review of a book on Bosanquet, for example, he writes that the "so-called Idealist theory of the State is the only theory which has paid thoroughgoing attention to all the problems which must be considered by a theory of the State." And he goes on to say that Bosanquet's *Philosophical Theory of the State* remains "the most comprehensive account" of this idealist theory of the state, picking out for special emphasis the "philosophy of self" I underlined above. "[I]t is its thorough consideration of the self which distinguishes [Bosanquet's] theory from the so-called 'individualistic' theories, which are inclined to treat the self as something too important to be examined."[96]

Clearly Oakeshott has much sympathy with the idealist project in political philosophy. Nevertheless, it is not to be inferred from this that he finds nothing wrong with the idealist theory of the state as it stands with Bosanquet. In fact, he indicates pretty clearly that he does find something wrong with the theory, though exactly what he does not say. Here is the whole passage from which I have quoted only partially above:

> [The] so-called Idealist theory of the State is the only theory which has paid thoroughgoing attention to all the problems which must be considered by a theory of the State, *and at the same time is a theory which has yet to receive a satisfactory statement.* And any attempt to understand *The Philosophical Theory of the State*, which still remains (with all its defects) the most comprehensive account of this theory, is a useful preliminary to restatement.[97]

One reads this passage with the sense that it provides an important clue to the starting-point of Oakeshott's own reflections on law, politics, and the state. If only we knew what it was that he finds unsatisfactory about Bosanquet's theory! This we will not know definitively, however, until we have examined in detail Oakeshott's most complete statement of his political philosophy, *On Human Conduct*, which I take to be the restatement of the idealist theory of the state demanded in the passage above. Here I can only anticipate.

We will find, I think, that Oakeshott departs from his idealist predecessors in his greater skepticism toward the state and its role in what is called "self-realization." This is not to say that he retreats to the negative "individualism" criticized by the idealists or denies the correlativity of state and individual. But he does reject the substantive theory of human nature which seems to lurk in the idealist doctrine of self-realization and of the "real will." And he rejects the substantive or purposive character this doctrine of human nature seems to impose on the state.[98] There is in thinkers like Bosanquet and Green – Hegel is, of course, much more ambiguous – a tendency to identify the "real will" which the state embodies with wisdom.[99] And it is precisely this identification of the state with reason or wisdom that we will see Oakeshott vehemently deny. Indeed, we already have some indication of this in Oakeshott's writings on Hobbes, where authority and wisdom are sharply distinguished. That he displays such a positive attitude toward Hobbes is yet another indication of Oakeshott's divergence from Bosanquet and Green, who tend to see Hobbes as an absolutist.[100] For Oakeshott, Hobbes's skeptical doctrine of authority seems to serve as an antidote to the "telocratic" tendencies of the idealists. And Oakeshott's political philosophy may perhaps be understood as an attempt to synthesize these two seemingly divergent strands of thought.

But that is the burden of another chapter. For the moment I would like to conclude this one by considering briefly a long review Oakeshott wrote of J. D. Mabbott's *The State and the Citizen*.[101] The book may no longer be familiar to political theorists today (though it is a good book), but the review conveniently brings together many of the themes which have flickered through this chapter. It also serves to underline the deep Hegelian strains we have been pursuing in Oakeshott's political thought.

The review begins, conveniently enough, where we have just left off: with Bosanquet. Oakeshott remarks that since "the publication of Bosanquet's *The Philosophical Theory of the State* no general work on political philosophy by an English writer has impressed those interested in the subject as being of first-class importance." This fact he finds remarkable "because Bosanquet's work did not leave the subject in so firm a state of equilibrium that it was difficult to know in what direction advance was to be made: the book was recognised to have grave defects, though its most important shortcomings were not those which its contemporary critics fastened on."[102] The reference to Bosanquet is not irrelevant to the book under consideration. Mabbott himself acknowledges that Green and Bosanquet have provided the starting-point for his reflections on the state.[103] And the main theme of the book, the limits of state activity, as well as Mabbott's general approach to the question, certainly bespeaks their influence.

Mabbott takes as his starting-point the Hegelian doctrine of the

state, which he characterizes as locating the whole of a man's duty in
service to the common good, and which he seems to associate with
political absolutism or "totalitarianism." Rejecting this doctrine of
the "maximum city" (as Oakeshott calls it), he sets out "to determine
the principle of the *limits* of State activity." He finds such a principle –
after rejecting the doctrine of natural rights and Green's and Bosanquet's doctrine of the immorality of compulsion – in the notion of non-
social goods or values; goods or values which either lie beyond social
control (like motives) or are ends in themselves and therefore exempt
from social control (like truth, beauty, and religion). The state is
limited by its inability to procure such non-social goods. Further, it is
limited by duties such as keeping promises and paying back debts
which are not in the service of any association but owed to human
beings as human beings. Finally, Mabbott argues that even certain
social goods lie beyond the capacity of the state to procure. Foremost
among these is that solidarity of feeling which we generally associate
with the family or a small community. The state is too large, and
relies too much on compulsion, to promote this kind of solidarity. In
this connection, Mabbott severely criticizes the notion that the unity
of the state springs from a general will, a corporate self, or a group
mind.[104]

Oakeshott has three general criticisms of Mabbott's argument,
all of which reveal something important about his own approach to
political philosophy. The first concerns Mabbott's idea of political
philosophy, in particular his understanding of the relationship of
political philosophy to the other social sciences. Political philosophy is
said to be a "part" of social theory (anthropology, social psychology,
economics, and jurisprudence being other "parts") with a subject-
matter and method of its own.[105] And it comes as no surprise, after
following the arguments of *Experience and its Modes* and "The Concept
of a Philosophical Jurisprudence," that Oakeshott finds this emphasis
on "exclusive areas" "unfortunate." For him, as we have learned,
political philosophy is not simply one mode of inquiry among others;
it doesn't simply occupy its own exclusive "field." Nor does political
philosophy simply lie alongside other types of inquiry into law and
politics; it somehow supersedes them. Whatever the relationship between anthropology and economics is, Oakeshott argues, "it cannot
. . . be the same as the relationship of either to political philosophy.
Whatever else it is, political philosophy cannot be what is left over
when the social sciences have staked their claims."[106]

Oakeshott also objects to the fact that Mabbott sometimes speaks
as though the principles discovered by the political philosopher were
capable of being "applied" or "followed." And yet Mabbott begins
his book with the rather Oakeshottian image of the philosopher as
climbing the stairs of a cathedral tower. As he climbs, all the things

which were apparent at ground level (conscience, duty, law, liberty) are completely transformed or shrink to invisibility.[107] But, Oakeshott asks, if philosophy has this transformative effect on our commonsense concepts (as he thinks it does), how can we speak of "applying" the view we had from the top of the tower after reaching the ground again?[108] The concrete knowledge of the philosopher has no relevance to the abstract world of common sense or practice; to pass directly from one world to the other is, in the language of *Experience and its Modes*, to commit an *ignoratio elenchi*.

Mabbott does not draw the line between theory and practice quite as sharply as Oakeshott would have it drawn, and his "lapses into an irrelevant practical attitude" are duly noticed. The "doctrine of the 'maximum city' (which Mr. Mabbott attributes to Hegel) is desig- nated as 'political absolutism' or 'totalitarianism', and its professors are said 'to *make* the State . . . the supreme and unique focus of man's loyalty and affection' and to *advocate* complete government control of all activities." Mabbott discusses the theory of natural rights "as if it were . . . an attempt to *set* a limit to the activity of the State." And finally, "Hobbes is said to have 'a low and cynical view of human nature'." Now, Oakeshott finds in all this a confusion of between the practical and philosophical attitudes. Philosophy he defines here as "saying something such that, if true, things would be as they are";[109] the transformation it effects is in the realm of thought, not in the realm of practice. Philosophy does not *make*, *advocate*, or *set limits* to anything. There is a crucial difference, Oakeshott writes,

> between the point of view from which one might assert that "the State is an association of a certain character, therefore its place in our lives is such and such, and if we observe it to be taking a place which *ex hypothesi* it cannot take then there is something wrong with our observation", and the point of view from which one might assert that "the State is an association of a certain character, but since the exercise of that character is not necessarily beneficial, we need to consider what it should be permitted to do and for this we require some information beyond our information about its character". The first of these points of view I believe to be philo- sophical, and it is the point of view of Plato, of Hobbes, of Spinoza and of Hegel. The second is merely a view of the proper functions of government, and if we adopt it we may hope to be able to say whether a law is good or bad but we cannot prevent ourselves being led into all sorts of cir- cumstantial considerations, and our conclusions . . . will be far from permanent.[110]

So far we have considered only the first of Oakeshott's criticisms of Mabbott's book, his criticism of Mabbott's idea of political philos- ophy. His second criticism is closely connected with it, going to what seems to be the "root presupposition" of Mabbott's philosophical method: namely, that "everything is what it is, and not another thing."[111] Mabbott never really frees himself from this "realistic" premise (which is also the premise of much analytic moral and political philosophy). "Everywhere there is an attempt to circumscribe, to determine limits; and the relations between things are always taken to be external to the things themselves." As a consequence, his world has "a strangely atomistic appearance: external and internal, self and others, social and non-social, are assigned separate compartments"; and "no activity is permitted to have any relevant consequences beyond its intended consequences."[112]

For Oakeshott, this atomistic presupposition is particularly evident in the way that Mabbott handles "the individual" and his relationship to the state. And here Oakeshott's criticism closely parallels Bosanquet's criticism of the "individualism" of Bentham and Mill. For Mabbott, the individual is what he *prima facie* appears to be, namely, private and self-contained. "Each self is what it is, and not another thing. Its relations with other selves may determine what it does, but not what it is." But this private and exclusive individual of which we are immediately aware, Oakeshott argues, is an abstraction; it is what appears (returning to the metaphor of the cathedral tower) at ground level. A more concrete view discloses that this "private individual" is by no means absolute or self-contained. The "private individual" as Oakeshott understands him

> is an institution, a social, indeed, for the most part a legal, creation, whose desires, emotions, ideas, intelligence, are social in their constitution. Nothing, I take it, is more certain than that this individual would collapse, like a body placed in a vacuum, if he were removed from the "external" world which is the condition of his existence.[113]

And he denies that this philosophical – one might also say historical – conception of the individual has anything to do with psychological notions of a "group mind" or "corporate personality" associated with thinkers like Gierke. Indeed, it is just such bogus notions that he considers to have hindered genuine reflection on the nature of the individual.[114]

Oakeshott's third and final criticism concerns Mabbott's distinction between social and non-social goods and his belief that there are certain duties which human beings owe to one another as human beings and not as members of a particular association. Once again he finds a certain amount of abstraction and atomism here. Is there any human activity or value which is simply non-social, that is, without social consequences and insulated from social conditions? Oakeshott does not think so. Neither art nor religion, for example, is isolable from social consequences or able to be insulated from social conditions in this way. And the same goes for the motives which accompany our actions. "[N]o association and certainly not the State, is indifferent to the motives of its members." Certain motives (like conscientiousness, for example) are sanctioned by the state and considered to be social goods. And in the absence of social sanction or recognition such motives will lose their value. For Oakeshott, no value is "naturally" or "intrinsically" or "absolutely" valuable. To posit "absolute values" or "intrinsic goods" is to relapse into the same error that is involved in the error of "natural rights." Even where artistic, scientific, and religious activity is "free" of government control, such freedom "is the gift of the State"; just as the freedom of the individual is the gift of the state and not a natural inheritance. Given this radically historical view of the nature of value, Oakeshott's rejection of the notion of duties human beings owe to one another as human beings and not as members of a particular association should not be difficult to understand.[115]

Oakeshott concludes his review by saying that though he too does not believe that service to the common good adequately expresses the whole of a man's duty, he does not think that Mabbott "has succeeded in detecting the principle of its inadequacy."[116] The positive element in this statement, as well as the critical assessment, must be attended to. Oakeshott obviously sympathizes with Mabbott's attempt to define the limits of state activity, or at least the limited role the state can play in man's overall practical destiny. And the fact that Mabbott rejects "natural rights" as a principle of limitation also seems to appeal to him. In this regard, Mabbott can be seen as continuing the line of thought taken by Green and Bosanquet (though in Bosanquet the *limits* of the state are not always emphasized). Nevertheless, it is clear from his review that Oakeshott does not think Mabbott has completely freed himself from the abstraction and atomism which characterize the "natural rights" approach. The abstract notion of the "private" self and of "private" spheres of activity creeps into his theory and is really at the core of his distinction between social and non-social goods. A more concrete solution to the problem of the state and its relation to the individual must be sought. In what direction we do not as yet know. We must follow Oakeshott in his reflections on rationalism to see if they provide a clue.

IV

RATIONALISM, TRADITION, AND POLITICS

In this chapter I will concern myself with Oakeshott's critique of rationalism and the account of practical (mainly moral and political) activity which emerges in the course of it. This, of course, is more familiar ground than that covered in the previous two chapters, and it has already provoked considerable discussion amongst philosophers and scholars. Nevertheless, it does not seem to me that Oakeshott's position has been completely understood, and I wish at the outset to point out some of the more common errors which my exposition seeks to avoid.

Perhaps the greatest obstacle to understanding Oakeshott's critique of rationalism has been the failure to grasp its distinctiveness. Too easily has his critique been assimilated to the multitude of attacks on rationalism, scientism, and utopianism which our century (especially since World War II) has produced. As we shall see, Oakeshott himself takes some care in specifying what he means by "rationalism" and in distinguishing his critique from others resting on different (or less) philosophical premises. For now it is enough to indicate that the distinctiveness of his critique lies in its being rooted in the general philosophical view we have already spent a considerable amount of time analyzing. Consequently, a good deal of my analysis in this chapter will be devoted to bringing out this philosophical root and continuity.[1] In trying to understand Oakeshott's critique of rationalism, it is not enough to fix exclusively on what it is directed *against*; the distinctiveness of the critique lies in the reasons (as Oakeshott himself might put it) upon which it rests.

A similar consideration applies when we turn to the positive doctrine which lies behind Oakeshott's critique of rationalism, the positive account of practical activity which this critique implies. Here too a concern with conclusions instead of reasons has predominated. For many, "What is Oakeshott *for?*" seems to be the only interesting question. And we do not have to wait long for the answer that he is "for" tradition; that he "appeals to" or "celebrates" tradition; that he is a "traditionalist." Comparisons with Burke inevitably follow. Once again the distinctiveness of Oakeshott's position is swallowed up in the chatter of pro and con. Few take time to figure out what he might mean by "tradition" or to wonder whether it even makes sense to describe him as "appealing" to it. It must be admitted, though, that the word "tradition" lends itself to this sort of unphilosophical inter-pretation; and this no doubt is one of the reasons why Oakeshott later chooses to abandon it.[2] Be that as it may, it is still quite clear from the essays in *Rationalism in Politics* that "tradition" for Oakeshott is a philosophical concept and not simply a practical option; and it is as such that I intend to approach it in my discussion. There are, of course, critics who question whether Oakeshott's analysis is "purely philosophical," and I shall try to address this point in the course of my discussion.

This approach ultimately bears on the question as to whether Oakeshott is to be considered a "Burkean conservative" or not. That Oakeshott has affinities with Burke is indisputable. Nevertheless, it seems to me that Oakeshott's "traditionalism" ultimately has a different source than that of Burke. Oakeshott's notion of tradition arises, as we shall see, out of a philosophical analysis of human activity; it has nothing to do (as Burke's notion of tradition does) with a belief in the goodness, wisdom, rationality, or providential character of history. Nor is Oakeshott's "conservatism" ultimately to be identi-fied with that of Burke, as Oakeshott himself makes clear in his essay "On Being Conservative." Oakeshott's conservatism has more in common with the skeptical conservatism of Montaigne, Hobbes, and Hume than with the religious or cosmic conservatism of Burke.[3] The exact nature of Oakeshott's conservatism and how it differs from other current conceptions is a theme that will occupy us throughout this chapter.

In thus distinguishing Oakeshott, I do not mean, however, to isolate him from current philosophical debate. It is quite clear that his reflections on rationalism are extremely pertinent to the whole issue of human rationality that has moved to the center of philosophical debate. This debate over the nature of human rationality has recently been canvassed by Richard Bernstein in his book *Beyond Objectivism and Relativism*.[4] And though Bernstein focuses on Hans-Georg Gadamer, Jürgen Habermas, Richard Rorty, and Hannah Arendt in his analysis, the common tendencies that he discerns in these writers – the rejection of the Cartesian preoccupation with certainty and method, the replacement of a technical conception of rationality with a more practical and contextual conception, the emphasis on *phronēsis* and judgment – could all be ascribed to Oakeshott in one form or another. Indeed, Bernstein's formula of "beyond objectivism and relativism" is about as good as any in characterizing Oakeshott's overall philosophical project. Among the writers Bernstein discusses, it is probably Gadamer – with his rejection of the Enlightenment contrasts of reason and prejudice, reason and tradition, and reason and authority[5] – with whom Oakeshott shares the most. In any event, it is a comparison I pursue briefly below. Closer to home, I also note where Oakeshott's reflections on rationality parallel those of certain of his contemporaries in England such as Gilbert Ryle, Michael Polanyi, and Friedrich Hayek.

Apart from these very general considerations, it should be kept in mind that the analysis of *Rationalism in Politics* in this chapter is intended ultimately to shed light on the questions raised toward the end of the last chapter and on the answers Oakeshott provides in *On Human Conduct*. Though initially we must concern ourselves with Oakeshott's concept and critique of rationalism in general, gradually our focus will narrow to politics and political philosophy. The transition to more political themes takes place in the third section of this chapter. In the first two sections the meaning of rationalism and the critique of rationalism are explored.

1. Rationalism and the Predicament of Our Time

For Oakeshott, our predicament, both moral and political, is characterized in terms of "rationalism"; and our first task must be to figure out what he means by "rationalism" and the grounds upon which he rejects it. In carrying out this task, however, a small difficulty confronts us – a difficulty of exposition really. Oakeshott's definition and critique of rationalism is contained for the most part in *Rationalism in Politics*. But *Rationalism in Politics* is a collection of essays written at different times and for different occasions. Each essay takes up the problem of rationalism from a slightly different vantage point and with a slightly different interest. This makes for some difficulty in expounding Oakeshott's doctrine. Should the essays be melted down in a single pot and made to compose (what Oakeshott himself says they do not) a single, settled doctrine? This is the procedure that is usually followed. But I have chosen instead to leave the essays as much integrity as possible. This results in a certain amount of repetition, but I also think it gives a better picture of the manner of Oakeshott's argument, of the way he goes about considering the problem. I begin with the earlier essays "Rationalism in Politics" (1947) and "The Tower of Babel" (1948), in which the nature of our predicament and rationalism are for the most part described and defined. In the next section I take up in somewhat greater detail the more philosophical essays "Rational Conduct" (1950) and "Political

Education" (1951), in which Oakeshott's critique of rationalism is fully developed. At the end of the second section I consider some of the more common criticisms that have been made of Oakeshott's critique of rationalism and of the concept of tradition which is correlative to it.

Let us start with "Rationalism in Politics." The essay is concerned with considering "the character and pedigree of the most remarkable intellectual fashion of post-Renaissance Europe," namely, rationalism, more specifically, modern rationalism. Further, it is concerned with considering the impact of this intellectual "fashion" or "style" on European politics, where it seems to have had its greatest influence.[6] Let us look at the intellectual style, rationalism in general, first.

Rationalism involves, of course, the belief that all activity should be guided by reason, by the belief that reason alone is sovereign and authoritative. But it is not simply this belief in reason but the particular way in which reason is understood that defines rationalism. The "hidden spring" of rationalism, Oakeshott argues, is a doctrine about human knowledge. In order to explicate this doctrine, he distinguishes two sorts of knowledge, both of which he says are involved in all concrete activity. The first sort – which he calls technical knowledge or knowledge of technique – consists entirely of formulated rules, principles, or maxims. It is the sort of knowledge which can be found in and learned from books, whether they be legal codes, cookbooks, or books containing the rules of method for an intellectual discipline. The second sort of knowledge in all concrete activity Oakeshott calls "practical" knowledge (also "traditional" knowledge), "because it exists only in use, is not reflective and (unlike technique) cannot be formulated in rules." No concrete activity, whether it be cookery, art, science, or politics, can be carried on simply with a knowledge of the technique. There is always something else – Oakeshott calls it variously style, connoisseurship, artistry, judgment – which tells us not only how and when to apply the rules but also when to leave the rules behind.[7]

I will have occasion to return to and expand upon this notion of practical or traditional knowledge – which not only recalls Aristotle's notion of *phronēsis* but also has obvious parallels with Ryle's "knowing how"[8] and Polanyi's "tacit knowledge"[9] – in the course of my discussion. For now it is important only to point out that Oakeshott identifies rationalism with the denial of the epistemic value of such practical knowledge. The only sort of knowledge the rationalist recognizes is technical knowledge. Thus, the rationalist's belief in the sovereignty of reason really turns out to be a belief in the sovereignty of technique. It is this belief in the sovereignty of technique, not the belief in reason per se, which fundamentally defines rationalism for Oakeshott.[10]

Why is the rationalist so bewitched by technique? Oakeshott argues that the reason has to do with the rationalist's preoccupation with certainty. The charm of technique lies in its apparent certainty and self-completeness. Technical knowledge seems to rest on nothing outside of itself, building directly on pure ignorance, the empty (or emptied) mind. But this apparent certainty and self-completeness of technical knowledge is an illusion. Knowledge of a technique does not spring from pure ignorance; it presupposes and is a reformulation of knowledge which is already there. "Nothing, not even the most nearly self-contained technique (the rules of a game), can in fact be imparted to an empty mind; and what is imparted is nourished by what is already there." It is only by ignoring or forgetting the total context of our knowledge that a technique can be made to appear self-contained and certain.[11]

This is but the kernel of Oakeshott's critique of rationalism, a kernel which he develops more philosophically and at greater length in later essays. But here he says he is not concerned to refute rationalism; he is concerned to specify its character more precisely. Rationalism, as we have learned, consists essentially in the belief in the sovereignty of technique. What is the historical genesis of this belief? And how and with what effect did it come to invade European politics? These are the questions Oakeshott addresses next.

Though the exact origins of rationalism cannot be fixed (to seek origins is always a "misdirection of inquiry"),[12] the moment of its "unmistakable emergence" can. For Oakeshott (as for so many other critics of rationalism), this moment is the early seventeenth century, when the project of finding a "consciously formulated technique of research," a mistake-proof method, first took hold. Bacon and Descartes are the dominating figures in setting this project on foot, though their writings also indicate (besides a belief in the sovereignty of technique) a certain awareness of the limitations of technical knowledge. It was more what was made of their teachings by lesser men, Oakeshott argues, rather than what these great men themselves actually believed that gave unmistakable rise to modern rationalism. Bacon and Descartes are among "les grands hommes" mentioned in the epigraph to the essay who, "en apprenant aux faibles à réfléchir, les ont mis sur la route de l'erreur."[13]

So much for the historical genesis of rationalism in general. But Oakeshott is concerned to tell the story not simply of the emergence of a new intellectual fashion or style but of its invasion into other departments of life, most importantly politics. No area of human activity, he maintains, has been more affected by rationalism than politics. Contemporary politics he believes are thoroughly rationalistic; no party, project, or political programme seems to have escaped its insidious influence. "Rationalism has ceased to be merely one style in politics and has become the stylistic criterion of all respectable politics."[14] But what exactly does rationalism in politics consist in?

Oakeshott characterizes rationalistic politics in a number of different, though connected, ways in the essay. They are characterized in the first place as the "politics of the felt need": politics as the discontinuous application of "reason" to the felt (and sometimes manufactured) need, problem, or crisis of the moment. They are also characterized as "the politics of perfection" in combination with "the politics of uniformity": the rationalist believes not only that there is a single best (i.e., "rational") solution for every political problem but that this solution should be universally applied. But by far the most significant characterization of rationalist politics for Oakeshott is that they are ideological politics, "the politics of the book." The rationalist's belief in the sovereignty of technique translates in politics into the belief in the superiority of an ideology over a tradition or habit of behavior. The superiority of an ideology, like that of a technique, is thought to lie in its being self-contained, "rational" through and through. But this we know not to be true. An ideology, far from being self-contained or independently premeditated, itself presupposes a tradition of behavior and is merely an abridgement of it.[15]

What circumstances, then, account for rationalism's overwhelming success in dominating European politics? Oakeshott traces the appeal of rationalism (i.e., of ideologies and of technique) in politics to the incursion of the politically inexperienced into politics. He gives three examples: the new ruler, the new ruling class, and the new political society. In the case of the new ruler it was Machiavelli who supplied the need for a technique of politics, a "crib" to make up for the ruler's lack of political education and traditional knowledge. Machiavelli thus takes his place alongside Bacon and Descartes as one of "les grands hommes." And like them, he too shows an awareness of the limitations of technical knowledge which his followers lack: "to the new prince he offered not only his book, but also, what would make up for the inevitable deficiencies of his book – himself: he never lost the sense that politics, after all, are diplomacy, not the application of a technique." As examples of cribs for new and politically inexperienced social classes, Oakeshott cites Locke's *Second Treatise* and the work of Marx and Engels, the latter two providing "for the instruction of a less politically educated class than any other that has ever come to have the illusion of exercising political power." Finally, Oakeshott shows how the circumstances of a new political society such as the United States at its founding favored the emergence of a rationalistic politics based on self-conscious reflection and abstract principles.[16]

Political inexperience, then, has led to the dominance of the rationalistic attitude in European and American politics. What has been the effect of this dominance? Oakeshott is strangely brief on this score, though the conviction that it has been disastrous lies barely beneath the surface of the entire essay. One could, of course, point to the examples of the Communist regime in the Soviet Union and the then recently defeated National Socialist regime in Germany, but Oakeshott seems to have more than these disasters in mind. "The view I am maintaining is that the ordinary practical politics of European nations has become fixed in a vice of Rationalism," and "that much of their failure (which is often attributed to other and more immediate causes) springs in fact from the defects of the rationalist character when it is in control of affairs."[17] The crux of Oakeshott's diagnosis of our current political predicament here seems to be that we have lost control over our affairs; that European politics have come to be characterized by an ever increasing irrationality and arbitrariness. This has happened because what the rationalist takes for the whole of knowledge is really only a part, and not the most important part at that. The more we have become enslaved to technique and ideology, the more impoverished our concrete knowledge of how to act and conduct our affairs has become. To paraphrase a passage from another essay of Oakeshott's: the political energy of our civilization has for many centuries been applied to building a Tower of Babel; and in a world dizzy with political ideologies we know less about how to behave in the public realm than ever before.[18] Our moral and political predicament, then, is one of great confusion; and this confusion stems not so much from a pervasive relativism (as some writers have suggested)[19] as from an erroneous belief about the self-sufficiency of technical or ideological knowledge. So Oakeshott seems to argue.

And what of the prospects of escaping this predicament? Given that political inexperience has promoted rationalism in politics, it does not seem likely that we will escape our predicament as long as this circumstance remains unchanged. And Oakeshott sees little chance that it will change. The peculiar viciousness of rationalism is that it destroys the only knowledge which could possibly save it from itself, namely, concrete or traditional knowledge. Rationalism only serves to deepen the inexperience out of which it was originally generated.[20]

What bodes particularly ill for an early release from our predicament is the increasing hold rationalism has taken on education itself. For the rationalist, education is not "an initiation into the moral and intellectual habits of his society, an entry into the partnership between present and past, a sharing of concrete knowledge"; it is a "training in technique." Oakeshott has, of course, written some eloquent essays defending the universities from the rationalistic attempt to transform them into "training" centers.[21] But here he is more concerned to point out the victory rationalism has won in the field of morality and moral education, a victory he finds particularly disturbing because the opponent of rationalism "hardly recognizes it as a defeat." The morality of the rationalist is, of course, "the morality of the self-conscious pursuit of moral ideals," and the education which belongs to it is an education by precept and in moral principles. And though this self-conscious morality is often thought to be superior to habit or "the unselfconscious following of a tradition of moral behaviour," Oakeshott argues that it is really only "morality reduced to a technique, to be acquired by a training in an ideology rather than an education in behaviour"; it is "the desiccated relic of what was once the unselfconscious moral tradition of an aristocracy who, ignorant of ideals, had acquired a habit of behaviour in relation to one another and had handed it on in a true moral education." Moral ideals are no more independent and self-contained than a political ideology or technique of research; they are a "sediment," having significance "only so long as they are suspended in a religious or social tradition." By "drawing off the liquid in which our moral ideals were suspended (and pouring it away as worthless)," Oakeshott argues, the rationalists have succeeded in destroying "the only living root of moral behaviour."[22]

In some ways this latter consideration of the morality of the rationalist leads in a direction slightly different from the rest of the essay. Indeed, it leads in the direction of "The Tower of Babel," an essay in which our current predicament is given a slightly different interpretation than it is in "Rationalism in Politics." Before going on to this essay, I would like to dwell for a moment on the diagnosis of our predicament in "Rationalism in Politics" and on how it differs from another (and more common) diagnosis – and one with which it could easily be confused.

Oakeshott has not, of course, been the only one to diagnose our current predicament in terms of "rationalism." Nevertheless, his diagnosis does not exactly coincide with that of other writers who can be found deploying this term or its equivalents.[23] Typically these critics of "rationalism" or "scientism" trace our predicament to the rise of the authority of natural science in our civilization and to the consequent application of its methods to human affairs. Oakeshott, however, finds this simple view of the matter mistaken.[24] Indeed, as we have already seen, he tells quite a different story of the historical genesis of rationalism. He also rejects the critique which usually accompanies this simple diagnosis: the argument that a science of society or politics is impossible because of the inherent irrationality, unpredictability, intractability, contingency, complexity, subjectivity, or tragedy of human affairs.[25] (Hayek, whose critique of "scientism" parallels Oakeshott's critique of rationalism in so many ways, sometimes lapses into this view.)[26] We have already seen in *Experience and its Modes* that Oakeshott rejects any argument denying the possibility of a science of man or society which rests on the Kantian (or neo-Kantian) distinction between the realms of "spirit" and "nature."[27] Science is not a separate *kind* of experience concerned with a separate *part* of reality; it is the whole of experience (or reality) viewed from a limited or abstract standpoint. Oakeshott does not abandon his original view when he comes to consider modern rationalism. He does not attribute our predicament to science but to the belief in the sovereignty of technique. It is not the application of scientific methods to non-scientific material, nor the application of reason to what is inherently irrational, which fundamentally defines rationalism. Rationalism consists, rather, in a misunderstanding of reason itself, the mistaken identification of knowledge (even of scientific knowledge) with technique.

It has been argued by some that Oakeshott's characterization of rationalism is too wide or abstract to be useful.[28] This I think is wrong. That practically all our current political projects and deliberations are rationalistic is, of course, part of Oakeshott's point. But it does not follow from this that rationalism has no precise meaning or that Oakeshott does not envisage any alternative to it. As it is presented in "Rationalism in Politics," rationalism involves a definite belief about the nature of knowledge and reason (not some vague belief in reason simply) which emerged at a definite time in a definite place (early modern Europe) under the influence of some specific thinkers (Descartes and Bacon) who are by no means to be identified with the whole of modern European thought (Pascal is mentioned as an early critic of rationalism, and Hobbes we know Oakeshott does not put in the rationalist camp).[29] Oakeshott may, of course, be wrong about all this, but imprecise he is not.

Related to the above criticism is the charge that Oakeshott's rationalist represents a "fictitious adversary," a straw man, a mere caricature; that no sane person – certainly no thinker of any stature – has ever held such a ridiculous doctrine as "Rationalism."[30] Here I think the character of Oakeshott's portrait has been mistaken. The rationalist is not essentially defined by his extremity; he is defined by *what* he believes, not the excesses to which he carries his belief.[31] Once again the distinctiveness of Oakeshott's notion of rationalism has not been fully grasped. It is not simply reason (or the excesses of reason) which is under attack but a certain conception of reason – and one which I think Oakeshott rightly claims has "a respectable place in the history of philosophy" and has influenced the way ordinary men think and speak.[32]

Having specified a little more precisely the nature of Oakeshott's diagnosis of our predicament and what he means by rationalism, we may now turn to "The Tower of Babel." Here we encounter yet another diagnosis of our predicament, a diagnosis which, while not unrelated to that found in "Rationalism in Politics," seems to probe the condition of the modern European consciousness even more deeply. The essay takes up where "Rationalism in Politics" left off – with the morality of the rationalist. It will be remembered that Oakeshott observed there that what makes the victory of rationalism in the field of morality and moral education particularly dangerous is that the non-rationalist "hardly recognizes it as a defeat." It is not just the rationalist who finds the self-conscious pursuit of moral ideals to be a higher morality than that of the unselfconscious following of a tradition of moral behavior. The belief in the superiority of the former seems to be more deeply embedded in the European consciousness than even the seventeenth century and the rise of the intellectual fashion of rationalism. It is to this belief and its criticism that Oakeshott addresses himself in "The Tower of Babel."

His purpose, he tells us at the start of the essay, "is to consider the *form* of the moral life, and in particular the form of the moral life of contemporary Western civilization." But he begins first by making a crucial point about the nature of moral activity in general. Moral activity, he says, is

> activity which may be either good or bad. . . . It is conduct to which there is an alternative. This alternative need not be consciously before the mind; moral conduct does not necessarily involve the reflective choice of a particular action. Nor does it require that each occasion shall find a man without a disposition, or even without a predetermination, to act in a certain way; a man's affections and conduct may be seen to spring from his character without thereby ceasing to be moral. The freedom without which moral conduct is impossible is freedom from a natural necessity which binds *all* men to act alike.[33]

This is a crucial point because Oakeshott will be describing the moral life largely in terms of habit or custom, and it is important to realize from the start that this does not mean that he fails to notice a distinction between moral activity and a natural process, or (as he will later put it in *On Human Conduct*) between human conduct and mere behavior. Moral conduct for Oakeshott is art, not nature; it is the exercise of an acquired skill. But that moral conduct is conduct to which there is an alternative does not mean that this alternative need be consciously before the mind, or that our actions be preceded by self-conscious reflection and choice. There is nothing in the notions of habit, disposition, custom, or character which is inconsistent with the freedom presupposed by moral conduct or by human conduct in general.[34]

Now, the form of our (Western) moral life, Oakeshott maintains, is a mixture of two ideal extremes – a mixture in which one extreme predominates over the other – and he proposes first to consider each of these two ideal forms of morality separately. The first form he considers is that of customary morality, the morality of a habit of behavior. It is perhaps most easily described in terms of what it is not: it is not self-conscious, it is not reflective, it knows nothing of moral ideals or principles. It is, in short, simply "acting in accordance with a certain habit of behavior"; "the unreflective following of a tradition of conduct in which we have been brought up." Nor (Oakeshott is quick to point out) is this a merely primitive form of morality; it is in fact "the form which moral action takes . . . in all the emergencies of life when time and opportunity for reflection are lacking." The kind of education which belongs to this form of morality – and of course education is necessary, since we have to do here with art, not nature – is not an education in principle or by precept; we do not acquire habits of conduct by learning rules. Rather, we acquire habits of conduct in much the same way that we learn our native language – continuously, unselfconsciously, imitatively. Indeed, the analogy with language informs Oakeshott's entire account of customary morality. Like a language, a tradition of customary behavior is highly elastic and adaptable, and from this stems its remarkable stability. Oakeshott denies the common view that customary behavior is rigid and unstable. "[C]ustom, we have been taught, is blind. It is, however, an insidious piece of misobservation; custom is not blind, it is only 'blind as a bat'." Nevertheless, he does admit that, because it is unselfconscious and unselfcritical, this form of morality is incapable of defending itself should crisis or superstition supervene.[35]

The second form of morality Oakeshott considers involves "the reflective application of a moral criterion," and can appear as either "the self-conscious pursuit of moral ideals" or as "the reflective observance of moral rules." This form of morality is in many ways simply the opposite of the first: where the first was all habit, this form is all reflection. Reflection is called for not only in determining and formulating the rules or ideals to be followed but also in applying them to concrete situations. Nor is it enough simply to know *what* to do, it is also important to know *why*, and therefore a good deal of energy is devoted in this form of morality to being able to defend the rules or ideals against criticism. The education which belongs to this form of morality is, accordingly, an education in the detection and appreciation of moral ideals, in the application or translation of these ideals, and finally in their intellectual management.[36]

Reflective morality, Oakeshott confesses, certainly has one advantage over customary morality: it is better equipped to defend itself against superstition and crisis. But it also has its dangers. Chief amongst these is its tendency to inhibit, undermine, or otherwise paralyze action.

[T]ogether with the certainty about how to *think* about moral ideals, must be expected to go a proportionate uncertainty about how to *act*. The constant analysis of behaviour tends to undermine, not only prejudice in moral habit, but moral habit itself, and moral reflection may come to inhibit moral sensibility.

Beyond this fundamental defect, a morality of ideals (not so much of rules) is also perfectionist, and this makes it particularly dangerous for a whole society (as opposed to an individual) to adopt. Also, unlike a morality of custom, a morality of ideals is relatively inelastic and incapable of adapting to change; its virtue and its vice is its rigidity, its imperviousness to change. Finally, in a morality of ideals a single moral ideal is liable to become an obsession to the exclusion of other ideals; purity and intellectual coherence are prized above the impure coherence of a complex whole or system.[37]

Though it may seem from this that Oakeshott prefers the first form of morality to the second, in fact he regards neither, taken alone, as a likely (or even a desirable) form of the moral life. They are ideal extremes, concrete morality consisting in some sort of combination of them both.[38] Oakeshott does, however, wish to recommend a mixture in which the first extreme is dominant. In such a mixture, he argues,

[a]ction will retain its primacy, and, whenever it is called for, will spring from habit of behaviour. Conduct itself will never become problematical, inhibited by the hesitations of ideal speculation or the felt necessity of bringing philosophic talent and the fruits of philosophic education to bear upon the situation.

Reflection and criticism will of course have roles in this form of moral life, but they will not usurp the place of moral habit; they will supplement it in the same way that a theology supplements a religious way of life.[39]

A less happy fate is envisaged for the mixed form in which the second extreme dominates. Moral criticism and speculation, Oakeshott believes, will have a disintegrating effect on moral habit. "When action is called for, speculation or criticism will supervene. Behaviour itself will tend to become problematical, seeking its self-confidence in the coherence of an ideology." In this mixed form of morality, moral ideals usurp the place of habits of behavior, and it is a role Oakeshott does not believe they can sustain. Why not? Because moral ideals are themselves the products of a habit or tradition of behavior. Here Oakeshott's argument parallels the argument he made in "Rationalism in Politics" against the supposed self-completeness and independence of technique. Moral ideals, he argues, do not exist in advance of moral activity; they "are not, in the first place, the products of reflective thought . . . they are the products of human behaviour, of human practical activity, to which reflective thought gives subsequent, partial and abstract expression in words." Torn from the concrete context of a tradition of behavior, moral ideals become increasingly incapable of determining behavior. What efficacy and determinacy they retain derives entirely from the traces of traditional behavior which continue to operate in them. "[T]he capital . . . upon which a morality of the pursuit of moral ideals goes into business has always been accumulated by a morality of habitual behaviour." By themselves, moral ideals cannot determine or generate human behavior; and a morality in which moral ideals are dominant "is not something which can stand on its own feet." "In such a morality, that which has power to rescue from superstition is given the task of generating human behaviour – a task which, in fact, it cannot perform."[40]

This critique of the morality of ideals (or of the morality in which ideals are dominant) recalls the critique of technique in "Rationalism in Politics," and I will have more to say about it when we come to consider "Rational Conduct" and "Political Education." But there are other and more famous echoes to be discerned in this critique of the morality of the self-conscious pursuit of moral ideals. The most notable of these is, of course, Hegel's critique of Kantian ethics and of the whole notion of "reflection" in morality. To the "subjectivity" of Kantian moral reflection Hegel opposed his notion of "objective spirit," expressing his position in the "provokingly simple formula" (as Gadamer puts it): morality is living in accordance with the customs of one's land.[41] This same hostility to subjective "reflection" informs Oakeshott's critique in "The Tower of Babel"; and the notion of tradition which he opposes to it in many ways resembles Hegel's notion of *Sittlichkeit*. Along the same lines, one can also hear in Oakeshott's critique echoes of Bradley's *Ethical Studies*, in which Hegel's critique of reflective morality is largely repeated.[42]

Of course, "The Tower of Babel" is not simply, or even primarily, a philosophical critique of a moral theory; it is a diagnosis of the moral predicament of our civilization. It is Oakeshott's view that the form of the moral life in the West is one in which the self-conscious pursuit of moral ideals is dominant, and that this fact accounts for much of its moral distraction. "The moral energy of our civilization has for many centuries been applied mainly (though not, of course, exclusively) to building a Tower of Babel; and in a world dizzy with moral ideals we know less about how to behave in public and in private than ever before."[43] When did this project get its start? As I have already indicated, Oakeshott goes well beyond the seventeenth century and the rise in the belief in the sovereignty of technique to discover the seeds of our morality of ideals. He goes, indeed, all the way back to the first four centuries of the Christian era – to the age in which the customary morality of the Greco-Roman world was losing its vitality and the age in which Christianity was transforming itself from a "way of life" for small communities into a world religion. Both circumstances, he argues, were met by an increase in moral self-consciousness and the construction of ideologies. Thus, practically from the start, European morality was determined by a morality of ideals instead of a morality of habitual behavior. Such a legacy is not to be easily overcome. But what makes it practically impossible to overcome, according to Oakeshott, is the pride and superiority with which we now regard this dominance of ideals in our moral life. And it is against this self-deception more than anything else that he writes.[44]

This, then, is Oakeshott's reading of the predicament of Western morals. It is a reading of our predicament which differs slightly from that found in "Rationalism in Politics," being in some ways more comprehensive. But the two accounts are not irreconcilable. The sources of our present discontents are multiple. The emergence in post-Renaissance Europe of the intellectual style of rationalism still seems to be the decisive event. But a belief in the superiority of the self-conscious pursuit of moral ideals – a belief with a slightly different provenance than that of rationalism itself – has made the rationalist's rhetoric and projects seem less strange. Both essays, of course, trace our current problems, moral and political, to the same fundamental source: namely, the belief in the sovereignty of technique or ideology over tradition or habit in the conduct of our affairs. In both essays Oakeshott has also indicated why he considers this belief to be erroneous; but his primary emphasis has been to characterize rather than to critique. It is to his critique of rationalism that we must now turn.

2. The Critique of Rationalism

In "Rationalism in Politics" and "The Tower of Babel" the alleged certainty, self-completeness and independence of a technique or ideology is denied. A technique or ideology is not certain, self-contained or self-complete; it depends on, implies or presupposes another kind of knowledge, of which it is only an abridgement or abstract or partial expression. In short, a technique or ideology does not disclose a concrete (that is to say, a self-complete or self-contained) manner of activity. This is the gist of Oakeshott's critique of rationalism, and it is time now to examine it more closely. I will do so, first, by considering the essays "Rational Conduct" and "Political Education," in which the critique is most fully and philosophically elaborated; and secondly, by considering some of the more common criticisms that have been made of this critique and of the notion of tradition which it presupposes.

It has already been pointed out that Oakeshott's critique of rationalism is not directed against reason per se but against a certain interpretation of reason, namely, the identification of reason with technique. It is this interpretation of reason (and of the epithet "rational" which goes along with it) that Oakeshott sets out to criticize and replace with a more adequate understanding in the essay "Rational Conduct." This done, he goes on to apply his understanding of rationality in general to human (i.e., moral and social) conduct in particular.

The view Oakeshott wishes to reject (and which for convenience we may attribute to Max Weber) "takes *purpose* as the distinctive mark of 'rationality' in conduct: 'rational' activity is behaviour in which an independently premeditated end is pursued and which is determined by that end."[45] To illustrate this view he takes the not simply amusing but genuinely illuminating example of bloomers, which in Victorian times were asserted to be the "rational" form of dress for girl bicyclists. Bloomers were thought to be especially "rational" because their design seemed to spring solely from independent reflection – undistracted by "irrelevant" considerations such as fashion, custom, or prejudice – on the specific problem of efficiently propelling a bicycle. Whether this was in fact the case will occupy Oakeshott later; for the moment he is interested only in the view of "rationality" disclosed in the example – a view which takes premeditated purpose as the hallmark of "rationality."[46]

What are the assumptions that lie behind this view of "rational" conduct? Oakeshott picks out one assumption in particular to emphasize, and it is to this assumption that a good part of his critique will be addressed. This view assumes, he argues, "that men have a power of reasoning about things," and "that this is a power independent of any other powers a man may have, and something from which his activity can *begin*." This power, sometimes hypostatized as "Reason," is assumed to be independent "not only of tradition . . . but also of the activity itself to which it is a preliminary." In short, what is being assumed here is a doctrine of the mind: the mind as a "neutral instrument," a "piece of apparatus," "intelligence," something that "can be separated from its contents and its activities." Oakeshott does not stint in evoking the image of the mind which lies behind the view he is considering, and perhaps quotation is unavoidable.

> The mind, according to this hypothesis, is an independent instrument capable of dealing with experience. Beliefs, ideas, knowledge, the contents of the mind, and above all the activities of men in the world, are not regarded as themselves mind, or as entering into the composition of mind, but as adventitious, posterior acquisitions of the mind, the results of mental activity which the mind might or might not have possessed or undertaken. The mind may acquire knowledge or cause bodily activity,

but it is something that may exist destitute of all knowledge, and in the absence of any activity; where it has acquired knowledge or provoked activity, it remains independent of its acquisition or its expression in activity. It is steady and permanent, while its filling is fluctuating and fortuitous.[47]

A doctrine of the mind, then, stands at the center of the view Oakeshott is considering, and it is on this doctrine that his criticism first fastens. He declares this neutral mind which only comes in time to acquire a "filling" to be a "fiction." "The instrumental mind does not exist." The mind cannot be separated from its contents or activities; it does not exist prior to these, it is constituted by them. "Mind as we know it is the offspring of knowledge and activity; it is composed entirely of thoughts." Take away the "filling" or the "knowledge" and what is left "is not a neutral, unprejudiced instrument, a pure intelligence, but nothing at all."[48] If Oakeshott's remarks here have the appearance of sheer assertion, it is because many of the arguments have already been disclosed in *Experience and its Modes*. Indeed, it is only in these critical passages on the rationalistic doctrine of the mind that the relationship between Oakeshott's critique of rationalism and his first work becomes clear. For if there is a view of the mind which may be said to inform the whole of *Experience and its Modes*, it is the view that the mind is inseparable from its contents, subject is inseparable from object. "Experience" in that book, it will be remembered, "stands for the concrete whole which analysis divides into 'experiencing' and 'what is experienced'." The relationship between "experiencing" and "what is experienced" is not that of cause and consequent but of complete and utter interdependence.[49]

The second criticism Oakeshott makes of the rationalistic view of rationality in conduct follows from the first and is already familiar to us from "Rationalism in Politics" and "The Tower of Babel." It, too, goes to the apparent independence and self-completeness of self-conscious reflection on conduct. The rationalist assumes that men have a power of reflecting abstractly about conduct, of considering and contemplating abstract propositions about conduct. That such a power exists Oakeshott does not doubt; but, he argues, "its prerequisite is conduct itself. This activity is not something that can exist in advance of conduct; it is the result of reflection upon conduct, the creature of subsequent analysis of conduct." And as such it can never be the *spring* of conduct. The spring of conduct is always a knowledge of how to go about an activity, and this "knowing how" (to use Ryle's apposite expression) can never be completely reduced to a set of propositions or a technique. Oakeshott invokes the familiar examples of the carpenter, the scientist, the painter, and the cook to show that it is not knowledge of propositions but a knowledge of how to decide (and even recognize) certain questions which governs their activity. "A cook is not a man who first has a vision of a pie and then tries to make it; he is a man skilled in cookery, and both his projects and his achievements spring from that skill."[50]

It is important to be clear as to the nature of Oakeshott's critique to this point. It goes not to what the rationalist is actually doing but to what he thinks he is doing. What is being criticized is not an actual way of behaving but an erroneous theory of behavior, a misdescription of concrete human behavior. What this theory takes to be a "rational" (that is, a valuable and desirable) mode of conduct Oakeshott does not regard as even a possible form of conduct. But if what the theory recommends cannot really be fulfilled, it will be asked, then what is the danger? Why bother criticizing the theory at all? Oakeshott answers this not unimportant question briefly, being more concerned with the theory than its practical effects. "The practical danger of an erroneous theory," he writes, "is not that it may persuade people to act in an undesirable manner, but that it may confuse activity by putting it on a false scent."[51]

We will have occasion later on to return to this point in connection with some criticisms that have been made of Oakeshott's critique. Now, though, we must follow Oakeshott as he tries to construct a more concrete view of human activity, a view which better describes what is actually going on in human conduct. It is only on the basis of what it is possible to do and what, in fact, we do do that a true understanding of rationality in conduct can be achieved. To carry us toward a more concrete view of human activity Oakeshott returns to the discussion of Victorian bloomers which he previously left unfinished.

Bloomers, it will be remembered, were asserted to be the "rational" form of dress for girl bicyclists. They were thought to have successfully solved the specific problem of efficiently propelling a bicycle; and this success was largely attributed to the fact that the designers of bloomers proceeded "rationally," allowing no irrelevant considerations (such as fashion or custom) to deflect them from pursuing the simple end in view. But was this in fact the case? Would not "shorts" have been a more "rational" solution to the problem? Why did the minds of the designers pause at bloomers instead of running on to shorts? Oakeshott interprets this arrest of invention not as a failure of "rationality" on the part of the designers but as an intimation of a more profound understanding of it. Though they themselves did not realize it, he argues, the question these designers were really trying to answer was not, "What garment is best adapted to the activity of propelling a bicycle of a certain design?" but the question, "What garment combines within itself the qualities of being well adapted to the activity of propelling a bicycle and of being suitable, all things considered, for an English girl to be seen in when riding a bicycle in

1880?" And it is this question, complex (involving more than a single simple consideration) and tied to time and place, that they succeeded in answering.[52]

But does this really carry us beyond the view that takes purpose and premeditation as the distinctive marks of rationality? Though this end, so much more complex and circumstantial than the original one, was not in fact premeditated by the dress-designers, there seems to be no reason why in principle it could not have been. We still have not achieved a concrete view of human activity, according to Oakeshott, though we have reached the limits of the bloomers example.[53] Accordingly, he turns his attention to the concrete activity of the historian, the scientist, the cook – these are his favorite examples – as well as to that of the politician and the man engaged in the ordinary conduct of his life. What can we learn about human activity from these examples?

In some ways Oakeshott simply reiterates in regard to these activities what he has already said about the priority of conduct to propositional or technical knowledge about conduct. The spring of the activity of these men is a non-technical, practical knowledge about how to go about answering and even asking certain questions. But he presents this view (which can easily degenerate into a meaningless formula) in such a way as to shed a little more light on how he is approaching the whole issue of rational conduct. If what he says about human activity is true, he asks, how have we gotten "the illusion that the activity of these and other men could spring from and be governed by an end, a purpose, or by rules independent of the activity itself and capable of being reflected upon in advance?" He suggests that the illusion is a product of that process of neglect and abstraction which attends any particular engagement of human activity. A man engaged in answering a particular question does not consider the implications of his project; he supposes this project to be the spring of his activity. "No man engaged in a particular task has in the forefront of his attention the whole context and implications of that engagement." If he did, Oakeshott argues, he would realize, first, that "in pursuing his particular project, his actions were being determined not solely by his premeditated end, but by what may be called the traditions of the activity to which his project belonged" – his skill in or knowledge of how to go about conducting the activity. Secondly (and more radically), though, he would realize that his project itself, and not simply the means by which he pursues it, derives from this knowledge of how to conduct an activity; it depends, in other words, on his being already *within* an activity. A problem is not something pre-given; it is itself the product of a skillful knowing how. A man who is not already a scientist, Oakeshott says, cannot formulate a scientific problem; and the same goes for history, cookery, etc.[54] This more radical implication takes us beyond the difficulty encountered in the bloomers example above. Whether the purpose is premeditated or not, it is never the *spring* of our activity, only a consequence.

As I mentioned above, Oakeshott's discussion here reveals how he is approaching the problem of rational conduct in general. More specifically, it reveals the connection between his reflections on activity in *Rationalism in Politics* and the view of philosophy (and experience) he expounded in *Experience and its Modes* and "The Concept of a Philosophical Jurisprudence." Oakeshott is concerned in this essay to elucidate the *implications* of human activity; and he frankly admits the discrepancy (which we have already seen to be a prominent feature of his philosophy of explanation) between the conclusions of such reflection and the beliefs of ordinary consciousness. The scientist, the historian, or the practical man is seldom aware of "the whole context and implications" of his actions or engagements. In philosophy, however, this normal process of neglect and abstraction is reversed and a concrete view of human activity disclosed. This critical or corrective feature of philosophical analysis is vividly illustrated when Oakeshott tells us that the question the Victorian designers of bloomers thought they were answering was not the question they were in fact answering.

But it is not only in philosophy that we pass beyond the abstract and foreshortened self-understanding of ordinary experience to a more concrete view of human activity. In history as well this concrete movement of thought takes place. And it is as much to historical experience as to anything else that I think Oakeshott's critique of rationalism and his positive account of rationality are owing. This is evident in the bloomers example above, which strictly speaking is an historical example. But in other places as well Oakeshott uses historical understanding to repair the abstraction which inevitably accompanies any particular engagement of human activity. Take for instance what he says about the historical naïveté of the American founders, who regarded as "the creation of their own unaided initiative" political arrangements which derived from "habits of behaviour they had in fact inherited."[55] A similar historical-mindedness reveals itself in marginal comments on the French and Russian revolutions. Regardless of what their leaders believed, historical analysis reveals these "revolutions" to be modifications of past circumstances rather than implementations of abstract designs or creations *ex nihilo*.[56] In short, history for Oakeshott discloses the degree to which our actions are governed, not by abstract ideas or purposes, but by concrete situations. The study of history leads away from the belief in the primacy of abstract ideas and purposes in generating human activity toward a more circumstantial and contextual view of human rationality.

Let us return from this methodological digression to "Rational Conduct." What Oakeshott's reflections on the implications of human activity has disclosed is that particular actions, problems, and projects all presuppose activity itself. "A particular action . . . never begins in particularity, but always in an idiom or a tradition of activity." We do not begin by independently premeditating an end or purpose to which we then self-consciously direct our activity; we begin with a knowledge of how to go about an activity, and all our purposes, problems, and projects derive from that original knowledge. Rationality is, accordingly, defined by Oakeshott as "faithfulness to the knowledge we have of how to conduct the specific activity we are engaged in." Such "faithfulness," however, does not imply that there is nothing more to be achieved in activity, no improvement to be made. The knowledge with which we begin is never "fixed and finished"; it is fluid, both coherent and incoherent, and rational conduct is conduct which contributes to and enhances its coherence. It is only when this "knowledge how" is mistakenly conceived in terms of fixed and finished rules and principles that "faithfulness" becomes mere and deadly imitation.[57]

Oakeshott's account of rationality here contains many echoes of the logic of *Experience and its Modes*, especially in its reference to the notion of coherence. It might be well to recall the significance of this term in that work. When Oakeshott designated coherence as the criterion of experience in *Experience and its Modes*, he meant to differentiate the unity which belongs to a world or system of ideas from that which belongs to a class. The unity of a world or system, unlike that of a class, does not have its seat in an "essence" or a fixed, central "principle."

> It is a unity . . . in which every element is indispensable, in which no one is more important than any other and none is immune from change and rearrangement. The unity of a world of ideas lies in its coherence, not in its conformity to or agreement with any fixed idea.[58]

In short, by coherence Oakeshott meant to designate the concrete universal as opposed to the abstract universal of a class. And it is this notion of coherence or concrete universality which continues to inform his thinking in *Rationalism in Politics*. The criterion of activity, its rationality, does not consist in conformity to some overall purpose; rather, it consists in the coherence of a complex whole in which every element is indispensable and nothing is fixed or absolute.

Having sketched an alternative view of rationality in conduct, Oakeshott proceeds to apply it, first to scientific activity, then to practical activity. Of scientific activity he writes:

> [I]t is not the pursuit of a predetermined end; nobody knows where it will reach. There is no achievement, prefigured in our minds, which we can set

up as a criterion by which to judge current achievements or in relation to which current engagements are a means. Its coherence does not spring from there being an over-all purpose which can be premeditated.... Nor does [it] lie in a body of principles or rules to be observed by the scientist, a "scientific method".

The coherence of scientific activity lies in the knowledge a scientist has of how to conduct a scientific investigation, and the rationality of his conduct lies in his adherence to this knowledge and his enhancement of its coherence. The irrational scientist is the man whose activity shows no sign of being in touch with the tradition (not simply the rules or methods) of scientific inquiry.[59] Here Oakeshott shows himself in tune with such recent post-empiricist philosophers of science as Kuhn, Feyerabend, Lakatos, and especially Polanyi, who also see science as an historic activity in which there are no determinate rules laid down in advance which serve as necessary and sufficient conditions for its pursuit. Like them, he too seeks to elaborate a model of "practical" rationality which emphasizes judgment, imagination, and tacit knowledge, a model of rationality which is in some sense "beyond objectivism and relativism."[60]

What about moral or social conduct (which is referred to here as "human conduct")? Granted that Oakeshott's view of rationality in conduct has a certain plausibility with respect to scientific activity, but is science a special case? Some critics have complained that the bulk of Oakeshott's examples in *Rationalism in Politics* are drawn from the "non-political arts and sciences" – from natural science, cookery, dress-design, and so forth; and that there is little in the book in the way of actual moral or political discussion.[61] This is not exactly true (see, for example, the essays "Rationalism in Politics," "The Political Economy of Freedom," "Political Education," and "On Being Conservative"), but the criticism does underline an important assumption of Oakeshott's approach in *Rationalism in Politics*: namely, that there is a fundamental analogy with respect to form between the various departments of human activity. This assumption of course informed *Experience and its Modes* as well, and in that work Oakeshott tried to vindicate it by considering scientific, historical, and practical experience. It is with much the same intention that he now turns in "Rational Conduct" to consider briefly moral or social conduct. And what he has to say interests us not only because it supports the general view of rationality he has been defending, but also because it is the first positive account of practical activity he has given since *Experience and its Modes*. As we shall see, it provides further evidence of the continuity between Oakeshott's critique of rationalism and his view of experience in that earlier work.

The main point Oakeshott wishes to make here with respect to practical activity is that it begins and ends in – and is characterized throughout by – coherence. This coherence is not introduced from the outside; it does not come from some external source – a rule, or principle, or premeditated purpose; it is coeval with the activity of desiring itself. Desire, according to Oakeshott, is not an "empirical" or "natural" state antecedent to activity; "desire is being active in a certain manner"; it already exhibits a knowledge of how to manage practical activity. This knowledge can, of course, take the form of moral approval or disapproval. But again, approval and disapproval are not to be understood as somehow coming after desire. We must remove from our minds the picture of practical activity as a linear process. Approval and disapproval do not supervene

> upon the activity of desiring, introducing norms of conduct from some external source; they are inseparable from the activity of desiring itself. Approval and disapproval are only an abstract and imperfect way of describing our unbroken knowledge of how to manage the activity of desiring, of how to behave.[62]

Practical activity, then, according to Oakeshott, "is always activity with a pattern; not a superimposed pattern, but a pattern inherent in the activity itself." He refers to this pattern also as a "current" or a "prevailing sympathy," and he defines a rational action as one which can maintain a place in this current or flow of sympathy. "No action is by itself 'rational', or is 'rational' on account of something that has gone before; what makes it 'rational' is its place in a flow of sympathy, a current of moral activity." Oakeshott acknowledges that this current or flow is subject to clog or compromise – "loss of confidence in the direction of moral activity." But he insists that this condition cannot be cured by a transfusion of ideals, principles, rules, or purposes, for these cannot generate behavior. Recovery ultimately "depends upon the native strength of the patient; it depends upon the unimpaired relics of his knowledge of how to behave."[63]

This brings to a conclusion my discussion of "Rational Conduct." I have spent a fair amount of time on the essay because it goes deeper than the other essays, revealing more clearly the philosophical roots of Oakeshott's antagonism to rationalism. In "Rationalism in Politics," Oakeshott stated that a doctrine about human knowledge lay at the heart of rationalism, and he went on to indicate (in that essay, as well as in "The Tower of Babel") the direction criticism might take. But it is only in "Rational Conduct" that his critique of the rationalist doctrine of knowledge, reason, and the mind is fully and philosophically elaborated. It is in this essay, too, that the relationship between his critique of rationalism and the theory of knowledge elaborated in *Experience and its Modes* becomes transparent. The deeply contextual view of knowledge which was presented in *Experience and its Modes* is precisely what is denied or overlooked in the rationalist view of human activity as the pursuit of independently premeditated ideals or purposes. Finally, and closely related to the last point, "Rational Conduct" offers a positive account of human activity, and in particular of practical activity. This positive account follows, as we have seen, *Experience and its Modes* in its emphasis on context, coherence, the immanence of thought, and the interdependence of subject and object.

As we turn to "Political Education" we find these positive and philosophical tendencies of "Rational Conduct" maintained and extended. But whereas in the latter essay Oakeshott applied his view of human activity and of rationality to moral or social conduct in general, in "Political Education" he applies it directly to political activity. Nevertheless, the theoretical orientation remains the same: to achieve a *concrete* understanding of the activity in question. A concrete understanding of an activity is one which recognizes "the activity as having the source of its movement within itself. An understanding which leaves the activity in debt to something outside itself is, for that reason, an inadequate understanding."[64]

The activity in question here is, of course, politics, which Oakeshott defines as "the activity of attending to the general arrangements of a set of people whom chance or choice have brought together." The sort of community he specifically has in mind is a "state," and by "general arrangements" he seems to mean mainly legal arrangements. As he later clarified his concern in the essay: "[W]hat we are considering here is a legally organized society and we are considering the manner in which its legal structure ... is reformed and amended." This delimitation of "politics" must be kept in mind as we follow the argument of the essay. Now, the activity of attending to the arrangements of society obviously makes some call upon knowledge, and a concrete understanding of politics must try to comprehend it. By inquiring into the nature of this knowledge, Oakeshott also hopes to gain a better understanding of the nature of political education (the somewhat recessed theme of the essay); that is, of the kind of education without which political activity would be impossible.[65]

He begins, in dialectical fashion, by considering two partial or inadequate understandings of political activity – one in which politics is conceived as empirical activity, the other in which it is conceived as ideological activity – and then goes on to suggest a third, more concrete understanding which overcomes the defects of the first two. Empirical politics are characterized as the pursuit of momentary desires without any overall plan or purpose: "politics without a policy." The defects of this view of politics lie pretty much on the surface, especially since we are already familiar with Oakeshott's general argument against empiricism. The momentary desires that are pursued in an empirical politics are never merely momentary; they are, like everything else, infected with thought, significance. No activity, not even the activity of desiring, is absolutely capricious. Though approximation to an empirical politics is certainly possible in practice, no politics can be simply empirical; no politics can be totally devoid of thought or knowledge. And this at once convicts the empirical understanding of politics of abstraction in Oakeshott's eyes. It is not simply that purely empirical politics are undesirable, they are strictly speaking impossible. Of course, Oakeshott adds that "to try to do something which is inherently impossible is always a corrupting enterprise" (echoing the assertion in "Rational Conduct" that the "practical danger of an erroneous theory is not that it may persuade people to act in an undesirable manner, but that it may confuse activity by putting it on a false scent"); but it is with empiricism as a *theory*, not as a practical *style*, that he is concerned here. The understanding that politics is an empirical activity fails because it is a misdescription of what actually goes on in political activity; it does not disclose a concrete or self-moved manner of activity. Something must be added to empiricism to set it to work.[66]

Oakeshott next explores the suggestion that this something else is a premeditated end to be pursued, a purpose, or an ideology. When empiricism is preceded by ideological activity, it is asserted, then politics appears as a concrete or self-moved manner of activity. In much the same way that hypothesis is thought to operate in science, a political ideology is said to set empiricism to work, guiding and directing it. "It supplies in advance of the activity of attending to the arrangements of a society a formulated end to be pursued, and in so doing it provides a means of distinguishing between those desires which ought to be encouraged and those which ought to be suppressed or redirected." In short, it is claimed for political ideology that it provides the impetus for political activity, that it is something from which political activity can begin.[67]

Because Oakeshott's reasons for rejecting such a claim on behalf of ideology have already been discussed at length, we need not go into detail. The main problem with the ideological understanding of politics is that what it takes to be the spring of political activity is really only the product of subsequent reflection on it. As Oakeshott succinctly puts it: "[P]olitical activity comes first and a political ideology comes after." A political ideology "merely abridges a concrete manner of behaviour." Such is the case, for example, with the Declaration of the Rights of Man and with Locke's *Second Treatise*. These did not exist in advance of political practice, they were abridgements of it; they were not prefaces to political activity but postscripts. Oakeshott concludes his criticism with a crucial observation on "freedom," perhaps the most idealized of our political ideals. Freedom, he argues, is not an abstract ideal or a dream, a bright idea or a speculative idea; it is a concrete manner of living.

The freedom which we enjoy is nothing more than arrangements, procedures of a certain kind: the freedom of an Englishman is not something exemplified in the procedure of *habeas corpus*, it *is*, at that point, the availability of that procedure. And the freedom which we wish to enjoy is not an "ideal" which we premeditate independently of our political experience, it is what is already intimated in that experience.[68]

So far Oakeshott has concerned himself with ideological politics only as a *theory*, not as a practical *style*. As a theory it suffers from the same defect that the empirical understanding of politics suffered from: it does not disclose a concrete, self-moved manner of activity. Nevertheless, Oakeshott does go on to say a few things about ideological politics as a practical style. He admits (as he did in "The Tower of Babel") that in certain circumstances an ideology can be useful, giving "sharpness of outline and precision to a political tradition." But the ideological style can be deeply corrupting too, for it deludes us into thinking that ideological knowledge alone is sufficient for conducting the activity of attending to the arrangements of a society; "it suggests that a knowledge of the chosen ideology *can take the place of* understanding a tradition of political behaviour." This corruption is perhaps best exemplified in what Oakeshott later in the essay calls "one of the most insidious current misunderstandings of political activity" – the misunderstanding in which the "arrangements of a society are made to appear, not as manners of behaviour, but as pieces of machinery to be transported about the world indiscriminately."[69]

Having exposed the partiality and abstractness of both the empirical and ideological understandings of politics, Oakeshott now turns to give a more positive account of political activity. The view he wishes to recommend has, of course, already been indicated in his critique of ideological politics. Political activity, he has argued, does not spring from, nor does it begin in, ideological activity; every ideology rests on or presupposes an already existing tradition of behavior. It is in terms of such traditions of behavior that political activity must be understood. And because no tradition is simply fixed or finished, an inflexible manner of doing things, political activity must be the exploration and pursuit of what is intimated in a tradition. Oakeshott describes the process in this way:

> The arrangements which constitute a society capable of political activity, whether they are customs or institutions or laws or diplomatic decisions, are at once coherent and incoherent, they compose a pattern and at the same time they intimate a sympathy for what does not fully appear. Political activity is the exploration of that sympathy; and consequently, relevant political reasoning will be the convincing exposure of a sympathy, present but not yet followed up, and the convincing demonstration that now is the appropriate moment for recognizing it.

He cites the example of women getting the vote. Here was a case in which what was already intimated in the already achieved legal status of women had yet to be recognized; here was an incoherence calling out for remedy. Natural right or abstract "justice" had nothing to do with it. The only relevant reason for enfranchising women "was that in all or most other important respects they had already been enfranchised."[70]

Politics is (in the now famous phrase) "the pursuit of intimations." Oakeshott uses the word "intimations" because he wants to emphasize that what we have to do with in political activity is something less precise and more elusive than "logical implications" or "necessary consequences." This ultimately relates back to the notion of tradition. A tradition of behavior for Oakeshott is not something fixed and finished; it does not point in a single direction, nor is it entirely self-consistent. A tradition of behavior is, in fact, a somewhat miscellaneous composition (in one place he calls it a "multi-voiced creature");[71] it consists of a variety of beliefs, many pulling in different directions or competing with one another. It has identity, but this identity is of a complex and not a simple nature. A tradition of behavior is, in short, a concrete universal, and Oakeshott evokes its complex many-in-oneness in the following way. He begins by pointing out (as I have just pointed out) that a tradition of behavior

> is neither fixed nor finished; it has no changeless centre to which understanding can anchor itself; there is no sovereign purpose to be perceived or invariable direction to be detected; there is no model to be copied, idea to be realized, or rule to be followed. Some parts of it may change more slowly than others, but none is immune from change. Everything is temporary.

But that everything is temporary in a tradition does not mean that it provides no criterion for distinguishing between good and bad political projects. To be sure, this criterion cannot lie in correspondence to a fixed purpose, rule or principle. But by denying such objectivism, Oakeshott does not lapse into a featureless relativism. The criterion which governs a tradition of behavior is (as we should have expected) coherence. He writes:

> [T]hough a tradition of behaviour is flimsy and elusive, it is not without identity, and what makes it a possible object of knowledge is the fact that all its parts do not change at the same time and that the changes it undergoes are potential within it. Its principle is a principle of *continuity*: authority is diffused between past, present and future; between the old, the new, and what is to come. It is steady because, though it moves, it is never wholly in motion; and though it is tranquil, it is never wholly at rest. Nothing that ever belonged to it is completely lost; we are always swerving back to recover and make something topical out of even its remotest

moments: and nothing for long remains unmodified. Everything is temporary, but nothing is arbitrary. Everything figures by comparison, not with what stands next to it, but with the whole.[72]

It is because a tradition of behavior is a whole in this complex and concrete way – because it does not disclose a single, unambiguous norm or principle – that politics is said to be the pursuit of "intimations," or (in another famous phrase) "a conversation, not an argument."[73] Since the image of "conversation" has been a feature much commented upon (as well as appropriated) in Oakeshott's philosophy, we would do well to clarify here what he means by it. The image is designed to evoke the quality of relationship subsisting between the members of a complex whole. It is used by Oakeshott in two separate but related contexts. In the first, conversation is used to refer to the quality of relationship subsisting between the multiplicity of considerations which compose a single tradition or activity. In the second, it is used to refer to the quality of relationship subsisting between the various activities and modes of discourse which compose a civilization, for example, "the conversation of mankind." Oakeshott uses the word "conversation" instead of "culture" to refer to this manifold of activities and modes because he thinks the latter suggests a consistency and homogeneity which does not belong to any complex civilization.

> [A] civilization (and particularly ours) may be regarded as a conversation being carried on between a variety of human activities, each speaking with a voice, or in a language of its own. . . . And I call the manifold which these different manners of thinking and speaking compose, a conversation, because the relations between them are not those of assertion and denial but the conversational relationships of acknowledgement and accommodation.[74]

The image of conversation in this second sense appears most frequently in Oakeshott's writings on university education (the passage above, for example, comes from "The Study of 'Politics' in a University"); for he believes that it is in a university that this conversational character of a civilization is most apparent.[75]

Clearly, it is "conversation" in the first sense mentioned above that is being used in "Political Education." The point Oakeshott is trying to make is that in political activity we do not have to do with deduction, subsumption, or demonstration; these belong to argumentative discourse. Rather, we have to do with a tradition of behavior which presents us with a number of different, frequently competing, always circumstantial considerations or "intimations" which have to be attended to, weighed, and balanced. "Conversation," like "intimation," evokes the open-endedness and flexibility of this engagement: there is no simply right or necessary response. What he does not mean to imply is that there are no "arguments" in politics.[76] And he certainly does not conceive of politics "in terms of the pleasant, somewhat idle but also valuable, civilized talk of university dons over their afternoon sherry."[77]

We have now arrived at what Oakeshott takes to be a concrete view of political activity. But it must be pointed out that he is not here recommending a certain style of politics. Politics for him can never be anything but the pursuit of intimations. Even so-called "revolutionary situations" or "foundings" do not escape this condition; for historical analysis reveals every such "founding" to be a modification of past circumstances and not creation *ex nihilo*.[78] The ideological style no less than any other style of politics is bound to tradition and confined to exploring its intimations. The ideological style is, in short, implicitly traditionalist, which is but the other side of Oakeshott's earlier contention that ideological politics are, theoretically speaking, impossible.

This "epistemological" aspect of Oakeshott's critique of rationalist or ideological politics has caused many commentators difficulties. Does it not, they ask, undermine or at least jar with the normative intention which lies behind the critique? If in the end all politics are traditionalist, as Oakeshott seems to maintain – if ideological politics are simply impossible – then there would seem to be no reason for preferring one style of politics to another; rationalist politics, though theoretically naive, would seem to pose no great danger and therefore not to need to be criticized.[79] The difficulty, though, is largely a manufactured one. Oakeshott is quite clear, if somewhat brief, on the relationship between his critique of rationalism as a theory and his critique of the practical style which bases itself on this theory. Though he asserts the ultimate impossibility of rationalist or ideological politics, he does not deny that belief in this erroneous theory can have practical consequences. Although the theory can produce no concrete piece of behavior to match its prescriptions, it can confuse, throw off, or otherwise corrupt activity. As Oakeshott puts it early on in "Political Education": "[T]o try to do something which is inherently impossible is always a corrupting enterprise." In the terminal note to the essay he restates this practical point, while at the same time downplaying it. If his understanding of political activity is true, he says, "it may be supposed to have some bearing upon how we conduct ourselves in political activity – there being, perhaps, some advantage in thinking and speaking and arguing in a manner consonant with what we are really doing." He goes on to say, however, that he does not hold this proposition to be very important; the essay is more concerned with the bearing of his understanding of political activity on political education than with its bearing on political practice.[80] Since I have said nothing about this aspect of Oakeshott's essay, I would like to summarize it briefly before going on to consider some criticisms that have been made of his basic notion of tradition.

Undoubtedly the most important consequence of Oakeshott's understanding of political activity for our understanding of political education is that an education in a political ideology can no longer be considered sufficient. To know a tradition of behavior is always to know it in detail. "What has to be learned is not an abstract idea . . . but a concrete, coherent manner of living in all its intricateness." Of course, at first and for a long time, this education is not a theoretical or self-conscious engagement but simply a haphazard "finding our way about the natural-artificial world into which we are born"; it is "learning how to participate in a conversation." As he did in "The Tower of Babel," Oakeshott compares this initiation into a tradition of behavior to the acquisition of our native language. We begin learning from the day we are born, and we do so (obviously) not by studying the alphabet or a book of grammar, but by observing, imitating, and interacting with our elders.[81]

But apart from this inevitable initiation, politics can also be a subject of academic study; and this, it may be assumed, is Oakeshott's main concern (although he does not devote much space to it). He mentions two modes of inquiry as being especially appropriate to the study of politics at this level: historical study and philosophical study. Historical study is, of course, for Oakeshott the very model of getting to know something in detail. But it is not to be supposed that it in any way helps us to pursue the intimations of our tradition. From *Experience and its Modes* we know that Oakeshott does not think that the study of history has any practical bearing; it does not teach "lessons," nor does it disclose "trends" (much less "progress"). Here he distinguishes himself from Mill, who, "when he abandoned reference to general principle either as a reliable guide in political activity or as a satisfactory explanatory device, put in its place a 'theory of human progress' and what he called a 'philosophy of history'." For Oakeshott, "neither 'principle' . . . nor any general theory about the character and direction of social change seems to supply an adequate reference for explanation or for practical conduct."[82] If history can be said to "teach" us anything, it is that institutions and procedures are not "pieces of machinery designed to achieve a purpose settled in advance" but "manners of behaviour which are meaningless when separated from their context."[83]

Political philosophy, too, "must be understood as an explanatory, not a practical, activity." It "cannot be expected to increase our ability to be successful in political activity. It will not help us to distinguish between good and bad political projects; it has no power to direct us in the enterprise of pursuing the intimations of our tradition." The purpose of political philosophy, as Oakeshott describes it here – pretty much consistent with his view in "The Concept of a Philosophical Jurisprudence," though with greater emphasis on the "analytical" aspect of philosophy – is "to consider the place of political activity itself on the map of our total experience"; to remove "some of the crookedness from our thinking"; and to promote "a more economical use of concepts." Such study, he suggests, may have an indirect effect on the way we conduct political activity – thinking and speaking correctly about politics may keep us from attempting the impossible – but this practical benefit seems to be incidental to his overall purpose. As he emphasizes in both his prefatory and terminal notes, his principal concern in the essay is with *understanding* and *explaining* political activity, not with judging it.[84]

The radical disjunction of theory and practice which Oakeshott observes here does not come as any surprise. It is, as we have seen, a central feature of his theory of knowledge from *Experience and its Modes* onwards. But it should not be concluded from this (as it often is) that Oakeshott sees thinking or reasoning or argument as foreign to practical discourse; or that he reduces practical activity to "following intuitions."[85] One of the main contentions of *Experience and its Modes*, it will be remembered, was that no human activity or form of experience is devoid of thought; and notions such as "intuition" or "insight" were explicitly rejected.[86] Oakeshott's point is not that reasoning is foreign to practical discourse, but only that the reasoning that is appropriate to practical discourse is of a different sort than explanatory reasoning.

Now let us turn to the issue on which criticism has chiefly centered, namely, Oakeshott's use of tradition. Criticism has generally taken one of two closely related forms. In the first, it is said that Oakeshott's notion of tradition does not provide a basis for distinguishing a good tradition from a bad one; it does not supply a standard by which an entire tradition might be evaluated. Not all traditions are good. We need a criterion to distinguish the tradition of, say, British parliamentary democracy from that of Soviet Communism or South African apartheid.[87] Secondly, it is argued that no tradition is univocal. A tradition always intimates many (and frequently contradictory) things. Tradition alone cannot tell us which of these intimations to pursue; an external standard is needed.[88]

As I say, these two criticisms are closely related to one another, and it is not uncommon to find a single critic deploying them both. Nevertheless, I think it is useful to distinguish them. And I will take up the second criticism first because it recognizes what in fact Oakeshott also recognizes: namely, that no tradition intimates a single thing; that every tradition contains within itself a multiplicity of different (and sometimes colliding) intimations. The question then arises: how do we know which intimation amongst this multiplicity to pursue? And Oakeshott has no ready practical answer to it. "Do you want to be told," he asks, "that in politics there is, what certainly exists nowhere else, a mistake-proof manner of what should be done?"[89] This does not mean that anything goes, or that there is no criterion for distinguishing between good and bad political projects. The criterion to be satisfied in political activity is, as we have learned, coherence. But what specifically this predicates is something that cannot be settled in advance of activity. There is no single principle, ideal, or norm from which we can deduce which intimation to pursue. Practical reasoning is always a matter of attending to the multiplicity of considerations which compose a tradition and of striking some sort of balance; it is always a contingent and circumstantial engagement.

We may now turn to the first criticism mentioned above, the criticism which poses the question of the "bad" tradition. Oakeshott nowhere really addresses this criticism directly, but this may be because it so misconceives what he is trying to say with the word "tradition." Tradition here seems to be equated simply with "what is" or the status quo – which may, of course, be "bad" – and to afford no standpoint outside itself by which to criticize itself. But it is quite clear that Oakeshott does not simply identify tradition with the status quo, and he certainly allows for the possibility of criticizing "what is." His point is not that the criticism of current arrangements is impossible, but only that such criticism must come from within a tradition itself. No matter how bad things are, there is no remedy outside the resources of a tradition of behavior. Even in the extreme case of political crisis, there is no appeal to a neutral, independent guide, for

> no such guide exists; we have no resources outside the fragments, the vestiges, the relics of [a] tradition of behaviour which the crisis has left untouched.... [P]olitical crisis ... always appears *within* a tradition of political activity; and "salvation" comes from the unimpaired resources of the tradition itself.[90]

But what if an entire tradition is "bad," rotten through and through? What if the "tradition" we are talking about is that of German National Socialism, or Soviet Communism under Stalin, or South African apartheid? It is, of course, a question whether it is even appropriate here to speak of "traditions" at all, since in most of these cases we have to do not with political deliberation but with brute force. But even putting this objection to one side, we may still wonder whether Oakeshott's "traditionalism" is incapable of accounting for resistance to these forms of tyranny. Was German National Socialism, for example, to be identified with the whole German political tradition at the time? And is it really to be supposed that Germans in the thirties completely lacked traditional resources with which to meet Hitler? The same goes for Stalin and South African apartheid. With respect to the latter, are we really to think that the South African political tradition is utterly lacking in resources with which to respond to or resist the tyranny of the present?

The criticism that Oakeshott does not adequately take into account the possibility of a "bad" tradition fails, then, in too narrowly construing what he means by "tradition" and in ascribing to him a determinism or fatalism which is no part of his doctrine. As he puts it toward the end of "Political Education": "A tradition of behaviour is not a groove within which we are destined to grind out our helpless and unsatisfying lives." Oakeshott's "traditionalism" has nothing to do with glorifying the past or defending the status quo. And it in no way denies the possibility of change or criticism. He acknowledges that some may find depressing the doctrine that what we have, and all we have, are traditions of behavior; but he maintains that such

> depression springs from the exclusion of hopes that were false and the discovery that guides, reputed to be of superhuman wisdom and skill, are, in fact, of a somewhat different character. If the doctrine deprives us of a model laid up in heaven to which we should approximate our behaviour, at least it does not lead us into a morass where every choice is equally good or equally to be deplored. And if it suggests that politics are *nur für die Schwindelfreie*, that should depress only those who have lost their nerve.[91]

The criticism that tradition alone provides no practical guidance in the case of a "bad" tradition or of a total breakdown of tradition is, of course, one that every defender of tradition must meet. And here it may be instructive to compare Oakeshott's response to this criticism (as I have constructed it) with that of another recent defender of tradition, Hans-Georg Gadamer. As I have already suggested, there is much that links these two thinkers together with respect to the issue of rationality, even if their respective philosophical approaches differ radically. Like Oakeshott, Gadamer rejects the Enlightenment contrast between reason and tradition, maintaining that reason always functions within traditions. He also emphasizes the importance of practical knowledge or *phronēsis* over against the modern belief in the sovereignty of method or technique (*technē*).[92] And like Oakeshott, Gadamer too has been criticized (by Habermas, among others) for absolutizing tradition and denying the power of critical reflection. He too has been faulted for not taking seriously enough the possibility of a "bad" tradition: the possibility of a tradition which rests on exploitation and systematically distorted communication.[93]

What is interesting about Gadamer's responses to these criticisms from our point of view is that in many respects they parallel Oakeshott's own. In the first place, he denies that his rehabilitation of tradition involves a denial of the possibility of critical reflection. "It is a grave misunderstanding to assume that emphasis on the essential factor of tradition which enters into all understanding implies an uncritical acceptance of tradition and sociopolitical conservatism."[94] And secondly, he rejects the notion that our tradition is characterized by systematically distorted communication and a total absence of the community or solidarity required for the exercise of *phronēsis*. Such a critique, he argues, overlooks the remnants of genuine solidarity and *praxis* which still inform our attitudes and discussion. And it is only on the basis of such solidarity and *praxis* that rational criticism of social arrangements can take place.[95] Oakeshott would, I think, agree with Gadamer's response to one critic who argues that traditional knowledge and *phronēsis* are no longer enough in a world characterized by a total chaos of norms and principles. Gadamer writes:

> Clearly your decisive argument is the collapse of all principles in the modern world, and I certainly agree with you that, if this were correct, my insistence on *phronēsis* would be nothing more than pure declamation. But is this really the case? Don't we all then run the risk of a terrible intellectual hubris if we equate Nietzsche's anticipations and the ideological confusion of the present with life as it is actually lived with its own forms of solidarity? Here, in fact, my divergence from Heidegger is fundamental. . . .
> I am concerned with the fact that the displacement of human reality never goes so far that no forms of solidarity exist any longer. Plato saw this very well: there is no city so corrupted that it does not realize something of the true city; that is what, in my opinion, is the basis for the possibility of practical philosophy.[96]

On account of their attempted rehabilitations of tradition, both Gadamer and Oakeshott have been compared to Burke. And it is important for us to be clear about the relationship – at least so far as it concerns Oakeshott – that is being asserted here. That there are certain similarities between the "traditionalism" of Oakeshott and that of Burke is indisputable. But the no less important differences also need to be pointed out. The most fundamental of these concerns the degree of contingency each accords to tradition. For Burke, of course, a tradition is not a very contingent thing; rather, it possesses an inherent rationality, and it unfolds with all the necessity of a natural "growth." Thus, in one of the more famous passages of the *Reflections on the Revolution in France*, he speaks of tradition as a kind of storehouse of wisdom, opposing it to the narrow reason of individual men.

> We are afraid to put men to live and trade each on his own private stock of reason; because we suspect that this stock in each man is small, and that the individuals would do better to avail themselves of the general bank and capital of nations and of ages.[97]

No such doctrine of the wisdom or rationality of tradition is implied in Oakeshott's notion of tradition. For him (as I have tried to emphasize in my interpretation), a tradition is an eminently contingent thing; it is miscellaneous and incoherent; and its deliverances are never unambiguous, containing within itself a multiplicity of different (and frequently conflicting) intimations.[89] Nor is tradition for Oakeshott something solid to be opposed to the waywardness of individual reason; it is not something different from ordinary human rationality but itself the ground of such rationality. Insofar as he emphasizes the contingency of tradition, Oakeshott joins such thinkers as Alasdair MacIntyre and Gadamer, who also emphasize the elements of freedom and conflict in a tradition against the necessity and stability of a Burkean tradition.[99]

Before leaving the subject of Oakeshott's "traditionalism," there is one final criticism I would like to consider, closely connected with the others we have been discussing: namely, the charge that Oakeshott's view of political activity leads to the denial or devaluation of political philosophy itself; that it denies the possibility of a theoretical understanding of politics and society.[100] This criticism generally rests on a presupposed notion about the nature of political philosophy: namely, that it is normative activity. It is a view we know Oakeshott rejects. He has a different understanding of the nature and task of political philosophy. This understanding I have already discussed in previous chapters, and I will not rehearse it here. Whether or not it maintains political philosophy as a genuine and constructive possibility can in some ways only be decided by looking at Oakeshott's practice as a political philosopher (and, of course, confirming that his practice corresponds to his theory).[101] Any final decision, therefore, must be postponed until we consider *On Human Conduct*. Here it is only necessary to point out that there is nothing in Oakeshott's understanding of political activity which inherently denies the possibility of a theoretical understanding of politics.

3. Rationalist and Non-Rationalist Politics:
Oakeshott's Skeptical Conservatism

It is time now to see how Oakeshott's view of practical activity applies to politics as we know it. It is true that, with "Political Education," we have already begun to make the transition from a theory of practical activity in general to a theory of political activity. Still, that essay remains at a fairly general level; it does not really address specific problems arising from our own political tradition, nor (it must be added) was it meant to. In order to determine what exactly follows from Oakeshott's view of practical activity for our understanding of concrete governmental activity and projects, we must turn to another set of writings, again drawn from *Rationalism in Politics* or written at roughly the same time as the essays in that volume. By examining these writings, I hope to construct some sort of bridge from Oakeshott's reflections in *Rationalism in Politics* to his full-blown political philosophy in *On Human Conduct*.

A potential difficulty, however, confronts us at the outset. It will be noticed from what I have said above that my emphasis in what follows falls on the continuity or consistency of Oakeshott's writings – not only between the various writings from the time of *Rationalism in Politics* but between those writings and *On Human Conduct*. That such a continuity or consistency exists amongst these writings, however, has recently been denied. Charles Covell argues that there is a tension in Oakeshott's postwar writings between the Hegelian historicism of his critique of rationalism, on the one hand, and the skeptical, individualistic, Hobbesian politics defended in the writings I am about to discuss, on the other.[102] It must be admitted there is a certain plausibility to this argument. The writings I am about to consider – and even more extremely *On Human Conduct* – do seem to move in a different direction from the writings I have already considered in this chapter: not only are they more political, they are also more libertarian, less historicistic or Hegelian. Nevertheless, I believe this discrepancy or tension to be only superficial. In what follows I try to bring out the profound continuity between Oakeshott's critique of rationalism and his skeptical, individualistic politics.

Indications of Oakeshott's outlook on the actual conduct of affairs are, of course, to be found in his earliest essay on the theme of rationalism, "Rationalism in Politics." There he characterizes rationalist politics as (among other things) "the politics of the felt need." By this he means to denote a style of politics in which a single problem or purpose is isolated and the entire resources of a society are mobilized to solve or pursue it. Though Oakeshott doesn't specify any further here, one need only look at some of his other essays from this period to determine what current policies and attitudes he has in mind. In "Contemporary British Politics" (1948), for example, he criticizes both the Labour and the Conservative parties for their exclusive preoccupation with the problem of mass unemployment. "Obsession with a single problem," he writes, "however important, is always dangerous in politics; except in time of war, no society has so simple a life that one element in it can, without loss, be made the centre and circumference of all political activity."[103] And it is precisely the recent experience of war, he goes on to argue, which has caused so many minds to be bewitched by the ideal of central social planning. Here and elsewhere Oakeshott, like Hayek, rejects the view (much put about at the time) that takes society in wartime as the model for society in peacetime.[104]

> In war all that is most superficial in our tradition is encouraged merely because it is useful, even necessary, for victory. . . . There are many who have no other idea of social progress than the extrapolation of the character of society in time of war – the artificial unity, the narrow overmastering purpose, the devotion to a single cause and the subordina-

tion of everything to it – all this seems to them inspiring: but the direction of their admiration reveals the emptiness of their souls.[105]

Mention of such terms as "war," "mass unemployment," and "central social planning" suggests that we have entered a more familiar – certainly a more political – world than the one in which he hitherto dwelled. The topical and practical character of Oakeshott's reflections here is undeniable. And before proceeding, it is perhaps not going too far out of our way to mention an objection that is frequently raised against Oakeshott, but one which I think is without basis. I mean the charge (or nest of charges) that Oakeshott's political philosophy somehow constitutes a "denial of politics"; that his is an essentially non-political or anti-political political theory; that he is uninterested in politics; that his political outlook is determined by aesthetic or Epicurean considerations.[106] Some of the things Oakeshott has from time to time said about politics, especially when taken out of context, might suggest this view. Take, for example, this sentence from his introduction to *Leviathan*:

> For politics, we know, is a second-rate form of human activity, neither an art nor a science, at once corrupting to the soul and fatiguing to the mind, the activity either of those who cannot live without the illusion of affairs or those so fearful of being ruled by others that they will pay away their lives to prevent it.[107]

But here, as elsewhere, Oakeshott does not mean to deny the value or necessity of politics; he simply wants to indicate their limits. He asserts what he thinks every great political philosophy has always maintained: that politics alone is not sufficient for man's salvation; that it contributes to this end but cannot itself bring it about; "that the achievement in politics is a tangible good and not, therefore, to be separated from the deliverance that constitutes the whole good, but something less than the deliverance itself."[108] When Oakeshott does actually come to discuss politics, however, there is absolutely nothing to suggest the aestheticism, romanticism, Epicureanism, apoliticism, unrealism, insularity, and irrelevance with which he has been charged. His discussion is, in fact, remarkably down-to-earth and shows a keen appreciation for current political realities. This, of course, awaits further proof, but I believe careful examination of what Oakeshott says about politics will show him to be what he frequently credits Hegel with having been: namely, "a supremely observant man."[109]

Nor must it be thought that in responding to current social and political circumstances Oakeshott is contradicting his view of the relationship between theory and practice. This view, as we have already seen, does not deny the continuity between practical or pre-philosophical reflection on politics and philosophical reflection, as we ascend from the one to the other. It only denies that the process is reversible; that having ascended we can descend again and "apply" the conclusions of philosophy to the world of practice.[110] Now it is some such movement from the practical to the theoretical that I intend to follow in this section. I will begin with the more practical essays, "Contemporary British Politics" and "The Political Economy of Freedom" (1949), and then go on to consider the more theoretical "On Being Conservative" (1956) and "The Masses in Representative Democracy" (1957), both of which intimate the teaching of *On Human Conduct*. Of course, these labels "practical" and "theoretical" are to be taken only as very rough and relative distinctions. In even the most "practical" of these essays there is philosophical sophistication and detachment; none are merely partisan.

This is well illustrated in the first essay I wish to consider, "Contemporary British Politics." Oakeshott approaches his subject by way of considering two recent books, one on British socialism by a socialist, the other on British conservatism by a conservative. And though he shows a clear preference for conservatism over socialism, this does not prevent him from subjecting the former to rather relentless criticism in the course of the essay. He begins with the "doctrine of natural law" (really of natural rights) upon which conservatives frequently call to support their position. He concedes that this doctrine, which essentially puts limits on the claims the group or majority may make on the individual, is superior to "the philosophy of the Mandate" espoused by socialists. Nevertheless, "as a philosophy it leaves much to be desired." "So simple a doctrine of natural law cannot ... survive the criticism ... of Burke and of Hegel." It is "too abstract to offer much practical guidance," and "the notion of a criterion which is merely an external *limit* is scarcely good enough."[111] These are criticisms our previous researches would lead us to expect, and Oakeshott returns to them at several points in the course of the essay. For us now, though, they serve notice that his political point of view does not always or exactly coincide with what frequently passes for conservatism today, a point to which I will have occasion to return several times in the course of my discussion.

The issue which dominates "Contemporary British Politics" is the issue of central planning, both in the economic realm and with respect to society at large (for a centrally planned economy for Oakeshott, as for Hayek, necessarily involves a centrally planned society). We have already seen that Oakeshott identifies central planning with the politics of the felt need; here he calls it "the ideal of all rationalistic politics." It is, of course, primarily the ideal of the socialists, though the conservatives have not altogether escaped its allure. What does this ideal involve? At least on the British socialist's view of it (as interpreted by Oakeshott), a centrally planned society is "a society in which everyone is an employee of the government, a society upon which has been fixed and riveted the deadly grip of the corporation employee mentality, a society in which everyone has a 'post' given him by 'the community'." It is also a society in which the government has a monopoly of power; in which "the power which is at present widely distributed throughout our society" is concentrated "in the hands of the Government." Oakeshott sees no reason not to call this state of affairs "despotism" or "tyranny," but the really interesting question to him is why it has not been recognized as such by the denizens of the twentieth century. He cites a number of reasons, perhaps the most important being "the vast emotional and intellectual confusion there is with regard to the nature and conditions of freedom." It is not sufficiently understood that what the socialist offers (though does not necessarily supply) is not more freedom but something quite different, namely, security and prosperity. And the passion for security has long since come to dominate European life and politics.[112]

What of the alternative offered by conservatism? It differs from the vision of the socialist in two fundamental ways. In the first place, it is not utopian; politics are understood to be, not the pursuit of a dream or an abstract ideal, but "a limited activity, a necessary but second-rate affair." Secondly, whereas the socialist seeks to concentrate power in the hands of the government, the conservative seeks "to prevent the concentration of power in a society and to break up all concentrations of power which have the appearance of becoming dangerous." The "politics of the diffusion of power," both Oakeshott and the conservative agree, "are the only guarantee of the most valuable and substantial freedom known to human beings." And the concentration of power in the hands of the government poses no less a threat to this freedom than the concentration of power in the hands of an individual, a corporation, a party, or a union.[113]

But how is the politician to carry out this function of breaking up dangerous concentrations of power in a society, of diffusing power? On this point Oakeshott detects a certain amount of intellectual confusion on the part of the conservative. For Oakeshott, the main integration of our society is in terms of rights and duties – what he calls the rule of law. It is the rule of law and not some mythical laissez-faire which he opposes to central social planning, and he understands these two modes of social integration to be categorially distinct: no conceivable extension of the rights and duties which comprise the rule of law "will ever produce a centrally planned society, which is something of an altogether different nature." The integration provided by the rule of law is of course never perfect or final. Enjoyment of the rights and duties which comprise it can lead to dangerous concentrations of power, and such "maladjustments" call out for remedy or readjustment. This gets us to Oakeshott's difference with conservatism. Both he and the conservative agree that "the necessary re-adjustments must be *in pari materia* with the integration itself – that is, an adjustment which, at any point, replaces rights and duties by an overhead plan, is destructive of an integration based upon rights and duties." Where they differ is in how they conceive these rights and duties and how they characterize their readjustment. Put simply, for the conservative these rights and duties are "natural" and absolute, whereas for Oakeshott they are historical and relative. The conservative, Oakeshott argues,

> as a relic of an old intellectual error . . . thinks of these rights and duties as "limitations" and of their adjustment as "interference". It is an unfortunate way of thinking which is inherent in the simpler forms of a natural law conception of society. The truth is, however, that we do not begin by being free; the structure of our freedom is the rights and duties which, by long and painful effort, have been established in our society. The conditions of individuality are not limitations; there is nothing to limit. And the adjustments of those conditions are not interference (unless they are overhead adjustments); they are the continuation of the achievement.[114]

Once again we are back to the criticism of natural rights with which the essay began. The passage also recalls some of the criticisms we found Oakeshott making toward the end of chapter 3 of the "private individual" and the notion of "limits." This is obviously an important point for him, and yet it is primarily a *philosophical* point; its connection to the dominant theme of central planning in this essay is not immediately clear. Oakeshott seems to think, however, that the conservative's intellectual confusion on this point ultimately makes him more susceptible to the idea of planning. "[T]he step from these ideas of limitation and interference," he writes, "to the idea of adjustment by means of overhead planning, with physical controls, is as short as it is disastrous."[115] By thinking of our rights as "limitations" and of their adjustment as "interference" the conservative becomes less able to distinguish between adjustment by means of the rule of law and adjustment by means of an overhead plan; both are seen to be "intrusive." In some ways the conservative still participates in the old liberal opposition of "government" and "individual," and this prevents him from discerning what Oakeshott takes to be the truly significant opposition. The true opposition is not between "government" and "individual" but between two categorially distinct modes of government: between central social planning and the rule of law.

It is interesting that the remarks with which Oakeshott concludes the essay are directed more against the notion of abstract natural rights than against central planning per se. Once again he seems to be saying that the greatest danger lies in misunderstanding the nature of our own political tradition. (Oakeshott writes specifically of the British political tradition, but what he says is I think applicable to the American political tradition as well.) And the most important thing to recognize about our political tradition is that *it is a tradition*, something living and changing, and not simply a fixed body of abstract rights. "British democracy," he writes, "is not an abstract idea. It is a way of living and a manner of politics which first began to emerge in the Middle Ages." The problem now is that we have lost this sense of British democracy as a tradition or a "way of living." How did this happen?

> So convincing was this subtle manner of integrating a society that it became the model for peoples whose powers of social and political invention were unequal to their needs. The common law rights and duties of Englishmen were transplanted throughout the civilized world. . . . In this process some of their flexibility was lost; the rights and duties were exported; the genius that made them remained at home. Peoples, desirous of freedom, but dissatisfied with anything less than the imagination of an eternal and immutable law, gave to these rights the false title of Nature. Because they were not the fruit of their own experience, it was forgotten that they were the fruit of the experience of the British people. For many years now, these children of our own flesh have been returning to us, disguised in a foreign dress, the outline blurred by false theory and the detail fixed with an uncharacteristic precision. What went abroad as the concrete rights of an Englishman have returned home as the abstract Rights of Man, and they have returned to confound our politics and corrupt our minds.[116]

The need now, according to Oakeshott, is to recover the sense of British democracy as a tradition; of law "as a living method of social integration" and "not simply as an achieved body of rights and duties." The hope is, presumably, that with this more profound understanding of our tradition we will be less apt to be bewitched by simpler and more alien modes of social integration.

The considerations with which "Contemporary British Politics" concludes in some ways form the starting point for "The Political Economy of Freedom." Inquiry into the political economy of freedom obviously presupposes some notion of freedom, and Oakeshott quickly points out at the start of the essay that the freedom he (and the economist whose book he is discussing)[117] has in mind is not an abstract idea but a concrete "way of living." The political economy of freedom begins not with an abstract definition of freedom but with the way of living we currently enjoy and which we are accustomed to call a free way of living. "The purpose of the inquiry is not to define a word, but to detect the secret of what we enjoy, to recognize what is hostile to it, and to discern where and how it might be enjoyed more fully."[118]

With this radically unspeculative attitude toward the object of his inquiry, Oakeshott proceeds to ask after the essential characteristics of the freedom or way of living we currently enjoy. And as he did in "Contemporary British Politics," he points to "the absence from our society of overwhelming concentrations of power" as "the most general condition of our freedom." Not the separation of church and state, nor the rule of law, nor private property, nor parliamentary institutions, but the diffusion of power which each of these "signifies and represents" is the most general condition of our freedom. Of course, such a society in which power is widely diffused requires a government to keep it from disintegrating, but this government need not possess "overwhelming power" vis-à-vis the rest of society but "only a power greater than that which is concentrated in any one other centre of power on any particular occasion." And, as in "Contemporary British Politics," the method of government recommended as being peculiarly suited to preserve freedom thus understood is the rule of law. Non-arbitrary, binding on governors and governed alike, economical in its use of power, and not requiring extraordinary power, the rule of law is "the emblem of that diffusion of power which it exists to promote"; it is "the greatest single condition of our freedom."[119]

From these general reflections on the freedom which characterizes our way of living and on the mode of social integration corresponding to it, Oakeshott moves on to consider the economic question. His concern is to find a form of economic organization which is compatible with the freedom and form of social integration he has just sketched. This way of proceeding is significant. The question of economic organization is not considered by itself, apart from politics and social organization; the economic is set in the wider context of an entire concrete manner of living. As Oakeshott says toward the end of the essay: "[T]he political economy of freedom rests upon the clear acknowledgement that what is being considered is not 'economics' (not the maximization of wealth, not productivity or the standard of life), but *politics*, that is, the custody of a manner of living."[120] We will return to this point shortly; for the moment I only want to draw attention to Oakeshott's concrete procedure, his refusal to treat things in abstraction from their concrete context.

The type of economic organization Oakeshott thinks is most compatible with the freedom we enjoy is the one which guarantees the widest possible diffusion of power. Since property is, from one point of view, "a form of power," the institution of property most favorable to freedom "will be one which allows the widest distribution, and which discourages most effectively great and dangerous concentrations of this power." For Oakeshott, this entails a right of private property. It also entails a resolute opposition to monopolies of any kind, or (more positively) "the establishment and maintenance of effective competition." Nor is this latter condition to be confused with a belief in laissez-faire; "effective competition is not something that springs up of its own accord, . . . both it and the alternative to it are creatures of law." Indeed, Oakeshott believes the current situation is not one to be inactive or complacent about, being characterized by an accumulated mass of maladjustments and widespread concentrations of power which call out for remedy. But the correction of these maladjustments must be carried out in a manner that is compatible with the structure of our liberty. For this reason he rejects such solutions to our economic problems as collectivism (i.e., central planning) and syndicalism, both of which reject the notion of the diffusion of power and recommend instead "the integration of society by means of the erection and maintenance of monopolies."[121]

Oakeshott's whole approach to the problem of economic organization reflects his belief that what is being considered is not simply economics "but *politics*, that is the custody of a manner of living." And before leaving "The Political Economy of Freedom" I would like to say a little bit more about this subordination of the economic to the moral and the political; for Oakeshott seems to think it goes against the grain of much current thinking. In one place he writes that the belief in " 'maximum productivity' is one of the most damaging of the moral superstitions of our time."[122] What he calls in several places "the plausible ethics of productivity" is for him clearly an inadequate moral doctrine; indeed, it can hardly be called a moral doctrine at all, for "it turns out to have no criterion for helping us to know when we are not hungry."[123] Now all this would not need pointing out if the belief in "productivity" were not so prevalent today. But in some places Oakeshott indicates that this belief in "productivity," far from being the exclusive preserve of economists and the vulgar, actually runs quite deep in what might be called the "liberal" tradition. At one point, as we have already seen, he traces this materialistic element in liberalism back to Locke.[124] In another place he writes that "the most questionable element of Liberal Democracy" is "what may be called its moral ideal: 'the plausible ethics of productivity'." And he goes on to say that this moral ideal "was always the weakest part of the doctrine."[125] This is not to be taken as Oakeshott's last word on the liberal tradition, but it does indicate where he detects weaknesses in it, and where he thinks improvement might be made. In his own philosophical restatement of this tradition, as we shall see, he tries to make good this defect.

One final thing remains to be noticed about Oakeshott's procedure in both "The Political Economy of Freedom" and "Contemporary British Politics": namely, its non-ideological intent. In neither of these essays is Oakeshott concerned with defining a set of abstract beliefs by which to orient political activity. His reflections take their start from the concrete manner of living which we currently enjoy, and their purpose is to detect the secret of what we enjoy. All this is, of course, consonant with what we have already learned about the relationship of ideology to activity or practice in Oakeshott's critique of rationalism. Abstract ideas or ideals originate nothing; a firmer consciousness of the direction change should take is to be sought not in reflection on abstract ideals or purposes but in a more profound understanding of our own tradition. This non-ideological outlook clearly informs Oakeshott's procedure in "Contemporary British Politics" and "The Political Economy of Freedom." Though he points to a certain amount of intellectual confusion in these essays, he does not characterize our current crisis as being primarily philosophical. He certainly does not suggest that what is now needed is a new "philosophy of life" or *Weltanschauung.*"[126]

Nor is it simply the ideological propensities of the Left to which Oakeshott's non-ideological procedure opposes itself. Conservatives share with their otherwise opposite counterparts on the Left the same tendency to seek a remedy to our political predicament in general beliefs, doctrine, an ideology, or a *Weltanschauung.* This ideological tendency, however, Oakeshott does not believe is inherent in conservatism, and in the essay "On Being Conservative" he tries to disencumber conservatism of it: to define a conservatism which does not rest on natural law or any sort of general beliefs about human nature or the universe. His principal targets in this essay are Burke and his modern followers, whom he believes have tied political conservatism too closely to controversial and even anachronistic speculative and religious beliefs. In contradistinction to these "cosmic Tories" Oakeshott makes a thoroughly modern defense of the conservative disposition; he tries to make the conservative disposition in politics intelligible even (and especially) given current circumstances and beliefs.[127]

He begins with a characterization of the conservative disposition in general. The chief characteristic of this disposition, he maintains, is "a propensity to use and enjoy what is available rather than to wish for or to look for something else; to delight in what is present rather than what was or what may be." To be conservative is to prefer the present to the past or the future, the familiar to the unknown, the actual to the possible. Further, to be conservative is to have a certain attitude toward change and innovation. Change the conservative recognizes as inevitable, and he accommodates himself to it gracefully if somewhat regretfully. With respect to innovation – that is, self-induced change – the conservative will be cautious; for him there is much to lose, and this makes him unadventurous.[128]

Now, it is no part of Oakeshott's purpose to recommend, simply and unequivocally, this conservative disposition.[129] He acknowledges that with us this disposition is not – nor has it been for the last five centuries or so – notably strong, and he does not mean to suggest that we should completely change ourselves. Instead, he proposes to show that, even given our current disposition to change and innovation, a conservative disposition with respect to certain things – namely, the general rules of conduct or politics – is not necessarily unintelligible. For him it is not necessary to call upon general beliefs about human nature or the universe to make the conservative disposition in politics intelligible. What makes this disposition intelligible

> is nothing to do with a natural law or a providential order, nothing to do with morals or religion it is the observation of our current manner of living combined with the belief . . . that governing is a specific and limited activity, namely the provision and custody of general rules of conduct, which are understood, not as plans for imposing substantive activities, but as instruments enabling people to pursue the activities of their own choice with the minimum frustration, and therefore something which it is appropriate to be conservative about.[130]

This, then, is what Oakeshott wants to show, and he begins at what he takes to be the proper starting-place: "not in the empyrean, but with ourselves as we have come to be." The picture he draws is of an enterprising and self-directed, if somewhat superficial, fickle and acquisitive, race of human beings; a race of human beings engaged in a vast variety of enterprises and activities, entertaining a multiplicity of opinions, and in general exercising "an acquired love of making choices for themselves." There are, of course, those to whom all this over-activity appears a horrible waste. "It provides an excitement similar to that of a stock-car race; but it has none of the satisfaction of a well-conducted business enterprise." These are the rationalists; and, exaggerating the current disorder, their minds move to resolve it. They dream of a "collisionless manner of living proper to all mankind," of a society in which human activity is "co-ordinated and set going in a single direction." And it is to government that they entrust the task of making their dream actual. The office of government is understood to be "the imposition upon its subjects of the condition of human circumstances of their dream. To govern is to turn a private dream into a public and compulsory manner of living."[131]

The conservative's attitude toward the current condition of human circumstance, and hence his understanding of the office of government, is quite different, according to Oakeshott. He accepts the multiplicity of activity and diversity of opinion that currently constitutes our condition. And he understands the office of government to be, not to change this condition into something else, but simply to rule over it as a referee rules over a game. Such an attitude toward government need not invoke absolute values or natural rights; "something much

smaller and less pretentious will do: the observation that this condition of human circumstance is, in fact, current, and that we have
learned to enjoy it and how to manage it."[132] Oakeshott thus dis-
encumbers conservatism of any unnecessary moral and metaphysical
baggage. His understanding of government as a "ruler" or referee
rests entirely on the recognition of an historic condition of human
circumstance and of what is appropriate to it.

But what exactly does Oakeshott mean by "ruling"? Although he
generally characterizes it in terms of the custody of the general rules of
conduct, he makes it clear here (as he did in "Contemporary British
Politics" and "The Political Economy of Freedom") that to rule is not
simply to do nothing. Government plays a positive role in presiding
over the multiplicity of activities and beliefs which compose our current condition. The office of government is not simply to let things go
but "to resolve some of the collisions which this variety of beliefs and
activities generates." And it goes about doing this, Oakeshott argues,
not by arbitrating individual cases of collision (''the diseconomy of
such an arrangement is . . . obvious") but by making and enforcing
general rules of conduct. It is true that the conservative will not tinker
lightly with these rules of conduct, for "familiarity is a supremely
important virtue in a rule." Nevertheless, mere conservation is not
enough. The changefulness inherent in our current condition of human
circumstance calls for continual adjustment and modification of the
rules of conduct to bring them into line with novel conditions. One
thinks back to the example of the enfranchisement of women in "Political Education." And here, as there, Oakeshott emphasizes the "pursuit of intimations": "modification of the rules should always reflect,
and never impose, a change in the activities and beliefs of those who
are subject to them, and should never on any occasion be so great as
to destroy the *ensemble*."[133]

There are, then, according to Oakeshott, two opposed attitudes toward politics and the activity of governing. The first, what may be
called the rationalistic attitude, sees politics as the pursuit of a single
comprehensive end and government as the imposition of this end or
purpose on society. Government is recognized as "an instrument of
passion; the art of politics is to inflame and direct desire." The second,
the conservative, attitude toward politics, on the other hand, recognizes governing as a secondary and specific activity. The business of
government is "not to inflame passion and give it new objects to feed
upon, but to inject into the activities of already too passionate men an
ingredient of moderation." Not the charismatic "leader" or the "re-
deemer" but the "referee" is the image of the ruler here. These, then,
are the alternatives – "the politics of passion" versus "the politics of
scepticism" – and Oakeshott we know considers the second to be
more appropriate to our current circumstances. In a people that is

conservative in hardly any other respect, political conservatism (not even paradoxically) makes a great deal of sense. "[I]t is not at all inconsistent," he writes in a sentence that could stand as the motto for the entire essay, "to be conservative in respect of government and radical in respect of almost every other activity." And it is this peculiar mixture of political conservatism and radical individualism and skepticism which recommends Montaigne, Pascal, Hobbes, and Hume to him over the more old-fashioned Burke.[134]

Among the many questions Oakeshott's non-metaphysical vindication of political conservatism provokes, there is one in particular that nags. If political conservatism is so appropriate to our circumstances, why have we neglected it and made "the activist dreamer the stereotype of the modern politician?" Oakeshott says in a footnote that he has not neglected to ask himself this question, but that he has tried to answer it elsewhere.[135] The question is, where? It is possible that he is referring to "Rationalism in Politics," where he argues that the rationalist style in politics was generated out of political inexperience. But there is another essay, "The Masses in Representative Democracy," published just one year after "On Being Conservative," which also addresses this question, and in a slightly different way than it was addressed in "Rationalism in Politics."[136] Instead of political inexperience, the later essay points to moral and emotional inadequacy on the part of the "masses" – specifically a passion for security and uniformity – as the crucial circumstance giving rise to the activist style of politics.[137]

Whether it is to "Rationalism in Politics" or to "The Masses in Representative Democracy" that Oakeshott is referring in his footnote, it is to the latter essay that I would now like to turn; for it clearly attempts to answer the question raised above about the relationship between rationalist politics and modern circumstances. There are two other reasons that make this essay worth considering at this point. In the first place, it carries us well into the argument of *On Human Conduct*, where substantial portions of the essay are incorporated. Secondly, and more importantly, it fills out what might have seemed in "On Being Conservative" a too one-dimensional and sanguine view of the individualistic basis of our political tradition. The essay reveals, I think, Oakeshott's deep affinity with some of the less sanguine but more profound moralists and political thinkers of the nineteenth century.

He begins his historical inquiry into the "masses," interestingly enough, not with the emergence of the "mass-man" but with the emergence of the "individual" at the dawn of the modern era. This reflects the general point of view of the entire essay: the pre-eminent event in modern European history is the emergence of the "individual"; the "mass-man" is a wholly derivative character. The story

Oakeshott has to tell about the emergence of the "individual" in his modern idiom is not entirely unfamiliar. He fixes the event roughly toward the end of the medieval period when the tight-knit character of corporate and communal life was beginning to break up. Italy figures prominently in the story, and he quotes Burckhardt, to whom his account obviously owes a great deal: "At the close of the thirteenth century Italy began to swarm with individuality; the ban laid upon human personality was dissolved; a thousand figures meet us, each in his own special shape and dress." This historic disposition to cultivate and enjoy individuality gradually spread to Northern Europe, and Montaigne is cited as one of its earliest and greatest exemplars. The disposition certainly had its vicissitudes over the course of the next four centuries, but ultimately it imposed itself profoundly on European conduct and belief. No department of life remained unaffected by it.[138]

There are two areas, according to Oakeshott, in which this experience of individuality was clearly reflected. It was reflected, first, in the field of ethical theory, and he cites Hobbes and Kant as notable theorists of the morality of individuality.[139] It was also reflected in a certain manner of governing and being governed, a manner which came to be called "modern representative democracy," and which received its most perfect expression in "parliamentary government." Oakeshott's account of this manner of governing and being governed characteristically does not emphasize political participation so much as it emphasizes the necessity of "an instrument of government capable of transforming the interests of individuality into rights and duties." Individuality is not natural, it is a great human achievement; and what this achievement required in the first place was an instrument of government capable of asserting the interests of individuality against already existing feudal rights and privileges. Such an instrument was ultimately found in "sovereign" legislative bodies. From these came a law "favourable to the interests of individuality," providing "the detail of what became a well-understood condition of human circumstance, commonly denoted by the word 'freedom.'" Oakeshott goes on to point out that this manner of governing was partnered by an understanding of the office of government as

> the maintenance of arrangements favourable to the interests of individuality, arrangements (that is) which emancipated the subject from the "chains" (as Rousseau put it) of communal allegiances, and constituted a condition of human circumstance in which the intimations of individuality might be explored and the experience of individuality enjoyed.[140]

Such was the "revolution" which overtook European sentiments, morals, and politics from roughly the thirteenth century to the seventeenth. But not everyone responded to the new circumstances in quite the same way. What excited some appeared to others as a burden. And in these latter Oakeshott discerns the outline of a character quite opposed to the emergent "individual": namely, the "individual *manqué*." This character is, of course, the seed from which the "mass-man" we are seeking eventually grew. But before he could become the "mass-man," one further ingredient (besides his native incapacity) was needed: a feeling of moral inferiority. This feeling of moral inferiority was the inevitable consequence of the moralization of the pursuit of individuality. To the "individual *manqué*'s" already acute feelings of inadequacy in the field of conduct was now added "the misery of guilt." And from this feeling of guilt sprang a new and more militant disposition:

> the impulse to escape from the predicament by imposing it upon all mankind. From the frustrated "individual *manqué*" there sprang the militant "anti-individual," disposed to assimilate the world to his own character by deposing the individual and destroying his moral prestige.

It is this passion for uniformity, fueled by *ressentiment*, which is the key to the character Oakeshott is investigating. The "anti-individual" did, of course, eventually discover that he belonged to the most numerous class in European society, thus becoming the "mass-man"; but Oakeshott insists that it is his resentful, anti-individualistic disposition, not his numbers, which defines the "mass-man."[141]

Oakeshott goes on to argue that the "anti-individual," like the "individual," also generated a morality to correspond to his character. Instead of celebrating "liberty" and "self-determination," though, the "anti-individual" stressed "equality" and "solidarity." And though at first this morality of equality and solidarity drew from the vocabulary of "the morality of the defunct communal order," Oakeshott insists it never really had anything to do with that morality. This new morality was anti-individualistic; it presupposed the existence of an individuality which it sought to suppress. The nucleus of the new morality "was the concept of a substantive condition of human circumstance represented as the 'common' or 'public' good, which was understood, not to be composed of various goods that might be sought by individuals on their own account, but to be an independent entity." And the repository of this "common good" was of course understood to be the "community."[142] Apart from calling it "a rickety construction," Oakeshott does not really subject this morality of the common good to criticism here. His engagement is descriptive, not critical. We must wait until *On Human Conduct* for a full philosophical critique of the notions of the "common good" and the "community" (or "society") which comprise this morality.

Besides a morality, the "anti-individual" also generated a distinctive manner of governing and a distinctive understanding of the office of government. And Oakeshott is at some pains to distinguish these from the manner of governing and the understanding of the office of government evoked by the "individual." The distinctions he draws are, for the most part, already familiar to us from the other essays we have considered in this section. With respect to the "anti-individual's" understanding of the office of government, it corresponded on the whole to his understanding of morality: "To govern was . . . to impose and maintain the substantive condition of human circumstance identified as 'the public good.'" The "anti-individual's" image of the ruler was, "not the referee of the collisions of individuals, but the moral leader and managing director of 'the community.'" This understanding of the office of government expressed itself in a manner of governing quite opposed to "parliamentary government," which, with its ancient procedures and inherent skepticism about final goals, proved to be peculiarly unsuited for the imposition of a uniform and substantive condition of human circumstance.[143] Far better suited to the aspirations of the "mass-man" was "popular government," which for Oakeshott is not the same thing as "democracy." Whereas "democracy" properly refers to a manner of constituting the authority of government, "popular government" is defined by the substantive engagements it undertakes, the substantive interests it promotes.[144] The end-result of the changes made in the name of "popular government" was an immense increase of power for governments. That "the people" inherited this power was, of course, an illusion. The "masses," not having desires or opinions but only impulses, were incapable of making choices on their own; they needed "leaders" to tell them what to think. It was these latter who were the real beneficiaries of the new, "popular" manner of governing. Politics under the influence of the "masses" became, not the art of "ruling," but the art of "leading" in the modern sense.[145]

Once again we come back to the observation with which "On Being Conservative" concluded, and which informed "Contemporary British Politics" and "The Political Economy of Freedom" as well: that there are two categorially distinct attitudes toward the activity of governing, one corresponding to the character and morality of the "individual," the other corresponding (as we have learned from this essay) to the character of the "mass-man." The distinction between these two understandings of government in some ways forms the starting-point of Oakeshott's reflections in *On Human Conduct*, and its clear recognition marks an appropriate stopping-point for this chapter. Before concluding, though, I should point out that Oakeshott in "The Masses in Representative Democracy" does not simply leave it at the recognition of a duality in our tradition. One moral and political disposition – that corresponding to the "individual" – is recognized to be dominant. "[T]he event of supreme and seminal importance in modern European history remains the emergence of the human individual in his modern idiom." The "mass-man," on the other hand, is depicted as a wholly "derivative character, an emanation of the pursuit of individuality, helpless, parasitic and able to survive only in opposition to individuality." And the morality of the "mass-man" is said to be a "rickety construction," incapable of resisting "relapse into inappropriate concepts of individuality."[146] In short, it might be said that this morality is not a concrete morality, and the "mass-man" is not a concrete character. And it is in terms of concreteness or self-sufficiency that the dominance of the "individual" is also to be understood. The morality of individuality is dominant in our tradition in the sense of being original, positive, and self-sufficient, not in the sense of being currently more popular or powerful than the morality of the "mass-man." Indeed, Oakeshott admits that in recent times the numbers are all on the side of the "mass-man." But this does not take away from the fact that the morality of the "mass-man" is derivative, reactive, and ultimately incoherent. This question of dominance will occupy us in chapter 5 in connection with the third essay of *On Human Conduct*, where Oakeshott retells at somewhat greater length the history we have just considered.

This brings us to the end of this section on rationalist and non-rationalist politics, as well as to the end of this chapter. And in conclusion I would like once again to underline the relationship between the two; the relationship, that is, between Oakeshott's skeptical, non-purposive politics, on the one hand, and his critique of rationalism as a whole, on the other. At the beginning of this section I denied that there was a tension between these two aspects of Oakeshott's thought, and I think my analysis has borne this out. Oakeshott's antagonism to the view that sees government as an instrument for the achievement of a single substantive purpose – the common good – reflects the rejection of self-conscious purpose as the ground of human activity which runs through his entire critique of rationalism. To this rationalistic view of government and politics he opposes another view which does not take purpose as the fundamental principle of social and political organization. Non-rationalist politics do not deny that society must be integrated in some way, only that this integration must be in terms of a single overarching purpose. Running through Oakeshott's critique of rationalism – and, indeed, going all the way back to the concrete logic of *Experience and its Modes* – is the idea of a complex mode of integration which is not reducible to the simpler and more familiar mode of integration in terms of a fixed, central purpose. The implications of this idea for our understanding of politics and political philosophy are only suggested in his writings on rationalism. For its complete elaboration we must turn to *On Human Conduct*.

V

ON HUMAN CONDUCT: *OAKESHOTT'S THEORY OF CIVIL ASSOCIATION*

On Human Conduct is a résumé and restatement of the several themes we have been following through Oakeshott's career. The ideas of philosophy, political philosophy, practical activity, and political activity which we have explored are all to be found there, as well as the distinction between rationalist and non-rationalist politics. It is the latter theme, though – the distinction between two categorially opposed modes of government – which provides the most convenient access to this rather dense and difficult work.

The distinction by now is familiar enough. In the essays we have examined so far Oakeshott expresses it in a number of different ways: the rule of law versus central planning; British democracy versus socialism; the politics of the diffusion of power versus collectivism; the politics of skepticism versus the politics of passion; the morality of individuality versus the morality of the common good; representative democracy or parliamentary government versus popular government. And of course his preference for the former member of each of these antitheses is never in doubt. It may seem that there is little in all this to distinguish Oakeshott's political outlook from the run-of-the-mill anti-socialism and anti-totalitarianism which characterizes so much postwar conservative or libertarian thought. But as we have seen, Oakeshott is always fighting a two-front battle. It is not only socialism or collectivism that comes in for criticism; what conservatives and libertarians generally oppose to these ideologies – whether it be the free market, natural rights, fundamental values, or religion – is also criticized. Indeed, it sometimes seems that Oakeshott spends more time criticizing those with whom we might expect him to have something in common than he does criticizing the socialist or collectivist "enemy." This suggests, perhaps, that he thinks certain defenses of liberalism have done more to strengthen the opposing camp than to consolidate its own resources. It certainly suggests that he thinks these defenses rest on an inadequate understanding of the nature of liberalism.

In *On Human Conduct* the distinction between rationalist and non-rationalist politics variously expressed above appears as the distinction between *universitas*, or enterprise association, and *societas*, or civil association. Here again the reader with an ear only for the commonplaces of practical politics might be led to conclude that Oakeshott's primary concern is to critique the notion of the state as a *universitas* and to recommend *societas*. But this is not the aim of the book at all. Though Oakeshott does indicate that there are serious problems with the understanding of the state as a *universitas*, his primary concern is to make clear the categorial distinction between this mode of association and civil association or *societas*. And once again much of what he has to say seems to be addressed, not to the proponents of *universitas*, but to the advocates of *societas* who nevertheless fail to grasp what exactly this mode of association consists in and the grounds upon which it is to be distinguished from *universitas*. Oakeshott writes in one place that civil association or *societas* has been "grossly misunderstood and misdescribed both by those who think it a desirable mode of association for a state and those who do not. For the most part we know it only in the parodies it has evoked." And he goes on to mention some of the more common of these misunderstandings: the identification of civil association with "democracy," with the enjoyment of "rights," with the "minimal state," with "free enterprise" or "capitalism"; finally, "the saddest of all misunderstandings," in which civil association is correctly understood as association in terms of non-instrumental law, "but defended as the mode of association more likely than any other to promote and to go on promoting the satisfaction of our diverse and proliferant wants."[1]

In connection with these misunderstandings a number of contemporary writers immediately come to mind: Dworkin, Nozick, Friedman, perhaps Hayek. Oakeshott's relationship to these and other contemporary writers I will be pursuing throughout this chapter, as well as in my conclusion. For now, though, I only want to emphasize that the principal concern of *On Human Conduct* is to understand *societas* or civil association, not to criticize the state as a *universitas*. Its argument is addressed to the friends of liberalism as much as (if not more than) to its enemies. If we are to preserve this "most notable human invention," civil association, Oakeshott writes, "we must get to know, not only our opponents, but ourselves more exactly than we do at present; we must defend our position with reasons appropriate to it."[2] It is to this project of getting to know ourselves more exactly that *On Human Conduct* is first and foremost to be seen as a contribution.

I have been using the term "liberalism," and Oakeshott's position with respect to this term and what it stands for deserves at least some preliminary comment. In some ways Oakeshott's attitude toward "liberalism" displays the same ambivalence as his attitude toward the anti-socialism and anti-totalitarianism of his contemporaries. On the one hand, he defends what might be called the "liberal tradition" against anti-liberal alternatives such as socialism or fascism. On the other, though, he rejects much of what the term "liberalism" generally connotes: for example, a belief in natural rights or a "crude and negative individualism."[3] He also rejects the materialism or economism which seems to be so closely entwined with the idea of "liberalism." It will be remembered that Oakeshott once stated that "the most questionable element of Liberal Democracy" has been "what may be called its moral ideal: 'the plausible ethics of productivity'."[4] And we shall see that one of the major thrusts of *On Human Conduct* is to purge liberalism of the materialism and economism with which it has been historically connected. Because Oakeshott finds the word "liberalism" loaded down with meanings that do not convey his own, he generally avoids it and uses instead "Representative Democracy" or (in the case of *On Human Conduct*) "civil association" or *societas* to denote the tradition he wishes to expound and defend. Nevertheless, I do not think it entirely misleading to regard his political philosophy as in some sense a restatement or reformulation of liberalism: a restatement in which the negative individualism and materialism mentioned above have been thoroughly criticized and superseded.

Let me further specify my understanding of Oakeshott's "liberalism" by contrasting it to two recent discussions of the matter. Kirk Koerner's *Liberalism and its Critics* and Charles Covell's *The Redefinition of Conservatism* take two quite different positions with respect to Oakeshott's attitude toward liberalism. In Koerner's book, Oakeshott is depicted (along with C. B. Macpherson, Herbert Marcuse, and Leo Strauss) as an essentially anti-liberal thinker. Whether the label "anti-liberal" adequately describes Strauss's complex attitude toward liberalism is questionable, but the label is absolutely misleading when applied to Oakeshott. Koerner errs when he equates Oakeshott's critique of rationalism with a critique of liberalism simply. Though liberalism historically has exhibited certain rationalistic and universalistic tendencies, there is no evidence that Oakeshott regards these tendencies as in any way necessary or intrinsic to liberalism. Indeed, in his own reformulation of the doctrine (as we shall see) he attempts to grasp liberalism as a living, vernacular tradition – what Hegel called a *Sittlichkeit* – instead of as a fixed body of abstract or natural rights.

More plausible than Koerner's characterization of Oakeshott as an anti-liberal thinker is Covell's characterization of him as a liberal in a rather conventional, Hobbesian sense. Nevertheless, I think he goes too far in the other direction and fails to grasp what is distinctive and original in Oakeshott's restatement of the liberal tradition. Covell argues that there is a tension in Oakeshott's postwar writings between his Hegelian emphasis on tradition, on the one hand, and his Hobbesian defense of civil association, on the other; and that in *On Human Conduct* he all but abandons the former for the latter. That there is no such tension between Oakeshott's Hegelian critique of rationalism in *Rationalism in Politics* and his advocacy of a skeptical, individualistic politics was in some ways the burden of my fourth chapter. In this fifth chapter I shall emphasize the Hegelian elements of *On Human Conduct* as much as (if not more than) the Hobbesian ones. For me, Oakeshott's Hobbesianism or liberalism is not in tension with his Hegelianism. What makes his restatement of liberalism interesting is precisely that it successfully synthesizes these two strands of thought, combining liberalism with a sophisticated historical outlook.

This returns us to the theme pursued in chapter 3 regarding Oakeshott's relationship to the tradition of modern political philosophy. In that chapter, it will be remembered, we found Oakeshott celebrating Hobbes for making will the basis of the state but also criticizing him for lacking a coherent theory of volition. We also found him looking to the idealist theory of the general or rational will as pointing the direction in which this defect might be remedied. In this chapter I try to show that *On Human Conduct* may be understood as a further development of this idealist reflection on will and the state. In the spirit of idealist political philosophy, the book attempts to overcome the oppositions between individual and government, will and law, freedom and authority, which have dogged liberal thought ever since Hobbes. Oakeshott's relationship to his idealist predecessors is of course not of a simple nature. We will find, for example, that he diverges sharply from the teleological tendencies of his British predecessors, Green and Bosanquet; and that, in the case of Hegel, he provides us with a highly original and productive rereading. But the important point is that he continues to move within the horizon of problems first set to political philosophy by idealism.

Given this understanding of Oakeshott's project, it is not surprising that I begin my analysis (in section 2 below) by considering his views on freedom and agency, and develop his theory of civil association (in sections 3 and 4) from there. In section 5 I take up some common criticisms of the theory in an effort to clarify its meaning. But before taking up the details of Oakeshott's theory of civil association, I would like to consider briefly the "meta-political" doctrine with which *On Human Conduct* begins. This doctrine not only defines the idea of philosophy which will govern Oakeshott's whole approach in *On Human Conduct*; it also carries us back to the idea of philosophy in *Experience and its Modes* with which this study began.

1. The Idea of Philosophy Revisited

In the preface to *On Human Conduct*, Oakeshott gives a good one-sentence definition of the idea of philosophy which informs the work: "Philosophical reflection is recognized here as the adventure of one who seeks to understand in other terms what he already understands and in which the understanding sought (itself unavoidably conditional) is a disclosure of the conditions of understanding enjoyed and not a substitute for it."[5] In this definition we recognize the two cardinal features of Oakeshott's idea of philosophy as it was originally expounded in *Experience and its Modes* and "The Concept of a Philosophical Jurisprudence." In the first place, there is the Socratic notion of philosophy, not as some esoteric activity totally divorced from our ordinary pre-philosophical experience, but as the exploration of the implications of knowledge we already possess. And second, there is the (not very Socratic) idea that the knowledge gained through philosophical reflection cannot be *applied* to the experience reflected upon; in short, the distinctively Oakeshottian gulf between theory and practice. Oakeshott proceeds to flesh these ideas out in the next thirty pages by giving an account of the nature of understanding in general. It is an account which in many respects parallels the account of experience in *Experience and its Modes*. Nevertheless, it contains nuances and even some slight deviations which make it worth examining in its own right.

The foundations of Oakeshott's account of understanding in *On Human Conduct* remain recognizably idealist. As he did in *Experience and its Modes*, he begins by rejecting the empiricist distinction between mediate and immediate experience, between understanding and the datum of understanding. There is no "immediate datum" from which understanding may be said to begin. Understanding always "begins in an already understood."[6] And the process of understanding is basically one in which this already understood comes to be more profoundly and explicitly understood.

Oakeshott distinguishes three different stages or levels in this process of understanding: recognition, identification, and theorizing. Recognition involves the noticing, comparing and distinguishing of characteristics (sizes, shapes, colors, etc.). And because it is concerned exclusively with characteristics, such recognition confers only a limited and somewhat arbitrary intelligibility on "goings-on." These characteristics may, however, be put together to form an "ideal character," which may then be used to identify goings-on. Here what was previously recognized as purple, hard, or tall is now identified as a wild flower, a hammer, or the Empire State Building. Further, the identities which emerge in this process of identification may be explored in terms of their relationships to one another. Here we have arrived at a kind of theorizing, but one which is confined to what Oakeshott calls a "platform of conditional understanding" (what he earlier in *Experience and its Modes* called a mode of experience). On such a platform of conditional understanding, every going-on is identified in terms of an unquestioned ideal character – this, indeed, constitutes its conditionality. And though relationships between these identities may be explored and mapped, the identities themselves remain unproblematic and unquestionable.[7]

A more critical attitude toward these identities, however, is also possible. Instead of simply relating them to one another as unproblematic "facts," a theorist may also try to enhance their intelligibility by understanding them in terms of their conditions or postulates. Oakeshott uses the example of reading a clock. Reading a clock postulates but does not question the idea "time." "Time" may, however, itself be interrogated and become the subject of inquiry. Here one subject of inquiry ("What is the time?") is replaced by another ("What is time?"), and the theorist comes to occupy a new and in some sense superior platform of conditional understanding. To understand a going-on in terms of its postulates, then, is to understand something familiar "in terms different from those in which it is already understood." And examples of this theoretical engagement include the natural sciences, the historical sciences, and philosophical disciplines such as ethics, aesthetics, and political philosophy.[8]

Nor is this the end of the process. For these new platforms of conditional understanding may themselves be questioned and investigated in terms of their postulates. To this unconditionally critical process of exploring experience in terms of its postulates Oakeshott gives the name "philosophy." The accord here with *Experience and its Modes* is both deep and clear. Where in that earlier work philosophy was defined as "experience without reservation or arrest, experience which is critical throughout, unhindered by what is subsidiary, partial or abstract," here it is understood as "an unconditional adventure in which every achievement of understanding is an invitation to investigate itself and where the reports a theorist makes to himself are interim triumphs of temerity over scruple." And as in *Experience and its Modes* (though perhaps more unambiguously here in *On Human Conduct*), philosophy is understood to be unconditional not because it is completely free of conditions, or because it issues in unconditional theorems; "what constitutes its unconditionality is the continuous recognition of the conditionality of conditions."[9]

This is not to suggest that there are no differences between *Experience and its Modes* and *On Human Conduct* with respect to the idea of philosophy. Indeed, a subtle shift does seem to have occurred in Oakeshott's thinking about the relationship between philosophy as the unconditional engagement of understanding and the various arrests of this engagement. In *Experience and its Modes* this relationship was conceived largely in antagonistic terms. The abstract modes of experience, lacking self-consciousness about their abstract character, were said to be unable to resist putting themselves in competition with the concrete whole and thus falling into actual error.[10] The modes constituted a denial of the unqualified quest for a completely coherent world of experience, and it is for this reason that the primary emphasis in *Experience and its Modes* is on avoiding or rejecting them. In *On Human Conduct*, on the other hand, Oakeshott doesn't characterize the various arrests of understanding as necessarily lacking self-consciousness or denying the unconditional engagement of philosophical understanding. The philosophical "engagement to be perpetually *en voyage*," he writes,

> may be arrested without being denied. The theorist who drops anchor here or there and puts out his equipment of theoretic hooks and nets in order to take the fish of the locality, interrupts but does not betray his calling. And indeed, the unconditional engagement of understanding must be arrested and inquiry must remain focused upon a *this* if any identity is to become intelligible in terms of its postulates. An investigation which denies or questions its own conditions surrenders its opportunity of achieving its own conditional perfection; the theorist who interrogates instead of using his theoretic equipment catches no fish.[11]

Perhaps the main significance of this shift in Oakeshott's thinking relates to what he earlier in *Experience and its Modes* called "pseudo-philosophy." In that work, it will be remembered, fields such as ethics, political philosophy, and theology were characterized as "pseudo-philosophical" because in them the unconditional pursuit of an absolutely coherent world of ideas was qualified or arrested. And Oakeshott argued that such qualification or arrest constituted a form of philosophical error. Pseudo-philosophical experience failed to recognize clearly the world to which it belonged and therefore was convicted of abstraction; it was not completely self-conscious experience.[12] In *On Human Conduct*, however, in keeping with his new understanding of the relationship between philosophy and other forms of experience, Oakeshott no longer characterizes arrests such as ethics or political philosophy as defective, abstract, or incompletely self-conscious forms of experience. Instead, he calls the theorist who turns aside from the unconditional engagement of interrogating conditions in order to theorize a particular identity such as moral conduct or civil association a "self-consciously conditional theorist." Such a theorist, he says, "has a heavenly home, but he is in no hurry to reach it. If he is concerned to theorize moral conduct or civil association he must forswear metaphysics."[13] This notion of self-consciously conditional theorizing, then, marks something of a change from the notion of pseudo-philosophy in *Experience and its Modes*. Nor is this change entirely fortuitous, since it is in just such self-consciously conditional theorizing that Oakeshott will be engaging in *On Human Conduct*.

There are two further points Oakeshott wishes to make about this sort of conditional engagement to understand an identity in terms of its postulates, both of which are relevant to his own conditional engagement to theorize "human conduct." The first concerns the distinction (as it is now frequently formulated) between interpretive "understanding" and scientific "explanation." Oakeshott argues that in order to become a subject of theoretical inquiry, a going-on must be unambiguously identified as belonging to one of two categories: either it must be identified as an exhibition of intelligence (e.g., a biologist at work), or it must be recognized as a non-intelligent instance (e.g., a wave breaking on the shore). Each of these two categories of identities predicates very different sorts of inquiry, very different conditions to be inquired into. In the first case, the conditions will be "practices" which require to be learned or understood in order to be participated in (e.g., religious beliefs, rituals, traditions of inquiry, etc.). In the second, the conditions to be inquired into will be "processes" which need not be learned or understood in order to be operative (e.g., the law of gravitation, chemical decomposition).[14]

In many respects the distinction Oakeshott draws here between goings-on identified as exhibitions of intelligence and goings-on recognized as instances of non-intelligent processes parallels the distinction he drew between history and science in *Experience and its Modes*.[15] And as he did there, he insists here that the distinction he is drawing is not to be understood as an ontological distinction between objects or things, such as between spirit and nature. The distinction "is not a distinction between mental or physical or between minds and bodies regarded as entities. It is a distinction within the engagement of understanding, a distinction between 'sciences' (that is, ideal characters) and the identities with which they are concerned."[16] Again as he did in *Experience and its Modes*, Oakeshott here discusses two modes of inquiry which he believes suffer from categorial confusion and ambiguity: psychology and sociology. In the case of psychology, he argues that it is perfectly within its rights when it concerns itself with causal processes, but that it goes wrong when it applies its causal laws to goings-on identified as exhibitions of intelligence. Sociology, on the other hand, he recognizes as a legitimate though limited form of historical understanding which is fatally corrupted when it conceives the intelligent procedures with which it is properly concerned in terms of "systems" with causal conditions and "structures" displaying functional relationships.[17]

The second point Oakeshott makes with respect to the theoretical engagement to understand an identity in terms of its postulates concerns the relationship between such theoretical understanding and the uncritical understanding which it seeks to theorize. Here we link up once again with the familiar distinction between theory and practice. And as we would expect, Oakeshott draws it sharply. He argues that, though the understanding of the theorist is undoubtedly superior to the practical or commonsense understanding which he seeks to theorize, it nevertheless cannot take its place. The theorist is concerned with something quite different from relating or integrating the unproblematic identities of a platform of conditional understanding; he is concerned to interrogate these identities and understand them in terms of their postulates. And postulates are not principles from which correct performances may be deduced. To use theoretical knowledge in this way to direct practical activity is the spurious engagement of the "theoretician."[18]

Oakeshott goes on to illustrate his view of the relationship between theory and practice in an interesting interpretation and criticism of Plato's allegory of the cave. His main criticism (which owes something to Aristotle) concerns Plato's contention that the understanding of the philosopher (alleged to be unconditional) is not only superior to, but a substitute for, every other conditional or cave understanding.[19] We have already seen why Oakeshott rejects this contention. Apart from this criticism, though, it is perhaps worth noting just what Oakeshott's account of philosophy shares with Plato's: most importantly, the denial of the unconditionality of the cave; and the recognition of philosophy as the critical inquiry into the conditions of conditions. It is, I think, no accident that Oakeshott speaks of the platforms of conditional understanding as "prisons" from which the theorist makes at least a partial escape (if only to occupy another such platform). This Platonism in Oakeshott's thought goes all the way back to *Experience and its Modes*, and his insistence that the furthest thing from our needs is that philosophers should be kings should not be allowed to obscure it.

One of the reasons I underline this Platonic element in Oakeshott's thought is to prevent his idea of philosophy from being too easily assimilated to the anti-foundationalism of a thinker like Richard Rorty. In chapter 2 I pointed out that Oakeshott's idea of philosophy, while showing certain affinities with Rorty's anti-foundationalist conception, could not be identified with it. In that work Oakeshott certainly rejects the notion of philosophy as foundational in the sense of being a master-discipline which legitimates and ultimately dictates to other disciplines. Nevertheless, he does not follow Rorty in his skeptical and pragmatist attempt to de-privilege philosophy by blurring the line between it and other disciplines.[20] Much the same can be said about Oakeshott's conception of philosophy in *On Human Conduct*.

While rejecting the foundational notion of philosophy as a substitute for other modes of knowing, Oakeshott here nevertheless sees philosophy as a distinct form of understanding which is in some sense superior to other modes of understanding. And while he does not conceive of philosophy as being "transcendental" in the sense defined by Rorty (and ascribed to Plato, Kant and Hegel), he does conceive it (along the lines of Plato, Kant, and Hegel) as the transcendental inquiry into the conditions of conditions.

Of course, it is Oakeshott's notion of "conversation" that Rorty invokes for his anti-foundationalist conception of philosophy, and the question arises whether this notion of conversation does not in some way represent a divergence from the view of philosophy articulated in *Experience and its Modes* and, of course, re-articulated in *On Human Conduct*. This has been suggested by some commentators. Citing the non-hierarchical image of "the conversation of mankind" (without symposiarch or arbiter), as well as Oakeshott's characterization of philosophy as a "parasitic" activity springing from the conversation but making no specific contribution to it, they argue that the idea of philosophy in *Rationalism in Politics* represents something of a retreat from the large claims made on behalf of philosophy in *Experience and its Modes*. Of course, this retreat was only temporary, since in *On Human Conduct* Oakeshott seems to return to something like his original view.[21]

I must say I do not find this interpretation of the development of Oakeshott's view of philosophy very persuasive. In the first place, the vacillating pattern of "original view – retreat – and return" does not strike me as ultimately intelligible. In the second, most of the statements about philosophy in *Rationalism in Politics* (which are, for the most part, incidental) can I think be rendered compatible with the general view of philosophy articulated in *Experience and its Modes* and *On Human Conduct*. The idea of philosophy as a parasitic activity seems to me perfectly compatible with the understanding of philosophy as inquiry into the conditions or postulates of other modes of knowing. And that philosophy is not seen as the symposiarch or arbiter of "the conversation of mankind" need not imply that it does not represent a superior understanding to that of other voices in the conversation; it only implies that it cannot dictate to them. All this (again) is not to suggest that there has been no change in Oakeshott's views. In *On Human Conduct*, as I have already argued, there does seem to be less emphasis on philosophy's judging and rejecting other modes of knowledge. And this shift is undoubtedly intimated in the image of conversation in *Rationalism in Politics*.

Having expounded Oakeshott's idea of philosophy in *On Human Conduct* and disclosed its relationship to his earlier views, we may now turn to his theory of civil association and the view of human conduct which lies behind it.

2. The Idea of Freedom and the Idea of a Practice

Oakeshott begins his inquiry into civil association with a lengthy consideration of "human conduct" and the freedom which distinguishes it. In other words, like Hobbes, Rousseau, Kant, and Hegel before him, he takes will or freedom as the starting point for his political philosophy.[22] It will be remembered that Oakeshott early on in his career celebrated Hobbes for making will the basis of the state; but he also criticized Hobbes for not having a coherent theory of volition. He went on to cite Rousseau's doctrine of the "general will," Hegel's doctrine of the "rational will," and Bosanquet's doctrine of the "real will" as notable attempts to overcome this deficiency in Hobbes's political philosophy. The first essay of *On Human Conduct* can, I think, be seen as Oakeshott's own contribution to this effort. In it he tries to conceive will or freedom in such a way that its qualification by law or morality need not entail its being compromised. Let us follow him in this attempt.

The first thing to notice is that the freedom with which Oakeshott is concerned here is the freedom which is inherent in human conduct. "Freedom" here denotes a formal condition of all conduct recognized to be human; it does not refer to "the quality of being substantively 'self-directed' which an agent may or may not achieve" – what is more properly called "self-determination" or "autonomy."[23] In what, then, does this formal freedom inherent in human agency consist?

Oakeshott discusses it largely in terms of what he calls "reflective consciousness." Human conduct is "free" because it is recognized to be an expression or exhibition of intelligence. We do not attribute freedom to the setting sun because we do not recognize it as an exhibition of intelligence. It is intelligence, then, and not "free-will," which ultimately distinguishes the freedom inherent in agency. "Indeed, what is called 'the will' is nothing but intelligence in doing; in denying 'will' to an ebbing tide we are refusing to recognize it as an exhibition of intelligence."[24]

Of course, by specifying human conduct in terms of reflective consciousness or intelligence, Oakeshott does not mean to suggest that human conduct is notably reflective, self-conscious, or rational; only that it involves understanding (which may, of course, be implicit), that it must ultimately be learned. His concern is to distinguish human conduct, not from spontaneous, habitual, or irrational conduct, but from a genetic, psychological, or otherwise non-intelligent "process."[25] Human conduct is a matter of beliefs, understandings, and meanings, not of biological impulses, organic tensions, or genetic urges. It is the thoroughly meaningful or intelligible – one might say "hermeneutical" – character of human conduct that Oakeshott wants to emphasize here. In this regard his account recalls the account of practical activity in *Experience and its Modes* with its emphasis on practice as a "world of ideas." The "free" agent postulated in human conduct is one "who inhabits a world of intelligible *pragmata*, who is composed entirely of understandings, and who is what he understands (or misunderstands) himself to be."[26] No aspect of human conduct – neither situation, response, nor satisfaction – is allowed to escape this minimal condition of understanding or intelligibility.

Oakeshott considers each of these aspects of human conduct separately, beginning with the situation which the agent confronts in action. This situation is not a brute or natural datum; it is what the agent understands (or misunderstands) it to be, what it means to him. Again, it is because his situation is an understanding and not a mere "organic tension" that the agent can be said to be "free." "He is 'free' not because his situation is alterable by an act of unconstrained 'will' but because it is an understood situation and because doing is an intelligent engagement."[27] As an understanding, the agent's situation is necessarily his own. But Oakeshott is quick to point out that this does not mean that it is either "merely subjective" or that it cannot include the wants or interests of others. As he did in *Experience and its Modes*, he argues here that nothing in experience is "merely subjective," subjectivity or "mineness" being only an abstract aspect of experience. Because an agent's diagnosis of his situation is an understanding and not a mere "feeling" or "organic tension," it cannot be simply subjective. An agent's understanding of his situation is an "objective" conclusion which may be questioned by himself or by others. If upon examination this understanding reveals itself to be a misunderstanding, it does not thereby cease to be "objective." "'Objectivity' is not an attribute of correct understanding, it is an attribute of understanding distinguished from mere 'feeling'." By the same token, the intelligent character of human conduct releases it from necessary egocentricity or instinctive self-gratification.[28]

An agent's understanding of his situation is always a diagnosis; and this diagnosis, Oakeshott maintains, is always made in specific terms. The situation is not simply unacceptable, it is unacceptable in some specific way. The specificity of the situation is again tied to its being an understood, and not simply a "felt," situation. Now the specific unacceptability of a situation invites some sort of response. This response is, of course, related to the diagnosed unacceptability, but (Oakeshott argues) it is neither caused by nor deducible from it; it is a "genuine answer or rejoinder which must be chosen by the agent concerned." Once again we reach the definite border of Oakeshott's understanding of the freedom intrinsic to agency: an agent "is not 'free' because he is able (or because he believes himself to be able) to 'will' what he shall do or say; he is 'free' because his response to his situation, like the situation itself, is the outcome of an intelligent engagement."[29]

In acting, an agent of course seeks a satisfaction, and this "imagined and wished-for" satisfaction constitutes the "meaning" or "intention" of his action. According to Oakeshott, the satisfaction sought in conduct is simply the specific unacceptability of an agent's current situation "remedied and abated." It is thus an understood, and not a merely "natural," satisfaction. It is also specific, being tied to a specific situation. Conduct is not the pursuit of ideal satisfactions but of ends already implicit in it. Nor is there a putative substantive end such as "happiness" which is pursued in all conduct. "I cannot *want* 'happiness'; what I want is to idle in Avignon or hear Caruso sing." Of course, the word "happiness" (Oakeshott also mentions expressions such a "survival," "pleasure," "the desirable," and "the good") is not meaningless; but it refers to a common formal character of actions, not to a common substantive end; it refers to "the ideal condition, impossible to be made the substantive outcome sought in conduct, in which the performances of agents continuously achieve their wished-for outcomes (whatever they may be), and in which these specific outcomes are not found to be unduly disappointing." The affinity with Hobbes, who defined felicity as "continual success in obtaining those things which a man from time to time desireth," is here unmistakable. Oakeshott allows nothing to qualify what he sees as the inherent "endlessness" (which we saw was such a prominent feature of his analysis of practical activity in *Experience and its Modes*) of conduct. Conduct for him contains no "final solutions"; "and 'happiness' is not a substantive condition to be aimed at but merely not to be thwarted in this engagement."[30]

One other aspect of the satisfaction sought in human conduct (relating more to its content than to its form) adds to the contingency and diurnality Oakeshott sees at the heart of human conduct: namely, that such satisfaction consists largely of the contingent responses of other agents. In conduct *inter homines* the imagined and wished-for outcomes of actions are the actions of other agents. This is what makes conduct *inter homines* particularly hazardous; it involves "making a bargain with an imperfectly imagined future," a future "composed of the actions and choices of other agents." In short, conduct *inter homines* consists mainly of transactions between agents. And when Oakeshott speaks of "conduct *inter homines*," it is this transactional character of human conduct that he chiefly has in mind.[31]

What Oakeshott has so far described as human conduct – "agents responding to their own understood contingent situations by choosing to do or say *this* rather than *that* in relation to imagined and wished-for outcomes"[32] which are themselves composed of the actions of other agents – he refers to under the general rubric of "self-disclosure." There is, as we shall see, another aspect of human conduct to be considered – namely, "self-enactment" – but insofar as an agent responds to his understood contingent situation by choosing an action with a specific meaning he is said to "disclose" himself. This does not mean that he somehow makes actual what is already potential or latent within him. The self that is disclosed in conduct is not to be thought of as something already there, a "nature" or a potentiality or a latency. Oakeshott's historical and hermeneutical conception of human conduct will not allow for that. For him, as we have seen, a man is what he understands himself to be, and his contingent situations are also what he understands them to be. These understandings and self-understandings do not occur naturally; they can only be come by in a process of learning. "A man is what he learns to become"; "he has a 'history' but no 'nature'." Thus, what a man discloses in conduct is his own historic beliefs about himself and the world around him. It is this emphasis on the historicity of human being and conduct that distinguishes Oakeshott's notion of "self-disclosure" from the older idealist notion of "self-realization," to which it is of course akin. "Self-disclosure" avoids the teleological suggestion inherent in the notion of "self-realization." Oakeshott stresses that "there is no ultimate or perfect man hidden in the womb of time or prefigured in the characters who now walk the earth."[33]

As was pointed out above, conduct *inter homines* according to Oakeshott consists mainly of transactions between agents. But these transactions, he goes on to argue, are not by themselves self-sufficient or self-explanatory. Such "*ad hoc* terminable encounters postulate more durable relationships between agents which are not themselves transactions but are the conditional context of all such transactions."[34] It is to this most important postulate of human conduct, then, that we must now turn.

The more durable relationships presupposed by conduct *inter homines* and within which individual transactions take place Oakeshott calls "practices." A "practice" he defines as any set of considerations, manners, uses, customs, conventions, maxims, principles, or rules which governs or "adverbially" qualifies human actions and relationships. And he cites a number of different examples, varying in size and complexity: relationships involving abstract *personae* such as those of friends, of neighbors, of husband and wife, teacher and pupil, master and servant; ways of life such as the stoic *apatheia* and medieval chivalry; complex modes of discourse such as science, history, poetry, and philosophy. What these all have in common is that they specify procedural or adverbial conditions to be subscribed to in acting; they do not specify substantive performances or actions.[35]

What more than anything else Oakeshott wants to emphasize about these practices is that they in no way compromise what he has already defined as the freedom inherent in agency. They do not do so for two reasons. In the first place, a practice is not a biological, psychological, or unspecified "social" relationship; it is "an understood relationship,

capable of being engaged in only in virtue of having been learned." It
is a relationship based, not on natural propensities (such as greg-
ariousness) or physical propinquity, but on mutual understandings.
The practice of a neighborly relationship, for example, does not
simply consist in people living next door to one another; rather, it
consists in their understanding themselves to be neighbors. The
second reason a practice does not compromise the freedom inherent in
agency relates to its adverbial or procedural character. A practice
"prescribes conditions for, but does not determine, the substantive
choices and performances of agents." The "practical," according to
Oakeshott, is only an aspect of any action; it must always be accompanied by a substantive choice or action. A rule or maxim, for
example, does not "tell a performer what choice to make"; "it only
announces conditions to be subscribed to in making choices." This
applies even to those rules and procedures which have the appearance
of forbidding (and not merely adverbially qualifying) substantive
actions and choices, for example, criminal laws. "A criminal law . . .
does not forbid killing or lighting a fire, it forbids killing 'murderously'
or lighting a fire 'arsonically'." Because they are adverbial qualifi-
cations and not specific commands, the requirements of a practice
cannot simply be "obeyed" or "disobeyed," according to Oakeshott;
"they are subscribed to or not subscribed to." Similarly, they cannot
be "applied" to conduct; they can only be "used" in conduct.[36]

What Oakeshott here theorizes under the rubric of "practice" is
quite obviously what he once theorized under the rubric of "tradition." And what he says can be understood as a clarification of what
he previously was trying to express with that word. His principal
point, as we have just seen, is that the customs, rules, maxims, and so
forth, which compose a practice (or tradition) are not commands to
perform specific actions but adverbial considerations to be taken into
account when acting. It is never enough simply to know what the
rules are; one must also know how to "illustrate" (and not merely
"apply") them in substantive actions. The "practical" is only an
aspect of action; it must always be partnered by a substantive action
which it itself cannot specify. A practice cannot be performed; it can
only be subscribed to. All this was implicit – and more than implicit –
in the view of human activity Oakeshott presented in *Rationalism in
Politics*. As we saw, it was not a doctrine about the rationality of
history that lay at the heart of his notion of tradition there, but rather
a doctrine about the ultimate indeterminacy of rules and general
principles, and the necessity of supplementing them with "practical"
or "traditional" knowledge. Nevertheless, it was difficult to disengage
the word "tradition" from its conventional association with the past
and the ancestral, and this no doubt is what led Oakeshott to abandon
it for "practice" in *On Human Conduct*.[37]

The continuity between the notion of tradition in *Rationalism in Politics* and the notion of a practice in *On Human Conduct* is perhaps most clearly evinced in Oakeshott's use of the analogy of language. In *Rationalism in Politics*, it will be remembered, the acquisition and practice of a tradition of behavior was compared to the acquisition and practice of a language.[38] In *On Human Conduct* the analogy of language becomes even more prominent. A practice is described as "a language of self-disclosure." And what Oakeshott chiefly has in mind when he makes this analogy is again the adverbial or formal character of a practice. Like a language, a practice

> does not impose upon an agent demands that he shall think certain thoughts, entertain certain sentiments, or make certain utterances. It comes to him as various invitations to understand, to choose, and to respond. It is composed of conventions and rules of syntax, and it is continuously invented by those who speak it, and using it is adding to its resources. It is an instrument to be played upon, not a tune to be played.[39]

We will be returning to this analogy of language shortly in connection with Oakeshott's notion of a moral practice; but for the moment, I only want to indicate the continuity between his notion of a practice in *On Human Conduct* and his earlier notion of a tradition in this regard.

One other, more historical antecedent of Oakeshott's notion of a practice must here be mentioned: namely, Hegel's notion of *Sittlichkeit*. In an earlier chapter I compared Oakeshott's notion of tradition to the Hegelian notion of *Sittlichkeit*. It should therefore come as no surprise that I now see "practice" as a further interpretation of this untranslatable German term. For Hegel, as for Oakeshott, the individual, ad hoc transactions which comprise conduct *inter homines* "postulate more durable relationships between agents which are not themselves transactions but the conditional context of all such transactions." And the name he gives to these more durable relationships is *Sittlichkeit*. That Oakeshott sees an intimate connection between Hegel's notion of *Sittlichkeit* and his own notion of a practice becomes clear in his interpretation of the *Philosophy of Right* in the third essay of *On Human Conduct*. I take this interpretation up in some detail below. For now let me simply mention that Oakeshott emphasizes there with respect to *Sittlichkeit* what he emphasizes here with respect to a practice: namely, that it in no way compromises the freedom inherent in agency. A *sittlich* relationship is an understood, not a "natural," relationship; and it is a relationship which prescribes not substantive choices or actions but only procedural conditions to be taken into account when choosing and acting. The connection between Hegel's notion of *Sittlichkeit* and Oakeshott's notion of a practice will become clearer in the course of my discussion of the latter's notion of a specifically moral practice.

So far Oakeshott has distinguished two sorts of human relationship: what he calls "transactional" relationship, in which agents seek substantive satisfactions in the responses of other agents; and "practical" relationship, in which these transitory transactions are adverbially qualified by procedures. He now proceeds to draw a further distinction between two sorts of "practical" relationship, two sorts of practices. On the one hand, he says, there are practices "which are designed to promote the success of the transactions . . . they govern," practices which are "instrumental to the achievement of imagined and wished-for satisfactions." An office routine, the rules for making pastry, and the arrangements composing an economy would all be examples of such instrumental or "prudential" practices. On the other hand, there are practices which are not instrumental to any particular purpose or enterprise. Such practices Oakeshott calls "moral" practices. What is characteristic of a morality or a moral practice is that "it is not instrumental to the achievement of any substantive purpose or to the satisfaction of any substantive want," not even to such generalized purposes as are represented by the "common good," the "human good," or "human excellence." These latter expressions, Oakeshott argues, do not properly refer to substantive purposes or satisfactions which may or may not be chosen by an agent, but rather (like "happiness") they refer to the formal character of conduct. In short, a morality is "a practice without any extrinsic purpose," whose conditions are subscribed to "in seeking the satisfaction of any want." It is "the *ars artium* of conduct; the practice of all practices; the practice of agency without further specification."[40]

A number of critics have found Oakeshott's identification of morality with a non-purposive or non-instrumental practice here arbitrary and questionable.[41] And it must be admitted that he does not provide much argument for it. He seems to assume, with Kant, that there must be a distinction between moral and prudential conduct. If moral conduct is reduced to prudential conduct, as in utilitarianism, the force and meaning of the adjective "moral" is still to seek.[42] There is something profoundly Aristotelian in Oakeshott's procedure here, as in the rest of *On Human Conduct* (as he himself points out).[43] It is a procedure, not of reduction, but of progressive differentiation and specification, in which the intuitive distinctions of ordinary consciousness are more precisely and explicitly formulated. With respect to morality, this procedure initially leads him to side with Kant over the utilitarians. But as we shall see, his final position is less Kantian than Hegelian.

A certain negativity characterizes Oakeshott's discussion of morality to this point. He has told us that a moral practice is not an instrumental practice, but not much more. What he positively conceives a moral practice to be only becomes clear when he returns once again to the analogy of language. A moral practice is like a language, he writes, "in being an instrument of understanding and a medium of intercourse, in having a vocabulary and a syntax of its own, and in being spoken well or ill." And like a language, it is a wholly historic achievement, reflecting the historic self-understandings of its speakers. There are many such moral languages in the world, he insists; and this "plurality cannot be resolved by being understood as so many contingent and regrettable divergencies from a fancied perfect and universal language of moral intercourse (a law of God, a utilitarian 'critical' morality, or so-called 'rational morality')." That such a resolution should have been attempted, however, he does not find surprising, since "human beings are apt to be disconcerted unless they feel themselves to be upheld by something more substantial than the emanations of their own contingent imaginations." But for the "modest mortal with a self to disclose and a soul to make," the availability of a "familiar and resourceful moral language (and one for which he may hope to acquire a *Sprachgefühl*)" will be more than enough.[44]

What Oakeshott most wants to emphasize with his analogy of language is the wholly colloquial or vernacular character of a morality – an emphasis which marked his analysis of morality in *Rationalism in Politics* as well. A morality is not something "above" our daily existence which we only bring to bear on our actions through an act of reflective effort; rather, it is a medium for conduct without which no action or utterance could take place. A morality does not somehow supervene on the more primary or "natural" activity of desiring or of instinctual gratification; it is a language within which the pursuit of any satisfaction takes place, a knowledge we are never completely without. "There is no agency which is not the acknowledgement of a moral practice, and no moral conduct which is not an exercise of agency." Over and over again Oakeshott stresses this vernacular and colloquial character of a moral practice; the fact that it is a "living and vulgar language" continuously used by agents to disclose and enact themselves, to understand and interact with others. Moral conduct is not "lurching from perplexity to perplexity," nor is it "solving problems"; "it is agents continuously related to one another in the idiom of a familiar language of moral converse."[45] It is just this living, vulgar, mundane, vernacular character of morality which constitutes (as I have already pointed out in connection with *Rationalism in Politics*) one of the most purely Hegelian elements in Oakeshott's thought. Morality is recognized to be, not the strenuous and reflective affair it was for Kant, but something much more ordinary and vital.

Oakeshott sums up his entire point of view in a passage criticizing the romantic notion of "moral autonomy" implicit in Kant's writings and more explicit in vulgar versions of existentialism. Because the passage encapsulates so well his view of the relationship between a moral practice and the autonomy or freedom intrinsic to agency, I quote it at length:

> What is called "moral autonomy" does not require moral choice to be a gratuitous, criterionless exercise of a so-called "will" (an isolated *meum*) in which a lonely agent simultaneously recognizes or even creates a "value" for which he is wholly responsible and places himself under its command, thus miraculously releasing himself from organic impulse, rational contingency, and authoritative rules of conduct. Nor is it conditional upon an agent's critical consent or approval of a rule of conduct in terms of a recognition of purported reasons for considering it to be desirable. Nor, again, does it require some other release from having to recognize a rule of conduct merely in terms of its being a rule; that is, in terms of its authority. Indeed, strictly speaking, there is no such experience as "moral choice". What is chosen in conduct is a substantive action or utterance in which an agent embarks upon the adventure of seeking an imagined and wished-for satisfaction in the response of another. And his "moral autonomy" lies, first, in his character as an agent (that is, in his action or utterance being a response to an understood want and not the consequence of an organic impulse), and secondly, in his action or utterance as self-disclosure and self-enactment in a contingent subscription of his own to the conditions of a practice (which cannot tell him what to do or to say) recognized in terms of its authority. Human conduct is not first having unconditional wants (individual or communal) and then allowing prudential reason and moral sensibility to indicate or to determine the choice of the actions in which their satisfaction is sought; it is wanting intelligently (that is, in recognition of prudential and moral considerations) and doing this successfully or not so successfully.[46]

Having stressed the vernacular character of a moral practice, Oakeshott goes on to consider an aspect of morality which at first seems to contradict this character: namely, moral rules. The relationship of rules to a tradition of behavior is, of course, a subject which was discussed at length in *Rationalism in Politics*, and Oakeshott's argument here for the most part parallels what he said there. Moral rules, he argues, are "abridgements" of a concrete moral practice; they "concentrate into specific precepts considerations of adverbial desirability which lie dispersed in a moral language." In rules (and *a fortiori* in "duties," i.e., obligations owed in respect of occupying a specific position or office) a moral language loses some of its characteristic flexibility or "play." General moral considerations or "intimations" are transformed into relatively precise prescriptions. But these more stringent considerations are not self-contained or self-sufficient; they are abstractions which cannot survive apart from the concrete vernacular language from which they derive. Moral rules and duties give only an abbreviated account of the conditions containing the continuous flow of diurnally enacted genial relationships which constitute unaffected moral association; no moral practice can be reduced to the rules, the duties or the "ideals" it obtrudes, and *rightness* is never more than an aspect of moral response.

Further, Oakeshott argues, rules and duties, though relatively specific, remain "unavoidably indeterminate." They do not specify choices or performances, only considerations to be taken into account in choosing and acting. "They are not commands to be obeyed but relatively precise considerations to be subscribed to. They are used in conduct, not applied in conduct." In short, Oakeshott maintains (as he did in *Rationalism in Politics*) that rules alone are never enough to determine concrete activity; they "are not criteria of good conduct . . . they are prevailing winds which agents should take account of in sailing their different courses."[47]

There is one more point Oakeshott wishes to make about a moral practice, concerning an aspect of human conduct which he has hitherto said little about. Up to this point, he has discussed human conduct largely in terms of "self-disclosure," that is, agents disclosing themselves in actions aimed at procuring satisfactions composed primarily of the responses of other agents. And a moral practice he has identified mainly as a "language of self-disclosure," a language in terms of which these transactions between agents may be understood to take place. He now tells us, though, that there is another aspect of conduct to be taken into account. This aspect concerns, not the "intention" of an action, that is, its imagined and wished-for outcome, but the "motive" or "sentiment" with which an action is performed. In acting, an agent not only chooses an action aimed at some specific satisfaction, he also chooses a sentiment or motive with which to perform that action (e.g., fear, benevolence, pity, compassion, envy). Neither consideration is directly related to or deducible from the other. A man may kill, for example, out of a variety of motives – love, hatred, compassion, and so forth; he may perform the duties of an office out of pride or fear. Actions do not specify motives, and motives do not specify actions.[48]

To this second aspect of human conduct – relating to the sentiments or motives with which actions are performed – Oakeshott gives the name "self-enactment"; and he maintains that a moral practice is no less concerned with it than with self-disclosure. A moral practice specifies the conditions not only of moral self-disclosure but also of worthy or "virtuous" self-enactment. Oakeshott rejects the idea that there is anything merely "private" or "subjective" in motives; they no less than actions are governed by the compunctions of a common language and practice. Nevertheless, he does admit that the conditions of virtuous self-enactment "are apt to be less emphatic than those of moral self-disclosure"; and that we tend to judge our fellows less strictly or exactingly with respect to the former than with respect to the latter. But he insists that this greater tolerance does not stem from indifference to one another's exploits in self-enactment, but rather from "a recognition of our hardly avoidable ignorance" and from "the conviction that in ordinary intercourse a man's choices of what to do and the compunctions they exhibit matter more than the sentiment in which he makes them."[49]

What is the relationship between these two sorts of compunction, the one concerned with moral self-disclosure, the other with virtuous self-enactment? Oakeshott argues that since both compose a single language of moral intercourse, "the considerations they specify cannot be discrepant in any important respect; nevertheless, they concern different things." And because they concern different things, faithful observance of the compunctions of either cannot be thought to license or compensate "for the neglect of the compunctions of the other." Here Oakeshott is concerned to refute (much as Hegel was in the second part of the *Philosophy of Right*) the extreme Kantian view that the wrongfulness of an act contravening the compunctions of self-disclosure may be cancelled by the virtuousness of the motive with which it is performed. Neither the sincerity, conscientiousness, benevolence, or "authenticity" of conduct can absolve it of the imputation of fault. Virtuous self-enactment alone does not suffice (not even in Rabelais's Abbaye de Thélème); it must be accompanied by the faithful observance of the compunctions of a language of self-disclosure.[50]

What exactly is Oakeshott up to in his discussion of the relationship between self-disclosure and self-enactment? I do not think his meaning can be fully grasped unless it is set against the background of the understanding of the relationship between law and morality of his predecessors Green and (to a lesser extent) Bosanquet. As I pointed out in chapter 3, these writers, following Kant, held that the moral value of an action lay exclusively in its motive (what Oakeshott calls "self-enactment"), and that law or state action (concerned mainly with the compunctions of self-disclosure) was destructive of morality insofar as it substituted fear and compulsion for the freedom intrinsic to moral agency. For this reason Green limited law "to those actions better done from a bad motive than not done at all," and Bosanquet confined state action to the largely negative role of "hindering hindrances" to self-realization.[51]

Oakeshott's discussion of the relationship between self-disclosure and self-enactment intimates a different understanding of the relationship between civil law and motives. Not that he rejects the principle that laws cannot concern the sentiments or motives in which actions are performed; we shall see that he does not. But he puts this limitation of civil law on a different basis from that of his British

Hegelian predecessors. For him, it is not that the compunctions of self-disclosure are antagonistic to the compunctions of virtuous self-enactment, but (as we have seen) that they concern different things. And self-disclosure is no less a part of a moral practice than self-enactment. In some ways the British Hegelians' opposition of law and morality represents a relapse into the abstract individualism from which they were trying to escape. Viewed from this angle, Oakeshott's reformulation of the relationship between self-disclosure and self-enactment may be understood as an attempt to overcome this vestige of individualism in the idealist theory of the state. It represents a move back to Hegel himself without the British Hegelian (and hence Kantian) admixture.

These latter reflections on the relationship between self-disclosure and self-enactment in some ways return us to the larger theme of the first essay of *On Human Conduct*: namely, freedom or autonomy and its relationship to a moral practice. I have argued that this first essay is to be understood as an attempt to overcome the negative individualism which has dogged liberalism ever since Hobbes. In it Oakeshott provides the theory of volition which early on in his career he observed was lacking in Hobbes's political philosophy. For him, as we have seen, the freedom or will of an individual agent is not something unconditional or "natural" which comes to be diminished or limited by the conditions imposed by moral and social life. Rather, the freedom inherent in agency consists, first, in the fact that conduct is an exhibition of intelligence and not an organic or otherwise non-intelligent process; and second, in the fact that an agent's choice of a particular action is never completely specified or determined beforehand by the conditions or circumstances surrounding it. Now a moral practice does not compromise either of these conditions of free agency. It neither reduces conduct to a non-intelligent process, nor does it determine the substantive choices of agents; it only prescribes procedural or adverbial conditions to be taken into account when choosing and acting. Far from being an external limit on agency, a moral practice is indispensable to it. There is no agency which is not the acknowledgement of a moral practice, just as there is no individual utterance which is not in any language in particular. Will and morality mutually imply one another.

Oakeshott's thoroughly Hegelian conception of the relationship between freedom or will and a moral practice thus sets the stage for overcoming the opposition between individual and government, will and law, freedom and authority, which has dogged liberal thought ever since Hobbes. I say it only "sets the stage" because up to this point Oakeshott has not spoken of law or civil society per se, only of a moral practice in general. It is only in the second essay of *On Human Conduct* that the insights of the first are applied to the specific problems of political and legal philosophy. It is to this essay, then, that we must now turn.

3. The Theory of Civil Association

Everything we have considered so far – not only in this chapter but in all the previous ones as well – may be regarded as preliminary to Oakeshott's political philosophy proper. With the second essay of *On Human Conduct*, though, we finally arrive at the thing itself. The question Oakeshott sets out to answer in this essay is, What is the nature of civil association or the civil condition? Others have pursued this inquiry by asking themselves the question, What is the nature of the state? but Oakeshott purposefully avoids this formulation of the problem. The word "state" refers to certain complex, ambiguous, historic human associations, and it is not with these that he is here concerned. Rather, he is concerned with an ideal mode of human relationship which, while it may certainly be abstracted from historic states, cannot be identified with any single one of them. The civil condition is an "ideal character." This does not mean that it is some sort of utopia, only that it is an identity that has been purged of the contingencies and ambiguities of historic conditions. Civil association is ideal "not in the sense of being a wished-for perfect condition of things but in being abstracted from the contingencies and ambiguities of actual goings-on in the world."[52]

It is quite clear from the argument of *On Human Conduct* that this notion of the ideality of civil association is of crucial importance to Oakeshott. It expresses itself most immediately at the level of language, where much of the ambiguous vocabulary of modern European politics is eschewed and either replaced by archaic Latin expressions or qualified by unnaturally precise definitions. Oakeshott is convinced that the inquiry into civil association has suffered mainly because writers have concerned themselves too much with contingent considerations such as how civil association might be actualized, or because they have surrendered too easily "to the ambiguities of historic conditions."[53] Aristotle, Hobbes, and Hegel he mentions as notable exceptions; but even Hobbes and Hegel later come in for minor criticism for having written about civil association "as if it were the kind of association which a modern state only distantly resembled but which it should be made to become" – a way of thinking which "made the use of the ambiguous vocabulary of a modern state almost unavoidable and encouraged rather than excluded the consideration of contingencies."[54]

This idealistic feature of Oakeshott's argument in *On Human Conduct* has been remarked by many commentators, and it has been referred to pejoratively as "formalism." The question of whether the argument of *On Human Conduct* is formalistic or not I take up in the final section of this chapter. Here I only want to repudiate the further contention that it somehow represents a methodological departure from Oakeshott's earlier emphasis on complexity, contingency, and ambiguity in *Rationalism in Politics*.[55] Such a contention, when it does not rest on the elementary confusion of an ideal character with an ideal or a utopia, ignores what must be seen as one of the most persistent features of Oakeshott's idea of philosophy from *Experience and its Modes* onwards: namely, the detachment of philosophy from the contingencies of both historical and practical reality. It is not lack of historical sense but precisely a heightened historical awareness which impels Oakeshott to make this move. Because he sees historical and practical life as pre-eminently contingent, he thinks philosophy must operate at a level of considerable abstraction from it; otherwise it will be led "into all sorts of circumstantial considerations," and its conclusions "will be far from permanent."[56]

The key to Oakeshott's understanding of civil association is, of course, the idea of a moral practice which he developed in the first essay of *On Human Conduct*. Civil association for him is, most fundamentally, association or relationship in terms of a moral (i.e., non-instrumental) practice. There are and have been, of course, alternative identifications of civil association, the most common being that it is association in terms of the joint pursuit of a common purpose or interest. To this latter mode of association Oakeshott gives the name "enterprise association." And since it is in terms of enterprise association that civil association has been most frequently understood, he spends some time at the outset discussing what it involves and why he considers it inadequate to identify civil association.

In the first essay of *On Human Conduct*, Oakeshott distinguished two modes of human relationship: "transactional" relationship, in which agents seek substantive satisfactions in the responses of other agents; and "practical" relationship, in which these individual transactions are adverbially qualified by procedures. One of the main points he now wishes to make with respect to enterprise association is that it belongs to the former, substantive mode of human relationship. It is association in terms of a common substantive purpose and in terms of substantive actions and utterances (managerial decisions) designed to promote that purpose. And the most important condition of such substantive relationship is that it be chosen by an agent. An agent must not only acknowledge the common purpose as his own, he must be able to extricate himself from the relationship at any time by a choice of his own. To make enterprise association compulsory would be to deprive an agent of that "freedom" or "autonomy" which is the condition of agency. This in the end is one of the principal reasons why Oakeshott rejects the identification of a state with enterprise association. A state is a compulsory association. As such it cannot be an enterprise association without compromising the moral autonomy of its members.[57]

But this is to anticipate somewhat. Initially, Oakeshott is concerned to repudiate the identification of civil association with enterprise association. And foremost he mentions "the difficulty of specifying a common purpose in terms of which to distinguish civil association from all other enterprise relationship." There is nothing in such common purposes as general "prosperity" or devotion to a set of religious beliefs, for example, to distinguish *civil* association from a business enterprise or a religious community; "the force and meaning of the adjective 'civil' is to seek." Nor can this force or meaning be supplied by adding a compulsory character to these common purposes, since (as we have just seen) "compulsory enterprise association is a self-contradiction." Finally, Oakeshott denies that such ends as "security" or "peace" constitute the common purpose of civil association. "Security" and "peace," he argues, are not substantive purposes at all; they are not specific satisfactions sought for themselves, but conditions which make possible the pursuit of substantive satisfactions.[58]

Having rejected the identification of civil association with the substantial relationship of enterprise association, Oakeshott turns to formal or "practical" relationship as a more fruitful direction in which to pursue the nature of civil association. But "practical" relationship alone does not serve to identify civil association, since a practice may be a procedure instrumental to the achievement of a substantive satisfaction or common purpose. Since civil association is not enterprise association, however, it cannot be identified with an instrumental practice (such as an "economy," *the* instrumental practice, according to Oakeshott, with which civil association is most frequently confused). Rather, civil association is a practice which is "subscribed to in all or any of an agent's actions or utterances," and which is not instrumental to the achievement of any substantive purpose – what Oakeshott has called a "moral" practice.[59]

A moral practice, as we have seen, is to be understood as a vernacular language of intercourse, and it is precisely in these linguistic terms that Oakeshott now speaks of the civil condition. The "language of civility" is not, he concedes, spoken on every occasion (it is not, for example, the language in which lovers converse); nevertheless, "it is never wholly put by," and "there is no situation *inter homines* to which it cannot relate." Nor is this characterization of civil association in terms of a vernacular language of intercourse to be thought of as a mere or vague analogy. For Oakeshott, it constitutes "the essential character of the civil condition."

I think the investigation of this condition has flourished only when it has been tied to a reading of its character in which it is recognized as agents exploring their relations in terms of a language of understanding and intercourse which is native to and is continuously re-enacted by those who use it.[60]

It is here in Oakeshott's evocation of the civil condition as a vernacular language of intercourse that we are once again reminded of Hegel's notion of *Sittlichkeit*. In this passage Oakeshott announces that he intends to grasp civil association as a living tradition, a way of life, and not simply as something fixed, finished, or essentially dead. And it is this same intention which informs Hegel's theorization of the state in terms of *Sittlichkeit* in the *Philosophy of Right*. I have already remarked that Oakeshott's "practice" can be understood as a translation and interpretation of the Hegelian *Sittlichkeit*, and this Hegelian reference must be kept in mind as we try to grasp the meaning of civil association. It is only by ignoring this connection between Oakeshott's "practical" relationship and Hegel's *sittlich* relationship that a commentator like Judith Shklar can assert that Oakeshott's civil association, lacking the "integrative force" of *Sittlichkeit*, corresponds more to Hegel's notion of "abstract right."[61] Other commentators have made similar points about the un-Hegelian character of *On Human Conduct*.[62] It should be clear by now that my interpretation of *On Human Conduct* goes in quite a different direction.

To have identified civil association as a moral (i.e., non-instrumental) practice is to have gone some distance toward understanding the nature of civil association. Nevertheless, this mode of association still remains incompletely specified, according to Oakeshott. There remains one last step in the Aristotelian process of specification and differentiation he has been pursuing. Civil association is to be understood, not simply as a moral practice, but as a special kind of moral practice: it is a moral practice "composed entirely of rules; the language of civil intercourse is a language of rules; *civitas* is rule-articulated association."[63] Other moral practices do not share this exclusively rule-articulated character. The considerations which comprise them are generally not so narrow or specific as rules. Of course, a moral practice may be abridged or reduced to a set of rules, but this does not seem to be what Oakeshott has in mind when he speaks of civil association as relationship solely in terms of rules. The rules which comprise civil association are not to be regarded simply as abridgements of a morality. Again, civil association is to be regarded as a genuine morality and a living tradition, not as an abridgement or a code.[64]

The difference between civil association and other moral practices will I hope become clearer in the course of discussion. By way of anticipation, though, let me quote a passage from Oakeshott's reply to some critics in which he briefly summarizes the differences between civil rules (or laws) and other moral considerations. The moral (non-instrumental) rules which comprise civil association differ from other moral considerations, he writes,

> in being subject to enactment, repeal and alteration in an authorized procedure, in that the conditions they prescribe are narrower, less demanding, and more precisely formulated, in there being an authoritative procedure for determining whether or not an agent in acting has adequately subscribed to these rules, and in there being known penalties attached to inadequate subscription and an apparatus of power to enforce them.[65]

Though differing from other moral considerations in this way, civil rules (or laws) are nevertheless – and this must never be forgotten – moral and not instrumental considerations. Oakeshott's understanding of civil association as relationship in terms of rules must not be severed from his more general understanding of it as a moral, that is, a non-instrumental, practice. Indeed, he criticizes those theorists (such as the theorists of the *Rechtstaat*) who identify civil association as relationship in terms of rules, or law, and leave it at that. What needs to be explained, he argues, is whether these rules or laws are moral or instrumental. Likewise, the expression "the rule of law" remains an ambiguous identification of civil association unless the *kind* of law – moral or instrumental – is also specified.[66] In Oakeshott's own interpretation of "the rule of law" (in the essay of that name), the non-instrumental character of the law is made explicit.

With the characterization of civil association as relationship in terms of non-instrumental rules (or laws) we have arrived at what might be called the *differentia* of civil association. Oakeshott himself considers this feature to be the most significant of civil association. It has also been, he comments, the most difficult feature "to identify and get into place." Aristotle, for example, to whom Oakeshott gives so much credit for having correctly identified the central features of civil association, is said to have recognized it as a system of rules "only indistinctly."[67] And Bodin, Hobbes, and the theorists of the *Rechtstaat* also come in for criticism, as we shall see. It is quite clear that one of Oakeshott's chief concerns in *On Human Conduct* is to get straight the nature of law, the rules appropriate to civil association.[68] It is therefore necessary that we follow him closely as he theorizes these rules and the conditions relating to them.

He begins by considering the nature of rules in general, of which the rules of a game provide a fairly clear picture.[69] Four basic features are indicated. In the first place, a rule is said to be an authoritative assertion and not a theorem. Unlike a maxim or a piece of advice, it is not an argumentative utterance, and its validity does not depend

upon its being found reasonable, worthwhile, or in some sense desirable. It may be argued about, and its desirability debated, but a rule
in itself does not invoke approval; it calls only for assent. Secondly, a
rule is general or abstract. Unlike a command, for example, it is not
addressed to an assignable agent. A rule "has a jurisdiction and it
relates indifferently and continuously to all who fall, or may in future
fall, within its jurisdiction." Again, unlike a command, a rule is not
tied to a particular situation, nor is it used up or exhausted in a
particular performance; "it remains 'standing' for unknown future
occasions." Thirdly, "rules do not enjoin, prohibit, or warrant substantive actions or utterances"; they prescribe adverbial considerations
to be subscribed to or taken into account in choosing performances –
considerations which "cannot themselves be either 'obeyed' or
performed." Once again a rule differs in this way from a command.
The fourth feature of rules concerns the terms in which they are
recognized. These terms, Oakeshott argues (briefly here, more extensively later in his discussion of civil authority and obligation), have
nothing to do with considerations of the consequences of observance
or non-observance. Authority and obligation – as distinguished from
compulsion and fear of punishment – are the terms in which rules are
recognized.[70]

It will be noticed that several of the features mentioned above point
up the difference between rules and commands. The reasons for this
are not obscure. Of all the types of human utterance, it is commands
with which rules (and law) have been most frequently confused. What
is called the "command theory" of law – a theory which received its
most unambiguous statement in the jurisprudence of John Austin,
and which has been criticized most persuasively by H. L. A. Hart[71] –
is here under attack. Oakeshott insists that what we have to do with in
civil association is a moral practice, and that the terms of this practice
(i.e., rules) are adverbial considerations and not substantive commands. Civil relationship in terms of rules may be "association in
somewhat more exactly specified terms than, for example, the intimations provided by general theorems about proper conduct or by
maxims of indeterminate jurisdiction." Nevertheless, the rules which
comprise civil association "are neither definitive principles of conduct
nor explicit injunctions addressed to assignable agents commanding
or prohibiting substantive actions or utterances." Oakeshott once
again reiterates that "nothing should be allowed to obscure the view
of civil association as relationship in terms of a language of understanding and intercourse continuously used in conduct and enacted
and re-enacted in being used."[72]

As has already been pointed out, the rules of civil association
resemble in many ways the rules of a game. But there is a crucial
difference to be observed, stemming from the fact that a game is an

engagement which itself constitutes a relationship whereas in the civil condition there is no such common engagement. *Cives*, unlike the players of a game, are related solely in terms of their common recognition of rules. (This also distinguishes *cives* from the members of an enterprise association, who may observe rules but are not related in terms of rules; they are related instead in terms of a common choice or purpose.) According to Oakeshott, "the most important postulates of *civitas* stem from this consideration" that rules are the sole terms in which *cives* are related; the first being that the rules of civil association (which Oakeshott chooses to call "*lex*" instead of "law," "so that they may not be confused with the heterogeneous collection of rules and rule-like instructions, instruments, provisions, etc. which constitute the conditions of those ambiguous associations we call states") compose a self-contained system identifying its own jurisdiction. It is necessary that the laws of civil association compose such a system because they (unlike the rules of a game or an enterprise association) "are not imposed upon an already shaped and articulated engagement"; because they must "relate to the miscellaneous, unforeseeable choices and transactions of agents . . . who are joined in no common purpose or engagement, who may be strangers to one another . . . and who may lack any but this moral allegiance to one another." In short, *lex* must be a self-contained system identifying its own jurisdiction "because it relates those who are not, as such, otherwise related."[73]

There are other conditions besides this systematic character of *lex* which civil association as a "durable and diurnal association" postulates. The first of these that Oakeshott takes up is adjudication. Because the rules of civil association are (as we have seen) general and abstract, there must be some procedure by which they are related to contingent situations. This is accomplished in adjudication. In adjudication the uncertainty which is intrinsic to *lex* as a set of general norms is authoritatively resolved. This relation of the general norms of *lex* to contingent situations is not, however, to be thought of as a matter of mere "application." Here Oakeshott's understanding of adjudication reveals itself to have a hermeneutic dimension. In adjudication something is added to *lex* which was not there to begin with; the meaning of *lex* is "significantly amplified." Of course, a judicial decision must always refer to *lex* in some way; it "cannot be understood as the arbitrary exercise of the so-called 'subjective will' of the judge." Nevertheless, adjudication is not a "deductive procedure." A judicial decision is always a novel "illustration" of *lex* and not simply a mechanical "exemplification" of it.[74]

Another condition of the durability of civil association is a procedure of legislation. Where "association is solely in terms of *lex*," a procedure is needed whereby the conditions of civil conduct may be altered in response to "notable changes of belief or sentiment" about

the desirability of these conditions. Legislation involves the deliberation of *lex* in terms of its desirability. Since this deliberative engagement belongs to what Oakeshott calls "politics," he postpones his
discussion of it until he takes up the latter theme. Here he only
mentions what it necessarily excludes. To deliberate about *lex* in
terms of its desirability necessarily excludes considering it in terms of
its propensity to promote a common purpose or in terms of its contingent outcomes (who gets what, when and how). "Legislative
opinion is concerned with the desirable composition of a system of
moral, non-instrumental, considerations."[75]

The third condition of civil association Oakeshott discusses is
"ruling." The durability of civil association depends upon its prescriptions being "generally and adequately subscribed to." Civil association thus postulates an apparatus of rule to enforce *lex* and to
exact penalties where the conditions of *lex* have been inadequately
observed. This engagement differs from any other in civil association
in that it commands and prohibits substantive actions; its idiom is not
adverbial but "injunctive." Nevertheless, the commands and prohibi-
tions which constitute the engagement of ruling "are not transactions
in which rulers seek imagined and wished-for satisfactions of their
contingent wants in the responses of other identified persons . . . ;
rulers are not persons with substantive wants, they are office-holders
with powers and obligations concerned with the observance of a procedure." Ruling is not a transactional or substantive engagement of
conduct; it is concerned with the maintenance of a procedure or
practice. Rulers may, of course – and inevitably do – engage in
enterprises and seek substantive satisfactions, but insofar as they do
they are not ruling, according to Oakeshott; they are participating
in the categorially different engagement of "lordship." The "private"
or transactional relationship of master and servant, manager and
role-performer, is to be categorially distinguished from the "public"
relationship of ruler and subject.[76]

Oakeshott's use of the ambiguous words "public" and "private"
here calls for some comment, since previously we have seen him
deprecate this distinction as an abstraction (e.g., in discussing such
notions as the "private" individual or "non-social" actions or goods).
But he makes it clear here that "public" and "private" do not refer
to concrete persons, performances, or places but to relationships –
"practical," on the one hand, and "transactional," on the other; and
that in the civil condition these two relationships meet in every substantive engagement. "Here every situation is an encounter between
'private' and 'public', between an action or utterance to procure an
imagined and wished-for substantive satisfaction and the conditions
of civility to be subscribed to in performing it; and no situation is
one to the exclusion of the other."[77] Oakeshott does not relapse into

the abstract individualism – with its "private" spheres, actions, and individuals – which characterizes so much liberal thought. By casting the distinction between "public" and "private" in terms of two categorially distinct but not necessarily exclusive modes of relationship, he retains an important distinction without falling into abstraction.

So far Oakeshott has concerned himself with civil association primarily as a system of rules – a manifold of laws and law-like conditions to which he now gives the name *respublica*, or the public concern. But civil association, he now goes on to argue, is not simply relationship in terms of a system of rules; it is relationship in terms of a certain manner of recognizing rules – namely, "the recognition of rules as rules." What such recognition involves he has already considered briefly in his discussion of rules in general, and here he simply amplifies what he said there. To recognize a rule as a rule is not to recognize it in terms of approval or disapproval; a rule does not cease to be obligatory simply because we do not approve of it. Nor is the recognition of a rule as a rule recognition of it in terms of the consequences – benefits or rewards – of subscribing or not subscribing to it; hope or fear may be *motives* for subscription, but they are not the *grounds* of the obligation to subscribe. To recognize a rule as a rule is to recognize it in terms of its *authority*, and it is to recognize subscription to it as an *obligation*. It is to these two most important postulates of civil association – civil authority and civil obligation – that Oakeshott now turns his attention.[78]

With respect to civil authority, he is particularly concerned to show that it has nothing to do with the desirability (i.e., utility, wisdom, rationality, or justice) of the conditions of *respublica*. "Recognizing the authority of *respublica* is not finding its conditions to be desirable or believing that others better than oneself approved of them: it does not concern the merits or otherwise of the condition." Recognizing the authority of *respublica* is simply accepting its conditions as binding regardless of whether one approves of them or not. *Respublica* is not a perfectly rational construction; it is

> a manifold of rules, many of unknown origin, subject to deliberate innovation, continuously amplified in judicial conclusions about their meaning in contingent situations, not infrequently neglected without penalty, often inconvenient, neither demanding nor capable of evoking the approval of all they concern, and never more than a very imperfect reflection of what are considered to be "just" conditions of conduct.

How such a motley assemblage could ever be acknowledged to have authority is not puzzling to Oakeshott: "authority is the only conceivable attribute it could be indisputably acknowledged to have."[79]

Oakeshott's sharp distinction here between the authority of

respublica and the desirability of its conditions inevitably recalls Hobbes. Hobbes, too, argued that the authority of the law did not, and could not, rest on its being found desirable or true; it rested solely on its being promulgated by an authorized ruler. Obedience was called for whether one approved of the law or not. Of course, Hobbes's doctrine of authority – his sharp distinction between the authority and the desirability of the law – was rejected by many of his successors as having absolutist implications. This, however, is not (and was never) Oakeshott's view. Indeed, he sees Hobbes's doctrine of authority as the other side of his individualism, and diametrically opposed to absolutism. As he put it in his introduction to *Leviathan*: "Hobbes is not an absolutist precisely because he is an authoritarian." We will be returning to this issue of absolutism – both with respect to Hobbes and with respect to Oakeshott – shortly. Here I only want to underline the continuity between their doctrines of authority.

A good deal that has had currency at one time or another in the history of political thought is being rejected in the pages devoted to authority in *On Human Conduct*. Oakeshott does not name too many names, but that he has identifiable historical doctrines in mind cannot be doubted. Perhaps the most important of these to be noticed is that form of natural-law teaching which argues that the authority or validity of *lex* derives from its conformity with some sort of "natural," "rational," or "higher" law, which conformity is said to endow *lex* with the quality of "justice." According to this view, which Oakeshott refers to in "The Rule of Law" as the "neoplatonic view of the matter," *lex injusta non est lex*. He goes on to mention a few figures who may be associated with this view: Samuel Rutherford, Montesquieu, and the early exponents of the *Rechtstaat* who ended up replacing the somewhat speculative natural law with a set of formulated, unambiguous principles.[80] As we have seen, Oakeshott rejects this "neoplatonic" view which makes the authority of *lex* contingent on it being found "just" or in conformity with a "higher law." Authority and desirability are not the same thing for him, and authority and justice (as we shall see more clearly later on) he sees as distinct considerations. *Lex injusta* may indeed still be authentic *lex*.

One important qualification of this doctrine of the relationship (or non-relationship) of authority and justice must, however, be noticed. Oakeshott himself mentions it only in passing in the section devoted to authority in *On Human Conduct*, but that should not dissuade us of its significance. He says there that the authority of *respublica* cannot lie in the identification of its prescriptions with a justice "other than that which is inherent in *respublica*." What he means by the justice "inherent in *respublica*" he explains in a footnote. This justice pertains to those conditions which are intrinsic to association in terms of non-prudential rules, such as: the quality of legal subjects; rules not arbitrary, secret, retroactive or awards to interests; the independence of judicial proceedings (i.e. all claimants or prosecutors, like defendants, are litigants); no so-called "public" or "quasi-public" enterprise or corporation exempt from common liability for wrong; no offence without prescription; no penalty without specific offence; no disability or refusal of recognition without established inadequacy of subscription; no outlawry, etc., etc.: in short, all that may be called the "inner morality" of a legal system.[81]

In "The Rule of Law" Oakeshott makes more of this justice inherent in *respublica* than he did in *On Human Conduct*, referring to it there as the *"jus* inherent in *lex."* Again he characterizes it as consisting of those formal considerations which distinguish a legal order and without which a legal order would cease to be a legal order. And he goes on to list roughly the same conditions he listed in *On Human Conduct*: rules not secret and retroactive, and so forth. The important point to be noticed, though, is that in both *On Human Conduct* and "The Rule of Law" Oakeshott recognizes certain conditions of justice to which a law must conform if it is to be a valid law. True, these conditions are only formal – intrinsic to *lex* as such – and not "independent principles which, if followed by legislators, would endow their laws with a quality of 'justice'." Nevertheless, they do significantly qualify – in a manner not totally unlike that of natural law – the authority of *lex*. It is in respect of these considerations – but only in respect of these considerations – "that it may perhaps be said that *lex injusta non est lex*."[82]

This brings me back to the issue of absolutism raised above in connection with Hobbes's doctrine of authority. It is clear that Oakeshott's recognition of certain principles of justice inherent in law as such insulates him from the charge of absolutism (and from the charge of positivism as well). But what about Hobbes? Does he recognize certain formal conditions inherent in *lex* to which laws must conform if they are to be considered valid? Oakeshott argues that he does in his "laws of nature," which he interprets as "no more than an analytic breakdown of the intrinsic character of law, what I have called the *jus* inherent in genuine law which distinguishes it from a command addressed to an assignable agent or a managerial instruction concerned with the promotion of interests."[83] Civil authority for Hobbes – no more than for Oakeshott – is not something unconditional, arbitrary, undifferentiated, or "total"; rather, it is something conditional. It is conditional, first, in its being recognized by those who are subject to it; and second, in its prescriptions being in conformity with the *jus* inherent in *lex*. Such authority does not have to be "limited" because – as Oakeshott puts it with reference to Bodin's notion of "absolute authority" – it is an authority "whose only conditions are inherent."[84]

Let us now turn to Oakeshott's idea of civil obligation, which can be discussed briefly because it is simply the counterpart of the idea of authority. To recognize the conditions of *respublica* as authoritative is also to recognize them as obligatory. Civil obligation thus relates to the authority of *respublica*, not to its power. This means that it cannot be identified with the feeling of "being obliged" or constrained. Nor does civil obligation have anything to do with approving or choosing the conditions prescribed by *respublica*. Just as the authority of these prescriptions does not lie in their having been chosen or approved of, so their obligatory character does not derive from this sort of consent. As with civil authority, civil obligation is absolutely distinguished from approval.[85]

Because civil authority and obligation do not argue, persuade, or seek to be approved, they have frequently been thought to pose some sort of threat to the moral autonomy of human beings. But Oakeshott argues that this is not so for reasons ultimately relating back to his distinctive understanding of the nature of moral autonomy and of the "freedom" inherent in agency. Civil authority and obligation do not compromise the moral autonomy of human beings in the first place, he argues, because they relate to *lex*, and *lex* (as we have learned) does not specify substantive actions but only adverbial considerations to be taken into account when choosing and acting. "It is true," he admits, "that authority and obligation do not argue or ask to be approved. . . . But their prescriptions are not expressions of 'will' and their injunctions are not orders to be obeyed." What takes the place of argumentative discourse in civil rule is not *voluntas* but *lex*.[86] It should be noted that Oakeshott here significantly diverges from his predecessor Hobbes. Hobbes – along with Bodin – did have a tendency to identify the exercise of authority with will and command.[87] Though this confusion is not crippling to either of their theories, according to Oakeshott, it nevertheless obscures the connection between authority and autonomy which he finds so important.

The second reason civil authority and obligation do not compromise the freedom or autonomy inherent in agency has to do with their being distinguished from approval and desirability. It is precisely because recognizing the authority of *respublica* does not involve approval of its conditions that the "freedom" inherent in agency – which Oakeshott here reformulates in terms of the "link between belief and conduct" – is preserved. "[I]n acknowledging civil authority *cives* have given no hostages to a future in which, their approvals and choices no longer being what they were, they can remain free only in an act of dissociation." This freedom which belongs to civil association Oakeshott calls "civil freedom," and he contrasts it

with the "not less genuine, but wholly different freedom which belongs to enterprise association." Actually, it is not so much "freedom"
that is different here as the manner in which the link between belief
and conduct which constitutes "freedom" is preserved. In enterprise
association the "freedom" of an agent depends on his having chosen
his situation and on his having the ability to extricate himself from it if
and when he chooses to do so. Only in this way – completely different
from civil association – is the link between belief and conduct which
constitutes "free" agency preserved. It is because "freedom" in enterprise association is conceptually tied to the choice to be and to remain associated that enterprise association has proved to be (as was
pointed out above) a dubious model for a state, which is a compulsory
association.[88]

In the passages of *On Human Conduct* under discussion we find
perhaps the clearest statement of the intimate relationship Oakeshott
sees between freedom and authority. This idea of the correlativity of
freedom and authority, which in many ways constitutes the heart of
Oakeshott's political philosophy, of course goes all the way back to
some of his earliest writings on political themes, especially those on
Hobbes. It receives expression in the statement (which I have already
quoted several times) that "Hobbes is not an absolutist precisely
because he is an authoritarian"; and that "it is Reason, not Authority,
that is destructive of individuality." It is Hobbes's thoroughgoing
understanding of and emphasis on authority, his detachment of the
idea of authority from the notion of consent (in the sense of approval),
that makes him for Oakeshott a far more profound philosopher of
freedom and individuality than, say, Locke.[89]

Oakeshott's reflections on freedom and authority here may also be
usefully compared with the tradition of idealist political philosophy I
considered in chapter 3. As we saw there, the core of the idealist
project consisted in an attempt to reconcile the authority of the state
with individual freedom by basing that authority, not on individual
consent, but on the general or rational will. The basic idea was that
the authority of the state rested on the will of the individual, not
insofar as it derived from his capriciously given consent, but insofar as
it corresponded to his "real" or "rational" will. Now, Oakeshott's
relation to this idealist tradition is somewhat complex. He certainly
follows Rousseau, Hegel, and Bosanquet in rejecting individual consent, "the will of all," as the basis of authority. Nevertheless, he
does not identify authority with the "real" or "rational" will of the
individual, at least not when this will is conceived teleologically. His
reconciliation of freedom with authority depends instead (as we have
seen) on showing that civil authority does not compromise the formal
freedom inherent in agency. In this latter respect, Oakeshott seems to
diverge most from his British Hegelian predecessors, whose notion of

the "real will" does seem to point to a substantialist and teleological doctrine of human nature, and whose doctrine of authority therefore does not clearly distinguish between authority and wisdom. Hegel's "rational will" is of course more ambiguous; it is more susceptible to the formal interpretation which we shall soon see Oakeshott gives to it.

There remains one final and very important postulate of civil association to be considered: namely, politics. So far Oakeshott has concerned himself with the manner of recognizing rules which constitutes civil association: namely, the recognition of rules as rules in terms of their authority. And he has been particularly concerned to show that this recognition of the authority of the rules of *respublica* has nothing to do with finding them desirable or approving of them. Nevertheless, he now goes on to argue, these rules may legitimately be considered in terms of their desirability. Though acknowledgement of the authority of the rules of *respublica* does not entail recognition of them as desirable, neither does it forbid the consideration of these rules in terms of their desirability. The only thing that is forbidden is that either of these considerations be confused or substituted for one another. In civil association authority and desirability (or approval) are always distinguished; and this is one of the things that differentiates it, not only from enterprise association, but also from other non-instrumental, moral practices, where authority and approval are difficult to distinguish. In most moralities the "recognition of a moral virtue is itself the approval of the conditions it specifies for conduct; these conditions may be forgotten or neglected, but to dislodge them is nothing other than a withdrawal or qualification of approval." In a morality there does not exist – as there does in civil association – an authorized procedure by which a virtue or a norm of conduct may be deliberately enacted or repealed. This is one of the significant differences between the specific moral practice of civil association and other, less specific moral practices.[90]

The engagement of deliberating on the conditions of *respublica* in terms of their desirability Oakeshott calls "politics." He puts this word in inverted commas to distinguish what he means by it from all the other meanings the word has accrued over time. For him "politics" relates exclusively to civil association, and this imposes certain conditions on it. Most importantly, it restricts the desirabilities in terms of which *respublica* may be deliberated to *civil* desirabilities, to *bonum civile*. "[E]ngagement in politics," Oakeshott contends,

> entails a disciplined imagination. It is to put by for another occasion the cloudy enchantments of *Schlafraffenland*, the earth flowing with milk and honey and the sea transmuted into ginger beer, it is to forswear the large consideration of human happiness and virtue, the mysteries of human destiny, the rift that lies between the aspiration of human beings and the

conditions of human life, and even the consideration of the most profitable
or least burdensome manner of satisfying current wants, and to focus attention upon civility; that is, upon a practice of just conduct and upon
the conditions which should be required to be acknowledged and subscribed to under threat of civil penalty or sentence of civil disability.[91]

A specifically "political" proposal, according to Oakeshott, "must
relate to a possible condition of *respublica* and to nothing else." And
what this excludes – besides the dreams and "cloudy enchantments"
alluded to above – he has already briefly considered in his discussion
of legislation. It excludes proposals designed to promote a common
purpose or any other substantive interest. This does not mean that a
"political" proposal may not emerge from an effort to procure a substantive satisfaction, or that it may not ultimately redound to some
particular person's or group's advantage or disadvantage; it only
means that it must lose this "interested" character before it can
become a specifically "political" proposal. Politics is not concerned
with the promotion of substantive purposes, interests, or doctrines
because *respublica* as such is not concerned with these things. Politics is
concerned with the custody, maintenance, and desirability of a system
of moral, non-instrumental, non-substantive considerations.[92]

Oakeshott concludes his discussion of politics (and, indeed, of civil
association as a whole) by considering what might be called the
process – as opposed to the formal conditions – of political deliberation or inference. He is concerned to show that political deliberation is
a contingent and circumstantial engagement, not a demonstrative or
deductive one.[93] This, of course, was the theme of a number of essays
in *Rationalism in Politics* (especially "Political Education"), and it is
here that Oakeshott most clearly reflects the concerns of those essays.
Once again he rejects natural law and unconditional principles as
criteria for political deliberation, and he defends instead a more
historical (though not necessarily relativistic) understanding of the
process in political activity. It is here, too, that he clarifies for us his
understanding of the problematic relationship between morals and
politics, morality and law.

He begins by rejecting a number of different principles from which
it has been suggested political conclusions might be deduced. He
denies, for example, that political conclusions (conclusions about the
desirability of civil prescriptions) can be deduced from theorems
about the natural conditions of human life (e.g., theorems about what
is necessary for survival given conditions of natural scarcity), since the
civil condition is not a natural or biological condition but a "condition of human conduct, of agents who are concerned with seeking
imagined and wished-for satisfactions." The view rejected here would
seem to include H. L. A. Hart's doctrine of natural law with a "minimum content."[94] Nor (Oakeshott goes on) can political conclusions

be deduced from theorems about the satisfaction of human wants, since civil association as a moral condition "is not concerned with substantive outcomes but with the terms upon which the satisfactions of wants may be sought."[95] What, then, of moral considerations?

Oakeshott also denies that the desirability of a civil prescription can be deduced from some "superior norm of unquestionable or acknowledged desirability, a moral rule, a prescriptive Law of Reason or of Nature, a principle of utility, a categorical imperative, or the like." And the reason he gives for this is both interesting and typical. It is not, he says, that such a Law may not exist or that such principles may not be desirable, but only that "inference of this kind is impossible: no civil rule can be *deduced* from the Golden Rule or from the Kantian categorical imperative." The argument here is brief, but it is essentially the one made repeatedly in *Rationalism in Politics*: abstract moral principles are incapable of determining actions; they do not direct human activity but are themselves the product of a more contingent "knowing how." Oakeshott repeats this argument about the indeterminateness of general principles in *On Human Conduct*. Acting, he says, cannot be "implementing" or "applying" general moral principles to contingent situations because these principles "are unable to specify actions. What the agent needs to know . . . is how to *illustrate* them in actions, and they do not themselves provide the directions about how this may be done."[96] It is the essential indeterminacy, then, of a Law of Nature or a categorical imperative which makes it impossible for a civil rule to be *deduced* from them.

This logical point, however, does not exhaust what Oakeshott has to say about the relationship between morals and politics. He goes on to argue that a civil prescription cannot be shown to be desirable simply because it is in conformity with what is held to be morally desirable. Because a rule or duty is recognized to be morally desirable (for example, the duty of parents to educate their children) does not mean that it should necessarily be made into a civil obligation. The civil and the moral are distinct considerations. Sometimes this distinction is expressed in terms of the "moral neutrality" of civil prescriptions, but Oakeshott believes that this way of speaking obscures the essential point that civil association is "itself a moral and not a prudential condition." Civil considerations are moral, that is, non-instrumental, considerations – of this fact Oakeshott never allows us to lose sight. Nevertheless, there is much that is moral that lies outside the capacity of civil rules to compel. A civil rule, for example, "cannot concern the supreme moral consideration which relates to the sentiments or motives in which actions are performed." That the civil and the moral do not exactly coincide, however,

> does not mean that civil desirabilities are unconnected with more intimate moral relationships; it means only that what is civilly desirable cannot be

inferred or otherwise derived from general moral desirabilities, that it is not necessarily a sign of something amiss if they are not found to be pulling in the same direction or even [if they are found] to conflict with such desirabilities, and that political deliberation and utterance (concerned with civil desirabilities) is concerned with moral considerabilities of its own.[97]

The desirability of civil prescriptions, then, according to Oakeshott, cannot be deduced or inferred from any of these theoretical, factual, or normative considerations. In arguing thus he does not mean to suggest, however, that political judgments are "mere opinions," that they are somehow "irrational" or "merely subjective."[98] He only wants to make clear that political deliberation is not a demonstrative or deductive undertaking but rather something more circumstantial and contingent. It was precisely this circumstantial and contingent character of political activity that he had emphasized in *Rationalism in Politics*. And as Oakeshott goes on to elaborate more positively here what he thinks is involved in political deliberation, it is perhaps not surprising that we find many echoes of that earlier work. He does not, it is true, use the word "tradition" here; but much of what he says parallels what he had earlier tried to express with that word.

The subject in political deliberation, he begins, is always an actual, historic practice of civil association composed of rules which have been elaborated over time by intelligent agents responding to their contingent situations. Such a practice composes "a more or less coherent system of rules." But this system "cannot be expected to display any notable elegance or economy of design; nor can it escape being ragged at the edges, intimating situations to which it has no precise response." And it is constantly undergoing modification and change. Besides rules, such an historic practice may also contain "some general theorems . . . about the conduct of *cives*." Oakeshott instances such legal concepts as a tort and a crime, and even "more general moral ideas (such as fairness and humanity) which have been 'civilized' by being given civil meanings." But these, he insists, are contingent products and subject, like everything else, to continuous change and modification.[99]

Given that the subject in politics is of such a contingent and circumstantial character, the considerations in terms of which innovation and change are deliberated cannot help but be contingent and circumstantial also. There are, to be sure, some general ideas which provide practical guidance; but these political considerations are to be thought of as no more than "aids to reflection" rather than as "indisputable criteria of choice." It is true that Oakeshott goes on to discuss three of the more solid (though far from unconditional) of these considerations: the consideration that a civil prescription be enforceable; the consideration (which Mill unfortunately elevated into an unconditional principle) that civil conditions relate to actions only insofar as they affect others; and the consideration that a projected innovation be continuous with and not disruptive of the ensemble of civil conditions. But for the most part his emphasis falls on the conditionality and contingency of political deliberation. He speaks of it (in language reminiscent of *Rationalism in Politics*) as "an exploration of intimations" for which there exists no "mistake-proof manner" of proceeding. Nor is there any end to this activity: "[E]very adjustment of a *respublica* is a disturbance of tensions which hold it together and is liable to bring thitherto concealed discrepancies to the surface." There are, in short, no "final solutions" in politics.[100]

This concludes Oakeshott's discussion of politics in *On Human Conduct*. But before leaving this topic, we would do well to consider Oakeshott's view in relation to what is perhaps the most important consideration in political deliberation, namely, the justice or "rightness" of a law. Oakeshott takes up this issue of the criterion by which the justice (or, as he likes to put it, the *jus*) of law is determined in "The Rule of Law." And what he says there serves to reinforce the complex view of the relationship between morality and law which he has set forth in *On Human Conduct*.

He begins by distinguishing the considerations of justice into which he is now inquiring from those considerations of justice (already discussed above) which are inherent in civil law or *lex*: "non-instrumentality, indifference to persons and interests, the exclusion of *privelege* and outlawry," and so forth. Though certainly important, these latter, formal principles inherent in *lex* do not exhaust the considerations in terms of which the justice of law may be deliberated. Oakeshott criticizes Hobbes for making just this identification of the justice of a law with its faithfulness to the intrinsic character of law. "[T]he *jus* of *lex* cannot be identified simply with its faithfulness to the formal character of law." And, contrary to Hobbes's belief, authentic *lex* can be *injusta*.[101] Of course, it is not just Hobbes that Oakeshott wishes to distance himself from here, but also positivist writers who deny that the moral consideration of justice extends any further than to the consideration of whether a law has been properly enacted or not.

The criterion by which the justice of a law may be determined, then, must be sought outside of positive law, according to Oakeshott. Nevertheless, he denies that natural law is an adequate interpretation of this criterion.[102] In *On Human Conduct* this denial was based on the indeterminateness of natural law, and in "The Rule of Law" a similar objection is implied. It is true that an attempt has been made to surmount this difficulty by formulating the Natural Law in terms of some readily available principles: a Bill of Rights or a Fundamental Law. But Oakeshott does not seem to think this solution helps much. We know from *Rationalism in Politics* that he regards the certainty provided by such ideologies as ultimately illusory. And here in "The Rule of Law" he characterizes them, along with the Natural Law itself, as "more often than not . . . the occasion of profitless dispute."[103]

But besides this more familiar criticism of natural law as the criterion of justice, Oakeshott puts another, and in some ways simpler, criticism in "The Rule of Law." Whether there exists a set of demonstrable, unambiguous, universal criteria by which to determine the *jus* of *lex* or not, he says, "association in terms of the rule of law [or civil association] has no need of them." Civil association does of course recognize, as has already been pointed out, certain formal principles inherent in the very notion of a legal order. But "beyond this it may float upon the acknowledgement that the considerations in terms of which the *jus* of *lex* may be discerned are neither arbitrary, nor uncontentious, and that they are the product of a moral experience which is never without tensions and internal discrepancies."[104] Oakeshott is saying two things here: first, that the criterion by which the *jus* of *lex* is determined is historical, the reflection of the historic moral-legal self-understanding of the association; and second, that this historic self-understanding is never monolithic, never without ambiguity or internal tension.

It is for this second reason that he goes on to say that what is needed more than anything else in determining the *jus* of *lex* is a "moral imagination more stable in its style of deliberation than in its conclusions."

> What this mode of association requires for determining the *jus* of a law is not a set of abstract criteria but an appropriately argumentative form of discourse in which to deliberate the matter; that is, a form of moral discourse, not concerned generally with right and wrong in conduct, but focused narrowly upon the kind of conditional obligations a law may impose, undistracted by prudential and consequential considerations, and insulated from the spurious claims of conscientious objectors, of minorities for exceptional treatment and, so far as may be, from current moral idiocies.[105]

As he did in *On Human Conduct*, Oakeshott here precisely delimits the moral considerations in terms of which civil conditions may be deliberated, distinguishing them not only from non-moral, instrumental considerations but also from more general moral desirabilities. Deliberation of the *jus* of *lex*, like all political deliberation, cannot concern itself with all the conditions of the moral life – conditions relating to the motives of our actions, for example – but only with those conditions which a law may impose. "To deliberate the *jus* of *lex*," Oakeshott insists,

> is to invoke a particular kind of moral consideration: neither an absurd belief in moral absolutes (the "right" to speak, to be informed, to pro-

create and so on) which should be recognized in law, nor the distinction between the rightness and wrongness of actions in terms of the motives in which they are performed, but the negative and limited consideration that the prescriptions of the law should not conflict with a prevailing edu- cated moral sensibility capable of distinguishing between the conditions of "virtue", the conditions of moral association ("good conduct"), and those which are of such a kind that they should be imposed by law ("justice").[106]

Oakeshott rejects, then, natural law as the criterion by which the justice of a law may be determined, and puts in its place a more historical criterion: the "prevailing educated sensibility" of a people, qualified of course by its capacity to make the distinctions mentioned above. In this he is in agreement with Hegel, and he acknowledged the fact. Hegel, he says, "also rejected the notion of 'natural law' as the standard by which *der Gerechtigkeit* of *das Gesetz* might be determined."[107] But recognition of this historical aspect of Oake- shott's teaching on justice and political deliberation in general should be accompanied by a recognition of the limits he places on such de- liberation. As we have just seen, he confines deliberation of the *jus* of *lex* to those considerations which relate to the kind of obligations a law may impose, excluding larger considerations such as those which relate to the sentiments or motives in which actions are performed. And beyond this there are those formal principles inherent in the notion of a legal order – the *jus* intrinsic to *lex* – which form a kind of natural limit to political deliberation and legislation. Oakeshott's re- placement of natural law with a more historical criterion of justice, then, does not commit him to an undifferentiated historicism with respect to law. And it is precisely this recognition of the historical, without falling into a radical historicism or relativism, which con- stitutes one of the most fascinating features of his political thought.

No contemporary account of justice would be complete without at least some mention of the notion of distributive justice, which has lately received so much attention. And I propose to conclude my ex- position of Oakeshott's theory of civil association by briefly consider- ing his views on this much-discussed topic. These are not difficult to ascertain, being clearly stated in a couple of footnotes in *On Human Conduct* and "The Rule of Law." In essence, he argues that there is no place for distributive justice in civil association. Distributive justice posits a substantive condition as the end of association, and this as we know is not civil association. With respect to the theories of distrib- utive justice of Rawls and Ackerman, Oakeshott writes: "Here, *lex*, if it exists at all, is composed of regulations understood in terms of the consequences of their operation and as guides to a substantive state of affairs."[108] Writers such as Rawls and Ackerman thus theorize a kind of enterprise association; they are engaged in exploring that idiom of the state to which Oakeshott gives the name "teleocracy." And this suggests that their own self-understanding of what they are doing may be somewhat mistaken. Claiming to have expelled teleology and utilitarianism entirely from their theories, it would seem that they end up incorporating these notions implicitly. On this view, Oakeshott may be seen as doing more consistently what these deontological liberals attempt – although I consider in section 5 below whether he too does not end up contradicting himself. There too – as well as in my conclusion – I consider whether Oakeshott is properly seen as a deontological liberal at all.

This brings us to the end of Oakeshott's philosophical theory of civil association. It is difficult to summarize this theory neatly, since it takes up and disposes of almost every important issue in contemporary legal and political philosophy. At the very heart of the theory lies, of course, the notion of civil association as a moral (i.e., noninstrumental) practice and the distinction between such association and enterprise association. I will be subjecting this distinction between civil association and enterprise association to critical scrutiny in section 5 below. Before that, however, there is one final step in Oakeshott's argument to be pursued: namely, the relationship of the ideal character of civil association to the historical state. The question nags as to whether this ideal of civil association is anything more "than a logician's dream, a kind of geometrical theorem composed of related axioms and propositions?" And if not, "what place, if any, does it occupy as a practical engagement in the history of human hopes, ambitions, expectations or achievements in respect of association?"[109] It is to this historical – and in some ways pre-eminently Hegelian – question that Oakeshott turns in the third essay of *On Human Conduct*.

4. The Equivocal Character of a Modern European State

In the third essay of *On Human Conduct*, Oakeshott is concerned, not (as he was in the second essay) with an ideal mode of human relationship, but with the kind of human relationship or association actual, historical states constitute. I have already remarked that the sharp distinction between these two themes constitutes one of the most distinctive features of Oakeshott's political philosophy. Unlike his predecessors Hegel and Bosanquet, Oakeshott does not allow us to forget that civil association is an *ideal* mode of association and in no way to be mistaken for a specification of a modern state. Why he so sharply distinguishes between civil association, on the one hand, and the historical state, on the other, it is perhaps not out of place to ask here. To a large extent the answer lies, as we shall see, in the historical description of the state he provides. The distinction can, of course, be traced to the more general distinction Oakeshott draws between the coherence of a philosophical concept and the contingency and ambiguity of historical reality. But it is only in the third essay of *On Human Conduct* that the ambiguity which constitutes the modern state is exactly specified. It is only in this third essay that we learn that the modern state is not a single, unambiguous type of human association but a tension between two different types, namely, civil association and enterprise association.

The business that remains, then, is to follow Oakeshott in his historical inquiry into the character of the modern European state. By the "character" of a modern European state he means specifically its mode of association. What sort of association the modern European state constitutes has been a question that has haunted it ever since it emerged in the sixteenth century. It is a question that has never received a definitive answer; the modern state has always remained an "association in the making." Nevertheless, the effort to understand just what sort of association the modern state constitutes has been continuous, and it is to the history of this inquiry – "one of a family of inquiries which together we are accustomed to call the political thought of modern Europe" – that Oakeshott turns his attention in his essay. He tells us, too, that closely related to this inquiry into the mode of association of the state is the inquiry into the office and engagements of government and the identity (or *persona*) these impose on its subjects. Indeed, it is largely in terms of the beliefs that have been entertained about the office and engagements of government that he constructs his history of thinking on the question of the character of a modern European state as an association of human beings.[110]

Much else besides this has, of course, been thought and said about the modern European state. And Oakeshott mentions two important themes in the history of European political thought which his own history will leave to one side. The first concerns the beliefs in virtue of which a government is recognized to have authority; beliefs relating to the "constitutions" of governments. When states were first emerging, Oakeshott tells us, this was the most important theme of political reflection, and it has never ceased to be important. Nevertheless, he does not intend to explore it because it does not bear on his stated concern with the character of a modern state as an association of human beings and with the office and engagements of its government. The categorial distinction between these two themes has, of course, been frequently overlooked, and the inquiry into the character of a state and the engagements of its government has frequently been conducted in terms of the vocabulary of authority and constitutional shapes (Oakeshott's favorite example is "democracy," which properly denotes a constitutional shape but which has now come to be used in connection with certain policies and substantive engagements of government). Nevertheless, Oakeshott insists that there is absolutely no connection whatever between the mode of association of a state and the manner in which the authority of its government is constituted. Nor is there any relationship between the constitutional shape of a government and the character of its engagements. And this has to be insisted upon because a history which fails to recognize these distinctions will inevitably fall victim to the confusion and ambiguity which it is to some extent meant to abate.[111]

About the second theme left out by Oakeshott's history less need be said, both because Oakeshott himself says less about it and because it has caused less confusion than the theme of the constitution of authority with respect to the inquiry into the character of a state as an association of human beings. This second theme concerns the power of a government, reflection about which is to be discovered in the administrative histories of European states. Oakeshott points out that, though there is no connection between the amount or kind of power at the disposal of a government and the manner in which a government is constituted, there is a connection between the former consideration and the mode of association of a state and the office of its government. In this the consideration of power differs from that of the constitution of an office of authority.[112] Nevertheless, it too lies to one side of Oakeshott's concern in *On Human Conduct*, which is with what has been thought and said about the character of a European state as an association of human beings and about the office and engagements of its government. It is to his historical treatment of this theme that we must now turn.

Oakeshott organizes his historical account around two ideas or analogies which were used early on to try to understand the puzzling and exceedingly ambiguous experience of the emergent state: the ideas of *societas* and *universitas*. Drawn from Roman private law, these words denoted two different modes of association. A *societas* was an association in which the members remained distinct despite their being associated; they were joined, not in the pursuit of a common purpose, but in the common acknowledgement of a set of non-instrumental rules of conduct. A *universitas*, by contrast, was an association in which the members to some extent gave up their distinctness and came to constitute in certain important respects a single "person." Oakeshott does not think that this many-in-oneness of a *universitas* needs to be understood in terms of such mystical, Gierkean notions as "corporate personality" or "corporate mind." Something more commonplace will do. The idea of a *universitas* is the idea of a many become one in the joint pursuit of a common substantive purpose: what Oakeshott earlier referred to as enterprise association. And examples of this sort of corporate association in late medieval life included collegiate churches, cathedral chapters, monastic houses, guilds, and universities.[113]

What these terms translated into when applied to the state is not difficult to guess. A state understood in terms of *societas* was a state governed by non-instrumental law: what Oakeshott in the second essay called a *civitas*, and what he here refers to as a "nomocracy." A state understood in terms of *universitas* was a purposive association in which law was understood to be instrumental to a purpose and government to be the management of that purpose: a "teleocracy." Oakeshott mentions that there were difficulties with this identification of a state with a *universitas*, the chief one being that the voluntary character of a *universitas* could not be made to fit with the compulsory character of the state. But if this difficulty were overlooked (as it frequently was), *universitas* proved to be a plausible analogy in terms of which to understand the state. Oakeshott himself does not really dwell on this difficulty (though neither does he allow us to forget it) until the end of the essay, where his tone becomes more critical.[114]

Now it is these two mutually exclusive understandings of the state in terms of *societas* and *universitas* which Oakeshott proposes to trace in what has been thought and said about the character of a state over the last five centuries or so. His view is that, while neither one of these understandings taken alone can identify the state, when taken together they provide a framework within which the complexity and essential ambiguity of the state may be understood. "A state," he writes,

> may perhaps be understood as an unresolved tension between the two irreconcilable dispositions represented by the words *societas* and *universitas*.... This tension, I contend, was inherited from earlier times. It has acquired some new features and has imposed a particular ambivalence upon all the institutions of a modern state and a specific ambiguity upon its vocabulary of discourse: the muddle in which we now live where "law", "ruling", "politics", etc., each have two discrepant meanings. At all events, the thesis I propose to explore is that it is this tension, and not any of the others celebrated in current political discourse, which is central to the understanding of a modern European state and office of its government.[115]

The thesis stated, Oakeshott descends into the detail of what has been thought and said. And he begins, not with the appearance of the tension between *societas* and *universitas* in the modern state, but with the intimation of this ambiguity in the late medieval realm. This institution, according to Oakeshott, contained intimations of both *societas* and *universitas*. On the side of *societas* there was the ruler of the medieval realm, the king, who was understood to be, not a *grand seigneur* or a lordly proprietor of a domain, but the keeper of the peace and (eventually) the supreme dispenser of justice. The slow

extension of royal justice in the medieval realm resulted finally in
its being recognized as an association in terms of law. It was this
legal or judicial aspect of the medieval realm which suggested *societas*
as the most plausible analogy in terms of which to understand its
character.[116]

But there were other features of the medieval realm which suggested *universitas* as the analogy in terms of which it should be
understood. To begin with, an "unpurged relic of lordship" remained
embedded in the office of a king. To be sure, the distinction mentioned
above between rulership and lordship constituted one of the great
achievements of medieval thought and practice, but (Oakeshott tells
us) it was never "more than a somewhat hesitating distinction."
Rulership and lordship were never completely separated. Nevertheless, this intimation of a realm as a *universitas* in the economic idiom
remained rather remote in the Middle Ages; for the most part it was a
dream that belonged to the future. Far more important for nourishing
the belief that a realm was a *universitas* was the sacerdotal authority of
its ruler. This authority was the relic of that *plenitudo potestatis* which
the medieval Church originally claimed for the Pope and which included (among other things) the power to control education (*potestas
docendi*). Now with respect to the Pope this *plenitudo potestatis* was
"never much more than a dream," according to Oakeshott; and it was
repudiated by almost every ruler in late medieval Europe. Nevertheless, it did not simply disappear. "What was lost to the Church was
acquired by the king and added to his office." The king came to be
concerned with the spiritual welfare of his subjects as well as their
temporal peace. And a good deal of the *potestas docendi* previously
claimed for the Pope now fell under his authority. It was this appropriation of the sacerdotal authority of the Church by the civil
ruler, according to Oakeshott, which more than anything else gave
credence to the understanding of a medieval realm in terms of a
universitas.[117]

Having disclosed the intimations of both *societas* and *universitas* in
the late medieval realm, Oakeshott now turns his attention to the
modern state. His concern, as we know, is with the character of the
state as an association of human beings and with the office and
engagements of its government. But before addressing this thematic
concern, he first considers certain administrative and constitutional
features of the modern state as it emerged in the sixteenth century
which did not impose on it any substantive character as an association
of human beings or specify the engagements of its government. One of
these features relates to the state as an association in terms of law. The
other concerns the state as a "free" or "sovereign" association. With
respect to the latter, two things were involved: first, the emancipation
of the state from external authorities (such as the Church or the

Empire) as well as from competitors at home (ungovernable feudal magnates, etc.); second, the power of the state to emancipate itself continuously from its legal past, that is, its imprescriptability.[118]

Oakeshott reiterates that neither of these features of the emergent state indicated anything one way or the other as to whether it was to be understood as a *societas* or as a *universitas*. A state may be an association in terms of law, but the important question is whether this law is instrumental to a common purpose or non-instrumental. By the same token, to say that a government is "sovereign" says nothing about its office and engagements. Is this "sovereign" government concerned with the custody of a system of non-instrumental rules, or is it concerned with the management of a common purpose? Is its engagement nomocratic or teleocratic? These, according to Oakeshott, are "the crucial questions to be answered" in trying to understand the character of a modern European state, and he proposes now "to consider what has been thought and said about them in modern times."[119]

He begins with the circumstances and beliefs which evoked the understanding of a modern European state in terms of *societas*. One of the most important of these had to do with the rather miscellaneous composition of most European states. Each was composed of a vast variety of persons and peoples differing in language, beliefs, customs, aspirations, and purposes. None even came close to constituting what might properly be called a "community," much less a "nation." In short, a European state, at least on the surface, did not appear to be very promising material from which a *universitas* might be made.[120]

But besides this somewhat external circumstance, Oakeshott mentions another which pointed even more positively in the direction of understanding a state in terms of *societas*. This circumstance had to do with the emergence of a new disposition or sentiment in Europe, namely, the disposition to cultivate and enjoy individuality. Oakeshott, as we know, had already discussed the emergence and significance of this historic disposition at some length in "The Masses in Representative Democracy." And his discussion here for the most part parallels his discussion there. There are some changes in expression, though; changes which reflect the somewhat more formal and philosophical idiom of *On Human Conduct*. Instead of speaking of the disposition to cultivate and enjoy individuality, for example, he speaks of the disposition to cultivate and enjoy the freedom inherent in agency, thus referring us back to his initial discussion of the postulates of human conduct. This freedom inherent in agency is, as we already know, something inescapable, something of which we cannot divest ourselves without at the same time ceasing to be human. Nevertheless, Oakeshott tells us, it may be greeted with varying degrees of revulsion, anxiety, or confidence; it may be found burdensome or exciting. It is his contention that toward the end of the Middle Ages, as the bonds of corporate, communal life were beginning to dissolve, this unsought and inescapable freedom inherent in agency came to be regarded not simply as a condition to be accepted and acquiesced in but as "the emblem of human dignity ... a condition for each individual to explore, cultivate, to make the most of, and to enjoy as an opportunity rather than suffer as a burden."[121]

In discussing the historic disposition to cultivate individuality, Oakeshott is particularly concerned that it not be confused with any sort of negative individualism, atomism, subjectivism, or romantic notion of self-expression. He denies, for example, that individuality is to be identified with notably egoistic or self-interested behavior. And he insists that the disposition to cultivate the freedom inherent in agency "is not to be understood as a surrender to so-called 'subjective will', or a relapse into the effortless indulgence of inclination, or as the canonization of 'conscience'; it is a difficult achievement." The self here is not something "natural," opposed to civilization and reflective consciousness; it is the "outcome of education." Nor does this disposition to be an individual have anything to do with the mindless "worship of nonconformity" or with gratuitous "self-expression." And it certainly does not imply an "unconcern with the conditions which specify the arts of agency"; subscribing to the conditions of a moral practice in no way compromises the pursuit of personal autonomy. Finally, Oakeshott rejects the identification of "authenticity" (which he finds in Rousseau, among others) "as a hypothetical organic feeling of self-identity, dissipated in reflective consciousness and unable to survive in conduct *inter homines*, or as the 'idiocy' of idiots."[122] In all this he shows himself the heir of the non-negative, deromanticized view of the self of his Hegelian predecessors.

Besides these elementary errors, Oakeshott is also concerned to repudiate the identification of the historic disposition to cultivate the freedom inherent in agency with so-called "bourgeois morality" or "possessive individualism." In an acerbic footnote he writes that the contraction of the history of this disposition

> into a history of so-called "bourgeois market-society capitalism" is a notorious botch. Of course, this disposition displayed itself in commerce. But anyone who believes the Frere Jean des Entommeurs or Parini were "possessive individualists", or that it was of such persons that Pico della Mirandola, or Montaigne or Hobbes or Pascal or Kant or Blake or Nietzsche or Kierkegaard wrote is capable of believing anything.[123]

Oakeshott's own brief sketch of the history of this disposition, with its invocation of the names of such figures as St. Francis, Cellini, Montaigne, Pico, Pascal, Rabelais, and Cervantes, is meant to evoke some of the variety and profundity contained in the historic experience of individuality. And he concludes by insisting, much as he did in "The Masses in Representative Democracy," that this disposition to cultivate individuality and to concede virtue to autonomy "has remained the strongest strand in the moral convictions of the inhabitants of modern Europe."[124]

As to the understanding of the state which corresponds to the "individual" thus understood Oakeshott thinks there can be no doubt. It can only be the state understood as a *societas*. "Individuals" are defined by their desire to make choices for themselves, and it is only in a state understood as a *societas* that this freedom to make one's own choices is not compromised. In order to emphasize its connection with "individuality," Oakeshott uses yet another Latin expression (this one deriving from Augustine) to designate the state as a *societas*. He calls it the *"civitas peregrina*: an association, not of pilgrims travelling to a common destination, but of adventurers each responding as best he can to the ordeal of consciousness in a world composed of others of his kind."[125]

Having disclosed the circumstances which promoted the reading of a modern European state in terms of *societas*, Oakeshott goes on to discuss some of the more notable writers in whom this understanding of the state has appeared. He divides these writers into three groups, each representing a different level of self-consciousness with respect to *societas*. First, he mentions the writers in whom the understanding of the state as a *societas* appears at the level of an "implicit assumption." For the most part practical men and concerned with other matters (such as the constitution of government), these writers assumed that the state either was or ought to be a *societas* without explicitly recognizing it to be so. Among these writers Oakeshott counts Machiavelli, the American Founders, Locke, Burke, Paine, Ranke, de Tocqueville, and Acton. In the second group of writers there is a more explicit recognition and characterization of the state in terms of *societas*. The writer Oakeshott here discusses at some length is Montesquieu, whose notion of "monarchy" he identifies with the ideal of civil association. (For Oakeshott, Montesquieu's "despotism," "republic," and "monarchy" stand for ideal modes of association and not for constitutional shapes.) The third group of writers consists of the genuine political philosophers. These writers not only explicitly identified the state as a *societas* but were also concerned to theorize this understanding of the state in terms of its postulates. Among the most accomplished of these writers Oakeshott names Bodin, Hobbes, Spinoza, Kant, Fichte, and Hegel.[126]

I do not intend to go into each one of Oakeshott's interpretations of these writers, which in most cases amounts to no more than a suggestive sentence or phrase anyway. But I would like to consider for a moment the seven or so pages of discussion he devotes to Hegel's

Philosophy of Right. This discussion is important for a couple of different reasons. First, it is the longest discussion to be found any-where in Oakeshott's writings of the philosopher for whom he most consistently expresses admiration and to whom his own philosophy seems to be most in debt. Second, it makes clear just what the con-nection is, at least in Oakeshott's mind, between his own political philosophy and that of Hegel. That the connection is quite close becomes evident as we follow him in his reconstruction of Hegel's argument.

I will quickly pass over what Oakeshott says about Hegel's under-standing of human beings in terms of *der Geist* and *das Subjektive* – briefly, the point he wishes to make is that for Hegel human beings are what they understand themselves to be, they are not the unwitting components of a natural process – and turn immediately to his inter-pretation of the breakdown of "abstract right" treated by Hegel in the section entitled "Wrong" in the *Philosophy of Right.* Oakeshott writes:

> "Wrong", here, is failure (of various kinds) of one or more persons related in a transaction to subscribe to its purported formal conditions, and its antithesis is a "right" identified merely as a faithful observance of these conditions. But no such transaction is isolated; it postulates relationship with persons other than the transacting parties whom it may injure. And the conditions of a transaction are not merely considerations which may be arbitrarily agreed between the parties immediately concerned, they postulate considerations (norms) in terms of which they themselves may be recognized to be "right" or "wrong". In short, the exercise of *der Wille* in postulating the possibility of a local "wrong" postulates a "right" which is not merely the antithesis of this local "wrong" but is composed of considerations not concerned with Objects willed but with the exercise of *der Wille* itself. These considerations of right conduct Hegel calls *das Recht*, and to be associated in these terms (the common recognition of *das Recht*) is to enjoy a *sittlich* relationship.[127]

The dialectical progression from "abstract right" to *das Recht* and *Sittlichkeit* which Oakeshott describes here is reminiscent of his own dialectical argument, made early on in *On Human Conduct*, that the individual, ad hoc transactions which comprise conduct *inter homines* "postulate more durable relationships between agents which are not themselves transactions but are the conditional context of all such transactions," namely, practices. And of course, Oakeshott's "prac-tice" is a translation and interpretation of the Hegelian *das Recht* or *Sittlichkeit.*

In describing the transition from "abstract right" to *das Recht*, Oakeshott has, of course, skipped over the entire stage Hegel calls *Moralität,* and he now swerves back to pick it up. For Hegel, he argues, human conduct is an engagement in which agents disclose and enact themselves in self-chosen actions, "an engagement in which Subjects continuously create and recreate themselves as the finite persons they wish to be." "And it is a necessary characteristic of the conditions of conduct which constitute *das Recht* that, however much they qualify this engagement, they do not deny or compromise it." Hegel recognizes this to be an important principle, but he also argues that it "has been made to yield conclusions it cannot sustain." This is the burden of his criticisms of the moral point of view in the *Philosophy of Right* (and elsewhere). The "good will" does not comprise the whole of morality. Benevolence, sincerity, conscientiousness, or authenticity alone do not identify or satisfy the conditions of *das Recht*. "So far from identifying *das Recht*, they merely deny it." But Hegel's treatment of *Moralität* in the *Philosophy of Right* is not simply negative (he does, after all, make it a necessary mediation in the development of the Idea of the state), and Oakeshott's interpretation captures this nuance of Hegel's analysis nicely. Though the "'authenticity' of conduct cannot be a sufficient identification of the conditions which constitute *das Recht*," he writes, it nevertheless

> stands for a principle of the highest importance; namely, that the only conditions of conduct which do not compromise the inherent integrity of a Subject are those which reach him in his understanding of them, which he is free to subscribe to or not, and which can be subscribed to only in an intelligent act of Will. The necessary characteristic of *das Recht* is not that the Subject must himself have chosen or approved of what it requires him to subscribe to, but that it comes to him as a product of reflective intelligence and exhibiting its title to recognition, and that it enjoins not a substantive action but the acknowledgement of a condition which can be satisfied only in a self-chosen action.[128]

Once again it will be noticed that the view of moral autonomy which Oakeshott here ascribes to Hegel is almost identical to the one he has himself defended in the first two essays of *On Human Conduct*.

Having elucidated the significance of *Moralität* for Hegel, Oakeshott returns to the third part of the *Philosophy of Right* and to *das Recht*. He turns his attention first to that form of *das Recht* in which people are associated in terms of the satisfaction of wants: what Hegel called *bürgerliche Gesellschaft* (which Oakeshott thinks has been unfortunately translated as "civil society") and what we know as an "economy." Here *das Recht* is a set of instrumental considerations. Oakeshott insists that "Hegel had profound misgivings about the manner in which this engagement to satisfy wants was being conducted in modern Europe," but that this is not his concern in the *Philosophy of Right*.[129] His concern here is with the self-sufficiency or self-completeness of association in terms of the satisfaction of wants, and his conclusion is that this mode of association "is a conditional, not an autonomous, mode of association. It postulates another mode of association in which *das Recht* is not composed of contrivances for satisfying wants but considerations to be subscribed to in choosing wants to satisfy and in performing actions to satisfy them." This non-instrumental (moral) mode of association postulated by *bürgerliche Gesellschaft* Hegel calls *der Staat*. In *der Staat, das Recht* appears not as a set of instrumental considerations but as a system of non-instrumental rules of law (*Gesetze*).[130]

Oakeshott goes on to summarize what is implied in this sort of relationship in terms of non-instrumental law (*das Gesetz*) for Hegel, and what he says bears very close comparison with his own elaboration of the conditions of *lex* in the second essay of *On Human Conduct*. He concludes by pointing to Hegel's contention that legislation is necessarily a deliberative and not a demonstrative engagement; which contention, it will be remembered, concluded Oakeshott's own theory of civil association. For Hegel, he writes, "the actual *Gesetze* governing the conduct of any historic set of persons . . . could not be deduced from the character of *das Gesetz*," or (for that matter) from natural law. "'Legislating' in these circumstances is necessarily a deliberative engagement reflecting the contingent moral self-understanding of the persons concerned."[131]

It is clear from his interpretation of the *Philosophy of Right* that Oakeshott sees Hegel as his true predecessor, and that he conceives *On Human Conduct* as in large measure a restatement of Hegel's political philosophy. But Oakeshott is not uncritical of Hegel, and he realizes to what extent he has, in interpreting Hegel, "Oakeshotteanized" him. He has Oakeshotteanized Hegel, however, not so much in failing to recognize the "integrative force" of *Sittlichkeit* (as Shklar suggests), but more importantly in sharply distinguishing Hegel's argument about *der Staat* as an ideal mode of association from more contingent considerations. Hegel only imperfectly separates his philosophical argument from his political opinions and preferences, and Oakeshott does not hesitate to point this out. He calls the *Philosophy of Right* a "dreadfully miscellaneous piece of writing" in which political opinions and "considerable excursions into matters of contingency" jostle for space with Hegel's philosophical argument about *der Staat* as a non-purposive or moral mode of association.[132] He finds the connections Hegel draws between this ideal mode of association and certain constitutional arrangements for the most part "far-fetched." He even criticizes Hegel for using the word *Staat* to designate the ideal mode of association he is trying to theorize, since it blurs the distinction between this ideal and the ambiguous, contingent, historic state.[133] In short, Oakeshott recognizes that Hegel's political philosophy is rather less pure than he would like, and in both his interpretation of Hegel and his restatement of Hegel's political philosophy he tries to remedy this defect. *On Human Conduct* may be understood as a purer, slimmed down version of the *Philosophy of Right*.

And when I characterize it as a "restatement," I mean that it is a genuine restatement: a total transformation in which the incoherencies and obscurities of the original are criticized and superseded.

Though Oakeshott criticizes Hegel for becoming involved with contingencies in the *Philosophy of Right*, there is one contingent contention which he considers to be a "legitimate extension of his argument": namely, Hegel's contention that the ideal mode of association *der Staat* "was at least intimated in the so-called states of modern Europe." It is obvious that the subject of this contention corresponds essentially to the subject of Oakeshott's essay; and it is important to be clear on where Oakeshott and Hegel differ in regard to this question of the character of the modern European state. Hegel's contention that *der Staat* is at least intimated in the states of modern Europe rests on two considerations, according to Oakeshott. First, there is the consideration that it would be difficult simply to deduce *der Staat* unless there existed some intimation of it in the real world. Second, there is Hegel's belief that the historic disposition postulated by *der Staat* to cultivate the freedom inherent in agency (which disposition he traced to Christianity) was coming more and more to characterize European peoples.[134] It is this second assumption that Oakeshott cannot so easily accept. Like de Tocqueville, Kierkegaard, Burckhardt, Nietzsche, and so many other moralists who came after Hegel, he recognizes that there is another disposition besides the one to be an individual at work in the modern world; a disposition evoking an altogether different understanding of government than that corresponding to *societas* or *der Staat*. Where Hegel sees a linear evolution toward individuality and *societas*, Oakeshott sees a tension between *societas* and *universitas*. And it is to the intimations of the latter in the modern European state that he now turns.

He begins, as he did with the analogy of *societas*, with the circumstances in early modern Europe which promoted the reading of the state in terms of *universitas*. He mentions first the creation and extension of a central administrative apparatus in modern states. Though this circumstance did not necessarily entail understanding the office of government in terms of management, it nevertheless "beckoned imagination" in this direction. The second circumstance Oakeshott believes nourished the understanding of a state in terms of a *universitas* was what he has already alluded to as the "unpurged relic of lordship embedded in the office of a king." Though in states emerging from medieval realms this element of lordship always remained subordinate to civil rule, in states emerging from landed estates this was not the case. And it was in these states that the idea of government as the management of an enterprise "most easily found a home." A third circumstance which acquainted governments with significant managerial experience, according to Oakeshott, was colonial adventure and administration. But even more important than this colonial experience, he argues, has been the experience of war in modern Europe. From Oakeshott's postwar writings we are already familiar with his belief that war, with its mobilization of a society toward a single, common purpose, is the worst model for understanding what civil society is or should be. Here he repeats this conviction – "War in a modern European state is the enemy of civil association; belligerence is alien to civil association" – and he argues that the experience of war in modern Europe has been the "chief nourishment" of the belief that a state is an enterprise association.[135]

In addition to these circumstances, Oakeshott mentions another, of a somewhat different kind, which promoted the understanding of the state in terms of *universitas*: namely, the emergence of the "individual *manqué*." We are already familiar with this character from the "The Masses in Representative Democracy," and what Oakeshott says here about him differs little from what he said there. Once again we hear that not everyone in late medieval Europe responded to the dissolution of communal life quite the same way. What excited some, depressed others. And from these latter sprang the "individual *manqué*," a character who "had needs rather than wants," and who "sought a patron rather than a ruler, a lord able to make for him the choices he was unable to make for himself rather than a law to protect him in the adventure of choosing." Quite obviously *universitas* and not *societas* was the understanding of the state which corresponded to this character. Oakeshott goes on to describe how the "individual *manqué*," resentful of his more enterprising counterpart and manipulated by unscrupulous "leaders," came to be transformed into the militant "anti-individual": "one intolerant not only of superiority but of difference, disposed to allow in all others only a replica of himself, and united with his fellows in a revulsion from distinctness." Here again the only kind of state which could accommodate such a character was a *universitas* in which individual choice was removed and a uniform substantive condition imposed upon all.[136]

These, then, are the circumstances which suggested a modern European state be understood in terms of *universitas*. And it remains for Oakeshott only to consider the attempts of governments to impose, and of speculative writers to project, such a character on the state. These attempts he separates into four different categories representing four different idioms of teleocratic belief. In the first idiom the state is understood as a cultural and religious *universitas*. In the second the state is understood as a corporate enterprise for exploiting the resources of the earth. In the third idiom the first two are said to be combined in the idea of "enlightened" government. And in the fourth the state is understood as a therapeutic corporation. Let us take up each of these idioms of teleocratic belief in a little more detail.

The cultural and religious integration of miscellaneously composed states, Oakeshott says, constituted the "earliest and least compromising" of the above-mentioned adventures in teleocracy. This integration involved the suppression of alien or eccentric beliefs, and on the positive side the appropriation of educational and religious institutions (the *auctoritas docendi* which had until then been the prerogative of the Pope) by the state. In Catholic countries such as France, Spain, Poland, and Portugal this annexation of the Papal *auctoritas docendi* to the state was carried out with some (not total) success in the sixteenth and seventeenth centuries. In England, on the other hand, "an official norm of educational and religious solidarity emerged slowly and never established itself conclusively." In Lutheran countries in the sixteenth century "a more decisive step" was taken "in the direction of teleocracy." Lutheran Princes acquired significant moral and religious authority. Nevertheless, Oakeshott maintains, Lutheran culture remained for the most part "insubstantial" and "liable to collapse." It was only in Calvinist states, he argues, that substantial (though still not unqualified) religious and cultural solidarity was achieved. For Oakeshott, sixteenth-century Geneva is the cultural and religious *universitas* par excellence.[137]

Traces of this teleocratic aspiration for cultural and religious solidarity can, of course, be found in Burke. And insofar as Oakeshott's position can be identified as non-teleocratic, we can see here again how his conservatism diverges from that of Burke. Unlike Burke (or, in the Catholic idiom, de Maistre), Oakeshott does not advocate the cultural and religious integration of the modern state. Such integration he seems to regard as impossible in modern circumstances. And where it has been attempted with a modicum of success (e.g., in National Socialist Germany and in Soviet Russia), the results have been disastrous.

The second idiom of teleocratic belief Oakeshott explores is that in which the state is understood as a corporate enterprise for the exploitation of the resources of the earth. Here the state is recognized not simply to *have* an "economy" but in fact to *be* an "economy." This understanding of the state sprang, according to Oakeshott, from the unpurged relic of lordship embedded in the office of ruler; and it received its earliest and most audacious expression in Bacon's *New Atlantis*. Bacon's technological vision of the state, however, remains in the theological idiom; productivity is still *ad majorem gloriam Dei*. It is only in Bacon's successors (such as St. Simon, Fourier, Owen, Marx, Webb, and Lenin) that anything like a full-fledged *civitas cupiditas* emerges. A *civitas cupiditas* Oakeshott defines as

a corporate productive enterprise, centered upon the exploitation of the material and human resources of an estate and managed by a government whose office it [is] to direct research, to suppress distracting engagements and to make instrumental rules for the conduct of the enterprise, and to assign to each of its "subjects" his role in the undertaking and to deploy their productive energies and talents according to a "scientifically" deliberated plan.

Nor did the exponents of this vision of the state confine themselves to the theme of productivity. Distribution (and "distributive justice") also became an important subject of reflection.[138]

It is clear, not only from his description here but also from what he has said before, that Oakeshott regards this technological or economistic conception of the state as the most serious opponent to civil association in the modern world. In his presentation of the idea of civil association, as we have seen, he is constantly distancing himself from the belief that this mode of association has anything to do with the quest for material prosperity. And I have already drawn attention to the numerous places in which he remarks the futility and self-defeat inherent in the bare ideal of productivity. That he sees devotion to productivity and prosperity as posing the greatest challenge to civil association today is confirmed by his observation in *On Human Conduct* that all the current versions of the state understood as a *universitas* are "indelibly Baconian."[139] Nor is he alone in this diagnosis of our current political predicament. One thinks here of (among many others) Hannah Arendt's historical excavation of modernity in terms of the rise of "the social" in which the distinction between the public and private realms is lost. Like Oakeshott, Arendt sees European history largely in terms of the incursion of the private "household" into the public realm and the replacement of genuine politics by the "economy" and the "administration of things." And like Oakeshott, she sees nothing but futility and meaninglessness in the modern (and Marxian) ideal of material abundance and a "socialized mankind."[140]

Despite Oakeshott's emphasis on the historic importance of the technological or economistic idiom of teleocratic belief, he goes on to describe a third idiom – a synthesis of the first two – which he says "now constitutes the strongest strand of teleocratic belief in modern European thought." This is the idiom of " 'enlightened' government," which emerged in the eighteenth century, and which Oakeshott sees as a kind of secularized version of a moral and religious *universitas* in which virtue is understood in relation to a secular instead of an otherworldly purpose. Enlightened government retains the essentially economic purpose of a *civitas cupiditas* but imposes on it a "quasi-moral" character. In the enlightened state, Oakeshott writes, virtue and cupidity "constitute a single engagement directed or managed by a lord and his agents."[141]

Apart from this "quasi-moral" character, Oakeshott points to some other important features of the enlightened state; first and foremost, its preoccupation with administration, its vast expansion of the "apparatus of lordship." In this connection he mentions the ideas of the Cameralists and the achievements of eighteenth-century Prussia. Another big concern of Enlightened government, Oakeshott maintains, was "the poor," who, along with the individual *manqué*, "composed the natural-born recruits for the army of retainers" required by the managerial state. This concern stemmed, he goes on to argue, not so much from charitable impulse or moral indignation as from a "'rational' horror of waste." For enlightened government the poor represented a "wantonly wasted asset," and it sought to recuperate the loss by "educating" them. This education was not, of course, to be an initiation into a moral and intellectual inheritance but an "apprenticeship to adult life" in which the poor would be equipped with skills that might make them more useful to society. Oakeshott's attitude toward the functionally integrated enlightened state here breaks out into a kind of Nietzschean contempt.[142]

Contempt, too, is evident in Oakeshott's treatment of the fourth idiom of teleocratic belief (in some sense the "residual belief hidden in all versions" of the state understood as a *universitas*) in which the state is understood as an association of invalids, of victims suffering from a common disease, and the office of government is understood as a remedial or therapeutic engagement. Of course, the idea that man is somehow diseased, Oakeshott says, is not a particularly new idea; it has received expression in much religious (especially Christian) doctrine. But the idea that the disease is somehow curable, that it is a "historic morbid" and not a "cosmic" condition, and that the function of government is to treat and cure the afflicted, is of more recent origin. It is this latter set of beliefs which characterizes the understanding of the state Oakeshott is presently exploring. He notes that numerous diagnoses of the disease have been suggested over the last 150 years: poverty, insecurity, frustration, alienation; and that currently the therapeutic elite consists of sociologists, psychologists, "trained social workers," et al., engaged in "counselling," "behavioural engineering," and "behaviour modification."[143] His contempt for this therapeutic understanding of the state and of the human condition in general is, as I have already pointed out, evident throughout his discussion of it. Again one is perhaps reminded of Nietzsche and his decrial of the "madhouses and hospitals of culture"; his denunciation of the conversion of society into a sanatorium for the sick and the suffering.[144] Less hysterical and perhaps more akin to Oakeshott in spirit is the sentiment Goethe expressed in a letter to a friend: "Also, I must say myself, I think it is true that humanity will triumph eventually, only I fear that at the same time the world will become a large hospital and each will become the other's humane nurse."[145]

These, then, are the four idioms of teleocratic belief Oakeshott sees as having distinguished themselves over the course of modern European history. And all the current versions of the state as a *universitas* he sees as simply combining in one form or another these older and in many respects more coherent doctrines. Certainly there have been some new expressions – "the welfare state," "communism," "collectivism," "National Socialism," – but no really new ideas: in the twentieth century "the repetition of *idées reçues* has taken the place of genuine reflection." Indeed, one of the unstated purposes of Oakeshott's account of the fortunes of *universitas* over the last five centuries of European history is to show that this understanding of the state is not something new, a response to recent developments in politics or the economy. This understanding of the state, he writes,

> is not (as is sometimes thought) the outcome of recent intellectual adventures, nor is it a response to a long age of governmental indifference and negligence, to so-called "capitalist" industrial undertaking, to more populous territories, to "atomized societies", or to lately "self-alienated" subjects. It is a manner of thinking which was coeval with the emergence of Europe as a manifold of states and it had already been explored in connection with the realms and principalities of medieval times. It reflects, not the fancies of visionaries, but some of the contingent features of these states and the circumstances of their emergence.[146]

Oakeshott goes on to say that this understanding of the state in terms of *universitas* "has bitten deep into the civil institutions of modern Europe," compromising its civil law and corrupting its vocabulary of civil discourse. But as deep as it has gone, this understanding of the state has never characterized a European state without qualification. "[N]o regime in the five centuries of modern European history has ever 'represented' this understanding of the state entirely without qualification; the voice of civil association has, here and there, sunk to a whisper, but nowhere has it been totally silenced."[147]

This last reflection raises the issue which in some ways hovers over the whole of Oakeshott's essay: Just what is the relative importance of these two understandings of a state – *societas* and *universitas* – in relation to actual, historic European states? Can one be said to be more dominant than the other? Oakeshott denies that these two characterizations of the state can be read in terms of a dominant/recessive scheme. He insists that a European state is an "ambivalent experience," an "unresolved tension" between *societas* and *universitas*. But in denying that either of these characterizations of the state can be seen as dominant or recessive, Oakeshott seems to be primarily concerned to refute the view (which he takes to be the more common) which identifies purposive association as the dominant characteristic of a European state and civil association as the recessive; and which furthermore sees this recessive, civil feature of the state in the process of passing away, leaving behind an unambiguous *universitas*.[148] He considers two forms of this view, and his criticisms of both reveal once again the underlying purposes of the history he has just narrated.

In the first, the trend towards teleocracy is seen to be historically inevitable on account of recent (mainly technological) developments; "it is alleged to be the destiny imposed upon Europe (indeed, upon the world) by the 'needs of the epoch'." In a world characterized by over-population and the undirected proliferation of technology, civil association is seen to be anachronistic and inadequate. What is needed is the planning and direction provided by teleocratic government.[149] Oakeshott's criticism of this view of teleocracy as unavoidable in the circumstances of modern life is essentially the one we saw him making above. The disposition in favor of teleocracy did not emerge in response to recent developments in technology or world population; it "has been a feature of the European political consciousness for more than five centuries and it received its definitive expression three hundred years ago in the idea of 'enlightened' government."[150] Nor is Oakeshott's criticism here of the view that teleocracy is a necessary adaptation to the needs of the epoch new with *On Human Conduct*. As far back as "Rationalism in Politics" he expressed suspicion about the "crises" and "needs of the New Age" to which the rationalist's activity purported to be a response.

The second form of the view that the modern European state is evolving toward an unambiguous *universitas* has a romantic rather than a rationalistic root. It sees the history of modern Europe as a long, painful effort to recover the warmth and intimacy of communal ties which modern individualism, cold and "possessive," reputedly destroyed. Oakeshott's criticism of this reading of the moral and political tradition of modern Europe is once again implicit in the history he has already narrated. In the first place, he argues that "medieval realms are parodied if we neglect their memorable achievements in exploring the intimations of civil association." Secondly, he argues that the achievements of modern European states with respect to civil association "are misrepresented by identifying them with the creation of so-called 'atomized' society." This latter misrepresentation is one that Oakeshott has opposed throughout the third essay of *On Human Conduct*, especially in his discussion of the ethos of "individuality." For him, as we have seen, neither civil association nor the "individual" corresponding to it is reducible to capitalism, "possessive individualism," or so-called "bourgeois morality." "The *persona* who is the counterpart of civil association," he writes, "he whom Montaigne and Rabelais celebrated, is neither a savage egoist, nor a cold 'capitalist', nor the contemptible bourgeois of legend who (having played his part) is now become a moral embarrassment." It is only these parodies of the individualist tradition which have allowed the longing for "community" to appear respectable and even dominant in our tradition. That he finds this longing to be neither respectable nor dominant, however, Oakeshott makes abundantly clear:

> The urge to impose upon a state the character of a *solidarité commune* is certainly a notable disposition but, so far from being the dominant disposition of the modern European political imagination, it is easily recognized as a relic of the servility of which it is proper for European peoples to be profoundly ashamed.

He grants that "the path marked *universitas: dominium* has been, in recent times, the more crowded with travellers." But he nevertheless maintains that "no European alive to his inheritance of moral understanding has ever found it possible to deny the superior desirability of civil association without a profound feeling of guilt."[151]

Is Oakeshott contradicting himself here? Setting out to show that the European political consciousness is a divided consciousness in which neither *universitas* nor *societas* can be regarded as dominant, he ends up asserting the disposition favoring *societas* to be the dominant disposition in our political tradition. How can these two positions be reconciled? I think the key is to recognize that Oakeshott is using the word "dominant" in two different ways here. He rejects the notion that either *societas* or *universitas* is dominant in the sense that the modern state is "evolving" unambiguously toward one or the other. With such philosophies or sciences of history he has no truck. But there is another sense of "dominant" which he does seem willing to invoke, though one has to look outside *On Human Conduct* to flesh it out.

It will be remembered that this whole issue of dominance came up in the essay "The Masses in Representative Democracy," where Oakeshott also asserted the moral and political disposition corresponding to the "individual" to be the dominant disposition in our tradition. In that essay he also gave some reasons for taking this position – reasons which had nothing to do with the belief that the morality of individuality would eventually "win out." The morality of individuality is dominant, he argued, because it is original, positive, and self-sufficient, whereas the morality of the "anti-individual" or "mass-man" is derivative, reactive, and ultimately incoherent. The "mass-man," he wrote, is a wholly "derivative character, an emanation of the pursuit of individuality, helpless, parasitic and able to survive only in opposition to individuality." And the morality of the "mass-man" is a "rickety construction," incapable of resisting "relapse into inappropriate concepts of individuality."[152] It is precisely in the sense of being less derivative, more coherent, that Oakeshott seems to assert the dominance of individuality and civil association over communal solidarity in *On Human Conduct*. (Indeed, in a footnote to the passage discussed above he cites some egregious examples of self-contradiction on the part of teleocrats who unavoidably invoke inappropriate concepts of freedom and individuality in defending their conception of the state as an enterprise association.)[153] Nor, it must be emphasized, does the dominance of civil association in this sense in any way imply that the modern state is evolving toward an unambiguous *societas*; it in no way implies the elimination of the ambivalence of the modern European state, as the view of dominance Oakeshott rejects does.

There is, of course, another sense in which a state understood as a *universitas* is revealed to be self-contradictory, "a somewhat rickety moral construction."[154] As we learned in the second essay of *On Human Conduct*, enterprise association is necessarily chosen relationship: not only must an agent choose to be so associated, he must be able to extricate himself from such relationship whenever he chooses to do so. A compulsory enterprise association is a contradiction in terms and an affront to the "freedom" inherent in agency. But the state is a compulsory association. Therefore it cannot be an enterprise association without falling into self-contradiction and depriving its members of their "freedom" and "autonomy." Oakeshott makes this argument in the second essay of *On Human Conduct*.[155] In the third essay he tells us he has refrained from exploring this contradiction inherent in a state understood as a *universitas* in order not to prejudice his historical investigation of this understanding of a state. It must be said, however, that though he does not explore this self-contradiction in detail in the third essay, he alludes to it on several occasions and never allows us to lose sight of it completely.[156] It constitutes *the* central moral argument in *On Human Conduct* against conceiving the state as an enterprise association.

Oakeshott, as we have seen, insists upon the essential ambivalence of the modern European state; and he rejects the notion that such a state will ever come to be characterized unambiguously by either *societas* or *universitas*. Nevertheless, he warns that *societas* and *universitas* are not

> to be understood as complementary characteristics – both required (like the two dimensions of a plane figure) for the specification of a modern European state. *Societas* and *universitas* stand, each, for an independent, self-sustaining mode of association; and my contention is that they are both characteristics of a state, not because they have an inherent need of one another (indeed, they deny one another), but because they have become contingently joined by the choices of human beings in the character of a modern European state.[157]

The word "contingently" in this passage is somewhat ambiguous. Does Oakeshott mean to say that what has been contingently joined may be just as contingently unjoined? There is evidence that he does not think such a disjunction of *societas* and *universitas* possible or even desirable in our current circumstances. In a couple of places he indicates that, though *societas* and *universitas* may not have an inherent need of one another, in a modern European state *societas* must to some extent be qualified by *universitas*. This is the case, for example, with respect to national defense, which (especially in times of war) necessarily qualifies civil association and transforms the state into at least a partial enterprise association. And, of course, the need for defense has been an "unavoidable contingent circumstance," not only in our own time, but throughout the history of modern Europe.[158] Another circumstance which may be seen as requiring the qualification of *societas* by *universitas* is the problem of providing for the poor. Oakeshott himself does not say much about this problem, but he does invoke Hegel's view that it is necessary to exercise "a judicious 'lordship' for the relief of the destitute," if only to remove the temptation these might have to transform the state into an industrial *universitas* with equal rations and assured benefits for all.[159]

Just what the mixture of *societas* and *universitas* is or should be in a modern European state is, of course, a contingent question and not really Oakeshott's concern in this third essay. His concern, rather, is historical (i.e., theoretical, not practical), and the essay is to be understood as an historical essay. I emphasize this point because it is frequently denied. It is argued that Oakeshott's account of the modern European state is not historical at all; that it is a tendentious and ideological abridgement of the history of modern Europe, a myth, an exercise in the kind of rationalistic historicizing he elsewhere decries.[160] This charge, however, is sadly wide of the mark. The mere fact that Oakeshott sees the modern European state not as a simple thing but as an ambivalent experience, that he interprets its character in terms of tension between two things, and that he goes out of his way not to diminish the historical importance of either side of this tension – all this indicates that he has left rationalist abridgement and philosophy of history far behind. It is true that he leaves us in doubt in the essay as to where his preferences lie with respect to *societas* and *universitas*. But his obvious preference for the former in no way affects his central thesis, which (again) is not that the state is or ought to be identified with *societas*, but that the state is an "unresolved tension" between *societas* and *universitas*. Oakeshott is not concerned to resolve this tension but simply to explore it; to show that it is "*this* tension, and not any of the others celebrated in current political discourse, which is central to the understanding of the character of a European state and the office of its government." As he reiterates the thesis toward the end of the essay: "In short, my contention is that the modern European political consciousness is a polarized consciousness, that *these* are its poles and that all other tensions (such as those indicated in the words 'right' or 'left' or in the alignments of political parties) are insignificant compared with this."[161]

What these statements underline is that Oakeshott's primary concern in the third essay of *On Human Conduct* is not to defend a position in the current political debate – and again it is not denied that he has a position or preference which he reveals quite clearly – but to understand exactly and fundamentally just what the debate is. The current political debate, he maintains, concerns most fundamentally the mode of association to be attributed to the state. And this debate is seriously misunderstood when it is cast in terms of the "contrast between dictatorship and democracy" (words which do not even refer to modes of association but to manners of constituting the authority of the state),

> or between Left and Right (these merely represent an insignificant squabble about the common purpose to be imposed upon a state already assumed to be a purposive association). The words Liberal and Conservative are already so overloaded with meanings that they must fail to be explicit here. And those who understand it in terms of Communism and Capitalism, collectivism and free enterprise, centralism and pluralism, merely add to the confusion by suggesting a substantive purpose for civil association.

The debate over the mode of association to be attributed to the state is most clearly and coherently understood in terms of the contrast between *universitas* and *societas*, purposive and non-purposive association. And to avoid misunderstanding, Oakeshott adds that this "alignment of political belief is not between those who value purposive association [or "community"] and those who do not, or between those who have a compassionate regard for their fellow man and those who have none; it concerns only the character of a *state* as an association of human beings."[162]

Oakeshott's particular understanding of the modern European state and of the current political debate in terms of the opposition of *societas* and *universitas* of course owes much to his definition of civil association in the second essay of *On Human Conduct*. As I pointed out at the beginning of this chapter, and as the remarks quoted above confirm, Oakeshott believes that much of the confusion in the current political debate has come from a failure to grasp adequately the side of the opposition labelled *societas*. This mode of association, he argues, has been misunderstood by those who oppose it and by those who think it a desirable mode of association for a state. It is to these latter that many of his most critical remarks are addressed. He rejects, for example, the argument made by such libertarian thinkers as Robert Nozick that civil association is to be identified with a "minimal state." Such a view, he argues, totally misrepresents the distinction between civil and purposive association by making it appear "to be one of degree and not of mode." He also criticizes economists like Milton Friedman who describe civil association as a "free enterprise" association. These err by ascribing a substantive purpose to civil association. Properly speaking, civil association is not a free enterprise association but a no enterprise association. Finally he rejects what he calls "the saddest of all misunderstandings of the state as a civil association":

> that in which it is properly presented as association in terms of non-instrumental conditions imposed upon conduct and specified in general rules from whose obligations no associate and no conduct is exempt, but defended as the mode of association more likely than any other to promote and go on promoting the satisfaction of our diverse and proliferant wants.

Oakeshott does not attach a name to this "saddest of all misunderstandings," but I think it is not unlikely that he has someone like Hayek in mind. There is much that these two thinkers have in common – most importantly, the idea of a liberal social order as a non-purposive order governed by non-instrumental rules – but ultimately Oakeshott rejects the utilitarianism and economism which seems to creep into Hayek's political thought. "Prosperity," he writes, "may be the likely contingent outcome of civil association, but to recommend it in these terms is to recommend something other than civil association."[163]

Oakeshott's criticisms here are based, as I have already pointed out, on the definition of civil association which he sets forth most fully in the second essay of *On Human Conduct*. I will not rehearse the totality of that definition here, but only draw attention to its central feature: namely, the identification of civil association as a non-instrumental practice. In *On Human Conduct* we find civil association grasped as a purely moral idea without any utilitarian admixture. This I take to be one of the book's most significant achievements. In *On Human Conduct* Oakeshott has succeeded – as perhaps no other contemporary thinker has – in freeing liberalism from the utilitarianism, materialism, and economism which have dogged it since the seventeenth century, and which continue to find expression in such writers as Friedman and Hayek (and even Rawls and Nozick, who, despite their protests to the contrary, end up buttressing their deontological theories with substantial utilitarian appeals to economic efficiency and well-being). I have had occasion to refer more than once to this anti-materialistic, anti-economistic aspect of Oakeshott's political thought. As far back as 1939 he remarked that the weakest part of the liberal tradition was "what may be called its moral ideal: the plausible ethics of productivity." In *On Human Conduct* he undertakes to purge the liberal tradition of this most questionable element. It is not the only thing the book is about, as it is concerned with the whole range of theoretical issues confronting political and legal philosophy today; but it is perhaps the book's most persistent *political* theme. As such it is not superfluous to draw attention to it once more in concluding my exposition.

5. Criticisms of the Theory

In this final section I would like to take up some common criticisms of Oakeshott's theory of civil association. Most of these criticisms revolve around a single theme: namely, the formalism of the theory. It is objected that Oakeshott's distinction between civil and enterprise association is drawn too sharply; that civil association and civil law are never purely procedural or without purpose, as Oakeshott makes them out to be; and that even if civil association and civil law could be purged of purpose and made purely procedural, they should not.[164] In this section I intend to respond to these criticisms, not so much in an effort to vindicate Oakeshott's theory, as in an effort to clarify its meaning. In the preface to *On Human Conduct*, Oakeshott warns that he has left much to the reader, not staying to cross all the "ts" of the argument; and it must be admitted that it is not always clear what his abstract theory means for politics as we know it. By reconstructing Oakeshott's responses to the criticisms mentioned above, I hope to mitigate this abstractness somewhat. I begin by addressing the question of the tenability of the distinction between civil and enterprise association. From there I go on to consider the possibility of purely procedural laws and what they might include. And I conclude by considering the probing question of whether Oakeshott is advocating total neutrality in the law, and if so, whether he is not therefore vulnerable to some of the same criticisms that have been levelled by "communitarians" against "deontological" liberal theories.

Let us begin with the tenability of the distinction between civil and enterprise association. We want to know whether the distinction between these two modes of association is really as sharp as Oakeshott wants to draw it. Is not civil association dedicated to some purpose in the final analysis, whether it be peace, security, freedom, or (as the Declaration of Independence has it) life, liberty, and the pursuit of happiness? If purposes such as these can be ascribed to civil association, does not Oakeshott's whole distinction between civil association and enterprise association collapse? And if not, why not? These are obvious but important questions, going straight to the heart of Oakeshott's political philosophy. Because they are so obvious, I think it would be a mistake to suppose Oakeshott had not thought of them. Nevertheless, he does not spend a lot of time addressing them explicitly. I intend, therefore, to reconstruct what I think his responses to these questions and criticisms would be, taking some of the more common purposes that have been proposed for civil association and showing how they differ from the substantive purposes of enterprise association.

I will begin with what is perhaps the commonest purpose ascribed to civil association, namely, "peace" or "security." In a review of *On Human Conduct*, D. D. Raphael has argued that "security is a bedrock common interest in all civil association," and that this fact completely undermines Oakeshott's distinction between civil and enterprise association.[165] But does it? Oakeshott does not seem to think so, though his argument in refutation is rather brief and needs to be fleshed out. He simply asserts that peace and security "are not substantive purposes and they do not specify enterprise association."[166] What he means to argue, I think, is that peace and security are not specific satisfactions sought for themselves but rather conditions which make possible the pursuit of specific substantive satisfactions. Peace and security are not themselves substantive wants, nor do they specify substantive states of affairs; rather, they are formal conditions which allow agents to pursue their manifold wants and purposes with a minimum of frustration and collision. "Security" can, of course, have a more substantive meaning, suggesting assured benefits and equal rations. But Oakeshott's notion of civil association has nothing to do with security in this substantive and rather servile sense. Security is not an object of want but simply the minimum condition for the pursuit of wants.

Oakeshott follows a roughly similar strategy in rejecting "happiness," the "human good," and "human excellence" as substantive purposes for civil association. For him, these expressions do not specify substantive purposes at all but rather formal conditions inherent in human conduct. Thus with respect to happiness he writes: "I cannot *want* 'happiness'; what I want is to idle in Avignon or hear Caruso sing." Happiness is not a substantive end but rather (like Hobbes's felicity) a formal condition "in which the performances of agents continuously achieve their wished-for outcomes (whatever they may be), and in which these specific outcomes are not found to be unduly disappointing."[167] Similarly with respect to "human excellence" or the "human good": this "is not a substantive purpose to be achieved as the outcome of performances; it is not a purpose ... in terms of which [an agent] might or might not choose to be related with others in achieving ... like joining an expedition to climb Mount Everest or agreeing to settle in Katmandu."[168]

In this connection one thinks of – and Oakeshott obviously means us to think of – Aristotle, who throughout the *Politics* defines the end or purpose of a *polis* as the good life. It would seem that Aristotle fundamentally disagrees with Oakeshott insofar as he proposes such a purpose for civil association, but this is not Oakeshott's view of the matter. The end which Aristotle posits for civil association (he argues), namely, the good life or human excellence,

> is not for him a substantial purpose but a formal condition. He appears to have thought that *eudaimonia* was difficult if not impossible of attainment in the absence of certain substantive conditions (e.g. good health and adequate material means) but it is not itself a substantive condition of things. It is an agent continuously disclosing and enacting himself in his own chosen actions while subscribing adequately to considerations of moral propriety or worth.

In this regard, then, Oakeshott considers himself a follower of Aristotle. And, indeed, he credits Aristotle with identifying that feature of civil association which he himself considers to be of paramount importance: namely, *autarkeia*, or the quality of having no extrinsic substantive purpose.[169]

If "peace," "security," "happiness," and "human excellence" all fail to specify a purpose for civil association, there still remains "freedom" as a possible purpose for this type of association. But Oakeshott rejects the suggestion that "freedom" constitutes the purpose of civil association, and his reasons for doing so parallel those he gave for rejecting the other suggested purposes. "Freedom" for him, as we have seen, does not specify a substantive condition of things to be aimed at but rather a formal quality of conduct: the link between belief and conduct. In civil association this link is preserved because such an association does not prescribe purposes to be pursued or actions to be performed. In enterprise association, on the other hand, the link is preserved because an agent chooses to be so associated and may revoke this choice at any time. In neither civil association nor enterprise association is "freedom" a substantive purpose to be pursued; it is a formal feature which belongs to each. Thus Oakeshott can write with respect to civil association that, though "freedom" certainly characterizes civil association, it "does not follow as a consequence of this mode of association; it is inherent in its character."[170]

Neither freedom, nor peace, nor security, nor happiness, then, counts as a substantive purpose which may be ascribed to civil association; and thus far Oakeshott's distinction between civil association and enterprise association appears to hold. But there is yet one more condition which suggests itself as a purpose of civil association. I am thinking here of the idea of "individuality" which plays such a prominent role in the third essay of *On Human Conduct*, as well as in Oakeshott's other writings on politics. Individuality, unlike "freedom" or "happiness," does not refer simply to a formal feature of human conduct; it is a substantive, historic disposition; it is a particular way in which particular men at a particular time have conceived themselves and their happiness. Nevertheless, individuality does not specify a substantial purpose for civil association. It is not something (like material prosperity or empire) which can be jointly pursued, and it does not even remotely specify substantive actions or performances which could be conceived as instrumental to its achievement. That Oakeshott sees the historic disposition to cultivate individuality as a postulate of the state understood as a civil association certainly suggests that he does not conceive this type of association as a totally neutral idea, impartial with respect to different ways of life or types of character – a point I will be developing at greater length below. Nevertheless, it does not suggest that he is contradicting his view of civil association as a non-instrumental, non-purposive practice.

Having addressed the criticism that Oakeshott's distinction between civil and enterprise association does not hold, we may now pass to a second which is closely related to it. This criticism questions whether civil laws are or can be as procedural and purposeless as Oakeshott suggests. Judith Shklar argues, for example, that civil laws are never purely procedural, never completely without purpose. Even the rules of the road, which come closest to meeting this formalistic criterion, are not without a purpose, namely, to prevent collisions.[171] It is perhaps worth dwelling on this example of the rules of the road for a moment, in order to clarify what Oakeshott means by the non-purposiveness of civil laws. I do not think that Oakeshott would consider that, because the rules of the road are designed to prevent collisions, they are therefore purposive in the sense he means. The rules of the road do not impose destinations on drivers; they simply impose considerations to be taken into account by drivers whatever their destinations may be. The rules of the road do not determine choices; they simply allow individuals to pursue their individual courses without colliding with others as they pursue theirs. It is in this sense that the rules of the road are non-purposive; and it is in this sense that the rules of civil association in general are non-purposive. These rules are certainly designed (as Oakeshott himself frequently acknowledges) to prevent collisions between individuals pursuing their own individual courses, but they do not determine what courses or destinations they will pursue.

But beyond the rules of the road, what sorts of regulations does Oakeshott seem to think civil association allows for? Here we could wish that Oakeshott were more specific and provided more examples. In a couple of places he mentions the imposition of civil conditions on industrial enterprise, which conditions (he says) do not compromise the rule of law. In this regard he cites Henry Simons's *Economic Policy for a Free Society*, the book which formed the basis of his earlier article on "The Political Economy of Freedom," and a book which does not deny the importance of governmental activity in maintaining competition. Oakeshott also mentions civil conditions designed to prevent fraud and pollution of the atmosphere.[172] Admittedly, these references are not much, but they do suggest that Oakeshott does not see civil laws as doing nothing to regulate relationships between members of a civil association. In *Rationalism in Politics* (as I tried to show in chapter 4), Oakeshott did not envisage a completely passive role for civil government, and I think the same goes for *On Human Conduct*. I disagree with the commentator who suggests that *On Human Conduct* represents a more austere view of governmental action than *Rationalism in Politics*.[173] The non-purposiveness of civil laws is not inconsistent with governmental activity. As we have seen, the crucial consideration for Oakeshott is not the quantity of government but rather its mode.

This last consideration of the sorts of regulations civil laws might include leads to the question of how Oakeshott conceives the relationship between law and morality. Does his commitment to procedure and non-instrumentality lead him to advocate total neutrality in the law? Is his position to be equated with that of "deontological" liberals such as Rawls, Nozick, Dworkin, and Ackerman, who argue that the law must be absolutely neutral with respect to different ways of life, different conceptions of the good life?[174] And if so, is he not vulnerable to some of the same criticisms that have been levelled against these latter by "communitarians," who argue that the attempt to impose a neutral character on the liberal state and to purge its law of any substantive content can only serve to erode those moral and religious foundations without which liberalism cannot survive? What is now needed, these communitarian writers maintain, is not greater neutrality but a more profound understanding of the moral preconditions of liberalism and of the conception of the good implied in it. What is needed, in short, is the recognition of liberalism as a substantive way of life or regime.[175]

This is perhaps the most probing challenge that might be raised against Oakeshott's theory of civil association and its putative formalism. Let me begin to respond to it by observing that Oakeshott himself does not generally use the term "neutrality" to describe the laws of civil association. In the one place that he does, it is only to point out the inadequacy of the expression. "Civility," he writes in a passage I quoted at length above, "denotes an order of moral (not instrumental) considerations, and the so-called moral neutrality of civil prescriptions is a half-truth which needs to be supplemented by the recognition of civil association as itself a moral and not a prudential condition."[176] The civil condition is not a morally neutral condition; it is itself a morality with moral considerations of its own. And Oakeshott realizes that such an association presupposes certain moral and intellectual qualities in the human beings who comprise it: for example, an "exact focus of attention" and an "uncommon self-restraint" in politics; also the capacity to distinguish "between the conditions of 'virtue,' the conditions of moral association ('good conduct'), and those which are of such a kind that they should be imposed by law ('justice')."[177] These are examples of what might be called the moral preconditions of civil association. Oakeshott does not deny the importance of such preconditions for the maintenance of civil association or of liberalism, though they are not his immediate concern in *On Human Conduct*. (*Rationalism in Politics* is more concerned with these sorts of "regime" questions – questions of moral education.) There is nothing in his theory of civil association which denies the possibility of a liberal theory of virtue.

Now we may turn to the specific issue of the relationship between morality and the law. I want to argue that Oakeshott's understanding of this relationship is quite different from that of deontological liberals such as Rawls and Dworkin. Whereas these latter have argued that the law should be totally neutral with respect to questions of morality and thus avoid coming into conflict with different ways of life, Oakeshott does not seem to be committed to such sanitization of the law. Though his exact views on this subject are somewhat difficult to gather, the discussion of justice in "The Rule of Law" seems to indicate that he believes that the laws of civil association ought to reflect (more or less faithfully) the historic moral-legal self-understanding of its members. Of course, he places certain conditions on this moral deliberation of the law. In the first place, whatever moral content they are given, civil laws must remain non-instrumental. In the second, these laws must remain confined to a rather narrow band of the moral life; they cannot, for example, concern "the supreme moral consideration which relates to the sentiments or motives in which actions are performed." Though civil prescriptions should not conflict with the "prevailing educated moral sensibility," according to Oakeshott, this sensibility must be one capable of making the distinctions between "virtue," "good conduct," and "justice" mentioned above.[178]

As I have said, Oakeshott does not go into much detail with respect to his understanding of the relationship between morality and the law. Therefore, in order to flesh out this understanding, I would like to consider for a moment an essay by Shirley Letwin which nicely draws out the implications of Oakeshott's argument.[179] Arguing against those modern individualists who have tried to purify the law of any specific moral content, Letwin specifies two different moral commitments which are intrinsic to civil law. The first is a commitment to the non-instrumental character of law with which we are familiar from Oakeshott. The second is a commitment to the specific "standards of civility" which characterize a particular civil association. Every civil association, according to Letwin, has its own beliefs about what is decent or indecent, reasonable or unreasonable, offensive or inoffensive, behavior.

> Civil associations may be noisy or quiet, chaotic or orderly, businesslike or easy-going, excitable or stolid. What is considered a minimum of cleanliness in one place may feel like a hospital regime to another. A civil association may take great pains to cultivate public gardens or have none at all. It may relish large, fast motor-cars or ban them altogether. Its members may consider it indecent to walk about the roads without a hat, or decent to do so in a bikini.[180]

Some of these standards of civility – which might also include beliefs about pornography, abortion, criminal justice, and even religion – inevitably come to be reflected in the laws of a civil association; and Letwin argues that they do so without compromising the character of such an association. Standards of civility are to be distinguished from the regulations of a theocracy. They are not nearly so strict, nor do they specify anything so grand as moral virtue. They qualify but in no way compromise the freedom of the individual to live his life in his own way.

What Letwin says here about the standards of civility in a civil association is I think perfectly compatible with Oakeshott's understanding of the relationship between morality and civil law. His remarks about justice in "The Rule of Law" and about the desirability of a civil association's reflecting the moral-legal self-understanding of its members indicate that he does not seek to sever law completely from morality. In this he diverges from those deontological liberals who advocate total neutrality in the law and thus avoids some of the legitimate criticisms that have been levelled against these latter. Oakeshott's emphasis on the non-instrumentality of civil law is not to be confused with deontological neutrality. Non-instrumental civil law is perfectly capable of accommodating the substantive beliefs a community might have about what constitutes decent or indecent, reasonable or unreasonable, just or unjust, behavior. If it were not, it would be worthless.

This brings us to the end of the criticisms fastening on the formalism of Oakeshott's theory of civil association. We have seen that his limitations on what is to count as a civil law may not be as great as is often supposed, and his theory not so formalistic. Still, it must be admitted that the theory remains quite sketchy as to actual political practice. And this sketchiness becomes even more pronounced when one considers that all I have said so far concerns only the ideal character of civil association. Obviously Oakeshott's distinction between this ideal and the historical state makes for further difficulties in ascertaining what the theory means for actual political practice. We still need to know what the proper mix is between civil association and enterprise association in a modern European state. And on this issue Oakeshott provides little guidance, regarding it as a contingent and not a philosophical consideration.

The sketchiness of Oakeshott's theory of civil association with respect to actual political practice ultimately bears on the more general issue of theory and practice in his work. The sharp distinction Oakeshott draws between theory and practice has, of course, been one of the most seriously questioned aspects of his philosophy, and we have already encountered the common criticism that his own work fails to observe this distinction quite as nicely as it is drawn. This is said of *On Human Conduct* as well.[181] I do not intend to address this criticism in detail here, since I have already said enough to indicate my position on it. But I do wish to point out that the very difficulty of deducing any specific political agenda from the theory of civil association suggests that Oakeshott may be truer to the distinction than is sometimes supposed. *On Human Conduct* is, in the final analysis, a richly abstract and even laconic work whose implications for politics remain to be fully developed.

VI

CONCLUSION: OAKESHOTT AND THE CONTEMPORARY DEBATE OVER LIBERALISM

In the last chapter I argued that Oakeshott's theory of civil association could be understood as a restatement of liberalism – a restatement in which some of the more questionable ethical and metaphysical assumptions of the traditional doctrine have been criticized and superseded. I would like to conclude now by more explicitly considering Oakeshott's restatement in the context of the contemporary debate over liberalism. This debate has, of course, largely been framed in terms of the antinomy of "deontological" liberalism (as represented by, say, John Rawls, Robert Nozick, Ronald Dworkin, and Friedrich Hayek) and "communitarianism" (as represented by Michael Sandel, Charles Taylor, Richard Rorty, and Alasdair MacIntyre, among others). What I want to argue in this conclusion is that Oakeshott does not fit neatly into either of these camps, and that as a result he in many respects transcends the limitations of both. More specifically, I shall argue that, while Oakeshott's idea of civil association as a non-instrumental, non-purposive practice certainly has more in common with the procedural or juridical ideal of deontological liberals, it nevertheless seems to answer (and therefore be less susceptible to) the criticisms communitarians have levelled at the deontological project. Something like this conclusion began to emerge toward the end of the last chapter when we considered Oakeshott's position vis-à-vis the deontological principle of neutrality. In this concluding chapter I would like to take up some other communitarian criticisms – relating to the nature of the human subject, justification, and materialism – and show that Oakeshott provides a more satisfying response to them than other deontological liberals.

Let me begin with the communitarian criticism of the notion of the self or subject which is said to lie behind deontological liberalism. This criticism has been pressed most vehemently by Sandel and Taylor, who argue that deontological liberalism rests on an atomistic conception of the self as prior to and independent of society and its substantive commitments. Drawing on Hegel and the more recent hermeneutic tradition, these writers maintain that deontological liberals fail to grasp the constitutive role of the community in our self-understanding and ultimately in the construction of the persons that we are. Taylor presses this criticism (with justice) against Nozick and his atomistic doctrine of rights as side-constraints. And Sandel presses it against Rawls (who is somewhat more ambiguous on this point), to whom he attributes the notion of an "unencumbered self."[1]

Whatever the justice of this communitarian criticism of the liberalism of Nozick, Rawls, and Dworkin (and I think there is substantial justice in it), it in no way applies to Oakeshott's restatement of liberalism. It has been one of the main contentions of this book that Oakeshott's political philosophy rests on a thoroughly Hegelian rejection of the atomism and negative individualism of traditional liberal theory. This Hegelian attitude toward the self and its relationship to society we saw clearly reflected in Oakeshott's early writings on political philosophy; and it continues to inform his philosophical outlook in *On Human Conduct*. In that work, as we have seen, Oakeshott completely eschews any reference to natural rights, the private or isolated individual, consent, or contract and instead erects his liberal theory on a view of freedom or autonomy which is perfectly compatible with historicity, government, law, and civil authority.

By underlining this Hegelian and historical strain in Oakeshott's political philosophy, I do not, of course, mean to assimilate his position to that of the communitarians. Oakeshott's theory of civil association remains a *liberal* theory, even while incorporating a more Hegelian, historical, even hermeneutic conception of the self. This is what makes it (besides being more satisfying than other contemporary liberal theories) more satisfying than current communitarian theories, in which the relationship to liberalism is left highly ambiguous. Of all the writers on either side of the current debate, Oakeshott's position here probably comes closest to that of Hayek, who also grounds his liberal theory in a doctrine of procedural, non-purposive law rather than a doctrine of fundamental rights. But even this comparison cannot be pressed too hard, since Hayek can hardly be said to have a very Hegelian view of the self or of liberty. Indeed, in a number of places he seems to fall into precisely that negative individualism and atomism which Oakeshott seeks to escape.[2] And of course, as was noted in the previous chapter, Hayek fails to liberate himself completely from the materialism or economism which Oakeshott sees as so detrimental to a genuine understanding of liberalism.

I would like to turn now to another set of criticisms of deontological liberalism which can also be said to come from a roughly communitarian standpoint. These criticisms center on the issue of justification, attacking deontological liberals for seeking ahistorical criteria by which to justify liberalism instead of simply recognizing it as an historical (and valuable) practice characteristic of an historical community. Political philosophy, exponents of this view maintain, should be concerned, not with *justifying* liberalism, but with *articulating* our shared liberal intuitions and beliefs.

The thinker who has pressed this particular criticism of deonto-logical liberalism most vehemently is, of course, Richard Rorty. Ever since his influential *Philosophy and the Mirror of Nature*, Rorty has increasingly applied his critique of foundationalism to the field of political philosophy. Indicative of his general point of view is the article "Postmodernist Bourgeois Liberalism," in which he divides contemporary political theorists into three different groups: first, the "Kantians" (such as Rawls and Dworkin), who seek ahistorical cri-teria by which to justify and evaluate liberal institutions; second, the "Hegelians" (such as MacIntyre and Roberto Unger) who want to abandon these institutions; and third, the "Hegelians" who want to preserve liberal institutions but not on a Kantian (i.e., non-historical) basis. This latter group – to which Rorty assigns not only himself but also Oakeshott and (inevitably) John Dewey – is engaged in re-interpreting liberalism on a more Hegelian and historical basis, abandoning the unencumbered self of Kantian theory for a more historical and situated conception. To this "Hegelian" movement which he clearly favors, Rorty gives the (unfortunate) name of "post-modernist bourgeois liberalism."[3]

Rorty spells out his historicist (though not necessarily relativist) position in greater detail in a later article entitled "The Priority of Democracy to Philosophy." The great change in this article comes in Rorty's understanding of Rawls, around whom the article revolves. Rawls now is no longer seen as a Kantian absolutist (like Dworkin) but rather as one of those Hegelians (like Oakeshott and Dewey) who grasp liberalism as an historical and contingent tradition. Basing his interpretation on some of Rawls's more recent writings – the Dewey Lectures and "Justice as Fairness: Political not Metaphysical" – Rorty now sees Rawls, not as attempting to found liberal political institutions on a metaphysical theory of the self (as Sandel maintains), but rather as grounding them in our shared intuitions about justice and our historic self-understanding. Despite this change, however, Rorty's fundamental point about the relationship between liberalism and philosophy remains the same. Practice is prior to theory, liberal democracy is prior to philosophy. The task of political philosophy is not to *justify* political institutions but to *articulate* our shared intuitions and beliefs about politics.[4]

How does Oakeshott stand with respect to Rorty's historicist understanding of the relationship between liberalism and philosophy? It is especially important to answer this question since, firstly, Rorty invokes Oakeshott as an exemplar of the Hegelian or "pragmatist" brand of liberalism he himself is advocating, and secondly, his account of Oakeshott's political philosophy as steering a course between – and thus avoiding the pitfalls of – deontological liberalism and communitarianism in many respects resembles my own account. Here again, however, I must – as I have done at several other points in this study – warn against too close an identification of these thinkers. On the one hand, Oakeshott certainly agrees with Rorty that practice is prior to theoretical reflection on it, and that philosophy should concern itself with "articulation" instead of "justification"; he accepts, in other words, with Hegel, that philosophy is essentially a twilight affair. On the other hand, Oakeshott does not share Rorty's rather unproblematic attitude toward the thing that he is theorizing, namely, liberalism. I agree with the critic who says of Rorty that he "simply speaks globally about 'liberal democracy' without ever un-packing what it involves or doing justice to the enormous historical controversy about what liberal democracy is or ought to be."[5] Oakeshott in no way accepts Rorty's implication that "we" all have common intuitions about what liberal democracy means, nor does he assume consensus about the nature of our political tradition. As we have seen, he regards our political tradition as essentially ambivalent. And he arrives at his theory of civil association only by radically abstracting from the contingency and ambiguity of historical reality.

All this points to what for me is the fundamental difference between Oakeshott and Rorty: namely, that Oakeshott believes political philo-sophy to be something more than the mere expression of political opinion, whereas Rorty does not. For Oakeshott, though philosophy comes after and reflects upon liberal democracy, it is not confined simply to mirroring our ordinary practical understanding of this historic practice. Philosophy (and political philosophy) represents a form of understanding that is radically distinct from and in certain respects superior to our ordinary practical self-understanding. For Rorty, on the other hand, no such gulf between theory and practice exists. The result of such "pragmatism" is that political philosophy becomes indistinguishable from political opinion. Thus, when Rorty speaks of "liberal democracy," he leaves the word in roughly the same muddle as he found it in the practical realm. And when he later tries to clarify the term, he provides a rather banal list of political opinions which currently pass for "social democracy."[6] Ultimately such "prag-matism" leads to an historicism in which philosophy becomes indis-tinguishable from history, "cultural anthropology," and politics.[7] It is just such historicism – as I have pointed out at several points in this study – that Oakeshott seeks to avoid. While he incorporates the historical outlook and anti-rationalism which constitute Rorty's virtue, he never allows philosophy to be "liquidated" by history or practice.

Before turning to a third strand of communitarian criticism of liberalism, I wish briefly to consider Oakeshott's political philosophy in relation to Rawls's. This comparison is in part provoked by Rorty's historicist interpretation of Rawls, an interpretation which brings Rawls closer to Oakeshott than we might otherwise expect. It is perhaps a testament to Rorty's obsession with the meta-theoretical issue of the relationship between philosophy and practice that he can overlook the substantial differences between Rawls and Oakeshott and put them in the same "Hegelian" or "pragmatist" camp. Not that there are no similarities between these two writers, but the more important differences also need to be stressed. There are three such differences that I wish to mention (leaving aside the obvious difference with respect to distributive justice): the first relates to the issue of utilitarianism and teleology; the second relates to the issue of justification; and the third relates to the issue of political authority.

With respect to the first two, one might immediately be more inclined to note the similarities between Rawls and Oakeshott rather than to remark the differences. After all, both writers seem to want to eject utilitarianism and teleology from their views, and both seem to conceive political philosophy (as we have just seen) in terms of "articulation" instead of "justification." What I want to argue, however, is that Rawls only inconsistently holds to these positions. In the first place, his description of the "original position" in *A Theory of Justice* contains strong utilitarian elements; and in the second, the contract argument there functions at least as much to *justify* the principles of justice as to *elucidate* them. Of course, ever since *A Theory of Justice*, Rawls has sought to downplay the utilitarianism and instrumentalism of the original position by redescribing it as a "device of representation" for the fundamentally Kantian idea of an association of free and equal persons.[8] But his efforts in this direction I think have been only of limited success. In the first place, they have had the effect of making the original position – easily the most powerful intuitive idea of *A Theory of Justice* – superfluous. Second, insofar as the original position has been retained, it still seems to model utilitarian calculation, instrumental rationality, bourgeois hedonism, and even a kind of anti-liberal concern with security.[9] In short, I do not think Rawls has successfully resolved the tension between his utilitarianism, on the one hand, and his Kantianism, on the other. Nor do I think he completely abandons the justificatory intention his argument shares with other contract arguments. On both these scores I think Oakeshott's restatement of liberalism proves to be more sophisticated and consistent.

With respect to the issue of political authority, I only want to remark its glaring omission from Rawls's entire discussion of justice and of a liberal political order. In vain do we search *A Theory of Justice* for a sustained discussion of this absolutely critical concept (though we do find a rather lengthy defense of civil disobedience). Rawls is concerned exclusively with justice, but justice alone does not exhaust the considerations relating to a liberal social order, much less to the reality of the modern state. Authority, more austere and less inspiring than justice, is an essential component of any theory of the liberal state which aims to be complete. Here is where Oakeshott proves himself to be a more challenging and comprehensive theorist than Rawls. Like his masters Hobbes and Hegel, he recognizes the importance of the idea of authority and spends considerable time (as we have seen) distinguishing it from mere power and showing its essential connection to freedom and individuality. No other contemporary liberal theorist has given as much consideration to this crucial notion.

I turn now to a third and final strand of communitarian criticism of deontological liberalism – indeed, of liberalism in general. These criticisms are more radical than the ones we have considered so far, rejecting not simply certain untenable assumptions in traditional liberal doctrine (e.g., its theory of the self or its Enlightenment rationalism and universalism) but rather the liberal tradition itself with its individualism, acquisitiveness, and materialism. This type of criticism of liberalism of course goes back quite far – it can be found in Rousseau, Marx, and Nietzsche, for example – but it has found more recent expression in such writers as Alasdair MacIntyre and Roberto Unger.[10]

What does Oakeshott have in common with these radical critics of liberalism? Not a great deal, really. For he seeks to defend what they no longer find worth defending. Nevertheless, it seems to me his sensitivity to the problematic elements in the liberal tradition – especially its materialism and economism – makes him far more effective in responding to these radical communitarian critics than other contemporary liberals. As we have seen, Oakeshott is at great pains to purge liberalism of the materialism, economism, and "bourgeoisness" with which it has been traditionally associated and for which it has been so frequently criticized. As a result, his restatement of liberalism is much less vulnerable to anti-liberal attacks – much less likely to be confused with the grotesque parodies of liberalism which are to be found in critics such as MacIntyre – than the theories of Rawls or Nozick or Hayek.

This brings me to the end of my consideration of Oakeshott's political philosophy in the context of the contemporary debate over liberalism. I have focused for the most part on the achievement of this philosophy, but in doing so I have in no way meant to deny the need now for criticism. Perhaps even more important than criticism, however, is the need to develop what this philosophy means in concrete detail. As I remarked toward the end of the last chapter, Oakeshott's political philosophy is highly original and enormously suggestive, but it ultimately remains too sketchy and laconic on important issues. To begin to work out what this political philosophy means for political life as we know it is the next step in understanding and (more importantly) amplifying Oakeshott's thought.

NOTES

For those works of Oakeshott's cited most frequently in the book I have used the following abbreviations:

"CPJ" "The Concept of a Philosophical Jurisprudence." *Politica* 3 (1938): 203–22, 345–60.
EM *Experience and its Modes.* Cambridge: Cambridge University Press, 1933.
OH *On History and Other Essays.* Totowa, N.J.: Barnes and Nobles, 1983.
OHC *On Human Conduct.* Oxford: Clarendon Press, 1975.
RP *Rationalism in Politics and Other Essays.* London: Methuen & Co. Ltd., 1962.

CHAPTER 1

1. Maurice Cranston, "Michael Oakeshott's Politics," *Encounter* 28 (January 1967): 82.
2. E.g., W. H. Greenleaf, *Oakeshott's Philosophical Politics* (London: Longmans, 1966). This brief monograph is the only book on Oakeshott to be published to date. While it provides useful summaries of Oakeshott's early writings, it is severely hampered in its treatment of his political philosophy by having been written prior to the appearance of *On Human Conduct.*
3. In using this term I do not mean to refer simply to a certain school of American thought. I use it, analogously to "positivism" and "historicism," to refer broadly to that view which holds practice to be somehow fundamental or primordial. Such a view encompasses so-called "philosophers of life" and existentialists as well as the American pragmatists.
4. *EM,* p. 321.
5. Cf. *OHC,* pp. 1–31, especially Oakeshott's interpretation and criticism of Plato's allegory of the cave.
6. *OHC,* pp. vii, 9.
7. Some such assumption seems to lie behind Rawls's notion of "reflective equilibrium," though he also allows for the reaction of philosophy upon common sense.
8. *RP,* p. 115.
9. Cf. Charles Covell's chapter on Oakeshott in *The Redefinition of Conservatism: Politics and Doctrine* (New York: St. Martin's Press, 1986), pp. 93–143.
10. Cf. Covell, pp. 121, 136, 141, 142–43; also Hanna Pitkin, "Inhuman Conduct and Unpolitical Theory," *Political Theory* 4 (August 1976): 301–4.
11. Oakeshott alludes to both of these defects in traditional liberal doctrine in his introduction to *The Social and Political Doctrines of Contemporary Europe* (Cambridge: Cambridge University Press, 1939), pp. xvi, xvii–xviii, xx, xxi.
12. R. G. Collingwood, "Oakeshott and the Modes of Experience," *The Cambridge Review* 55 (February 16, 1934).

CHAPTER 2

1. *EM,* pp. 2–3.
2. W. Brock, *An Introduction to Contemporary German Philosophy* (Cambridge: Cambridge University Press, 1935).
3. Michael Oakeshott, review of *An Introduction to Contemporary German Philosophy,* by W. Brock,

The Cambridge Review 57 (1935–36): 195. On the revival of interest in the nature and task of philosophy in the late nineteenth and early twentieth centuries (after the dominance of science and history), cf. also R. G. Collingwood, *An Essay on Philosophical Method* (Oxford: Clarendon Press, 1933), pp. 5–6.

4. Brock, pp. 9–14. Both these conceptions of philosophy are picked out for ridicule by Nietzsche in his essay, "Schopenhauer as Educator," *Untimely Meditations*, trans. R. J. Hollingdale (Cambridge: Cambridge University Press, 1983), pp. 188–89.

5. *EM*, p. 2. In *Speculum Mentis, or the Map of Knowledge* (Oxford: Clarendon Press, 1924), a book resembling *EM* in many respects and to which I will be making frequent comparison in my discussion, R. G. Collingwood also warns against the temptation of science: "The cry that philosophy must accept the results of science and adopt scientific methods is quite sufficiently heard among us. In fact, it is the prime obstacle to the healthy development of modern philosophy. Philosophy has its own problems and methods, and must look for its own results . . ." (p. 281).

6. *EM*, p. 353. This quote eliminates the possibility of any confusion between Oakeshott's view of philosophy and the exclusively epistemological point of view of the neo-Kantians. For Oakeshott, philosophy is not merely methodology. Nor is it merely "analysis." I think Greenleaf is misleading when he attributes to Oakeshott a notion of philosophy as second-order experience such as is to be found in analytic philosophers such as T. D. Weldon. Cf. Greenleaf, "Idealism, Modern Philosophy and Politics," pp. 108–10; also *Oakeshott's Philosophical Politics*, pp. 95–6.

7. *EM*, p. 2.

8. Richard Rorty, *Philosophy and the Mirror of Nature* (Princeton: Princeton University Press, 1979), pp. 389–94.

9. Of course, it may be contended that Oakeshott's conception of philosophy changes from *Experience and its Modes* to "The Voice of Poetry in the Conversation of Mankind," and that it is the more "conversational" view of philosophy found in the latter which corresponds to Rorty's anti-foundationalist view. I will take up and reject the view that Oakeshott's conception of philosophy changes substantially from *Experience and its Modes* to "The Voice of Poetry in the Conversation of Mankind" in a later chapter.

10. For Rorty's view I am here drawing on not only *Philosophy and the Mirror of Nature* but also "Pragmatism and Philosophy," in *After Philosophy: End or Transformation?*, ed. K. Baynes, J. Bohman and T. McCarthy (Cambridge, MA: MIT Press, 1987): 26–66.

11. Rorty, "Pragmatism and Philosophy," pp. 56, 58.

12. Cf., for example, Rorty, *Philosophy and the Mirror of Nature*, pp. 131–36, where Rorty criticizes the Kantian attempt to distinguish philosophy and science.

13. *EM*, p. 6.

14. Cf. F. H. Bradley, *The Principles of Logic*, 2nd ed. (London: Oxford University Press, 1928), vol. 1, chap. 2, pp. 45 ff.; *Appearance and Reality*, 2nd ed. (Oxford: Oxford University Press, 1969), pp. 146–47, 201–9; *Essays on Truth and Reality* (Oxford: Clarendon, 1914), pp. 206–7, 297. For Hegel's critique of the notion that in sensation we have to do with an immediate datum or pure particularity, cf. *Phenomenology of Spirit*, trans. A. V. Miller (Oxford: Clarendon, 1977), A.I., "Sense Certainty."

15. The chapter entitled "The Search for a *Datum*" in Harold Joachim, *Logical Studies* (Oxford: Clarendon, 1948), pp. 62–178, is perhaps the most thorough of the idealist critiques of the empiricist notion of immediate experience. For Bosanquet's criticism of this notion, cf. *Knowledge and Reality* (London: S. Sonnenschein, 1892) p. 326; *Logic, or the Morphology of Knowledge*, 2nd ed. (Oxford: Clarendon, 1911), vol.1, pp. 29–31, vol. 2, pp. 281–88.

16. Of this picture of knowledge as a building resting on indubitable and incorrigible foundations Bradley says that it is "untenable, and the metaphor ruinously inapplicable. The foundation in truth is provisional merely. In order to begin my construction I take the foundation as absolute – so much certainly is true. But that my construction continues to rest on the beginnings of my knowledge is a conclusion which does not follow. It does not follow that, if these are allowed to be fallible, the whole building collapses. For it is in another sense that my world rests upon the data of perception. My experience is solid, not so far as it is superstructure but so far as in short it is a system" (*Essays on Truth and Reality*, pp. 209–10). Bosanquet makes a similar criticism of the simile of the foundations of knowledge: "Knowledge is not like a house built on a foundation which is previously laid, and is able to remain after the house has fallen; it is more like a planetary system with no relation to anything outside itself, and determined in the motion and position of every element by the conjoint influence of the whole" (*Knowledge and Reality*, p. 331).

17. For the most comprehensive statement (and questioning) of the coherence theory of truth, see Harold Joachim, *The Nature of Truth* (Oxford: Clarendon, 1906). Cf. also chap. 3 of his *Logical Studies*.

18. On the concrete universal, see Bosanquet, *The Principle of Individuality and Value* (London: Macmillan, 1927), lecture 2, pp. 31–81; also his *Implication and Linear Inference* (London: Macmillan, 1920), pp. 4–17. Cf. also Collingwood, *Speculum Mentis*, pp. 158–63, 195–200, 217–21.

19. Bradley, *Appearance and Reality*, pp. 433–34, 440–41.

20. Cf. Bradley, *Appearance and Reality*, chap. 15, "Thought and Reality." Bradley's most famous statement of his difference with Hegel on this point comes in *The Principles of Logic*: "Unless thought stands for something that falls beyond mere intelligence, if 'thinking' is not used with some strange implication that never was part of the meaning of the word, a lingering scruple still forbids us to believe that reality can ever be purely rational. It may come from a failure in my metaphysics, or from a weakness of the flesh which continues to blind me, but the notion that existence could be the same as understanding strikes as cold and ghost-like as the dreariest materialism. That the glory of this world in the end is appearance leaves the world more glorious, if we feel it is a show of some fuller splendor; but the sensuous curtain is a deception and a cheat, if it hides some colorless movement of atoms, some spectral woof of impalpable abstractions, or unearthly ballet of bloodless categories. Though dragged to such conclusions, we cannot embrace them. Our principles may be true, but they are not reality. They no more *make* that Whole which commands our devotion, than some shredded dissection of human tatters *is* that warm and breathing beauty of flesh which our hearts found delightful" (vol. 2, pp. 590–91).

21. Bosanquet is somewhat ambiguous on this point, but cf. *Knowledge and Reality*, pp. 16–26; *Logic*, pp. 292–94; and *The Principle of Individuality and Value*, pp. 54–68. For Joachim, cf. *Logical Studies*, pp. 276–92.

22. *EM*, p. 9. Oakeshott discusses the absolute correlativity and interdependence of experience and reality at some length at *EM*, pp. 49–61. There too he utters the sentence which in some ways sums up his entire outlook on the question: "Perhaps the only satisfactory view would be one which grasped, even more thoroughly than Hegel's, the fact that what we have, and all we have, is a world of 'meanings', and constructed its philosophy without recourse to extraneous conceptions which belong to other views" (p. 61).

23. For other idealist denials of this identification of their view with subjective idealism or solipsism, cf. Bradley, *Appearance and Reality*, pp. 128–29, 228–29; Joachim, *The Nature of Truth*, pp. 59–63; Collingwood, *Speculum Mentis*, pp. 311–12. The classic realist "refutation" of idealism is G. E. Moore's "Refutation of Idealism," *Mind* 48 (1903): 433–53; cf. also his "Proof of an External World," *Proceedings of the British Academy* (1939).

24. *EM*, p. 10.

25. *EM*, p. 348.

26. *EM*, p. 10. Oakeshott's discussion here of the mediacy of all experience recalls Joachim's much more detailed discussion in *Logical Studies*, pp. 62–178.

27. *EM*, pp. 11–14, 24.

28. R. Wollheim, *F. H. Bradley* (Harmondsworth: Penguin, 1959), p. 174. On the simile of the "foundations" of knowledge, cf. Bradley, *Essays on Truth and Reality*, pp. 209–10; Bosanquet, *Knowledge and Reality*, p. 331.

29. *EM*, pp. 18–20.

30. *EM*, pp. 32–33.

31. In *The Principle of Individuality and Value*, Bosanquet too uses the notion of a "world" to characterize the concrete universal; and he too opposes the unity which belongs to a "world" to the abstract unity which characterizes a class (cf. pp. 31–40). On the abstract universal as a class-concept versus the concrete universal, cf. also Collingwood, *Speculum Mentis*, pp. 158–63, 195–200, 217–21

32. *EM*, pp. 29–31.

33. *EM*, p. 43.

34. *EM*, pp. 43–44, 62–64. That individuality is to be identified, not with mere particularity, but with the concrete whole is a common theme in idealist thought. Cf., for example, Bradley, *The Principles of Logic*, vol. 1, p. 45; Bosanquet, *Logic*, vol. 2, pp. 260–62; Bosanquet, *The Principle of Individuality and Value*, p. 68 ff.; Collingwood, *The Idea of History* (Oxford: Clarendon, 1946), p. 162.

35. *EM*, p. 45.

36. *EM*, pp. 81–82.

37. *EM*, pp. 70–71.

38. *EM*, pp. 71, 73–75.

39. *EM*, pp. 78–79. Compare *and* contrast Bradley on the relationship of the absolute to its appearances, *Appearance and Reality*, pp. 407, 431–32. The major point of contrast seems to be that Bradley sees appearances as somehow "essential" and "indispensable" to the absolute.

40. *EM*, p. 80.

41. *EM*, pp. 4, 83. In *Speculum Mentis* Collingwood also emphasizes this active, critical character of philosophy. Characterizing philosophy as the attempt on the part of the mind to right itself in the midst of distorting influences from other abstract forms of experience, he comments: "It follows that the concrete life of philosophy is no mere haven of rest, but a ceaseless act of achieving this balance" (pp. 295–96).

42. *EM*, pp. 83, 84.

43. *EM*, pp. 83–84. For Collingwood's view on this matter, cf. especially *Speculum Mentis*, pp. 50–55. The belief that he expresses there – that the forms of experience "must form an order of some kind" – seems to provide the basis of his later criticism of Oakeshott in *The Idea of History*, pp. 156–57.

44. *EM*, p. 83.

45. *EM*, p. 4.

46. *EM*, p. 2.

47. *EM*, pp. 4, 71, 75. On philosophical criticism as immanent and not external, compare Collingwood, *Speculum Mentis*, p. 45.

48. *EM*, pp. 79–80, 328–29.

49. *EM*, pp. 81, 353–54. On the sovereignty of the modes (or "appearances") within their own sphere, compare Bradley, *Appearance and Reality*, pp. 250–52, 439–40; *Essays on Truth and Reality*, pp. 470–73.

50. For Oakeshott, each mode of experience is "wholly and absolutely independent of any other." There "is no direct relationship between any two of these modes of experience, for each . . . is a specific organization of the whole of experience exclusive of every other organization. Consequently, it is impossible to pass in argument from any one of these worlds of ideas to any other without involving ourselves in a confusion. The fallacy inherent in any such attempt is in the nature of *ignoratio elenchi*. And the result of all such attempts is the most subtle and insidious of all forms of error – irrelevance" (*EM*, pp. 75–76).

51. Besides the chapter in *EM*, there are three other major discussions of history in Oakeshott's *oeuvre*: "The Activity of Being an Historian," *RP*, pp. 137–67; *OHC*, pp. 91–107; and *OH*, pp. 1–118. Since these discussions are largely consistent with Oakeshott's original analysis of history in *EM*, I will take them up in later chapters only insofar as they bear on other issues.

52. *The Cambridge Review*, February 16, 1934. Collingwood, who was not always given to enthusiastic approval of the philosophical work of his contemporaries, went on to write: "Of this chapter, I can, in this brief notice, only say that it is the most penetrating analysis of historical thought that has ever been written, and will remain a classic in that hitherto almost unexplored branch of philosophical research." In *The Idea of History*, pp. 151–59, Collingwood treats Oakeshott's theory of history in *EM* at greater length and more critically, still calling it, however, "the high-water mark of English thought upon history."

53. Collingwood, *The Idea of History*, p. 170.

54. The affinity between the idealist theory of knowledge, on the one hand, and historical knowledge, on the other, is discernible not only in Oakeshott (and, of course, Collingwood) but also in Bradley. Bradley's first published work was an analysis of historical knowledge entitled *The Presuppositions of Critical History*, ed. Lionel Rubinoff (Chicago: University of Chicago Press, 1968). Of this work Bosanquet wrote: "[It] gives the best account known to me of the process by which *all* the parts of a whole can be criticized and adjusted *on the basis of each other*" (*Knowledge and Reality*, p. 332).

55. Arthur Schopenhauer, *The World as Will and Representation*, trans. E. F. G. Payne (New York: Dover, 1959), vol. 2, chap. 38, pp. 439–40 (translation slightly altered).

56. Bosanquet, *The Principle of Individuality and Value*, pp. 78–79.

57. *EM*, p. 89.

58. *EM*, pp. 90–92.

59. *EM*, pp. 92, 94.

60. *EM*, pp. 93–94.

61. *EM*, pp. 96, 55–56, 68.

62. *EM*, pp. 96–98.

63. *EM*, p. 96.

64. *EM*, p. 30.

65. *EM*, p. 41.

66. *EM*, pp. 98–99.

67. *EM*, pp. 114–17. On this view that historical truth consists in correspondence with the "original authorities," compare Collingwood, *The Idea of History*, pp. 234–38; also Bradley, *The Presuppositions of Critical History*.

68. *EM*, p. 113.

69. The distinction between the historical past and the practical past plays a large role in Oakeshott's later writings on history as well. Cf. "The "Activity of Being and Historian," and the first essay in *OH*, pp. 1–44.

70. *EM*, pp. 103–5. The "historical element" in religion (in particular, Christianity) is referred to several times in articles and reviews Oakeshott wrote (mostly for theological publications) during the twenties and thirties. Cf. especially "The Importance of the Historical Element in Christianity," *The Modern Churchman* 18 (1928–29): 360–71; and his review of Webb's *The Historical Element in Religion* (a book which, by the way, contains a lengthy discussion of Oakeshott's view of the relationship between history and religion), in *The Journal of Theological Studies* 37 (1936): 96–98. Oakeshott's interest in the whole question seems to stem from concern over the potential threat to religion coming from historical criticism (cf. *EM*, pp. 315–16). Such criticism, he argues, is irrelevant because the "historical element" in Christianity serves a wholly practical purpose; whether it is *historically* true is beside the point. The "historical element" in Christianity serves to make actual and impressive certain beliefs about the present practical world; it is in no way the ground or foundation of those beliefs. In the final analysis, the "historical element" is not indispensable to Christianity. Indeed, Oakeshott finds the current emphasis on history in Christianity ultimately unhealthy. This much he has in common with the existentialists.

71. *EM*, p. 106.

72. Cf. ibid., pp. 109–10. For Croce's view, cf. *History: Its Theory and Practice*, trans. D. Ainslie (New York: Russell & Russell, 1960), pp. 11–15. It might also be remarked that what Oakeshott understands by the historical past is precisely what Nietzsche finds questionable about history in his essay "On the Uses and Disadvantages of History for Life," *Untimely Meditations*, pp. 59–123. But it must be remembered that Nietzsche's essay is not so much concerned with the epistemological question of the nature and presuppositions of historical knowledge as with the practical "uses and disadvantages" of history. Nietzsche's concern is not the historical past but what Oakeshott calls the practical past.

73. *EM*, pp. 106–8, 110–11.

74. *EM*, p. 146.

75. *EM*, p. 147. Cf. Collingwood's criticism of this contention of Oakeshott's in *The Idea of History*, pp. 157–58.

76. *EM*, pp. 147–48. Collingwood's description of the breakdown of history in *Speculum Mentis* (pp. 231–39, 244–46) parallels Oakeshott's second criticism here. For Collingwood, the absolute and concrete whole of historical fact can never be achieved; "all history is fragmentary." This fact destroys any hope of discovering *was eigentlich geschehen ist* and ultimately leads to historical skepticism.

77. *EM*, pp. 44–45, 147; cf. also, pp. 62–65.

78. *EM*, pp. 119–22.

79. *EM*, pp. 122–23.

80. There are, of course, other characteristics of historical experience which Oakeshott discusses besides the ideas of the historical past and the historical individual. One of these, the idea of historical explanation, I will be taking up below in connection with the distinction between history and science. But it is the ideas of the historical past and the historical individual which best reveal the abstractness of historical experience and which are therefore most relevant to Oakeshott's main task of considering each mode of experience from the standpoint of the totality of experience, from the standpoint of its capacity to provide what is completely satisfactory in experience.

81. *EM*, p. 148.

82. *EM*, pp. 153–56.

83. Cf. Strauss's definition in *What Is Political Philosophy?* (Glencoe, Ill.: The Free Press, 1959),

p. 57: "Historicism is the assertion that the fundamental distinction between philosophical and historical questions cannot in the last analysis be maintained."

84. *EM*, p. 349.

85. Collingwood, *The Idea of History*, p. x; cf. pp. x–xv. This historicistic tendency is most evident in Collingwood's later works, *An Autobiography* (Oxford: Clarendon Press, 1939) and *An Essay on Metaphysics* (Oxford: Clarendon Press, 1940).

86. Michael Oakeshott, review of *The Idea of History*, by R. G. Collingwood, *English Historical Review* 62 (1947): 85.

87. Cf. Collingwood, *The Idea of History*, especially the chapter on "History as Re-Enactment of Past Experience," pp. 282–302.

88. Michael Oakeshott, "Mr. Carr's First Volume," *The Cambridge Journal* 4 (1950–51): 350.

89. *RP*, p. 164.

90. It is interesting, though, that Oakeshott credits Collingwood with a different view in his review of *The Idea of History* mentioned above: "The task of the historian of ideas, as [Collingwood] saw it, was precisely to understand a writer more profoundly than the writer understood himself, just as the task of the historian of feudal society (for example) is to understand that society more profoundly than anyone who merely enjoyed it could understand it" (p. 85). Here Oakeshott may have in mind Collingwood's *practice* as an intellectual historian, as opposed to his *theory* of historical knowledge. But he may also be referring to an ambiguity in the theory itself. For sometimes Collingwood speaks not only of re-enacting past thought but of criticizing it in re-enacting it. "The historian not only re-enacts past thought, he re-enacts it in the context of his own knowledge and therefore, in re-enacting it, criticizes it, forms his own judgement of its value, corrects whatever errors he can discern in it. This criticism of the thought whose history he traces is not something secondary to tracing the history of it. It is an indispensable condition of the historical knowledge itself" (*The Idea of History*, p. 215; cf. also pp. 60, 108, 135, 195, 248, 300–301, 304–5). In another place, though, Oakeshott explicitly rejects "the view favoured by Collingwood" of history "as the enterprise of resurrecting and reconstructing the thoughts, feelings and emotions of the past." The main difficulty with such a view, he writes (echoing the passages quoted above), is "that an historical account of the past at least purports to present something which was never in the mind of anybody at the time; the historian at least appears to have a way of thinking about the past which would have been impossible for anyone who lived in that past" (review of *An Introduction to the Philosophy of History*, by W. H. Walsh, *The Philosophical Quarterly* 2 [1952]: 276–77).

91. *EM*, p. 2.

92. *EM*, p. 354; cf. also, pp. 78–79, 218–19.

93. Cf. *EM*, pp. 250–51.

94. *EM*, p. 250.

95. This empiricist philosophy of science has, of course, been challenged by a number of recent writers, for example, Thomas Kuhn, Karl Popper, Michael Polanyi, Imre Lakatos, Paul Feyerabend, and Stephen Toulmin.

96. *EM*, pp. 169–70.

97. *EM*, pp. 170–72, 186. On the transformation of the world of perceived nature into the mathematical world of the natural sciences, compare Edmund Husserl, *The Crisis of European Sciences and Transcendental Phenomenolgy*, trans. David Carr (Evanston: Northwestern University Press, 1970), pp. 23–59; "Philosophy and the Crisis of European Man," in *Phenomenology and the Crisis of Philosophy*, trans. and ed. Quentin Lauer (New York: Harper & Row, 1965), pp. 182–83.

98. *EM*, pp. 181–86.

99. *EM*, pp. 186–7, 201, 206–7.

100. *EM*, pp. 175, 180, 190–91.

101. *EM*, pp. 209–10.

102. *EM*, pp. 208–9.

103. *EM*, pp. 187, 210, 211, 215. On the suppositional character of scientific knowledge, cf. also Collingwood, *Speculum Mentis*, p. 183.

104. *EM*, p. 215; also pp. 56–58, 189. Again, cf. Collingwood, *Speculum Mentis*, pp. 183–88. On the categorical nature of universal judgments, cf. Bosanquet, *Logic*, vol. 1, chaps. 3–6; also Bradley, "On Floating Ideas and the Imaginary," in *Essays on Truth and Reality*, pp. 28–64.

105. *EM*, p. 216; cf. also pp. 327–29.

106. *EM*, pp. 217–19.

107. And, it might be added, of the relationship between practice and science as well (mostly as it relates to the much discussed "conflict" between religion and science).

108. Mostly in Germany, but also in England with Bradley, and in Italy with Croce. On the history of this problem in late nineteenth- and early twentieth-century European philosophy, see Collingwood, *The Idea of History*, pp. 134–204.

109. *EM*, pp. 223–30. Oakeshott seems to change his mind about the "scientific" character of economics later on; cf. *OHC*, p. 20.

110. *EM*, pp. 178, 235–40.

111. Oakeshott does not mention the science of politics in *EM*; but in a review of Catlin's *The Principles of Politics*, in *The Cambridge Review* 51 (1929–30): 400, he discusses what the character of such a science must be. A science of politics, he writes, "must not be afraid of being abstract, and must free itself from all pretension of founding a science of history or of predicting historical events"; it must also be, as might be expected, quantitative.

112. *EM*, p. 8.

113. Collingwood observes in *The Idea of History* that it is characteristic of positivism that it distinguishes "between two kinds of history: empirical history, which merely discharges the humble office of ascertaining the facts, and philosophical or scientific history, which has the nobler task of discovering laws connecting the facts" (p. 176). And like Oakeshott, he rejects this distinction as involving a misconception of the nature of history.

114. *EM*, pp. 126–28.

115. *EM*, pp. 126–32. Criticism of causal explanation in history can also be found in Oakeshott's later work on history; cf. *OH*, pp. 72–88.

116. *EM*, p. 129.

117. *EM*, pp. 141–43.

118. Oakeshott writes, of course, about anthropology as it was defined and practiced at the beginning of the twentieth century. The bulk of his references, therefore, are to people like Frazer, Marett, and Tylor. This is not to deny the relevance of his criticisms to contemporary anthropology or to any other discipline which claims to unite historical and scientific thought.

119. *EM*, pp. 161–67. The dictum that anthropology must choose between being history or being nothing (apparently first pronounced by Maitland) is quoted approvingly by E. E. Evans-Pritchard in his essay on *Anthropology and History* (Manchester: Manchester University Press, 1961), pp. 20–21.

120. On this, see Collingwood's *The Idea of History* in general, especially p. 167.

121. *EM*, pp. 247–48.

122. *EM.*, p. 248.

123. I am thinking here not just of the pragmatists, but also of the so-called philosophers of life and the existentialists. In both Nietzsche and Heidegger, for example, there is, on the one hand, a profound appreciation of the truly limiting character of practical activity. But on the other, there is a tendency to reduce all thought to the horizon of "life" or "praxis." It should also be remarked that with respect to this issue of theory and practice Oakeshott diverges somewhat from Collingwood (to whom I have been comparing him). Collingwood begins *Speculum Mentis* in this rather un-Oakeshottian way: "All thought exists for the sake of action. We try to understand ourselves and our world only in order that we may learn how to live. The end of our self-knowledge is not the contemplation by enlightened intellects of their own mysterious nature, but the freer and more effectual self-revelation of that nature in a vigorous practical life" (p. 15).

124. *EM*, p. 251.

125. *EM*, pp. 251–52.

126. *EM*, pp. 252–53.

127. *EM*, pp. 253–54.

128. *EM*, pp. 299–300.

129. *EM*, p. 303.

130. *EM*, pp. 256–58.

131. *EM*, pp. 260–61, 262–63.

132. *EM*, pp. 261, 274, 289.

133. *EM*, pp. 274–78.

134. *EM*, pp. 278–88.

135. *EM*, p. 290.

136. *EM*, pp. 290–91.

137. *EM*, p. 304. Oakeshott's discussion of the endlessness and self-contradictoriness of practical experience has much in common with Bradley's criticism of the moral point of view in *Ethical Studies* (which, in turn, Bradley says owes much to Hegel's criticism of the same). The self-contradiction Bradley sees at the heart of morality consists in the fact that morality

presupposes what it attempts to negate, namely, the immoral or sensuous self. If the immoral or sensuous self did not exist, or if it were successfully negated by morality, then the very possibility of morality would disappear. Morality both negates *and* presupposes immorality. "[T]he non-moral and the immoral must exist as a condition of [morality], since the moral is what it is only by asserting itself against its opposite." Morality involves a contradiction because it tells you "to realize that which never can be realized, and which, if realized, does efface itself as such. No one ever was or could be perfectly moral; and, if he were, he would be moral no longer. . . . Morality aims at the cessation of that which makes it possible" (F. H. Bradley, *Ethical Studies* [Oxford: Clarendon Press, 1927], pp. 155, 233–34). For Bradley, the solution of the self-contradiction which is morality is religion. "Reflection on morality leads us beyond it. It leads us, in short, to see the necessity of the religious point of view." "Morality issues in religion" (*Ethical Studies*, p. 314). This view of morality and the relationship between it and religion is taken over almost whole in one of Oakeshott's earliest pieces, "Religion and the Moral Life," The "D" Society Pamphlets, no. 2 (Cambridge, 1927). And it is a view which continues to inform his discussion of practical experience in *EM* (cf. pp. 292–95).

138. *EM*, pp. 310–11.

139. *EM*, pp. 319–20.

140. Cf. *EM*, pp. 352–53. Cf. Collingwood, *Speculum Mentis*, pp. 256–57; *An Essay on Philosophical Method*, pp. 141–50, 164–74. Again contrast Greenleaf, "Idealism, Modern Philosophy and Politics," pp. 108–10.

141. Oakeshott, following Bradley, describes religion as the "completion" or "consummation" of practical experience. "Religion . . . is not a particular form of practical experience; it is merely practical experience at its fullest." Religion is practical experience pressed to its logical conclusion. Cf. *EM*, pp. 292–95; also "Religion and the Moral Life."

142. *EM*, pp. 208–9, 320–31. Nor, by the same token, can science or history make any relevant criticism of religious beliefs. Oakeshott at this point in his career appears to be quite concerned with the theological issues raised by positivistic and historicistic criticisms of religious ideas and beliefs. Cf., for example, his review of Needham's *Science, Religion, and Reality* (a book in which his assistance is acknowledged in the preface) in *The Journal of Theological Studies* 27 (1926): 317–19. He seems to be particularly concerned with the effect on Christianity of historical criticism of the New Testament. Cf. *EM*, pp. 315–16; also "The Importance of the Historical Element in Christianity."

143. *EM*, pp. 310, 320–31, 354–55.

144. *EM*, pp. 3, 355–56.

145. Cf. B. Parekh, "Review Article: The Political Philosophy of Michael Oakeshott," *British Journal of Political Science* 9 (1979): 487–88; T. Modood, "Oakeshott's Conceptions of Philosophy," *History of Political Thought* 1 (1980): 315–22.

CHAPTER 3

1. Cf. *EM*, pp. 331–35. By characterizing ethical thought and political philosophy as "pseudo-philosophical" forms of experience, Oakeshott means to indicate that they do not *fully* realize the character of philosophy. In both, the unconditional pursuit of an absolutely coherent world of ideas is qualified, arrested. And such qualification or arrest constitutes a form of philosophical error. Ethical thought and political philosophy fail to recognize the world to which they belong (i.e., philosophy) and are thus convicted of abstraction. Abstraction here, however, is not a special process (as in science or history) but a "mere inadvertence." Oakeshott later abandons this understanding of moral and political philosophy as incompletely self-conscious or pseudo-philosophical experience. In *OHC* he says that the unconditional pursuit of an absolutely coherent world of ideas "may be arrested without being denied" (*OHC*, p. 11). And he characterizes the political philosopher as a "self-consciously conditional theorist" (p. 25).

2. *EM*, pp. 336–40. Here Oakeshott follows Bradley, for whom, too, the business of ethics is not to prescribe or construct a morality. "All philosophy has to do is 'understand what is', and moral philosophy has to understand morals which exist, not to make them or give directions for making them. Such a notion is simply ludicrous. Philosophy in general has not to anticipate the discoveries of the particular sciences nor the evolution of history; the philosophy of religion has not to make a new religion or teach an old one, but simply to understand religious consciousness; and aesthetic has not to produce works of fine art, but to theorize the beautiful which it finds; political philosophy has not to play tricks with the state, but to understand it; and ethics has not to make the world moral, but to reduce to theory the morality current in the world" (*Ethical Studies*, p. 193).

3. *EM*, pp. 340–44.

4. "CPJ," p. 203.

5. "CPJ," p. 213.

6. "CPJ," pp. 205–12. Obviously Oakeshott associates each of these forms of explanation with specific writers. John Austin is of course the founder of the analytical school of jurisprudence. But Oakeshott elicits the presuppositions of this school mainly with reference to more recent writers such as Salmond and C. K. Allen. With respect to historical jurisprudence, he does not specifically say who he has in mind, but in the English context Henry Maine and Paul Vinogradoff would be obvious examples of this jurisprudential tradition. Finally, as an example of sociological jurisprudence, Oakeshott mentions E. Ehrlich's *Fundamental Principles of the Sociology of Law*.

7. "CPJ," p. 214.

8. "CPJ," pp. 215–16; cf. also p. 221.

9. Oakeshott takes his account of this view from Bryce's essay "The Methods of Legal Science," which is to be found in his *Studies in History and Jurisprudence*. Bryce claims to be describing the method of Kant and Hegel, but Oakeshott does not see much of a resemblance.

10. "CPJ," pp. 216–17.

11. "CPJ," pp. 217–18.

12. Oakeshott ascribes such a view to Roscoe Pound, among others.

13. "CPJ," pp. 219–20.

14. This view of philosophical jurisprudence is explicitly maintained in C. K. Allen, *Legal Duties* (Oxford: Clarendon Press, 1931), pp. 16–17. The passage is worth quoting because it embodies so perfectly the view of philosophy against which Oakeshott directs so much criticism. "Is not the business of philosophy (so far as it interests itself in law) to take the results of jurisprudence . . . and relate them to general philosophical principles? This is really what the great works of 'philosophy of law', such as Kant's and Hegel's, seek to do. In short, so-called philosophical or metaphysical jurisprudence seems to be the philosophical contemplation of the conclusions of a particular branch of knowledge."

15. "CPJ," p. 220.

16. "CPJ," p. 345. Compare *EM*, p. 82.

17. "CPJ," pp. 346–47. Oakeshott adds that the "so-called Socratic method is an example, though an imperfect example, of the process I have been trying to describe." On Socrates' discovery of this most important principle of philosophical procedure, see Collingwood, *An Essay on Philosophical Method*, p. 11.

18. "CPJ," pp. 348–49. Cf. also Collingwood, *An Essay on Philosophical Method*, pp. 170–74.

19. "CPJ," pp. 350–51.

20. "CPJ," pp. 350–51.

21. R. G. Collingwood, *The Principles of Art* (Oxford: Clarendon Press, 1938), p. 2. In this work Collingwood outlines a two-stage process of philosophical inquiry – involving "identification" and "definition" – along much the same lines as Oakeshott. It is perhaps worth noting that Oakeshott wrote a review of *The Principles of Art* in *The Cambridge Review* 59 (1937–38): 487. In it he picked out for special praise Collingwood's method of thought, his philosophical procedure, referring to it as a "Socratic method."

22. "CPJ," pp. 352–53.

23. Michael Oakeshott, "The Authority of the State," *The Modern Churchman* 19 (1929–30): 313–27, 614–15.

24. "Authority of the State," pp. 319–23.

25. "Authority of the State," p. 324. On the separation of the state from society, see also Oakeshott's review of Gierke's *Natural Law and the Theory of Society*, in *The Cambridge Review* 56 (1934–35): 11–12. There he rejects the distinction as a relic "of that 'individualism' in political theory which while it is explicitly fled from is implicitly succumbed to." Interestingly, he goes on to invoke, not Hegel, but Hobbes as providing a remedy. "[T]he notion of the State taking up and directing a separable part of the life of Society corresponds closely to the seventeenth-century notion that when man entered political society he surrendered, not the whole, but a part of his natural rights – and it is a notion from which Hobbes might have rescued us if we had listened to him."

26. "Authority of the State," pp. 325–27.

27. "CPJ," pp. 357, 360.

28. "CPJ," p. 357.

29. "CPJ," pp. 358–59.

30. Contrast this with what Oakeshott says in *EM* about the past as it is for the historian. The past for the historian, he says there, is a *dead* past, a past unlike the present (p. 106).

31. "CPJ," pp. 358–59.

32. Michael Oakeshott, "The New Bentham," *Scrutiny* 1 (1932–33): 114–31; "Thomas Hobbes," *Scrutiny* 4 (1935–36): 263–77.

33. "The New Bentham," pp. 119–21. For a similar assessment of Bentham's "originality" and his critical or philosophic powers, see E. Halevy's classic *The Growth of Philosophic Radicalism* (London: Faber, 1972), pp. 33–34.

34. "The New Bentham," p. 125.

35. "The New Bentham," pp. 127–28.

36. "The New Bentham," p. 128. Oakeshott's critique of anticipations here anticipates (if I may be excused the solecism) Q. Skinner's critique of the "mythology of *prolepsis*" in "Meaning and Understanding in the History of Ideas," *History and Theory* 8 (1969), pp. 22–24.

37. "Thomas Hobbes," pp. 264–65.

38. "Thomas Hobbes," p. 271.

39. "Thomas Hobbes," pp. 273–75. On the systematic character of Hobbes's thought, cf. also Oakeshott's introduction to Hobbes's *Leviathan* (Oxford: Basil Blackwell, 1946), p. xv.

40. "Thomas Hobbes," p. 275.

41. "Thomas Hobbes," p. 272. Cf. also the introduction to *Leviathan*, p. liv.

42. "Thomas Hobbes," pp. 275–76. Oakeshott's use of the term "naturalistic" should be noted here; we will have occasion to refer to it when comparing Oakeshott with Strauss on Hobbes.

43. "Thomas Hobbes," pp. 277, 271.

44. Michael Oakeshott, "Dr. Leo Strauss on Hobbes," originally published in *Politica* 2 (1936–37): 364–79; reprinted in *Hobbes on Civil Association* (Berkeley: University of California Press, 1975): 132–49. My references will be to the latter source. Oakeshott also published two shorter reviews of Strauss's book, one in *The Cambridge Review* 58 (1936–37): 150, and the other in *Philosophy* 12 (1937): 239–41.

45. Cf. "Dr. Leo Strauss on Hobbes," pp. 133–34.

46. Leo Strauss, *The Political Philosophy of Hobbes: Its Basis and its Genesis* (Chicago: University of Chicago Press, 1952), pp. ix–x.

47. Strauss, *Political Philosophy of Hobbes*, pp. 27–28. Cf. also "Dr. Leo Strauss on Hobbes," pp. 136–38.

48. Strauss, *Political Philosophy of Hobbes*, pp. ix–x.

49. "Dr. Leo Strauss on Hobbes," pp. 138–39.

50. "Dr. Leo Strauss on Hobbes," pp. 140–42.

51. "Thomas Hobbes," pp. 272, 275, 276.

52. "Dr. Leo Strauss on Hobbes," p. 142. In another review of Strauss's book, Oakeshott again expresses his dubiety about Strauss's interpretation of what Hobbes means by "science": "Hobbes's theory of the natural world is conceived always as a theory of knowledge, and is always determined by his fundamental concepts of the nature of reason and the character of philosophical explanation" (*Philosophy* 12 [1937]: 241). On the centrality of Hobbes's notions of philosophy and reasoning and the nascent distinction in his thought between philosophical and scientific explanation, see Oakeshott's introduction to *Leviathan*, pp. xx–xxiii.

53. "Dr. Leo Strauss on Hobbes," p. 143.

54. Strauss, *The Political Philosophy of Hobbes*, pp. vii–viii, 155–57. Of course, Strauss later come to see Machiavelli and not Hobbes as the originator of modern political philosophy (cf. the preface to the American edition), but his conception of the nature of the innovation involved did not change fundamentally.

55. Cf. "Dr. Leo Strauss on Hobbes," pp. 144–45; *The Cambridge Review* 58 (1936–37): 150; *Philosophy* 12 (1937): 240. But for Strauss's reasons for not identifying Hobbes with the Epicurean tradition, cf. *Natural Right and History* (Chicago: University of Chicago Press, 1953), pp. 168–70, 188–89. It should be pointed out that Oakeshott does not mean to belittle Hobbes's originality. And he certainly does not think the discovery of the link between Hobbes and scholasticism (one of the "significant results of present-day polymathy," as Strauss somewhat equivocally refers to it in *Natural Right and History*, pp. 166–67) exhausts the question of his originality. Cf. "Thomas Hobbes," p. 269.

56. "Dr. Leo Strauss on Hobbes," pp. 147–48.

57. Introduction to *Leviathan*, p. xii; cf. also pp. lii–liii.

58. Michael Oakeshott, introduction to Hobbes's *Leviathan* (Oxford: Basil Blackwell, 1946);

reprinted with some modifications in *Hobbes on Civil Association*, pp. 1–74. Except where the texts differ, my references will be to the former.

59. Introduction to *Leviathan*, pp. xii, lii–liii.

60. Introduction to *Leviathan*, pp. xviii–xxvii, liii. For an illuminating discussion of the differences between the pagan conception of reason and that of Hobbes, see S. Letwin, "Hobbes and Christianity," *Daedalus* 105 (Winter, 1976): 1–21.

61. Introduction to *Leviathan*, lix–lxi; Hobbes, *Leviathan*, chap. 21 (p. 141). Cf. also "The Moral Life in the Writings of Thomas Hobbes," *RP*, pp. 266, 282; "The Vocabulary of a Modern European State," *Political Studies* 23 (1975): 325.

62. Introduction to *Leviathan*, pp. lvi–lvii.

63. Introduction to *Leviathan*, pp. xliii–xliv. This passage is substantially changed in the later version of the introduction; cf. *Hobbes on Civil Association*, p. 45. On the relationship between the modern notion of law as command (vs. ancient *nomos*) and freedom, see Michael Foster, *The Political Philosophies of Plato and Hegel* (Oxford: Clarendon Press, 1935), pp. 110–21. There Foster argues that law as command (in contradistinction to *nomos* and custom) implies freedom in the subject in two ways: a) in its objectivity to the reason of the subject; and b) in the generality of its application. Oakeshott reviewed Foster's book in *The Cambridge Review* 57 (1935–36): 74.

64. Introduction to *Leviathan*, p. lvii

65. Michael Oakeshott, "The Moral Life in the Writings of Thomas Hobbes," *RP*, pp. 248–300 (hereafter "Moral Life"); reprinted in *Hobbes on Civil Association*, pp. 75–131. My references will be to the former.

66. "Moral Life," p. 260.

67. "Moral Life," pp. 266–73. On pp. 264–66 Oakeshott criticizes Strauss's attempt to show that there is a natural obligation to endeavor peace according to Hobbes, and that this obligation rests on the obligation of every man to endeavor to preserve his own nature.

68. "Moral Life," pp. 272–73, 286–88. The most systematic attempt to see the endeavor for peace in Hobbes as an obligation imposed by a more traditional Law of Nature can be found in H. Warrender, *The Political Philosophy of Hobbes* (Oxford: Clarendon Press, 1957), which Oakeshott treats on pp. 273–283.

69. The rationalism Oakeshott criticizes in *RP* is yet different from both the ancient and from Hobbes's skeptical rationalism, consisting in a kind of confusion between the two. "One important aspect of the history of the emergence of Rationalism is the changing connotation of the word 'reason'. The 'reason' to which the Rationalist appeals is not, for example, the Reason of Hooker, which belongs still to the tradition of Stoicism and of Aquinas. It is a faculty of calculation by which men conclude one thing from another and discover fit means of attaining given ends not themselves subject to the criticism of reason, a faculty by which a world believed to be a machine could be disclosed. Much of the plausibility of Rationalism lies in the tacit attribution to the new 'reason' of the qualities which properly belong to the Reason of the older intellectual tradition" (*RP*, pp. 17–18, n. 3). It is just this attribution to the new "reason" of qualities belonging to the older "Reason" that Oakeshott argues Hobbes avoids in "The Moral Life in the Writings of Thomas Hobbes."

70. Cf. Strauss, *Political Philosophy of Hobbes*, chap. 7, "The New Morality"; *Natural Right and History*, p. 189; *What Is Political Philosophy?*, p. 48. Cf. also C. B. Macpherson, *The Political Theory of Possessive Individualism* (London: Oxford University Press, 1962); "Hobbes's Bourgeois Man," in *Hobbes Studies*, ed. K. Brown (Cambridge, MA: Harvard University Press, 1965): 169–83.

71. "Moral Life," pp. 259–60, 289–94. Oakeshott also rejects this view of Hobbes as a bourgeois hedonist in his introduction to *Leviathan*: "Man, as Hobbes sees him, is not engaged in an undignified scramble for suburban pleasures; there is the greatness of great passion in his constitution" (p. lxv). On the non-bourgeois elements in Hobbes's political thought, see K. Thomas, "The Social Origins of Hobbes's Political Thought," in *Hobbes Studies*, ed. K. Brown, pp. 185–236.

72. "John Locke," *The Cambridge Review* 54 (1932–33): 73. On the dissatisfaction with liberalism because it has become boring, cf. Oakeshott's introduction to *The Social and Political Doctrines of Contemporary Europe*, ed. Michael Oakeshott (Cambridge: Cambridge University Press, 1939), pp. xi–xii.

73. "Thomas Hobbes," p. 272. Cf. also the introduction to *Leviathan*, p. lvii.

74. Cf. Oakeshott's review of Gierke, in which he criticizes the negative "individualism" involved in "the seventeenth-century notion that when a man entered political society he surrendered, not the whole, but a part of his natural rights." He goes on to add that this "is a notion from which Hobbes might have rescued us if we had listened to him" (p. 11). Cf. also

Oakeshott's introduction to *Leviathan*, p. lvii.

75. "Dr. Leo Strauss on Hobbes," pp. 147–48.

76. "Moral Life," p. 148.

77. Introduction to *Leviathan*, p. liv; cf. also pp. lv–lvi, where the atomistic and non-social character of Hobbes's theory of the self is particularly emphasized.

78. Cf. the implied criticism of Locke's doctrine of natural rights in Oakeshott's review of Gierke, p. 11.

79. On the idealist theory of the will in relation to the problem of political obligation, see J. H. Muirhead, "Recent Criticism of the Idealist Theory of the General Will," *Mind* 33 (1924): 166–75, 233–41, 361–68; J. Plamenatz, *Consent, Freedom and Political Obligation* (London: Oxford University Press, 1938), pp. 26–61; P. Riley, *Will and Political Legitimacy: A Critical Exposition of Social Contract Theory in Hobbes, Locke, Rousseau, Kant, and Hegel* (Cambridge, MA: Harvard University Press, 1982), chaps. 4 and 6. In his book Riley quotes Oakeshott's remark on the absence of an adequate theory of volition in Hobbes (pp. 98, 201–2, 240), but he does not seem to follow Oakeshott's suggestions as to a remedy.

80. Jean-Jacques Rousseau, *On the Social Contract*, ed. R. Masters, trans. J. Masters (New York: St. Martin's Press, 1978), bk. 1, chap. vii.

81. Rousseau, *Social Contract*, bk. 4, chap. ii.

82. Rousseau, *Social Contract*, bk. 1, chap. viii.

83. For example, *Social Contract*, bk. 2, chap. iii, where Rousseau speaks of the general will as what remains after differences in our private wills cancel each other out. Cf. also bk. 3, chap. xv, where Rousseau tries to find a guarantee for the expression of the general will in direct democracy.

84. G. W. F. Hegel, *Lectures on the History of Philosophy*, trans. E. S. Haldane and F. H. Simson (London: Routledge & Kegan Paul, 1968), vol. 3, pp. 401–2.

85. G. W. F. Hegel, *Philosophy of Right*, trans. T. M. Knox (Oxford: Clarendon Press, 1952), par. 258. Hegel's criticism of Kant's political philosophy (and of Fichte's, as is indicated in this passage) runs along the same lines. Cf. *Philosophy of Right*, par. 29; *Lectures on the History of Philosophy*, vol. 3, pp. 503–4.

86. Hegel, *Philosophy of Right*, par. 75 and addition; par. 258.

87. Hegel, *Philosophy of Right*, par. 258.

88. Hegel, *Philosophy of Right*, pars. 5 (and addition), 15, 29, 149; *Lectures on the History of Philosophy*, vol. 3, pp. 503–4; *Philosophy of History*, trans. J. Sibree (New York: Dover, 1956), pp. 38–41.

89. Hegel, *Philosophy of Right*, par. 124; cf. also pars. 121 (and addition), 185 (and addition), 206, 260–262 (and additions), 273 (and addition), 299 (and addition). For doubts as to whether Hegel succeeds entirely in preserving the will and individuality in his political theory, see Foster, pp. 121–41, 188–204; Riley, pp. 163–99.

90. Bernard Bosanquet, *The Philosophical Theory of the State* (London: Macmillan, 1965).

91. Bosanquet, *Philosophical Theory*, pp. 110–12.

92. Bosanquet, *Philosophical Theory*, pp. 136–39.

93. Bosanquet, *Philosophical Theory*, p. 140. For a similar view of the relationship between the state or social whole and self-realization, see Bradley, "My Station and its Duties," in *Ethical Studies*, pp. 160–213.

94. Bosanquet, *Philosophical Theory*, pp. xxxi–xxxix, 140–44, 172–87. Cf. also T. H. Green, *Lectures on the Principles of Political Obligation and Other Writings*, ed. P. Harris and J. Morrow (Cambridge: Cambridge University Press, 1986), pp. 18–22; Immanuel Kant, *The Metaphysical Elements of Justice*, trans. J. Ladd (Indianapolis: Bobbs-Merrill, 1965), pp. 13–21, 34–35.

95. Bosanquet, *Philosophical Theory of the State*, pp. 68, 52–79, 117–18.

96. Michael Oakeshott, review of *Bernard Bosanquet's Philosophy of the State: A Historical and Systematical Study*, by B. Pfannenstill, *Philosophy* 11 (1936): 482.

97. Review of Pfannenstill, p. 482 (emphasis added).

98. On the British idealists' substantive theory of human nature, cf. A. Vincent and R. Plant, *Philosophy, Politics and Citizenship: The Life and Thought of the British Idealists* (Oxford: Basil Blackwell, 1984), pp. 168–71.

99. Cf., for example, Bosanquet, *Philosophical Theory*, pp. 110–15, where he compares the "real will" with the function of Rousseau's Legislator.

100. Cf. Bosanquet, *Philosophical Theory*, pp. 97–99; Green, pp. 39–45. A more positive attitude toward Hobbes, however, is suggested in R. G. Collingwood, *The New Leviathan* (Oxford: Clarendon Press, 1942).

101. Michael Oakeshott, review of *The State and the Citizen*, by J. D. Mabbott, *Mind* 58 (1949): 378–89. Oakeshott wrote another shorter review of the book in *The Cambridge Journal* 2 (1948–49): 316, 318.

102. *Mind* 58: 378–79.

103. J. D. Mabbott, *The State and the Citizen* (London: Hutchinson's, 1948), p. 7.

104. This summary is for the most part derived from Oakeshott's, which is to be found on pp. 379–83 of his review.

105. Cf. Mabbott, pp. 7, 9, 171–72.

106. *Mind* 58: 383–84.

107. Mabbott, pp. 7, 9–10.

108. *Mind* 58: 383–84.

109. One is reminded of Wittgenstein's famous statement that philosophy "leaves everything as it is" (*Philosophical Investigations*, trans. G. E. M. Anscombe [New York: Macmillan, 1953], I: 124). But this applies to Oakeshott's conception of philosophy only if by leaving everything as it is the philosopher is understood not simply to accept things as they first present themselves to him or to confine himself to mere "analysis."

110. *Mind* 58: 384–85.

111. This dictum of Bishop Butler's forms the epigraph to G. E. Moore's *Principia Ethica* (Cambridge: Cambridge University Press, 1922). Cf. Collingwood, *Speculum Mentis*, pp. 256–57, where this premise of "realistic" philosophy is criticized.

112. *Mind* 58: 385.

113. *Mind* 58: 386. Cf. also Michael Oakeshott, "Contemporary British Politics," *The Cambridge Journal* 1 (1947–48): 488.

114. *Mind* 58: 386. Cf. Oakeshott's review of *Fundamental Problems of Life*, by J. S. Mackenzie, *Journal of Philosophical Studies* 4 (1929): 265, where he complains that Rousseau's notion of the general will and Hegel's notion of the rational will ought not to be confused with the notion of a "group mind." Cf. also Oakeshott's review of Gierke.

115. *Mind* 58: 387–89.

116. *Mind* 58: 389.

CHAPTER 4

1. I hope to avoid the error, though, of reading back into *EM* Oakeshott's entire critique of rationalism. I think J. L. Auspitz is guilty of this when he says, "*Experience and its Modes* is structured to convey a suppressed polemic against some of the most powerful dogmas of modern intellectual life, dogmas which Oakeshott later grouped under the head of Rationalism" ("Individuality, Civility, and Theory," *Political Theory* 4 [1976]: 265). *EM* is concerned with much else besides rationalism. And rationalism is not Oakeshott's term, as Auspitz suggests, "for a confusion of genres."

2. Cf. Michael Oakeshott, "On Misunderstanding Human Conduct: A Reply to My Critics," *Political Theory* 4 (1976): 364.

3. The idea that Oakeshott is a "Burkean conservative" is really a popular, and not a scholarly, idea. Oakeshott's more discriminating readers have always recognized the discrepancy between his conservatism and that of Burke. For a judicious recent discussion, see J. Rayner, "The Legend of Oakeshott's Conservatism: Skeptical Philosophy and Limited Politics," *Canadian Journal of Political Science* 18 (1985): 313–38. I do not, however, follow Rayner's understanding of the relationship between theory and practice in Oakeshott's later work.

4. Richard J. Bernstein, *Beyond Objectivism and Relativism: Science, Hermeneutics, and Praxis* (Philadelphia: University of Pennsylvania Press, 1985).

5. Cf. Hans-Georg Gadamer, *Truth and Method* (New York: Seabury Press, 1975), pp. 239–253.

6. *RP*, pp. 1, 20.

7. *RP*, pp. 7–11.

8. Cf. Gilbert Ryle, "Knowing How and Knowing That," *Proceedings of the Aristotelian Society* 46 (1945–46): 1–16; *The Concept of Mind* (London: Hutchinson, 1949), chap. 2.

9. Cf. Michael Polanyi, *Science, Faith and Society* (Chicago: University of Chicago Press, 1964); *Personal Knowledge* (Chicago: University of Chicago Press, 1958); *The Tacit Dimension* (New York: Doubleday, 1966).

10. *RP*, p. 11. Critics like M. Postan, "Revulsion from Thought," *The Cambridge Journal* 1 (1947–48): 395–408, fail to make clear that, not reason, but the identification of reason with

technique is the object of Oakeshott's attack on rationalism. It is this identification of reason with technique which seems to set modern rationalism off from ancient rationalism, which is not Oakeshott's concern in this essay; cf. *RP*, pp. 15–16, n. 3 on pp. 17–18.

11. *RP*, pp. 11–13.

12. To seek origins is to read the past backwards, which for Oakeshott signifies a practical, as opposed to a genuinely historical, attitude toward the past. Cf. "The Activity of Being an Historian" in *RP*, especially p. 160.

13. *RP*, pp. 1, 13–17.

14. *RP*, pp. 20–21.

15. *RP*, pp. 4–6, 12, 21–23.

16. *RP*, pp. 23–28.

17. *RP*, p. 28. In "Scientific Politics," *The Cambridge Journal* 1 (1947–48), Oakeshott seems to agree with the observation that modern politics is characterized by a "deplorable lack of success" (p. 347), but he is no more specific than in "Rationalism in Politics" as to what this lack of success actually consists in, being more concerned with its sources in rationalism. Interestingly, Oakeshott observes in this essay that German National Socialism, far from being a reaction against rationalist politics, was itself quite consistent with them (p. 351).

18. Cf. *RP*, p. 74.

19. E.g., Leo Strauss. See his characterization of "the crisis of modernity" in "The Three Waves of Modernity," in *Political Philosophy: Six Essays by Leo Strauss* (Indianapolis: Bobbs-Merrill, 1975), pp. 81–82.

20. *RP*, pp. 28–29, 30–32.

21. Cf. Michael Oakeshott, "The Universities," *The Cambridge Journal* 2 (1948–49): 515–42; "The Idea of a University," *The Listener* 43 (1950): 424–26; "The Study of 'Politics' in a University," in *RP*, pp. 301–33; "Education: The Engagement and its Frustration," in *Education and the Development of Reason*, ed. R. F. Dearden, P. H. Hirst, and R. S. Peters (London: Routledge & Kegan Paul, 1972), pp. 19–49; "A Place of Learning," *The Colorado College Studies*, no. 12 (1975). With the exception of "The Study of 'Politics' in a University," these essays have now been conveniently collected in Michael Oakeshott, *The Voice of Liberal Learning: Michael Oakeshott on Education*, ed. Timothy Fuller (New Haven and London: Yale University Press, 1989).

22. *RP*, pp. 32–36.

23. E.g., Hans Morgenthau in *Scientific Man versus Power Politics*. Oakeshott's "Scientific Politics" is a long review of this book.

24. *RP*, p. 29; "Scientific Politics," pp. 348–49.

25. "Scientific Politics," pp. 354–55, 356; "Science and Society," *The Cambridge Journal* 1 (1947–48): 694–95.

26. Cf. Friedrich Hayek, *The Counter-Revolution of Science* (Glencoe, IL: The Free Press, 1952); also "The Theory of Complex Phenomena," in *Studies in Philosophy, Politics, and Economics* (Chicago: University of Chicago Press, 1967): 22–42.

27. Cf. above, chap. 2, sec. 4, "History and Science." M. Postan, pp. 404–7, makes the mistake of tracing Oakeshott's anti-rationalism to the Kantian dualism of nature and spirit, science and morality.

28. Cf. B. Crick, "The World of Michael Oakeshott," *Encounter* 20 (1963): 72; H. V. Jaffa, "A Celebration of Tradition," *The National Review* 15 (October 22, 1962): 361; J. R. Archer, "Oakeshott on Politics," *The Journal of Politics* 41 (1979): 154.

29. On Pascal, cf. *RP*, pp. 19–20. On Hobbes, cf. n. 69 in chap. 3 above; "Moral Life" in general.

30. Cf. Postan, pp. 398–401; Archer, pp. 153–54; D. Kettler, "The Cheerful Discourses of Michael Oakeshott," *World Politics* 16 (1964): 488. Most recently K. Koerner, *Liberalism and its Critics* (New York: St. Martin's Press, 1985), pp. 282–295, has tried to prove that Oakeshott's rationalist is a "fictitious adversary" by showing that the alleged "rationalism" of Locke, the Founders, Godwin, and Bentham was never pure or unmixed with an appreciation of empirical experience, history, and tradition. But all of this is beside the point. Oakeshott's examples are meant as illustrations, not as definitive identifications; he too might agree that the "pure" rationalist is a fiction. Nor does he assert that the rationalist completely neglects experience, only that he seeks to reduce it (*RP*, p. 2).

31. W. Galston, *Justice and the Human Good* (Chicago: University of Chicago Press, 1980), p. 26, is I think misleading when he states that Oakeshott's "valid claims are directed against the excesses rather than against the essence of utopian thinking."

32. *RP*, pp. 87–88.

33. *RP*, p. 60; cf. also p. 248.

34. Peter Winch, in *The Idea of a Social Science and its Relation to Philosophy* (London: Routledge & Kegan Paul, 1958), pp. 57–65, argues that Oakeshott's critique of reflective morality is incompatible with this point about moral conduct being conduct to which there is an alternative, but I do not see that it is.

35. *RP*, pp. 61–65.

36. *RP*, pp. 66–68.

37. *RP*, pp. 68–70.

38. I do not follow Winch, p. 58, when he says that Oakeshott "seems to think that 'habitual' morality could exist in abstraction from 'reflective' morality."

39. *RP*, pp. 70–71.

40. *RP*, pp. 71–73.

41. G. W. F. Hegel, *Natural Law*, trans. T. M. Knox (Philadelphia: University of Pennsylvania Press, 1975), p. 115; cf. also pp. 70–115. Cf. also *The Phenomenology of Spirit*, trans. A. V. Miller (Oxford: Clarendon Press, 1977), pars. 349–52, 429–31, 596–671; *Philosophy of Right*, par. 153. For Gadamer's remark, as well as an account of Hegel's critique of subjective spirit, cf. *Philosophical Hermeneutics*, trans. and ed. David Linge (Berkeley: University of California Press, 1976), pp. 111–14.

42. Cf. especially the essay "My Station and its Duties," in which the Hegelian formula mentioned above is quoted several times with obvious relish.

43. *RP*, p. 74.

44. *RP*, pp. 75–79.

45. *RP*, p. 83. Oakeshott tells us in a footnote that an account of the view he is considering may be found in M. Ginsberg's *Reason and Unreason in Society* (London: Longman's, Green, 1948). And, indeed, in an essay entitled "The Function of Reason in Morals," we find Ginsberg writing that "the distinctive mark of rational behaviour is purpose. In other words, reasonable action is action for which a ground or reason can be given by reference to an end more or less consciously aimed at" (p. 240). He goes on to argue that "the function of reason in conduct is to clarify and define the ends of endeavour and to relate them to one another, to disclose the nature of the forces, internal and external, necessary for their realization," etc. (p. 245). For Weber's essentially similar view of rationality and the role of reason in conduct, see *The Methodology of the Social Sciences*, trans. and ed. E. Shils and H. Finch (New York: The Free Press, 1949), pp. 10–39, 52–60.

46. *RP*, pp. 81–83.

47. *RP*, pp. 85–86. A critique of this notion of the mind as something that can be separated from its contents, that lies *behind* its activities, can also be found in Gilbert Ryle's *The Concept of Mind*. Cf. Oakeshott's favorable review of this book in *The Spectator* 184 (1950): 20, 22.

48. *RP*, pp. 89–90, 91.

49. *EM*, p. 9. For a restatement of this view of the relationship between subject and object, self and not-self, see "The Voice of Poetry in the Conversation of Mankind," in *RP*, pp. 204–5.

50. *RP*, pp. 90–91.

51. *RP*, pp. 88–89.

52. *RP*, pp. 95–96. This reveals an important aspect of Oakeshott's philosophical procedure. He is far more interested in what the dress-designers actually *succeeded* in doing than in what they themselves thought they were doing. As he says of his analysis in "Political Education": "[I]t is neither intended as a description of the motives of politicians nor of what they believe themselves to be doing, but of what they actually succeed in doing" (*RP*, p. 133).

53. *RP*, p. 97.

54. *RP*, pp. 97–100.

55. *RP*, p. 27. Cf. also "The Customer is Never Wrong," *The Listener* 54 (1955): 302, where Oakeshott criticizes Walter Lippman for arguing that our free institutions were "founded" by men who held certain abstract beliefs about natural law. Here, he says, Lippman "speaks with the shortened perspective of an American way of thinking in which a manner of conducting affairs is inconceivable without an architect and without a premeditated 'dedication to a proposition'. But the fact is that nobody ever 'founded' these institutions. They are the product of innumerable choices, over long stretches of time, but not of any human design."

56. *RP*, p. 126; cf. also pp. 157–58.

57. *RP*, pp. 99–100.

58. *EM*, pp. 32–33.

59. *RP*, pp. 102–3. Though the account of science here for the most part accords with the

non-objectivist account of scientific experience in *EM*, there does seem to be some divergence. For in *EM* Oakeshott does speak of science, i.e., experience *sub specie quantitatis*, as in principle capable of completion (cf. p. 192).

60. Cf. Bernstein's account of recent post-empiricist philosophy of science in *Beyond Objectivism and Relativism*, pp. 51–108. For Polanyi, see *Science, Faith and Society* and *Personal Knowledge*. Cf. also Oakeshott's review of the latter book in *Encounter* 11 (1958): 77–80. In this review he makes some interesting remarks about Hegel's concept of the concrete universal as a solution to the problem of going beyond objectivism without subsiding into relativism or subjectivism.

61. Jaffa, p. 361.

62. *RP*, pp. 104–6.

63. *RP*, pp. 105–9.

64. *RP*, p. 113.

65. *RP*, pp. 112–13, 135.

66. *RP*, pp. 114–15, 89.

67. *RP*, pp. 116–18.

68. *RP*, pp. 118–21.

69. *RP*, pp. 122–23 (emphasis added), 130; cf. also p. 105.

70. *RP*, pp. 123–24.

71. Michael Oakeshott, "*Rationalism in Politics*: A Reply to Professor Raphael," *Political Studies* 13 (1965): 90. This brief response in fact clarifies a great deal about Oakeshott's notions of "tradition" and "the pursuit of intimations," and I have drawn on it liberally in what I have to say above. What makes it of particular interest is its emphasis on the miscellaneous and multifarious character of tradition. In this connection he mentions Aristotle; specifically, he compares his notion of tradition as a "multi-voiced creature" with Aristotle's recognition of the incommensurability of the "admitted goods" (I presume his reference here is to the *Rhetoric*, 1362a-b; cf. also *Politics*, 1282b–1283a; *Nicomachean Ethics*, 1094b, 1096a–b). He goes on to point out that the rationalist goes wrong by insisting on getting out of this "multi-voiced creature," tradition, what cannot in fact be gotten out of it, namely, a straight answer. Our "miscellaneous beliefs, preferences, approvals, disapprovals, etc. . . . do not provide a single unambiguous norm." The most we can expect from a tradition is a number of "intimations," which may serve as "aids to reflection."

72. *RP*, pp. 128, 134.

73. *RP*, p. 125.

74. *RP*, p. 304; cf. also pp. 197–99.

75. Cf. "The Universities," pp. 533–42; "The Idea of a University," p. 425; "A Place of Learning," pp. 16–17, 23–26.

76. Michael Walzer makes this criticism in his *Interpretation and Social Criticism* (Cambridge, MA: Harvard University Press, 1987), pp. 28–29. Walzer's interpretive model of moral reasoning does indeed bear a strong resemblance to Oakeshott's "pursuit of intimations."

77. Hanna Pitkin, "The Roots of Conservatism: Michael Oakeshott and the Denial of Politics," *Dissent* 20 (1973): 518.

78. *RP*, pp. 125–126, 133. For the criticism that Oakeshott does not adequately take into account such "revolutionary situations" or "foundings," cf. N. Wood, "A Guide to the Classics: The Skepticism of Michael Oakeshott," *The Journal of Politics* 21 (1959): 661; Jaffa, p. 361; Galston, *Justice and the Human Good*, p. 26.

79. Cf. J. W. N. Watkins, "Political Tradition and Political Theory," *The Philosophical Quarterly* 2 (1952): 333–37; J. C. Rees, "Professor Oakeshott on Political Education," *Mind* 62 (1953): 68–74; S. I. Benn and R. S. Peters, *Social Principles and the Democratic State* (London: George Allen & Unwin Ltd., 1959), pp. 312, 314–16; C. Falck, "Romanticism in Politics," *The New Left Review* (January-February 1963), pp. 64–65; J. G. Blumler, "Politics, Poetry and Practice," *Political Studies* 12 (1964): 357; Pitkin, "The Roots of Conservatism," pp. 500–503. Pitkin, after falling over backwards to point out this "ambiguity" in Oakeshott's critique of rationalism, ends up resolving it in pretty much the manner it was meant to be resolved.

80. *RP*, pp. 133–34.

81. *RP*, pp. 128–29.

82. *RP*, p. 136. Jaffa, pp. 361–62, totally misreads this passage and assimilates Oakeshott to Mill.

83. *RP*, p. 130.

84. *RP*, pp. 132–33, 111, 133–34.

85. Cf. "Reply to Professor Raphael," p. 89; *RP*, p. 134. For such criticism, cf. Benn and Peters, pp. 314, 316–17; Falck, pp. 71–72.

86. Cf. *EM*, pp. 10–26, 252–53, 302.

87. Cf. R. H. S. Crossman, "The Ultimate Conservative," *The New Statesman* 42 (1951): 61; Benn and Peters, pp. 316–18; Wood, pp. 660–62; Jaffa, p. 361; Pitkin, "The Roots of Conservatism," pp. 508–10; G. Himmelfarb, "The Conservative Imagination: Michael Oakeshott," *The American Scholar* (Summer 1975): 417–18; D. Spitz, "A Rationalist *Malgré Lui*: The Perplexities of Being Michael Oakeshott," *Political Theory* 4 (1976): 340; Galston, *Justice and the Human Good*, p. 26; Koerner, p. 296. Crick, pp. 73–74, and Spitz, pp. 340–41, add to this criticism the twist that since our tradition is rationalistic according to Oakeshott, we are condemned to pursue the intimations of rationalism.

88. Cf. Crossman, p. 61; Falck, p. 66; Jaffa, p. 361; Crick, p. 72; D. D. Raphael, "Professor Oakeshott's Rationalism in Politics," *Political Studies* 12 (1964): 212–15; S. Coleman, "Is There Reason in Tradition?," in King and Parekh, p. 250; Spitz, pp. 339–40; Galston, *Justice and the Human Good*, p. 26; Koerner, p. 296.

89. *RP*, p. 136.

90. *RP*, p. 126; cf. also pp. 107–8.

91. *RP*, p. 127.

92. On tradition, see Gadamer, *Truth and Method*, pp. 249–53. On *phronēsis*, see *Truth and Method*, pp. 278–89; Gadamer, "The Problem of Historical Consciousness," in *Interpretive Social Science: A Second Look*, ed. P. Rabinow and W. Sullivan (Berkeley: University of California Press, 1987), pp. 115–24; Gadamer, *Reason in the Age of Science*, trans. F. Lawrence (Cambridge, MA: MIT Press, 1981), pp. 115–37.

93. Cf. Jürgen Habermas, "A Review of Gadamer's *Truth and Method*," in *Understanding and Social Inquiry*, ed. F. Dallmayr and T. McCarthy (Notre Dame: Notre Dame University Press, 1977), pp. 357–61.

94. Gadamer, "The Problem of Historical Consciousness," p. 87; cf. pp. 137–38. Cf. also *Truth and Method*, p. xxv.

95. Cf. Gadamer, *Reason in an Age of Science*, 77–87; cf. also the editor's introduction, pp. xxiv–xxix.

96. From a personal letter Gadamer wrote to Richard Bernstein, reprinted in Bernstein, *Beyond Objectivism and Relativism*, pp. 263–64. Cf. also Gadamer's response to Leo Strauss, quoted in *Beyond*, p. 251. For Bernstein's criticisms, cf. *Beyond*, pp. 155–58. These criticisms parallel those of Himmelfarb of Oakeshott; cf. "The Conservative Imagination," pp. 417–18.

97. Edmund Burke, *Reflections on the Revolution in France*, ed. C. C. O'Brien (Harmondsworth: Penguin, 1968), p. 183; cf. also what Burke says about the "method of nature," pp. 119–22.

98. Apart from the passages I have already cited, see "Learning and Teaching," p. 162, for an evocation of the contingency of our traditional inheritance. In contrasting Oakeshott and Burke above, I diverge from Coleman, pp. 252–62, who places Oakeshott in the tradition of thought beginning with Moser and Burke and passing through Hayek and modern functionalists which sees tradition as inherently rational, a storehouse of wisdom.

99. Cf. Alasdair MacIntyre, *After Virtue: A Study in Moral Theory* (Notre Dame: Notre Dame University Press, 1981), chap. 15, especially pp. 206–7. When MacIntyre complains about the ideological uses to which the concept of tradition has been put by conservative political theorists who follow Burke, he certainly cannot have in mind Oakeshott. For a development of MacIntyre's views on tradition, see his recent *Whose Justice? Which Rationality?* (Notre Dame: Notre Dame University Press, 1988), especially chaps. 1, 17–20. For Gadamer's criticism of the romantic or Burkean understanding of tradition, cf. *Truth and Method*, pp. 249–50.

100. Cf. T. Peardon, "Two Currents in Contemporary English Political Theory," *American Political Science Review* 49 (1955): 487–92; Crick, p. 65; Falck, pp. 69–70; D. Germino, *Beyond Ideology: The Revival of Political Theory* (New York: Harper & Row, 1967), p. 139; Himmelfarb, "The Conservative Imagination," p. 159; Galston, *Justice and the Human Good*, pp. 26–27. Galston's comparison and contrasting of Oakeshott and Aristotle in this regard is highly reminiscent of Strauss's comparison/contrasting of Burke and Aristotle on theory and practice (*Natural Right and History*, pp. 302–12), suggesting that he (wrongly) identifies Oakeshott with Burke.

101. Some critics have denied that it does. Cf. Rees, pp. 68–74; Crick, pp. 66, 68; Raphael, p. 215; H. Pitkin, "Inhuman Conduct and Unpolitical Theory: Michael Oakeshott's *On Human Conduct*," *Political Theory* 4 (1976): 304–5; Spitz, pp. 340–41, 343, 346; Archer, pp. 154–55.

102. Charles Covell, *The Redefinition of Conservatism: Politics and Doctrine* (New York: St.

Martin's Press, 1986), pp. 99–102, 112, 120–21.

103. "Contemporary British Politics," *The Cambridge Journal* 1 (1947–48): 476.

104. "Contemporary British Politics," p. 477. Oakeshott quotes Mannheim: "By making the necessary adaptations to the needs of war one does not always realize that very often they contain also the principles of adaptation to the needs of a New Age." The book from which this quote comes, *Man and Society in an Age of Reconstruction* (1940), is picked out for criticism by Hayek as well in his own tract against central social planning, *The Road to Serfdom* (Chicago: University of Chicago Press, 1944). There, too, Hayek criticizes the then fashionable view that the lessons of war, in which everything is subordinated to a single purpose, should be applied to peacetime (p. 206). There are many similarities between Hayek's critique of central social planning and Oakeshott's. Nevertheless, Hayek's emphasis on the need to formulate a liberal ideology to combat collectivist ideologies (pp. 216–19) does not comport with Oakeshott's critique of all ideologies. Thus Oakeshott comments critically in *RP* that perhaps the main significance of Hayek's *Road to Serfdom* is "not the cogency of his doctrine, but the fact that it is a doctrine. A plan to resist all planning may be better than its opposite, but it belongs to the same style of politics. And only in a society already deeply infected with Rationalism will the conversion of the traditional resources of resistance to the tyranny of Rationalism into a self-conscious ideology be considered a strengthening of those resources" (*RP*, pp. 20–21).

105. "The Universities," p. 525. Cf. also *RP*, pp. 52–53; *OHC*, pp. 146–47, 27273; *OH*, pp. 163–64.

106. Cf. W. J. M. Mackenzie, "Political Theory and Political Education," *Universities Quarterly* 9 (1955–56): 359–360; Falck, p. 72; Crick, pp. 66, 6871; Blumler, pp. 355–61; Kettler, pp. 487–89; Pitkin, "The Roots of Conservatism," pp. 510–25, and "Inhuman Conduct and Unpolitical Theory," pp. 309–17; S. Wolin, "The Politics of Self-Disclosure," *Political Theory* 4 (1976): 323, 329–31.

107. Introduction to *Leviathan*, p. lxiv. This sentence does not appear in Oakeshott's revised version of the introduction in *Hobbes on Civil Association*.

108. Introduction to *Leviathan*, pp. lxiv–v. Cf. also "The Claims of Politics," *Scrutiny* 8 (1939–40): 146–51, where the "abstractness" and "vulgarity" of political activity is again evoked.

109. Michael Oakeshott, review of *Reason and Revolution*, by H. Marcuse, *The Spectator* 194 (1955): 404. Cf. also review of *Hegel's Theory of the Modern State*, by S. Avineri, *European Studies Review* 5 (1975): 217; *OHC*, pp. 256–57.

110. Cf. "Reply to Professor Raphael," p. 89.

111. "Contemporary British Politics," p. 475. For Burke's criticism of the doctrine of natural rights, see *Reflections on the Revolution in France*, pp. 148–54. For Hegel's, cf. the *Philosophy of Right*, pars. 155, 261.

112. "Contemporary British Politics," pp. 478–79, 482–85.

113. "Contemporary British Politics," pp. 485–87.

114. "Contemporary British Politics," pp. 479, 487–88.

115. "Contemporary British Politics," p. 488; cf. also p. 479.

116. "Contemporary British Politics," pp. 489–90.

117. This essay is an extended discussion of H. C. Simons's *Economic Policy for a Free Society* (Chicago: University of Chicago Press, 1948). But since Oakeshott for the most part endorses Simons's view, and since he recasts the argument largely in his own terms, I will discuss the essay without reference to Simons.

118. *RP*, pp. 39–40.

119. *RP*, pp. 40–43.

120. *RP.*, p. 58.

121. *RP*, pp. 45–48, 50–55.

122. Michael Oakeshott, review of *Modern Capitalism and Economic Progress*, by T. Wilson, *The Cambridge Journal* 4 (1950–51): 506.

123. "The Universities," pp. 522–23; cf. also "A Place of Learning," p. 14. Of the moral ideal of socialism as presented by one writer Oakeshott writes: "[T]he good life here is nothing other than the enjoyment by more and more people of more and more of everything.... In short, this is the plausible ethics of productivity, distinguished from 'capitalism' only by being alleged to be more successful. So far as I am concerned it involves a revolting nothingness, which has only to be successful in order to reduce human life to absolute insignificance" (review of *Socialism and Ethics*, by H. Selsam, *The Cambridge Journal* 2 [1948–49]: 693–94).

124. Cf. "John Locke," p. 73.

125. *The Social and Political Doctrines of Contemporary Europe*, pp. xx, xxi.

126. Cf. "The Universities" for a rather trenchant critique of the point of view which characterizes our predicament in terms of a lack of a "unified conception of life" or *Weltanschauung*, and which looks to the universities to supply the defect. This essay might usefully be contrasted with Allan Bloom's recent, and rather more alarmist reflections on higher education in *The Closing of the American Mind: How Higher Education Has Failed Democracy and Impoverished the Souls of Today's Students* (New York: Simon and Schuster, 1987).

127. In a highly critical review of R. Kirk's *The Conservative Mind*, Oakeshott gives a good summary of the point of view he presents in "On Being Conservative"; cf. *The Spectator* 193 (1954): 472, 474.

128. *RP*, pp. 168–73.

129. Many commentators, strangely, fail to recognize this. Cf., for example, B. Barber, "Conserving Politics: Michael Oakeshott and Political Theory," *Government and Opposition* 11 (1976): 456–57, where the "wary traditionalist" of "On Being Conservative" is said to be irreconcilable with the "adventurer" of *OHC*.

130. *RP*, pp. 174–75, 182–84.

131. *RP*, pp. 184–86.

132. *RP*, pp. 186–87.

133. *RP*, pp. 188–91. Oakeshott's generally positive account of government here recalls Hegel. And, indeed, in his review of Marcuse's *Reason and Revolution*, he gives an account of Hegel's understanding of the relationship between government and individual which sounds very much like his own account here (*The Spectator* 194 [1955]: 404–5).

134. *RP*, pp. 191–95. On the "politics of passion" versus the "politics of scepticism," cf. also "The Customer is Never Wrong" and Oakeshott's review of *Political Parties*, by M. Duverger, *The Spectator* 193 (1954): 94.

135. *RP*, p. 194, n. 1.

136. Michael Oakeshott, "The Masses in Representative Democracy," in *American Conservative Thought in the Twentieth Century*, ed. W. F. Buckley (New York: Dodd Mead, 1970), pp. 103–23. This essay was first published in German as "Die Massen in der repräsentativen Demokratie," in *Masse und Demokratie* (Erlenbach-Zürich und Stuttgart: Rentsch, 1957), ed. A. Hunold, pp. 189–214. An English translation appeared in *Freedom and Serfdom: An Anthology of Western Thought*, ed. A. Hunold (Dordrecht, Holland: Reidel, 1961), pp. 151–70.

137. Oakeshott remarks the growth of the passion for security in the nineteenth century in a number of different places, and he usually credits Jacob Burckhardt with having been the first to discern it clearly. Cf. "Contemporary British Politics," pp. 478, 484; review of *The Letters of Jacob Burckhardt*, ed. A. Dru, *Encounter* 2 (1954): 70, where Sorel is also mentioned as perceiving the subtle shift in mood from "prosperity" to "security"; *RP*, p. 51, where Oakeshott mentions Acton and Tocqueville along with Burckhardt.

138. "The Masses in Representative Democracy," pp. 103–7, 110, 122–23.

139. "The Masses in Representative Democracy," p. 107. Hobbes is here credited with having been "the first moralist of the modern world to take candid account of the current experience of individuality." Cf. also "Moral Life," *RP*, pp. 250–251.

140. "The Masses in Representative Democracy," pp. 108–10. Contrast with this historical view of the relationship between government and individual the view of the "anarchist," who (as Oakeshott writes somewhere else) forgets that the "'individual' is not a metaphysical entity but an historic achievement," and forgets also "how decisive a part 'government' has played in this achievement" (review of *Anarchy and Order: Essays in Politics*, by H. Read, *The Spectator* 192 [1954]: 593).

141. "The Masses in Representative Democracy," pp. 110–13, 121.

142. "The Masses in Representative Democracy," pp. 114–16. Cf. also Oakeshott's distinction between the morality of communal ties, the morality of individuality, and the morality of the common good in "Moral Life," *RP*, pp. 249–50. What distinguishes the third from the first is that it recognizes individuality and seeks to suppress it.

143. In several places Oakeshott insists on the opposition of parliamentary government to rationalist politics. Parliamentary government he identifies with the politics of skepticism. Cf. "Scientific Politics," pp. 356–58; "Contemporary British Politics," pp. 479–82, 489–90; "The Customer Is Never Wrong," p. 302.

144. Cf. "The Vocabulary of a Modern European State," *Political Studies* 23 (1975): 331. Oakeshott's use of the expression "popular government" recalls Henry Maine's book of the same name, and he points out that Maine used the expression "popular government" instead of

"democracy" because he recognized "that he was concerned with a method of governing and not a constitutional shape, with engagements and not authority."

145. The Masses in Representative Democracy," pp. 113–14, 117–21. Oakeshott's remarks about "leadership" here again recall Burckhardt (among others); cf. Oakeshott's review of *The Letters of Jacob Burckhardt.*

146. "The Masses in Representative Democracy," pp. 116, 122–23.

CHAPTER 5

1. Michael Oakeshott, "Talking Politics," *The National Review* 27 (December 5, 1975): 1426–27.

2. "Talking Politics," p. 1428.

3. *The Social and Political Doctrines of Contemporary Europe,* p. xvii. On "liberalism," cf. also *OHC,* p. 245, n. 2.

4. *The Social and Political Doctrines of Contemporary Europe,* p. xx.

5. *OHC,* p. vii.

6. *OHC,* p. 2.

7. *OHC,* pp. 3–8.

8. *OHC,* pp. 8–10.

9. *OHC,* p. 11.

10. Cf. especially *EM,* p. 330.

11. *OHC,* p. 11.

12. *EM,* pp. 331–35.

13. *OHC,* p. 25.

14. *OHC,* pp. 12–14.

15. Cf. chap. 2, sec. 5, above.

16. *OHC,* pp. 14–15.

17. *OHC,* pp. 20–25. On sociology as a limited form of historical understanding, cf. pp. 96–100.

18. *OHC,* pp. 25–26.

19. *OHC,* pp. 27–31. For Aristotle's criticism of the Platonic idea of the good, cf. bk. 1 of the *Nicomachean Ethics.*

20. For Rorty's anti-foundationalist conception of philosophy, see *Philosophy and the Mirror of Nature,* especially pt. 3; also "Pragmatism and Philosophy."

21. Cf. Parekh, pp. 487–88; T. Modood, pp. 315–22.

22. I am, of course, aware that Oakeshott does not generally speak of "will" in *OHC* except in contrast to his own view of human agency. His avoidance of this term, however, stems more from its identification as a faculty separate from the intellect than from a rejection of the notion of will altogether. For Oakeshott, as we shall see, will is simply intelligence in doing; it is not something unconditional or separate from thinking. This view of the will he enunciated as early as *EM* (cf. pp. 25–56, 251–52), and indeed it goes all the way back to Hegel (cf. the *Philosophy of Right,* addition to par. 4). Oakeshott's (and Hegel's) identification of thinking and willing is not to be understood as a rejection of the notion of will; it is itself a theory of will.

23. *OHC,* pp. 36–37.

24. *OHC,* pp. 32, 36, 39.

25. *OHC,* p. 89.

26. *OHC,* p. 36. Cf. also "Education: The Engagement and its Frustration," p. 21, where Oakeshott once again describes the human being as an inhabitant of a world, not of things, but of meanings and understandings. "To be without this understanding," he says, "is to be, not a human being, but a stranger to the human condition."

27. *OHC,* p. 36. For a similar view of human freedom and the constraint of a situation, cf. Collingwood, *The Idea of History,* pp. 316–17: "The hard facts of the situation, which it is so important for [a man] to face, are the hard facts of the way in which he conceives the situation."

28. *OHC,* pp. 51–53.

29. *OHC,* pp. 38–39.

30. *OHC,* pp. 39, 41, 45, 45–46, 53–54; Hobbes, *Leviathan,* chap. 6 (p. 39).

31. *OHC,* pp. 35–36, 39, 44, 54. It is interesting to note that Oakeshott later added a paragraph to his original introduction to *Leviathan* which gives more explicit recognition to Hobbes's comprehension of this transactional aspect of the human predicament; cf. *Hobbes on Civil Association,* pp. 35–36.

32. *OHC*, p. 50.

33. *OHC*, p. 41; "Education: The Engagement and its Frustration," pp. 19–22; "A Place of Learning," pp. 7–10. The terms "self-disclosure" and "self-enactment" are also used by Hannah Arendt, though not with exactly the same meaning, in her analysis of action in *The Human Condition* (Chicago: University of Chicago Press, 1958), pp. 175–88.

34. *OHC*, p. 54.

35. *OHC*, pp. 55–56.

36. *OHC*, pp. 55–58, 68, 90–91.

37. Cf. "On Misunderstanding Human Conduct," p. 364, where Oakeshott remarks the inadequacy of "tradition" to express any longer what he wants to express. The similarity between the list of historic practices on p. 99 of *OHC* and the list of historic traditions on p. 128 of *RP* only serves to confirm that what Oakeshott theorizes under the rubric of "practice" in *OHC* coincides with what he used to theorize under the rubric of "tradition" in *RP*.

38. *RP*, pp. 62, 129, 308–10.

39. *OHC*, p. 58; cf. also p. 91.

40. *OHC*, pp. 60–62.

41. Cf. Parekh, pp. 503–4; John Liddington, "Oakeshott: Freedom in a Modern European State," in *Conceptions of Liberty in Political Philosophy*, ed. Z. Pelczynski and J. Gray (New York: St. Martin's Press, 1984), p. 311.

42. For an analogous argument with respect *civil* association, cf. *OHC*, p. 119. The assumption that there must be a distinction between moral and prudential conduct also seems to underlie Oakeshott's discussion of moral obligation in "Moral Life."

43. Cf. "On Misunderstanding Human Conduct," p. 363.

44. *OHC*, pp. 62, 63–64, 80–81.

45. *OHC*, pp. 62–64.

46. *OHC*, pp. 79–80.

47. *OHC*, pp. 66–70.

48. *OHC*, pp. 71–73.

49. *OHC*, pp. 74–75, 77.

50. *OHC*, pp. 77–78, 260.

51. Cf. Green, pp. 18–22; Bosanquet, *Philosophical Theory*, pp. xxxi–xxxix, 140–44, 172–87. For a trenchant critique of this argument for limitation of state activity from the immorality of compulsion, see Mabbott, pp. 66–70. It is clear from the above, however, that Oakeshott does not follow Mabbott in exempting motives from the jurisdiction of state activity on the basis of their "non-social" character.

52. *OHC*, p. 109.

53. *OHC*, p. 109.

54. "On Misunderstanding Human Conduct," p. 364.

55. Cf. Pitkin, "Inhuman Conduct and Unpolitical Theory," p. 303; also Covell, pp. 120–21, 141, 142, 211.

56. These phrases come from Oakeshott's review of Mabbott in *Mind* 58: 384–85.

57. *OHC*, pp. 114–15, 119, 157–58. Cf. also "On Misunderstanding Human Conduct," pp. 355–56, 365–67.

58. *OHC*, p. 119. For a more general discussion of whether a common end or purpose can be attributed to civil association, see section 5 below.

59. *OHC*, pp. 119–22.

60. *OHC*, pp. 122–24.

61. J. Shklar, "Purposes and Procedures," *The Times Literary Supplement*, 12 September 1975, p. 1018.

62. Pitkin, for example, sees Oakeshott's interpretation of the *Philosophy of Right* in *OHC* (see below, section 4) as striking evidence of the general drying up of his earlier "dialectical richness" ("Inhuman Conduct and Unpolitical Theory," p. 304). Along the same lines, Covell sees the whole of *OHC* as an abandonment of the Hegelianism and skeptical historicism which animates Oakeshott's earlier work (*The Redefinition of Conservatism*, pp. 102, 120–21, 136–37, 141, 142, 211).

63. *OHC*, p. 124.

64. Cf. "The Rule of Law," in *OH*, pp. 134–35. Here I differ from Auspitz, who argues that civil association essentially differs from a morality in being a dead code. "For whereas the heart of a morality is a living tradition, a way of life, an only partially verbal language on which a code can at best be superimposed, civility, at its core, *is* a code" ("Individuality, Civility and

Theory," pp. 278–79).

65. "On Misunderstanding Human Conduct," p. 366.

66. *OHC*, pp. 245, 318; "The Vocabulary of a Modern European State," p. 339.

67. *OHC*, pp. 111, 181.

68. Oakeshott's close identification of political philosophy with the philosophy of law goes all the way back to the early essay on "The Concept of a Philosophical Jurisprudence." But it should be noted that what he offers us in the second essay of *OHC* is something broader than what is usually understood as a legal philosophy. And, indeed, he rejects the word "legal" to characterize the condition and relationship he is exploring (choosing the word "civil" instead) precisely because he finds it too narrow in reference (*OHC*, p. 108).

69. Although he does not proceed in this way in *OHC*, in "The Rule of Law" Oakeshott carries out his initial analysis of rules in terms of the rules of a game (pp. 125–33). In what follows I have drawn equally on this essay as well as *OHC*.

70. *OHC*, pp. 124–27; "The Rule of Law," pp. 126–30.

71. H.L.A. Hart, *The Concept of Law* (Oxford: Oxford University Press, 1961), chaps. 2–4. There are many similarities between Oakeshott and Hart on law, though they ultimately diverge with respect to natural law. Also, the non-instrumental character of law, which we have seen is absolutely central to Oakeshott's theory of law, does not play such a prominent role in Hart's.

72. *OHC*, pp. 127–28.

73. *OHC*, pp. 116–17, 128–30. Cf. also "The Rule of Law," pp. 131, 132.

74. *OHC*, pp. 130–37. On legal hermeneutics, see Gadamer, *Truth and Method*, pp. 289–305.

75. *OHC*, pp. 138–40; "The Vocabulary of a Modern European State," p. 414.

76. *OHC*, pp. 138–46.

77. *OHC*, pp. 146, 183.

78. *OHC*, pp. 147–49.

79. *OHC*, pp. 149–54.

80. "The Rule of Law," pp. 155–56.

81. *OHC*, p. 153, n. 1. On the "internal morality of the law," see Lon Fuller, "Positivism and Fidelity to Law," *The Harvard Law Review* 71 (1958): 644–48; also *The Morality of Law* (New Haven: Yale University Press, 1969), especially chap. 2.

82. "The Rule of Law," pp. 140, 159.

83. "The Rule of Law," pp. 157–59. Obviously, certain of Hobbes's laws of nature fit this description better than others. It should also be pointed out that Oakeshott criticizes Hobbes (as we shall see later on) for thinking that these formal conditions inherent in *lex* exhaust the considerations in terms of which the *jus* of *lex* may be deliberated.

84. *OHC*, p. 255. Cf. also "The Vocabulary of a Modern European State," p. 323.

85. *OHC*, p. 154–57.

86. *OHC*, p. 157.

87. *OHC*, p. 254; "The Vocabulary of a Modern European State," p. 323.

88. *OHC*, pp. 157–58; "The Vocabulary of a Modern European State," p. 340.

89. Oakeshott criticizes Locke's grounding of authority on consent in one of his earliest articles, "The Authority of the State," p. 326. Cf. Locke's *Second Treatise*, par. 149, where it is asserted that the authority of government and law ultimately rests on the consent (in the sense of approval) of the people.

90. *OHC*, pp. 158–61. On the difference between a morality and civil association, cf. also "The Rule of Law," pp. 135–36. The difference between laws and morals which Oakeshott mentions here is also mentioned by Hart, pp. 171–73. Both Hart and Oakeshott diverge from Kant here, who differentiated between laws and morals on the basis that one was concerned with "external" actions while the other was concerned with "internal" motives and intentions (cf. Kant's introduction to *The Metaphysics of Morals*).

91. *OHC*, p. 164.

92. *OHC*, pp. 168–73.

93. *OHC*, p. 173.

94. Cf. Hart, pp. 185–95. Hart ascribes such a doctrine of natural law to Hobbes and Hume.

95. *OHC*, pp. 173–74.

96. *OHC*, pp. 173, 90.

97. *OHC*, pp. 174–75; "The Rule of Law," p. 141. Oakeshott's complex understanding of the relationship between morality and law is taken up at greater length in section 5 below.

98. *OHC*, p. 176.

99. *OHC*, p. 177.

100. *OHC*, pp. 178–80.

101. "The Rule of Law," pp. 140, 157–60.

102. It should be pointed out that Oakeshott is not here criticizing the natural-law view which concerns the validity or authority of a law. This "neoplatonic" view he has already considered and rejected. It might also be pointed out that Oakeshott's general point about natural law here can be traced back at least as far as 1948, when, in a review of A. D. Ritchie's *Science and Politics*, he argued that a purely legal control of human affairs is impossible. Law alone, like any other "technology," is incapable of controlling human affairs because it is incapable of controlling itself. "A society always looks outside its positive law for a criterion of justice by means of which to control that law . . . and normally, says Professor Ritchie, it has found that criterion of justice in an ideal of natural law. I doubt whether this is either a satisfactory account of the direction in which the criterion of justice has been sought or of the direction in which a genuine criterion is likely to be found; this notion of a natural law is perhaps the least convincing of the current formulae of moral criteria" ("Science and Society," pp. 695–96).

103. "The Rule of Law," pp. 142–43, 156, 160.

104. "The Rule of Law," pp. 143, 159–60.

105. "The Rule of Law," pp. 143, 160–61.

106. "The Rule of Law," pp. 141, 160. Cf. also "Talking Politics," p. 1426.

107. "The Rule of Law," p. 161.

108. "The Rule of Law," p. 156, n. 13; also *OHC*, p. 153, n. 1.

109. "The Rule of Law," p. 149.

110. *OHC*, pp. 196–97; "On Misunderstanding Human Conduct," p. 359; "Talking Politics," p. 1424.

111. *OHC*, pp. 188–93; "The Vocabulary of a Modern European State," especially pp. 329–32, 337–39; "Talking Politics." In "The Vocabulary of a Modern European State" and "Talking Politics" Oakeshott is especially concerned with the ambiguity of our political vocabulary.

112. *OHC*, pp. 194–96. Cf. also "The Vocabulary of a Modern European State," pp. 332–36; "Talking Politics," pp. 1423–24.

113. *OHC*, pp. 199–206. On the distinction between *societas* and *universitas*, compare Maitland in his introduction to Gierke's *Political Theories of the Middle Ages* (Cambridge: Cambridge University Press, 1951), pp. xxii–xxiii; also Barker in his note on p. 45 of Gierke's *Natural Law and the Theory of Society*.

114. *OHC*, pp. 202–3, 204–6. In "The Vocabulary of a Modern European State" Oakeshott expresses reservations about the words "nomocracy" and "teleocracy." He considers them to be "etymologically unfortunate" because, while referring to modes of association and the engagements of a government, their "acy" endings suggest that they are authority words (pp. 339–40).

115. *OHC*, pp. 200–1.

116. *OHC*, pp. 206–13.

117. *OHC*, pp. 218–24. Oakeshott mentions Aquinas and Dante as writers who represented this understanding of the medieval realm as a *universitas*.

118. *OHC*, pp. 224–29.

119. *OHC*, pp. 231–32.

120. *OHC*, pp. 233–34. Cf. also "On Misunderstanding Human Conduct," p. 366.

121. *OHC*, pp. 234–36.

122. *OHC*, pp. 236–38; cf. also pp. 53, 250.

123. *OHC*, p. 242, n. 1; cf. also 321–22. The obvious reference in this passage is to Macpherson's *The Political Theory of Possessive Individualism*. But Oakeshott's criticism would also extend (as we saw in chapter 3) to Strauss, who saw Hobbes as the author of a new, bourgeois morality, and who interpreted the liberal tradition largely in the light of this fact. Cf. *The Political Philosophy of Hobbes*, chap. 7; *Natural Right and History*, p. 189; *What is Political Philosophy?*, p. 48. For Oakeshott's rejection of this view of Hobbes as a bourgeois hedonist, cf. the introduction to *Leviathan*, p. lxv; "Moral Life," in *RP*, pp. 259–60, 289–94.

124. *OHC*, pp. 238–42.

125. *OHC*, pp. 242–43.

126. *OHC*, pp. 243–52.

127. *OHC*, pp. 258–59.

128. *OHC*, p. 260.

129. Cf. Oakeshott's review of *Hegel's Theory of the Modern State*, by S. Avineri, *European Studies Review* 5 (1975): 217–20, where he distinguishes sharply between Hegel's political opinions and

sympathies, his responses to the *Zeitprobleme*, and the more philosophical, less contingent considerations of the *Philosophy of Right*. With respect to the latter Oakeshott says there are some "deep obscurities" in the *Philosophy of Right* – for example, "What really is the relation of *die bürgerliche Gesellschaft* and *der Staat?*" In his interpretation in *OHC* he offers a definite answer to this question.

130. *OHC*, p. 261.

131. *OHC*, pp. 261–62.

132. Review of Avineri, p. 219.

133. *OHC*, p. 262. Cf. also review of Marx's *Critique of Hegel's Philosophy of Right*, *Spectator* 226 (February 6, 1971): 193; "On Misunderstanding Human Conduct," p. 364. Oakeshott also rejects Hegel's view on the relationship between civil association and war. For him, unlike Hegel, war is the enemy of civil association ("The Rule of Law," p. 164; cf. also the *Philosophy of Right*, pars. 321–29).

134. *OHC*, pp. 262–63.

135. *OHC*, pp. 266–74. In seeing war as the enemy of civil association Oakeshott differs, as was noted above, from Hegel. Cf. "The Rule of Law," p. 164.

136. *OHC*, pp. 274–78.

137. *OHC*, pp. 279–85.

138. *OHC*, pp. 287–93.

139. *OHC*, p. 311. Cf. also "The Rule of Law," p. 153.

140. Cf. Arendt, *The Human Condition*, especially chaps. 2 and 3.

141. *OHC*, pp. 286, 297–99.

142. *OHC*, pp. 297–307. For an extended discussion of the idea of education as "apprenticeship to adult life" or "socialization," cf. also "Education: The Engagement and its Frustration." Here Oakeshott actually quotes Nietzsche, who spoke of this "socializing" engagement which has come to replace genuine education as an attempt "to rear the most 'current' men possible, 'current' in the sense in which the word is used of coins of the realm" (quoted on p. 34 from *Über die Zukunft unserer Bildungsanstalten*).

143. *OHC*, pp. 308–10.

144. Nietzsche, *The Genealogy of Morals*, in *The Basic Writings of Nietzsche*, trans. and ed. W. Kaufmann (New York: Random House, 1968), 3:14.

145. Quoted by Kaufmann in his translation of *The Genealogy of Morals*, in *The Basic Writings of Nietzsche*, p. 560.

146. *OHC*, pp. 310–12.

147. *OHC*, pp. 312–13.

148. *OHC*, p. 320; "The Vocabulary of a Modern European State," p. 341.

149. Weber, for example, believed that the increasing demand for bureaucratization of state administration in the modern world was owing to the "increasing complexity of civilization"; cf. "Bureaucracy," in *From Max Weber: Essays in Sociology*, ed. H. H. Gerth and C. W. Mills (New York: Oxford University Press, 1946), p. 212.

150. *OHC*, pp. 322–23; "The Rule of Law," p. 154.

151. *OHC*, pp. 320–22; "The Rule of Law," p. 154.

152. "The Masses in Representative Democracy," pp. 116, 122–23.

153. *OHC*, pp. 321–22, n. 1.

154. *OHC*, p. 317.

155. *OHC*, pp. 115, 119, 157–58.

156. *OHC*, besides pp. 316–17, pp. 206, 264, 298, 319.

157. *OHC*, p. 323.

158. "The Rule of Law," pp. 155, 162–64.

159. *OHC*, p. 305. Cf. also Oakeshott, review of *The Conservative Opportunity*, in *New Society* 6 (1965): 26. For Hegel's views on the "problem of the poor," see the *Philosophy of Right*, pars. 240–44, addition to 240.

160. Cf. Spitz, p. 343; Parekh, pp. 501–3; Covell, pp. 340–41.

161. *OHC*, p. 320.

162. "Talking Politics," p. 1428. Oakeshott makes a similar clarification in "On Misunderstanding Human Conduct." Responding there to the charge that he harbors an animosity toward the idea of community, he writes: "[T]he only 'animosity' I have ever entertained or expressed towards 'community' or association in terms of the pursuit of a substantive purpose is concerned with the attribution of this character to a *state* or the attempt to impose it upon a *state*. And, indeed, genuine purposive association can exist only when this character has *not* been

imposed upon a state" (p. 367).

163. "Talking Politics," pp. 1426–27; *OHC*, p. 319. For Hayek's utilitarian tendency to recommend the rule of non-purposive law in terms of prosperity, cf. *The Constitution of Liberty* (Chicago: University of Chicago Press, 1960), chaps. 2 and 3; *Law, Legislation and Liberty, I: The Rules of Order* (Chicago: University of Chicago Press, 1973), pp. 55, 110. For his "indirect" or "system" utilitarianism, cf. *The Constitution of Liberty*, pp. 158–59; *Law, Legislation and Liberty, I: The Rules of Order*, pp. 112–14; *Law, Legislation and Liberty, II: The Mirage of Social Justice* (Chicago: University of Chicago Press, 1976), pp. 17–23. On Hayek's utilitarianism and his ultimate affinity with Hume, cf. John Gray, *Hayek on Liberty* (Oxford: Basil Blackwell, 1984), pp. 58–61.

164. For some such criticisms, cf. Shklar, p. 1018; D. D. Raphael, *Political Quarterly* 46 (1975): 454; S. Miller, "The Rules of the Game," *Partisan Review* 44 (1977): 304–9; Pitkin, "Inhuman Conduct and Unpolitical Theory," pp. 301–320; Barber, pp. 457–63; Parekh, pp. 503–6; R. N. Berki, "Oakeshott's Concept of Civil Association: Notes for a Critical Analysis," *Political Studies* 29 (1981): 570–85; Liddington, pp. 311–14.

165. Raphael, p. 454.

166. *OHC*, p. 119; cf. also "The Rule of Law," p. 161.

167. *OHC*, pp. 53–54. Shklar, p. 1018, and F. Mount, "Oakeshott's Distinction," *The National Review* 27 (November 21, 1975): 1302, both argue that Hobbes, a philosopher Oakeshott claims for civil association, posited "commodious living" as the common purpose of such association. But it is difficult to ascribe a specific content to this expression; like "civilization" itself, it seems to describe a situation in which a manifold of purposes may be pursued unhindered rather than being an end or purpose itself.

168. *OHC*, pp. 61–62.

169. *OHC*, pp. 118–19, 110. Cf. also Oakeshott's review of *The Politics of Motion: the World of Thomas Hobbes*, by T. Spragens, *Government and Opposition* 9 (1974): 237–44, in which he criticizes a simplistic "teleological" interpretation of Aristotle's political philosophy.

170. "The Rule of Law," p. 161. Cf. also *OHC*, pp. 157–58; "The Vocabulary of a Modern European State," p. 340.

171. Shklar, p. 1018. Cf. also Miller, pp. 306–7; Parekh, pp. 504–6; Liddington, pp. 312–13.

172. *OHC*, p. 305; "The Rule of Law," pp. 162–63.

173. Parekh, p. 497.

174. Dworkin puts the neutrality thesis in this way: the liberal state "must be neutral on . . . the question of the good life . . . political decisions must be, so far as is possible, independent of any particular conception of the good life, or of what gives value to life" ("Liberalism," in *Public and Private Morality*, ed. Stuart Hampshire [Cambridge: Cambridge University Press, 1978]). Cf. also Rawls, *A Theory of Justice*, p. 19; Nozick, pp. 28–33; Bruce Ackerman, *Social Justice in the Liberal State* (New Haven: Yale University Press, 1980), p. 11.

175. Cf. Galston, "Defending Liberalism," *American Political Science Review* 76 (1982): 621–29; "Public Morality and Religion in the Liberal State," *PS* 19 (Fall 1986): 807–24. Though Galston himself cannot strictly be described as a communitarian, his critique of deontological liberalism shares much with the communitarian critique. Cf. also Barber, pp. 458–59, on the "defect of proceduralism" in Oakeshott's theory.

176. *OHC*, p. 175.

177. *OHC*, p. 180; "The Rule of Law," p. 160.

178. "The Rule of Law," pp. 141, 143, 160.

179. Shirley Letwin, "Morality and Law," *Encounter* 35 (November 1974): 35–43.

180. Letwin, "Morality and Law," p. 40.

181. Cf. Pitkin, "Inhuman Conduct and Unpolitical Theory," pp. 304–5; Spitz, p. 343; Barber, p. 463; Parekh, pp. 501–3.

CHAPTER 6

1. Cf. Charles Taylor, "Atomism," in *Philosophy and the Human Sciences: Philosophical Papers 2* (Cambridge: Cambridge University Press, 1985), pp. 187–210; Michael Sandel, *Liberalism and the Limits of Justice* (Cambridge: Cambridge University Press, 1982); "The Procedural Republic and the Unencumbered Self," *Political Theory* 12 (February 1984): 81–96. Rawls disclaims that any such metaphysical theory of an unencumbered self lies behind his theory of justice in "Justice as Fairness: Political not Metaphysical," *Philosophy and Public Affairs* 14 (1985): 223–51.

2. Cf., for example, *The Constitution of Liberty*, chaps. 1 and 9, where Hayek falls into the language of "limitation" and of "private spheres" in his discussion of freedom.

3. Richard Rorty, "Postmodernist Bourgeois Liberalism," *The Journal of Philosophy* 80 (1983): 583–89.

4. Richard Rorty, "The Priority of Democracy to Philosophy," in *The Virginia Statute for Religious Freedom: Its Evolution and Its Consequences in American History*, ed. M. Peterson and R. Vaughan (Cambridge: Cambridge University Press, 1988), pp. 257–82; cf. also "The Contingency of Community," *London Review of Books* 8 (July 24, 1986): 10–14, where Rawls is once again mentioned along with Oakeshott and Dewey as a writer who defends liberalism as a contingent tradition.

5. Richard Bernstein, "One Step Forward, Two Steps Backward: Richard Rorty on Liberal Democracy and Philosophy," *Political Theory* 15 (November 1987): 545–46.

6. Cf. Richard Rorty, "Thugs and Theorists: A Reply to Bernstein," *Political Theory* 15 (November 1987): 564–80.

7. For Rorty's view of philosophy as "cultural anthropology," cf. *Philosophy and the Mirror of Nature*, p. 381; cf. also "Pragmatism and Philosophy," pp. 55–59, where philosophy becomes indistinguishable from history or literary criticism, and the philosopher is described as an "all-purpose intellectual" and a "culture critic."

8. Cf. Rawls, "Justice as Fairness: Political not Metaphysical"; "Kantian Constructivism in Moral Theory," *Journal of Philosophy* 57 (September 1980): 515–72.

9. On Rawls's bourgeois hedonism, see Allan Bloom, "Justice: John Rawls vs. the Tradition of Political Philosophy," *American Political Science Review* 69 (1975): 648–62. On Rawls's anti-liberal concern with security, see Benjamin Barber, "Justifying Justice: Problems of Psychology, Politics and Measurement in Rawls," in *Reading Rawls: Critical Studies of A Theory of Justice*, ed. N. Daniels (New York: Basic Books, 1975), pp. 292–318.

10. Cf. MacIntyre, *After Virtue*, especially chap. 17; *Whose Justice? Which Rationality*, especially chap. 17; Roberto Unger, *Knowledge and Politics* (New York: The Free Press, 1975).

BIBLIOGRAPHY

Works by Oakeshott

This bibliography contains only those works of Oakeshott's that are cited in the book. For a more complete bibliography of Oakeshott's works up to 1968 (especially of his reviews), see W. H. Greenleaf's bibliography in *Politics and Experience: Essays Presented to Professor Michael Oakeshott on the Occasion of his Retirement*, ed. Preston King and B. C. Parekh. As a supplement to this, for works between 1968 and 1975, see J. L. Auspitz's "Bibliographcal Note," *Political Theory* 4 (August 1976): 295–300.

BOOKS

Experience and its Modes. Cambridge: Cambridge University Press, 1933.
Hobbes on Civil Association. Berkeley: University of California Press, 1975.
On History and Other Essays. Totowa, N.J.: Barnes and Noble, 1983.
On Human Conduct. Oxford: Clarendon Press, 1975.
Rationalism in Politics and Other Essays. London: Methuen & Co. Ltd., 1962.
The Voice of Liberal Learning: Michael Oakeshott on Education. Edited by Timothy Fuller. New Haven and London: Yale University Press, 1989.

BOOKS EDITED AND INTRODUCED

Hobbes, Thomas. *Leviathan*. Oxford: Basil Blackwell, 1946.
The Social and Political Doctrines of Contemporary Europe. Cambridge: Cambridge University Press, 1942.

ARTICLES

"The Authority of the State." *The Modern Churchman* 19 (1929–30): 313–27.
"The B.B.C." *The Cambridge Journal* 4 (1950–51): 543–54.
"The Claims of Politics." *Scrutiny* 8 (1939–40): 146–51.
"The Concept of a Philosophical Jurisprudence." *Politica* 3 (1938): 203–22, 345–60.
"Contemporary British Politics." *The Cambridge Journal* 1 (1947–48): 474–90.
"The Customer is Never Wrong." *The Listener* 54 (1955): 301–2.
"Dialectical Materialism and Official Philosophy." *The Cambridge Review* 56 (1934–35): 108–9.

"Education: The Engagement and its Frustration." In *Education and the Development of Reason.* Edited by F. F. Dearden, P. H. Hirst, and R. S. Peters. London: Routledge & Kegan Paul, 1972. Pp. 19–49.

"The Idea of a University." *The Listener* 43 (1950): 424–26.

"The Importance of the Historical Element in Christianity." *The Modern Churchman* 18 (1928–29): 360–71.

"John Locke." *The Cambridge Review* 54 (1932–33): 72–73.

"Learning and Teaching." In *The Concept of Education.* Edited by R. S. Peters. London: Routledge & Kegan Paul. Pp. 156–76.

"The Masses in Representative Democracy." In *American Conservative Thought in the Twentieth Century.* Edited by William F. Buckley, Jr. New York: Bobbs-Merrill. Pp. 103–23.

"Mr. Carr's First Volume." *The Cambridge Journal* 4 (1950–51): 344–52.

"Nazism." In *Chamber's Encyclopedia,* 9: 737–39.

"The New Bentham." *Scrutiny* 1 (1932–33): 114–31.

"On Misunderstanding Human Conduct: A Reply to My Critics." *Political Theory* 4 (August 1976): 353–67.

"A Place of Learning." *The Colorado College Studies,* no. 12 (1975).

"Political Laws and Captive Audiences." In *Talking to Eastern Europe.* Edited by G. R. Urban. London: Eyre & Spottiswoode, 1964. Pp. 291–301.

"*Rationalism in Politics*: A Reply to Professor Raphael." *Political Studies* 13 (1965): 89–92.

"Religion and the Moral Life." The "D" Society Pamphlets, no. 2 (Cambridge, 1927).

"Science and Society." *The Cambridge Journal* 1 (1947–48): 689–97.

"Scientific Politics." *The Cambridge Journal* 1 (1947–48): 347–58.

"Talking Politics." *The National Review* 27 (December 5, 1975): 1345–57, 1423–28.

"Thomas Hobbes." *Scrutiny* 4 (1935–36): 263–77.

"The Universities." *The Cambridge Journal* 2 (1948–49): 515–42.

"The Vocabulary of a Modern European State." *Political Studies* 23 (1975): 319–41, 409–14.

BOOK REVIEWS

Review of *Science, Religion and Reality,* ed. J. Needham. *Journal of Theological Studies* 27 (1926): 317–19.

Review of *Fundamental Problems of Life,* by J. S. Mackenzie. *Journal of Philosophical Studies* 4 (1929): 264–66.

Review of *The Principles of Politics,* by G. E. G. Catlin. *The Cambridge Review* 51 (1929–30): 400.

Review of *Natural Law and the Theory of Society, 1500–1800,* by Otto Gierke (translated by E. Barker). *The Cambridge Review* 56 (1934–35): 11–12.

Review of *Morals and Politics,* by E. F. Carritt. *The Cambridge Review* 56 (1934–35): 449.

Review of *The Political Philosophies of Plato and Hegel,* by M. B. Foster. *The Cambridge Review* 57 (1935–36): 74.

Review of *An Introduction to Contemporary German Philosophy*, by W. Brock. *The Cambridge Review* 57 (1935–36): 195.

Review of *The Political Philosophy of Hobbes*, by L. Strauss. *The Cambridge Review* 57 (1936–37): 150.

Review of *Bernard Bosanquet's Philosophy of the State*, by B. Pfannenstill. *Philosophy* 11 (1936): 482–83.

Review of *The Historical Element in Religion*, by C. Webb. *The Journal of Theological Studies* 37 (1936): 96–97.

Review of *The Political Philosophy of Hobbes*, by L. Strauss. *Philosophy* 12 (1937): 239–41.

Review of *The Principles of Art*, by R. G. Collingwood. *The Cambridge Review* 59 (1937–38): 487.

Review of *The Idea of History*, by R. G. Collingwood. *The English Historical Review* 62 (1947): 84–86.

Review of *Masters of Political Thought* (v. 2), ed. W. T. Jones. *The Cambridge Journal* 1 (1947–48): 636–37.

Review of *The State and the Citizen*, by J. D. Mabbott. *The Cambridge Journal* 2 (1948–49): 316, 318.

Review of *The State and the Citizen*, by J. D. Mabbott. *Mind* 58 (1949): 378–89.

Review of *Socialism and Ethics*, by H. Selsam. *The Cambridge Journal* 2 (1948–49): 763–74.

Review of *The Concept of Mind*, by G. Ryle. *Spectator* 184 (1950): 20, 22.

Review of *Modern Capitalism and Economic Progress*, by T. Wilson. *The Cambridge Journal* 4 (1950–51): 504–6.

Review of *An Introduction to the Philosophy of History*, by W. H. Walsh. *Philosophical Quarterly* 2 (1952): 276–77.

Review of *Anarchy and Order*, by H. Read. *Spectator* 192 (1954): 593–94.

Review of *Political Parties*, by M. Duverger. *Spectator* 193 (1954): 92–93.

Review of *The Conservative Mind*, by R. Kirk. *Spectator* 193 (1954): 472, 474.

Review of *The Letters of Jacob Burckhardt*, ed. A. Dru. *Spectator* 194 (1955): 404–5.

Review of *The Conservative Opportunity*, by the Bow Group. *New Society* 6 (1965): 26–27.

Review of *Critique of Hegel's Philosophy of Right*, by Karl Marx. Edited by J. O'Malley. *Spectator* 226 (1971): 192–93.

Review of *The Politics of Motion: the World of Thomas Hobbes*, by T. Spragens. *Government and Opposition* 9 (1974): 237–44.

Review of *Hegel's Theory of the Modern State*, by S. Avineri. *European Studies Review* 5 (April 1975): 217–20.

Works on Oakeshott

Archer, James. "Oakeshott on Politics." *Journal of Politics* 41 (1979): 150–68.

Auspitz, Josiah Lee. "Individuality, Civility, and Theory: The Philosophical Imagination of Michael Oakeshott." *Political Theory* 4 (August 1976): 261–94.

_____. Review of *On Human Conduct*. *Commentary* 61 (May 1976): 89–94.

Barber, Benjamin R. "Conserving Politics: Michael Oakeshott and Political Theory." *Government and Opposition* 11 (1976): 446–63.

Benn, S. R. and Peters, R. S. *Social Principles and the Democratic State*. London: George Allen & Unwin Ltd., 1959.

Berki, R. N. "Oakeshott's Concept of Civil Association: Notes for a Critical Analysis." *Political Studies* 29 (1981): 570–85.

Blumler, J. G. "Politics, Poetry, and Practice." *Political Studies* 12 (1964): 355–61.

Coats, Wendell John, Jr. "Michael Oakeshott as Liberal Theorist." *Canadian Journal of Political Science* 18 (December 1985): 773–87.

Coleman, Samuel. "Is There Reason in Tradition?" In *Politics and Experience*. Edited by Preston King and B. C. Parekh. Cambridge: Cambridge University Press, 1968. Pp. 239–282.

Collingwood, R. G. "Oakeshott and the Modes of Experience." *Cambridge Review* 55 (February 16, 1934).

Covell, Charles. *The Redefinition of Conservatism: Politics and Doctrine*. New York: St. Martin's Press, 1986. Pp. 93–143.

Cowling, Maurice. *Religion and Public Doctrine in Modern England*. Cambridge: Cambridge University Press, 1980. Pp. 251–282.

Cranston, Maurice. "Michael Oakeshott's Politics." *Encounter* 28 (January 1967): 82–86.

Crick, Bernard. "The World of Michael Oakeshott: Or the Lonely Nihilist." *Encounter* 20 (June 1963): 65–74.

Crossman, R. H. S. "The Ultimate Conservative." *The New Statesman and Nation* 42 (July 21, 1951): 60–61.

Falck, Colin. "Romanticism in Politics." *The New Left Review* 18 (January–February 1963): 60–72.

Fuller, Timothy. Review of *On Human Conduct*. *The Journal of Politics* 38 (1976): 184–86.

Galston, William. *Justice and the Human Good*. Chicago: University of Chicago Press. Pp. 25–27.

Germino, Dante. *Beyond Ideology: The Revival of Political Theory*. New York: Harper & Row, 1967. Pp. 131–39.

Greenleaf, W. H. *Oakeshott's Philosophical Politics*. London: Longmans Green, 1966.

———. "Idealism, Modern Philosophy and Politics." In *Politics and Experience*. Edited by Preston King and B. C. Parekh. Cambridge: Cambridge University Press, 1968. Pp. 93–124.

Himmelfarb, Gertrude. "The Conservative Imagination: Michael Oakeshott." *The American Scholar* (Summer 1975), pp. 405–20.

Jaffa, Harry V. "A Celebration of Tradition." *The National Review* 15 (October 22, 1963): 360–62.

Kettler, David. "The Cheerful Discourses of Michael Oakeshott." *World Politics* 16 (1964): 483–89.

King, Preston and Parekh, B. C., eds. *Politics and Experience: Essays Presented to Professor Michael Oakeshott on the Occasion of his Retirement*. Cambridge: Cambridge University Press, 1968.

Koerner, Kirk. *Liberalism and its Critics.* New York: St. Martin's Press, 1985. Pp. 270–308.

Kuhn, Helmut. Review of *Rationalism in Politics. Zeitschrift für Politik* 10 (1963): 194–97.

Liddington, John. "Oakeshott: Freedom in a Modern European State." In *Conceptions of Liberty in Political Philosophy.* Edited by Z. Pelczynski and J. Gray. New York: St. Martin's Press, 1984. Pp. 311–14.

Mackenzie, W. J. M. "Political Theory and Political Education." *Universities Quarterly* 9 (1955–56): 351–63.

Miller, Stephen. "The Rules of the Game." *Partisan Review* 44 (1977): 304–9.

Minogue, Kenneth. "Michael Oakeshott: The Boundless Sea of Politics." In *Contemporary Political Philosophers.* Edited by Anthony de Crespigny and Kenneth Minogue. New York: Dodd Mead, 1975. Pp. 120–46.

_____. "Oakeshott and the Idea of Freedom." *Quadrant* 19 (October 1975): 77–83.

Modood, Tariq. "Oakeshott's Conceptions of Philosophy." *History of Political Thought* 1 (1980): 315–22.

Mount, Ferdinand. "Oakeshott's Distinction." Review of *On Human Conduct. The National Review* 27 (November 21, 1975): 1301–5.

Parekh, B. C. "Review Article: The Political Philosophy of Michael Oakeshott." *British Journal of Political Science* 9 (1979): 487–88.

Peardon, Thomas P. "Two Currents in Contemporary English Political Theory." *The American Political Science Review* 49 (1955): 487–95.

Pitkin, Hanna Fenichel. "Inhuman Conduct and Unpolitical Theory." *Political Theory* 4 (August 1976): 301–20.

_____. "The Roots of Conservatism: Michael Oakeshott and the Denial of Politics." *Dissent* 20 (1973): 496–525.

Postan, M. "Revulsion from Thought." *The Cambridge Journal* 2 (1948–49): 395–408.

Raphael, D.D. "Professor Oakeshott's *Rationalism and Politics." Political Studies* 12 (1964): 202–15.

_____. Review of *On Human Conduct. Political Quarterly* 46 (October 1975): 450–54.

Rayner, Jeremy. "The Legend of Oakeshott's Conservatism: Skeptical Philosophy and Limited Politics." *Canadian Journal of Political Science* 18 (June 1985): 313–38.

Rees, John C. "Professor Oakeshott on Political Education." *Mind* 62 (1953): 68–74.

Sanderson, John. "Definitionism in Politics." *Durham University Journal* 57 (1964–65): 101–9.

Shklar, Judith. "Purposes and Procedures." Review of *On Human Conduct. Times Literary Supplement*, 12 September 1975, p. 1018.

Spitz, David. "A Rationalist *Malgré Lui*: The Perplexities of Being Michael Oakeshott." *Political Theory* 4 (August 1976): 335–52.

Watkins, J.W.N. "Political Tradition and Political Theory." *The Philosophical Quarterly* 2 (1952): 323–37.

Wolin, Sheldon. "The Politics of Self-Disclosure." *Political Theory* 4 (August

268

BIBLIOGRAPHY

1976): 321–34.

Wood, Neal. "A Guide to the Classics: The Skepticism of Professor Oakeshott." *The Journal of Politics* 21 (1959): 645–62.

Other Works

Ackerman, Bruce. *Social Justice in the Liberal State*. New Haven: Yale University Press, 1980.

Allen, C. K. *Legal Duties*. Oxford: Clarendon Press, 1931.

Arendt, Hannah. *The Human Condition*. Chicago: University of Chicago Press, 1958.

Aristotle. *Nicomachean Ethics*. Translated by Martin Ostwald. Indianapolis: Bobbs-Merrill, 1962.

——. *Politics*. Edited and translated by Ernest Barker. Oxford: Clarendon Press, 1946.

——. *Rhetoric*. Translated by J. H. Freese. Cambridge, Mass.: Harvard University Press, 1975.

Barber, Benjamin. "Justifying Justice: Problems of Psychology, Politics and Measurement in Rawls." In *Reading Rawls: Critical Studies of A Theory Justice*. Edited by N. Daniels. New York: Basic Books, 1975. Pp. 292–318.

Bernstein, Richard. *Beyond Objectivism and Relativism: Science, Hermeneutics, and Praxis*. Philadelphia: University of Pennsylvania Press, 1985.

——. "One Step Forward, Two Steps Backward: Richard Rorty on Liberal Democracy." *Political Theory* 15 (November 1987): 538–63.

Bloom, Allan. *The Closing of the American Mind: How Higher Education has Failed Democracy and Impoverished the Souls of Today's Students*. New York: Simon and Schuster, 1987.

——. "Justice: John Rawls vs. the Tradition of Political Philosophy." *The American Political Science Review* 69 (1975): 648–62.

Bosanquet, Bernard. *Implication and Linear Inference*. London: Macmillan, 1920.

——. *Knowledge and Reality*. London: S. Sonnenschein, 1892.

——. *Logic, or the Morphology of Knowledge*, 2nd ed. Oxford: Clarendon Press, 1911.

——. *The Philosophical Theory of the State*. London: Macmillan, 1965.

——. *The Principle of Individuality and Value*. London: Macmillan, 1927.

Bradley, F. H. *Appearance and Reality*. Oxford: Oxford University Press, 1969.

——. *Essays on Truth and Reality*. Oxford: Clarendon Press, 1914.

——. *Ethical Studies*. Oxford: Clarendon Press, 1927.

——. *The Presuppositions of Critical History*. Edited by Lionel Rubinoff. Chicago: University of Chicago Press, 1968.

——. *The Principles of Logic*, 2nd ed. London: Oxford University Press, 1928.

Brock, Werner. *An Introduction to Contemporary German Philosophy*. Cambridge: Cambridge University Press, 1935.

Burke, Edmund. *Reflections on the Revolution in France*. Edited by C. C. O'Brien. Harmondsworth: Penguin, 1968.

Collingwood, R. G. *An Autobiography*. Oxford: Clarendon Press, 1939.

_____. *An Essay on Metaphysics*. Oxford: Clarendon Press, 1940.

_____. *An Essay on Philosophical Method*. Oxford: Clarendon Press, 1933.

_____. *The Idea of History*. Oxford: Clarendon Press, 1946.

_____. *The New Leviathan*. Oxford: Clarendon Press, 1942.

_____. *The Principles of Art*. Oxford: Clarendon Press, 1938.

_____. *Speculum Mentis: Or the Map of Knowledge*. Oxford: Clarendon: Press, 1924.

Croce, Benedetto. *History: Its Theory and Practice*. Translated by D. Ainslie. New York: Russell and Russell, 1960.

Dworkin, Ronald. "Liberalism." in *Public and Private Morality*. Edited by Stuart Hampshire. Cambridge: Cambridge University Press, 1978. Pp. 113–43.

Evans-Pritchard, E. E. *Anthropology and History*. Manchester: Manchester University Press, 1961.

Foster, Michael. *The Political Philosophies of Plato and Hegel*. Oxford: Clarendon Press, 1935.

Fuller, Lon. *The Morality of Law*. New Haven: Yale University Press, 1969.

_____. "Positivism and Fidelity to Law." *Harvard Law Review* 71 (1958): 630, 648–57.

Gadamer, Hans-Georg. *Philosophical Hermeneutics*. Translated and edited by D. Linge. Berkeley: University of California Press, 1976.

_____. "The Problem of Historical Consciousness." In *Interpretive Social Science: A Second Look*. Edited by P. Rabinow and W. Sullivan. Berkeley: University of California Press, 1987. Pp. 82–140.

_____. *Reason in the Age of Science*. Translated by F. Lawrence. Cambridge, Mass.: MIT Press, 1981.

_____. *Truth and Method*. New York: Seabury Press, 1975.

Galston, William. "Defending Liberalism." *American Political Science Review* 76 (1982): 621–29.

_____. "Public Morality and Religion in the Liberal State." *PS* 19 (Fall 1986): 807–24.

Gierke, Otto von. *Natural Law and the Theory of Society, 1500–1800*. Translated by E. Barker. Boston: Beacon Press, 1957.

_____. *Political Theories of the Middle Ages*. Translated by F. Maitland. Cambridge: Cambridge University Press, 1951.

Ginsberg, Morris. *Reason and Unreason in Society*. London: Longmans Green, 1948.

Gray, John. *Hayek on Liberty*. Oxford: Basil Blackwell, 1984.

Green, T. H. *Lectures on the Principles of Political Obligation and Other Writings*. Edited by P. Harris and J. Morrow. Cambridge: Cambridge University Press, 1986.

Habermas, Jürgen. "A Review of Gadamer's *Truth and Method*." In *Understanding and Social Inquiry*. Edited by Fred Dallmayr and Thomas McCarthy. Notre Dame: Notre Dame University Press, 1977. Pp. 335–63.

Halevy, Elie. *The Growth of Philosophic Radicalism*. London: Faber, 1972.

Hart, H. L. A. *The Concept of Law*. Oxford: Oxford University Press, 1961.

Hayek, Friedrich. *The Constitution of Liberty*. Chicago: University of Chicago Press, 1960.

——. *The Counter-Revolution of Science*. Glencoe, Ill.: The Free Press, 1952.

——. *Law, Legislation and Liberty, I: The Rules of Order*. Chicago: University of Chicago Press, 1973.

——. *Law, Legislation and Liberty, II: The Mirage of Social Justice*. Chicago: University of Chicago Press, 1976.

——. *The Road to Serfdom*. Chicago: University of Chicago Press, 1944.

——. *Studies in Philosophy, Politics, and Economics*. Chicago: University of Chicago Press, 1967.

Hegel, G. W. F. *Lectures on the History of Philosophy*. Translated by E. S. Haldane and F. H. Simpson. London: Routledge & Kegan Paul, 1968.

——. *Natural Law*. Translated by T. M. Knox. Philadelphia: University of Pennsylvania Press, 1975.

——. *The Phenomenology of Spirit*. Translated by A. V. Miller. Oxford: Clarendon Press, 1977.

——. *The Philosophy of History*. Translated by J. Sibree. New York: Dover, 1956.

——. *Philosophy of Right*. Translated by T. M. Knox. Oxford: Clarendon Press, 1952.

Husserl, Edmund. *The Crisis of European Sciences and Transcendental Phenomenolgy*. Translated by D. Carr. Evanston: Northwestern University Press, 1970.

——. *Phenomenology and the Crisis of Philosophy*. Translated and edited by Quentin Lauer. New York: Harper & Row, 1965.

Joachim, Harold. *Logical Studies*. Oxford: Clarendon Press, 1948.

——. *The Nature of Truth*. Oxford: Clarendon Press, 1906.

Kant, Immanuel. *The Metaphysical Elements of Justice*. Translated by J. Ladd. Indianapolis: Bobbs-Merrill, 1965.

Letwin, Shirley. "Hobbes and Christianity." *Daedalus* 105 (Winter 1976): 1–21.

——. "Morality and Law." *Encounter* 35 (November 1976): 35–43.

Locke, John. *Two Treatises of Government*. Edited by Peter Laslett. Cambridge: Cambridge University Press, 1963.

Mabbott, J. D. *The State and the Citizen*. London: Hutchinson's, 1948.

MacIntyre, Alasdair. *After Virtue: A Study in Moral Theory*. Notre Dame: Notre Dame University Press, 1981.

——. *Whose Justice? Which Rationality?* Notre Dame: Notre Dame University Press, 1988.

Macpherson, C. B. "Hobbes's Bourgeois Man." In *Hobbes Studies*. Edited by K. Brown. Cambridge, Mass.: Harvard University Press, 1965. Pp. 169–83.

——. *The Political Theory of Possessive Individualism*. London: Oxford University Press, 1962.

Moore, G. E. *Principia Ethica*. Cambridge: Cambridge University Press, 1922.

——. "Proof of an External World," *Proceedings of the British Academy* 25 (1939).

——. "Refutation of Idealism." *Mind* 48 (1903): 433–53.

Muirhead, J. H. "Recent Criticism of the Idealist Theory of the General Will." *Mind* 33 (1924): 166–75, 233–41, 361–68.

Nietzsche, Friedrich. *Basic Writings of Nietzsche*. Translated and edited by Walter Kaufmann. New York: Random House, 1968.

_____. *Untimely Meditations*. Translated by R. J. Hollingdale. Cambridge: Cambridge University Press, 1983.

Nozick, Robert. *Anarchy, State, and Utopia*. New York: Basic Books, 1974.

Plamenatz, John. *Consent, Freedom and Political Obligation*. London: Oxford University Press, 1938.

Polanyi, Michael. *Personal Knowledge*. Chicago: University of Chicago Press, 1958.

_____. *Science, Faith and Society*. Chicago: University of Chicago Press, 1964.

_____. *The Tacit Dimension*. New York: Doubleday, 1966.

Rawls, John. "Justice as Fairness: Political not Metaphysical." *Philosophy and Public Affairs* 14 (1985): 223–51.

_____. "Kantian Constructivism in Moral Theory." *Journal of Philosophy* 57 (September 1980): 515–72.

_____. *A Theory of Justice*. Cambridge, MA: Harvard University Press, 1971.

Riley, Patrick. *Will and Political Legitimacy: A Critical Exposition of Social Contract Theory in Hobbes, Locke, Rousseau, Kant, and Hegel*. Cambridge, MA: Harvard University Press, 1982.

Rorty, Richard. "The Contingency of Community." *London Review of Books* 8 (July 24, 1986): 10–14.

_____. *Philosophy and the Mirror of Nature*. Princeton: Princeton University Press, 1979.

_____. "Postmodernist Bourgeois Liberalism." *The Journal of Philosophy* 80 (1983): 383–89.

_____. "Pragmatism and Philosophy." In *After Philosophy: End or Transformation?* Cambridge, MA: MIT Press, 1987. pp. 26–66.

_____. "The Priority of Democracy to Philosophy." In *The Virginia Statute for Religious Freedom: Its Evolution and its Consequences in American History*. Edited by M. Peterson and R. Vaughan. Cambridge: Cambridge University Press, 1988. pp. 257–82.

_____. "Thugs and Theorists: A Reply to Bernstein." *Political Theory* 15 (November 1987): 564–80.

Rousseau, Jean-Jacques. *On the Social Contract*. Edited by R. Masters and translated by J. Masters. New York: St. Martin's Press, 1978.

Ryle, Gilbert. *The Concept of Mind*. London: Hutchinson's, 1949.

_____. "Knowing How and Knowing That." *Proceedings of the Aristotelian Society* 46 (1945–46): 1–16.

Sandel, Michael. *Liberalism and the Limits of Justice*. Cambridge: Cambridge University Press, 1982.

_____. "The Procedural Republic and the Unencumbered Self." *Political Theory* 12 (February 1984): 81–96.

Schopenhauer, Arthur. *The World as Will and Representation*. Translated by E. F. G. Payne. New York: Dover, 1959.

Simons, H. C. *Economic Policy for a Free Society*. Chicago: University of Chicago

Press, 1948.

Skinner, Quentin. "Meaning and Understanding in the History of Ideas." *History and Theory* 8 (1969): 3–53.

Strauss, Leo. *Natural Right and History*. Chicago: University of Chicago Press, 1953.

——. *The Political Philosophy of Hobbes: Its Basis and Its Genesis*. Chicago: University of Chicago Press, 1952.

——. *Political Philosophy: Six Essays by Leo Strauss*. Indianapolis: Bobbs-Merrill, 1975.

——. *What is Political Philosophy?* Glencoe, Ill.: The Free Press, 1959.

Taylor, Charles. "Atomism." In *Philosophy and the Human Sciences: Philosophical Papers 2*. Cambridge: University of Cambridge Press, 1985. Pp. 187–210.

Thomas, Keith. "The Social Origins of Hobbes's Political Thought." In *Hobbes Studies*. Edited by K. Brown. Cambridge, MA: Harvard University Press, 1965. Pp. 185–236.

Unger, Roberto. *Knowledge and Politics*. New York: The Free Press, 1975.

Vincent, Andrew and Raymond Plant. *Philosophy, Politics and Citizenship*. Oxford: Basil Blackwell, 1984.

Walzer, Michael. *Interpretation and Social Criticism*. Cambridge, MA: Harvard University Press, 1987.

Warrender, Howard. *The Political Philosophy of Hobbes*. Oxford: Clarendon Press, 1957.

Weber, Max. *From Max Weber: Essays in Sociology*. Edited by H. H. Gerth and C. W. Mills. New York: Oxford University Press, 1946.

——. *The Methodology of the Social Sciences*. Translated and edited by E. Shils and H. Finch. New York: The Free Press, 1949.

Winch, Peter. *The Idea of a Social Science and Its Relation to Philosophy*. London: Routledge & Kegan Paul, 1958.

Wittgenstein, Ludwig. *Philosophical Investigations*. Translated by G. E. M. Anscombe. New York: Macmillan, 1953.

Wollheim, Richard. *F. H. Bradley*. Harmondsworth: Penguin, 1959.

INDEX

Absolutism, 99, 103, 104, 188, 189–90
Ackerman, Bruce, 198–99, 226
Acton, Lord, 206, 255n137
Adjudication, 185
Allen, C. K., 245n6, 245n14
American Founders, 125, 206
Anarchism, 255n140
Anthropology, 54–55, 243n118, 243n119
Apartheid, 136, 137
Aquinas, St. Thomas, 259n117
Arendt, Hannah, 108, 213, 257n33
Aristotle, 87, 88–89, 92, 110, 165, 179, 183, 223–24, 252n71
Atomism, *see* Individualism
Augustine, 206
Auspitz, J. L., 249n1, 257n64
Austin, John, 184, 245n6
Authority, 2, 104, 184, 187–92, 234–35;
   distinguished from desirability, 187–88;
   and freedom, 9–10, 90–91, 190–92; and
   justice, 188–89
Autonomy, 174–75, 190, 208; *see also* Freedom

Bacon, Francis, 111, 112, 115, 212
Barber, Benjamin, 255n129
Barker, Ernest, 259n113
Bentham, Jeremy, 80–82, 100, 105
Bernstein, Richard, 108–9
Bloom, Allan, 255n126
Bodin, Jean, 183, 189–90, 206
Bosanquet, Bernard, 18, 20, 88, 103, 105, 106,
   238n16, 239n28, 239n34, 240n54, 242n104;
   compared to Oakeshott, 101–2, 160,
   191–92; and concrete logic, 6; on concrete
   universal, 239n18, 239n31; on history, 33;
   and limits of state action, 99–100, 177;
   Oakeshott on, 101; and real will, 10, 87, 94,
   97–102, 167, 191–92; on self, 100; and
   state, 99, 199
Bradley, F. H., 98, 238n16, 239n23, 239n28,
   239n34, 242n104, 248n93; compared to

Oakeshott, 240n39, 240n49, 243n137,
   244n141, 244n2; and concrete logic, 6; and
   Hegel, 20, 239n20; on history, 240n54,
   241n67; and idealism, 18–20; influence on
   Oakeshott, 18; on morality, 119, 243n137;
   on religion, 243n137, 244n141; on theory
   and practice, 244n2
Brock, Werner, 14
Burckhardt, Jacob, 153, 210, 255n137,
   256n145
Burke, Edmund, 143, 206; compared to
   Oakeshott, 7, 108, 139–40, 149, 152, 212

Capitalism, 158, 216
Carr, E. H., 43
Central planning, 141, 142, 143–45, 148, 157,
   254n104
Civil association, 158, 159, 160, 179–99, 200,
   220–21; alleged formalism of, 11, 222–29;
   criticisms of Oakeshott's theory of, 222–29;
   distinguished from enterprise association,
   180–81; distinguished from other moral
   practices, 183, 192; and Hegelian *Sittlichkeit*,
   9, 182; as ideal character, 179; and
   liberalism, 2, 9–11, 230; as moral practice,
   180–82; and neutrality, 194, 225, 226–28;
   as relationship in terms of rules, 182–85;
   sketchiness of Oakeshott's theory of,
   228–29, 235–36; tenability of distinction
   between enterprise association and,
   222–25; as vernacular language of
   intercourse, 181–82
Cohen, Hermann, 15
Coherence: and experience, 24–25; and
   history, 36–37; and politics, 132–33; and
   reason, 126–28; and truth, 18–19
Collectivism, 148, 157, 215; *see also* Central
   planning; Socialism
Collingwood, R. G., 238n5, 239n23, 244n140,
   245n18; compared to Oakeshott, 20, 28–29,
   42–43, 240n41, 240n47, 241n67, 243n113,